Barney Kessel

A Jazz Legend

Other books by Maurice J. Summerfield:

The Jazz Guitar – Its Evolution, Players and Personalities since 1900
Ashley Mark Publishing Company (UK)

First Edition 1978

Second Edition 1979

Third Edition   1993

Fourth Edition 1998

The Classical Guitar – Its Evolution, Players and Personalities since 1800
Ashley Mark Publishing Company (UK)

First Edition 1982

Second Edition 1991

Third Edition   1992

Fourth Edition 1996

Fifth Edition 2002

BARNEY KESSEL

A Jazz Legend

by

MAURICE J. SUMMERFIELD

© 2008
Ashley Mark Publishing Company
Blaydon on Tyne, NE21 5NH, UK

BARNEY KESSEL - A JAZZ LEGEND
by Maurice J. Summerfield   © 2008.

All rights reserved. No part of this book may be used or reproduced in any manner whatsoever without written permission except in the case of brief quotations embodied in critical articles and reviews.

For information write to Ashley Mark Publishing Company, 1 & 2 Vance Court, Trans Britannia Enterprise Park, Blaydon on Tyne, NE21 5NH, United Kingdom.

OCTOBER 2008.
Typeset and printed in the United Kingdom.

HARDBACK   ISBN: 978-1-872639-70-3
PAPERBACK   ISBN: 978-1-872639-69-7

Front Cover Photo: Maurice J. Summerfield Collection.

Back Cover Photo: William Claxton.
Courtesy: Contemporary Records.

CONTENTS

Preface 7

Foreword by Howard Alden 9

Biography

    1. Muskogee 13

    2. Musical Beginnings 16

    3. Los Angeles and the Chico Marx Orchestra 21

    4. Back in Los Angeles 25

    5. Oscar Peterson Trio 33

    6. Contemporary Records 38

    7. Julie is Her Name 43

    8. Studio Musician 45

    9. Europe 52

    10. The Great Guitars 55

    11. The End of a Legendary Career 57

Barney Kessel – Honours & Awards 63

Comprehensive List of Barney Kessel Compositions 64

**Selected List of Jazz and Big Band Musicians
who have recorded with Barney Kessel** 65

Guitars and Equipment 71

Thoughts – On Music & Life 90

Bibliography 99

Sources for quotations in the text 100

Photo Gallery 104

Jazz Discography 144

Barney Kessel is a unique guitarist; he is an accomplished musician, well-endowed academically and intuitively. He swings like every member of a rhythm section wishes he could, he has a staggering amount of technique, a healthy respect for the traditional, a ceaseless curiosity for the experimental, and an admirable and lovely harmonic sense. In other words, he is a real artist, a commodity rare and not expendable in today's jazz field.

André Previn

Barney Kessel is a musician that swings so much he breaks down all the barriers, psychological and musicological that have been built up over the years. Jazz fans, no matter what their background, years of collecting King Oliver and Johnny Dodds, or a frantic race to keep up with the modern jazz of the Fifties, can all appreciate Barney Kessel. To each, of course, he says different things, but he meets all on the common ground of the great jazz artists, the area where Count Basie, Duke Ellington, Woody Herman, Erroll Garner, Benny Goodman have all made music you can play over and over again and never tire of, returning after ten years' absence to find still the freshness and vitality that characterize any art.

Ralph J. Gleason

As lyrical a guitarist as we have in jazz today, but also a rhythmic natural who can outswing any man in the house.

Leonard Feather

Barney Kessel is one of the most extraordinarily consistent and emotionally huge improvisers of our era.

Nat Hentoff

PREFACE

I began to play the guitar at the age of fifteen in 1955, and first became interested in jazz after hearing some marvelous Django Reinhardt records in 1956. A few friends (who had similar tastes in jazz as myself) and I decided to form a small modern jazz combo in 1957. One day the drummer in the group played us a September 1952 recording of the Oscar Peterson Trio featuring bassist Ray Brown and Barney Kessel on guitar. It was recorded at a live *Jazz at the Philharmonic* concert held at New York's Carnegie Hall. I was stunned by the group's performance as a whole, but especially with the incredible guitar playing of the then 29-year old Barney Kessel. Almost 50 years on I still find this historic recording a great inspiration and listen to it regularly. For me this is one of the best small group jazz recordings of all time. Hearing it inspired me to start what has become a 53-year study, and appreciation, of the music and life of Barney Kessel.

I originally took some lessons on the guitar with a well-known Newcastle upon Tyne guitar teacher Charles (Charlie) Smith. After playing him some of my Barney Kessel recordings, Charlie also became a fan appreciating the great spectrum of Barney's unique musical talents. By the time I was seventeen I was playing in several local jazz combos and dance bands. In 1957 Charlie said he had taught me all he could and recommended that if I wanted to extend my musical knowledge and guitar technique I should (1) Travel to London to have lessons with the great English guitarist Ivor Mairants, and (2) Write to Barney Kessel in Los Angeles for some tips and advice. Never dreaming that either of these great guitarists would respond, I still followed his advice and wrote to both. I was wrong! Ivor accepted me for some private lessons at his music school in Central London and eventually our families became good friends for over 40 years. Barney responded to me at length, answering in great detail all my questions. Over the next few years he always found time to respond to my new letters. Bearing in mind at that time Barney was regarded as the world's number one jazz guitarist, and one of Hollywood's top studio musicians, you can fully appreciate the measure of the man. This correspondence was the beginning of my lifelong association and close friendship with Barney Kessel. It was several years before we actually met face-to-face. Through a mutual friend, guitarist Ike Isaacs, we finally shook hands in 1972 over dinner at a London restaurant.

The music of Barney Kessel continues to be a major part of my life. I have been working on this book for over ten years and the comprehensive jazz discography for well over fifteen years. In some small way it my thank you to Barney for the pleasure his music has given, and still gives me, and his warm friendship over so many years. After his stroke, in May 1992, I visited Barney every year at his home in San Diego until his death in 2004. As a result he did see most of the detailed jazz discography in this book and confirmed that he was very pleased with it. The discography does not include the thousands of studio rock and pop recordings on which Barney played, however I have included a few worthy 'easy listening' recordings which have some jazz content. I know he would have loved to have worked on the rest of the book with me. Fortunately over 40 years he gave many interviews and I have therefore been able to include some quotations from these of Barney's own words, to help illuminate the story of his life. Phyllis Kessel also provided me with enormous support in supplying information, photographs and memorabilia.

I hope this book will inspire music lovers over the years to come to investigate and gain much pleasure from the great musical legacy that Barney Kessel, a true jazz legend, has left to the world.

Maurice J. Summerfield, September 2008

ACKNOWLEDGEMENTS

*A special thank you to Phyllis Kessel
for all her support and enthusiasm.*

My thanks also go to the following;

Dan Kessel

David Kessel

Adrian Ingram

Chuck Redd

Oscar Peterson

Ike Isaacs

Martin Taylor

Howard Alden

Bob & Cindy Benedetto

Ted O'Reilly

Ronald Gould

Simon Turnbull

Andrew Curry

Jaap van de Klomp

Terry Whitenstall

Robert Yelin

Contemporary Records – Lester Koenig

Verve Records – Norman Granz

Concord Records – Carl Jefferson

Gibson Guitar Corporation

Kay Musical Instrument Company

Downbeat Magazine

FOREWORD

When I was 12 years old, living in Southern California, I had been playing tenor guitar and tenor banjo for a couple of years, and starting to dabble in improvisation on the old tunes I was playing. I was at the home of a friend from a local banjo society, a part time guitarist named Jim Elsaas. I was checking out his record collection, digging out LPs of Benny Goodman and Count Basie, some of the jazz musicians I knew about at the time. Jim asked me, 'Why aren't you listening to my jazz guitar records?', and I asked him, 'What's jazz guitar?'. He immediately pulled out a Barney Kessel record, I believe it was *Barney Kessel Plays Standards*, and I was instantly captivated by the music coming out of the speakers. Even to my inexperienced ears, I loved the warm and robust sound, the organic exposition and development of melodies, the balance of chords, single-note lines and passages in thirds, the complex harmonic ideas and down-to earth blues phrases, and the infectious beat behind everything he played. Actually, I probably didn't use those exact words at the time, but I knew I loved it and couldn't get enough of it! I taped all of his Kessel records, and in the following years searched out every Kessel recording I could find in new and used record stores, both as a leader and a sideman. Mr. Elsaas also introduced me to many of the other greats of the jazz guitar, including Django Reinhardt, Charlie Christian, Tal Farlow, George Van Eps, Jim Hall, Kenny Burrell, Herb Ellis and Joe Pass. All of these incredible guitarists influenced and inspired me, but still to this day nobody has put it all together quite like Barney, and to me he is indeed the definition and epitome of 'Jazz Guitar'.

In following years, I kept discovering more and more aspects of Barney's playing, such as his beautiful obbligatos to Billie Holiday on her Verve recordings, where his short solos are little gems of melody and swing, his aggressive sparring with Oscar Peterson on Oscar's early trio recordings, the *Poll Winners* series of records with Ray Brown and Shelly Manne (which literally define how to play in a trio with guitar, bass and drums and maintain interest, excitement and textural variety with these three instruments), and the wonderful settings he creates for Julie London's voice with only his guitar and Ray Leatherwood's bass, to name just a few examples. I would listen to his memorable choruses on long *Jazz at the Philharmonic* jam sessions, where he would hold his own amongst a cast of some of the most legendary soloists of jazz (Lester Young, Charlie Parker, Flip Phillips, Ben Webster, Buddy Rich, Johnny Hodges to name a few). I would savor his arrangements for groups of various sizes on releases such as *To Swing Or Not To Swing* and *Music To Listen To Barney Kessel By*. I would be excited to hear his advancing vocabulary and newer compositions on the Concord Jazz records such as *Barney Plays Kessel*, his musical rendezvous with Django's old partner Stephane Grappelli, the guitar summit along with Herb Ellis and Charlie Byrd known as *The Great Guitars*, and even his interpretations of music from the rock musical *Hair*. He was playing in such a wide variety of settings, but always sounding fresh, inventive and timeless, and always definitely pure Barney Kessel. Also, more and more I saw how much he was admired and respected by so many musicians, not just guitarists - his musical spirit truly transcended his chosen instrument.

Barney Kessel has been such an important voice in the jazz world and the guitar community that it is almost overwhelming to contemplate all his contributions over the years. Maurice Summerfield's new book shows us that his involvement and influence over the music world goes much further than just the jazz field. He lovingly documents Barney's family background, his youth and musical start in Muskogee, Oklahoma, the big band days, his periods of studio work playing for movie sound tracks, various vocalists and pop groups, his contributions to jazz education, the guitars and equipment he used and developed throughout his career, and his thoughts on music and life, revealing Kessel's depth of thought and incredibly positive attitude, which remained with him up until his passing. I had met Barney a couple of times briefly over the years, getting to know him much more after his stroke in 1992. When visiting him and Phyllis in San Diego I was always moved by his interest, enthusiasm and complete lack of regret or bitterness about his condition. The discography is a major achievement, a catalogue listing a treasure of recorded works that is mind-boggling, even without listing the hundreds of pop and rock sessions on which Barney played. Maurice has also included an amazing collection of photographs which provide glimpses into various periods of Barney's life and career.

This is an important and exciting book, that let's us get to know even better the essence and legacy of a true giant of our music; Thank you Maurice, and thank you Barney!

Howard Alden, September 2008

Barney Kessel is one of my favorite guitarists. He's got a lot of feeling, he's got good conception of chords in a jazz manner. And he's trying to do a lot of things, not standing still at one particular level. He's trying to get away from the guitar phrase, to get into the horn phrase.

Wes Montgomery

Barney has a definiteness in his playing. When he plays a note, it really hits. Charlie Christian gave me that same feeling. The blues are a basic part of what Barney does. He's a terrific blues player. We've played together with just the two of us and with a rhythm section and in sessions with horns, and the blues especially always seem to be his vehicle. And he's certainly funky. He was funky long before it became a conscious thing to strive for. I also admire his continuity. His ideas hang together very well. Phrases are related but changed interestingly to follow the harmonic changes. There's logic there along with the earthiness.

Tal Farlow

I'd listen to records by Barney Kessel, for example, the great jazz guitarist who played at many Jazz at the Philharmonic concerts, and my jaw would drop. I was awe struck by the structure of his ad-libs. He had the gift of being complicated and simple at the same time. His amplified voice on guitar had a calm beauty that felt like poetry. I followed Barney Kessel's musical stories like a kid following a fairy-tale.

B.B. King

No one has done more to promote the image of the jazz guitar than Barney Kessel. Not only with his impeccable musical taste, but with his wit and humor.

Mundell Lowe

It's hard to describe in words what Barney Kessel means to me, both musically and personally. His fiery swing and lush chordal style define many of the qualities of bebop guitar. His melodic sense is second to none. With Barney, every tune has focus, with attention paid to even the smallest detail. I love how he treats each piece with consideration, not just the treatment of the head, but also in terms of setting up solo sections, interludes, and most importantly, intros and endings. He is to the guitar trio what Count Basie was to the big band.

Bruce Forman

Barney Kessel

A Jazz Legend

BIOGRAPHY

Barney Kessel c.1945 with the Artie Shaw Orchestra.

BARNEY KESSEL – *A Jazz Legend*
1. Muskogee

Barney Kessel was born Bernard Kessel in Muskogee on 17 October 1923. His birth certificate actually says that his name is Bernout but this is probably due to the fact that his mother, at that time, only spoke Yiddish and Russian. The way she pronounced Bernard sounded to the government official like Bernout when he was completing the birth certificate. Barney was the eldest son of Abraham and Ruth (nee Raisher) Kessel. Abraham's first wife Carolyn died in 1922, in Muskogee, leaving him with four children Rose (1910-1974), Harry, Jenny and Lee (1913-1996). Abraham Kessel married Ruth within a short period of time after Carolyn's death. Ruth and the Raisher family had settled in St. Louis after their arrival in the USA. Some members of her family became well-known builders and today there is a street in St Louis called Raisher Drive. Barney was born on 17 October 1923 and then Abraham and Ruth had another son, Lester, in 1926.

Abraham Kessel – formerly Kesselman - (1869-1941) was one of the two million or so East European and Russian Jews who emigrated to the USA at the end of the 19th century, and beginning of the 20th century, to escape anti-semitic pogroms and persecution. It seems Abraham had been living in Budapest, Hungary, but was probably born in southern Poland's Galicia region, for many years part of the Austro-Hungarian Empire. Ruth Raisher (1890-1968) was born in Minsk in Belorussia (now Belarus). Almost certainly Abraham landed at Ellis Island in New York around 1920 with his family where he received official entry into the USA. Muskogee was not an obvious place for him to go, particularly as the Jewish population there was very small. However he must have been advised there was a good opportunity in Muskogee for a shoe and boot maker to make a living.

Muskogee – A brief history.
In 1805 US President Thomas Jefferson addressed the United States Congress and seconded a Meriwether Lewis recommendation that a trading post be established near the modern day city of Muskogee. French fur traders had existed in the area for several years before the American

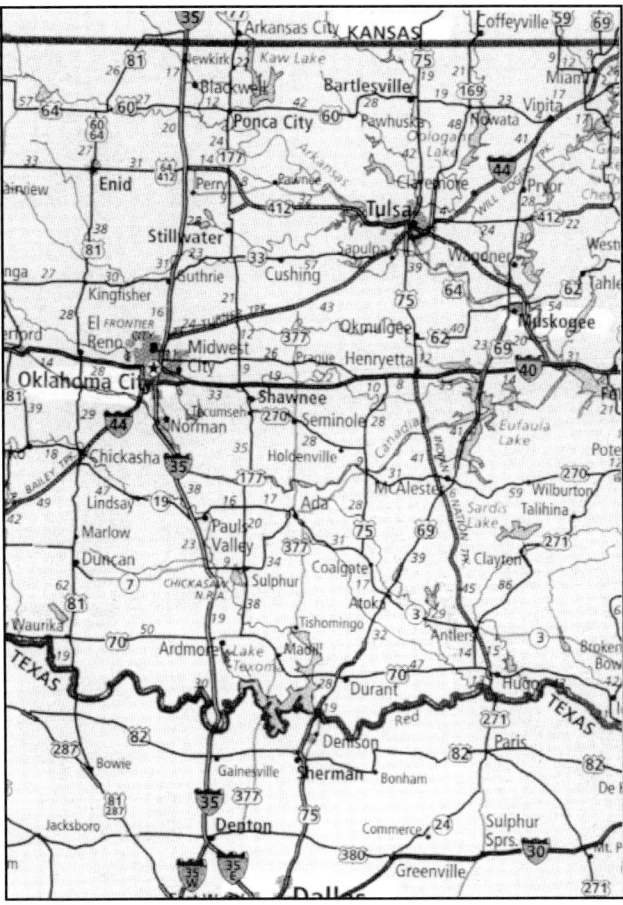

Map section showing the position of Muskogee in relation to Oklahoma City.

acquisition of the Louisiana Purchase. It is believed the French had established a small village near Muskogee in 1806, however the first permanent settlement was made in 1817 on the south bank of the Verdigris River, north of Muskogee. There were several Indian tribes living in and around that area but it was the Cherokee and Creek tribes that eventually established settlements near Muskogee. The Creeks recognized the importance of the settlement's position and in 1836 made Muskogee the Capital of the Creek Nation. In 1872, the Missouri-Kansas-Texas Railroad extended its line into this area and with Muskogee's growing economic and political value, a United States federal court was established there in 1889. This move opened Indian Territory to white settlers via land runs.

The City of Muskogee, as we know it today, was officially founded in 1876, even though settlements with the name Muskogee had existed in the area for many years. It was not until 1888 that a non-citizen of Indian Territory could legally own land in this area. It was an Ohio businessman Charles N. Haskell who, after he moved to Muskogee in March 1901, began the process of turning a small town of around 4000 people into the thriving city it is today of 38,000 people.

Main Street Muskogee 1930s.

Haskell built the first five-story business block in Oklahoma Territory. He organized and built most of the railroads running into that city. In total he built and owned 14 buildings in the city. As a result, Muskogee became an important business and industrial centre with a population of over 4000 inhabitants within a relatively short period. Muskogee is today an economic centre for eastern Oklahoma and is the eleventh largest city in the state with a total area of 38.8 square miles (100.4 km2). The population of Muskogee has remained relatively unchanged since the first half of the twentieth century. There are 24 different nationalities represented within in the city's limits as well as 17 non-English languages being spoken as first languages. Other famous jazz musicians who were born in Muskogee are Jay McShann, Don Byas and Claude Williams. Muskogee is also the home to the *Oklahoma Music Hall of Fame* in which great Oklahoma Musicians have been honoured since 1997. Barney Kessel was inducted into the *Oklahoma Music Hall of Fame* on 14 October 1999.

West Broadway and Second Street, downtown Muskogee in the 1930s.

Muskogee city skyline in the 1940s.

Part of Muskogee city business section in the 1940s.

BARNEY KESSEL – *A Jazz Legend*
2. Musical Beginnings

Having settled in Muskogee, Oklahoma, Abraham (Abe) Kessel soon owned a small shoe shop on South 2nd street right in the heart of the Afro-American commercial and entertainment district. He and his large family lived a few doors away at 128 South 2nd street. His reputation as a fair businessman, amongst both black and white populations, was soon established. The success of this shop led Abraham to open another small shop in a nearby district by the time Barney was in his teens.

Barney has described in many magazine articles and radio interviews how he became attracted to a guitar at the age of 12 in a music store window. He passed the store daily on his way to sell newspapers on the corner of Okmulgee Avenue and Third Street in downtown Muskogee. The guitar came with an instruction booklet titled *'How to Play the Guitar in Five Minutes'* and a bright red and yellow neck cord – with a tassel. With money earned as a newspaper boy he was able to purchase the guitar, cord and instruction book for one dollar:

It was quite by accident, really, that I became a guitarist. I was a newsboy, selling papers on a business corner, and there was a store there that had some guitars in the window. The look, the shape of them kinda fascinated me. I saved up enough money to buy a very modest-priced guitar. It had a little book with it, that I believed at the time 'How To Play The Guitar In Five Minutes' I really thought I could.[1]

Barney also related how his father did not want his son to play the guitar as in Budapest, where Abraham had lived, it was usual for beggars to play the guitar on street corners. He feared his son would end up on the street. Barney's mother gave him more encouragement. When asked in an interview if anybody else in his family was musical Barney responded:

My father was a professional boot maker and, as a matter of fact, both my parents were very much against me playing music. At first, he didn't mind me as a child just fooling around with the guitar. But when it looked like I was becoming serious about it, he became quite concerned. My parents felt I would spend all my time playing, and not develop the skills for a profession. They came from Europe, and in Europe most musicians sold pencils at the subway station besides playing. So, they had no way to relate to the fact that music could lead to anything of solid substance and success. My father broke my first guitar. He broke it for two reasons: He got tired of hearing me play the open E chord over and over again in some idiotic fashion, and also he was concerned that I was spending too much time with it. He wanted me to do my school work, have a profession and grow up and have a family.[2]

When asked if he had any formal music tuition Barney confirmed:

I had been exposed to music in public school, through singing and music appreciation. However, I was not really a good music student. I didn't sing well, and I didn't concentrate too much on the academic side of music in school. When I started playing the guitar at 12, I played cowboy music for about a year. But by the time I was 14, I was making my living at music - most of it jazz music. I left home and left school at the age of 14 to become a professional musician.[1]

Barney's teacher for three months under the Federal Music Project was a guitarist of Hawaiian origin called Charles Kiave.

For the most part, I've been self-taught on the guitar from the beginning. With the exception of when I first started; there was a Federal Music Project, sponsored by the Franklin D. Roosevelt government. They had a music grant which allowed certain teachers to devote time to under-privileged children; that is, those from poor families. Right after I bought the guitar, we entered a summer vacation, and I was able to study for about four hours a day, six days a week, with an instructor through the summer term.

And that gave me such a good foundation, because what he taught me was so valid that I even refer to it and use it today. I find that I cannot improve on

Muskogee High School.

that information I received, and I more or less pass this along to other people who start out. So I was fortunate that it was as valid as it turned out to be.[1]

Barney Kessel and his brother, Lester, attended Jefferson and Sequoyah elementary schools in Muskogee. He then attended Muskogee Central High School until the ninth grade. Barney remembered that he worked in his spare time for the Proctor and Marsh cinemas in Muskogee - the Ritz, Broadway, Yale and Roxy. He sold pop-corn and candy bars for five cents each. He later was promoted to an usher and had to take movie reels to the train station on his bicycle so that the films could get to the next town. By the time he was 13, Barney was a member of the band that played backup music for the Saturday morning cartoons on the stage of the Ritz Theatre. Barney explained in a *Muskogee Neighbours* newspaper article:

Through my job at the theater, I saw all the Hollywood musicals - the Busby Berkeley ones and the Fred Astaire 1930s musicals. I saw them over and over and learned the words and music to all the songs.[22]

It was in 1939 that Barney's mother, impressed with his progress, bought him a National electric guitar (with an amplifier) for $150 from Kroh's Music Store in Muskogee.

In a Guitar Player interview Arnie Berle asked Barney how he compared his instruction then with some of today's practices?

Looking back at it now, it was in 1935, and comparing it with the books I see on the market today, I know I couldn't have received better instruction. I learned major, minor, chromatic, and augmented scales; I learned how to read; I learned how to build up to four-note chords, and how to build diatonic scales. I also learned something that is a very important part of fingerboard study that I don't see being taught a lot today. My teacher insisted that as we learned to play each chord, we had to learn the name of each note in the chord, and we also had to know in which part of the chord each note was. Like, which note was the fifth of the chord, or the third. This all happened in just those three months in 1935. Little boys and girls learning all those things. And you know, all the time I was in the class, I felt like I was in the bottom five. I always felt like a real stumble-bum. I remember when I learned to play the six-string barre F chord, my fingers bled from working so hard at it. I had to work so hard to keep up with the rest of the class.[2]

17

When asked if he was playing mostly open-string chords when he first started playing Barney responded:

From the very first, even before I went to a teacher, I was extremely curious to find out how to play melodies that I heard in my head. I think that's a very vital thing to people who want to improvise. I wanted to play everything I heard - the music from the calliope at the fair, the tunes played by the organ grinder with his little monkey. I tried playing all those tunes on the guitar, and I would experiment on all the strings. In other words, the music was already in me. I wasn't looking for the guitar to tell me what I should look for. I already knew what I wanted to find, and I used the guitar to find it. The only thing that has happened through the years is that I learned more about music-developed certain inclinations, certain tastes, and wanted to go in new directions. It's been a matter of finding new material that's come to my heart and to my mind. [2]

Copying guitarists that he heard play on the radio helped the budding guitarist develop his technique. At the age of thirteen Barney played on KBIX, a local radio station, with his friend Coble Parker. By the time he was fourteen Barney played on a regular basis with three bands. Two of these were white bands, playing at 'White Only' dance halls and the other was a black 14-piece band led by Ellis Ezell. Ellis's father had a cleaning shop that was close to Barney's father's shop which was situated in the middle of the white and black areas of town. He used to pass Barney sitting on fenders of parked cars playing his guitar and recognized that he was capable of filling the guitar seat in his band. Barney played with Ezell's band from 1937 to 1939 – and was the only white musician in it. It was the musicians in Ezell's band that encouraged Barney to listen to Charlie Christian and play his guitar solos like a saxophone. The promotional advertisements for Ezell's band said in big letters – *Featuring the Electric Guitar of Barney Kessel*. Barney was always amused that his guitar was a bigger attraction than the player. Ezell's band was very popular and played in all-black clubs throughout Oklahoma. Barney's jazz guitar style was originally influenced by western-swing musicians but as he travelled around he developed a jazz style close to the sounds coming out of Kansas City.

Charlie Christian.

As I was learning those very first chords, I played the country-type music. But a fellow that I went to school with had an extensive jazz record collection. This was about 1935, and he had records by bands like Tommy Dorsey, Benny Goodman, Jimmy Lunceford, Duke Ellington, Count Basie. They didn't have guitar prominently featured on them; there were hardly any electric guitar players, and very few people aspiring to play guitar solos at the time. Even so, I was interested in the ensembles and the various tenor men and trumpet players. So it was through the bands, and not through any guitar players, that I became absorbed with jazz.

When I began to play with local bands in my home town, Muskogee, Oklahoma, it was for dances and private parties. In the course of the next few years, while I was living on the college campus and going to high school, I played with two different college orchestras. [1]

Barney greatly admired the playing of the young black jazz guitar sensation, Charlie Christian who in 1939 had shot to fame as a member of the Benny Goodman orchestra and sextet. There is no doubt that the recordings of this jazz genius profoundly affected Barney. He wrote in detail in two articles in the January and February 1977 issues of Guitar Player magazine about his experience in the spring of 1940 meeting Charlie Christian. In a May 1982 interview with Jas Obrecht, in Guitar Player magazine, Barney added more information:

Speaking about Charlie Christian is a matter of personal love for me. I have just a great personal affection and regard for Charlie and for what he stood for, and I'm even more moved by his music now than I was when I first heard it. His contribution to the electric guitar was as big as Thomas Edison's contributions and Benjamin Franklin's contributions in terms of changing the world: The music Charlie made changed the guitar world. Anyone who studies him can see where all of the guitar players that came afterwards evolved from his fountainhead. They went their own ways according to their own taste, but Charlie was as much a way-shower as any philosophical giant that people have patterned themselves after.

Charlie's tone was the concept for what is being used today in jazz. It is the antithesis of rock, pop rock, or punk rock guitar tones. It's more of an electric guitar sound than an electronic guitar sound. A lot of people think that what I want now and what Charlie Christian wanted then is simply to amplify the natural sound of the guitar - that's not true! That's a different sound entirely. The electric guitar as he played it had its own sound. Charlie's tone was more like the velvety tone of some of the saxophone and trombone players. As a matter of fact, many people that heard him play didn't even know that they were listening to an electric guitar. From a distance, almost everyone thought they were hearing a slightly percussive tenor saxophone. People didn't know what to expect from an electric guitar.

Before I met him, I had heard about Charlie Christian in several ways. First of all, I'm from Oklahoma, where he lived before joining Benny Goodman. Back then I was playing with a 14-piece black orchestra. Most of them knew his playing, and they were always telling me about him. The first record I heard him on was 'Soft Winds', with Benny Goodman. He didn't have a solo on it; he just played in the group and had a couple of little fills. But already I could tell that he was sounding different and good.

Then I heard 'Flying Home' It really knocked me out! It just thrilled me. It was the same kind of impact 16-year-olds felt later when they heard Elvis Presley the first time or the Beatles. It embodied everything I ever loved about the guitar and more, because I didn't realize that you could do all that on the instrument.

I immediately became a disciple of his. I would go down to the record store and just bug them to death: 'Do you have the new Benny Goodman Sextet album? Will you call me when you get one in?' If I didn't have the money to buy it, I'd just take it into the booth and play it over and over. They had to literally force me out of the store—that's the impact! I tried to learn every note I could—not so much to call it my own or to copy it, but because I loved to hear it so much that figured if I was in a place where I couldn't get to a record player, I could take out my guitar and play it. If I had been able to carry around a portable record player, I would probably have been playing the record over rather than trying to play it on guitar.

What knocked me out most was his time clarity, and the fact that everything he played made a statement. There weren't any throwaways, no little fills just to create a little side effect. There was no high-fidelity back then much less stereo or mixing down to different channels, yet he knew enough to get his solo on that record with a lot of presence. When it's time for him to play, he is on the scene. He certainly did not have the kind of technique people have today, or even a lot of people had during his day, because he didn't concentrate on that - it wasn't a big thing.[3]

In 1940 Barney was playing with the *Varsitonians*, a college band from Stillwater, Oklahoma (Oklahoma State University). This band played three nights a week at a club in Oklahoma City. A black waiter there took an interest in Barney's playing and told him during the intermission: *'I'm going to tell Charlie Christian about you. I think he'd like to know that there is a white boy around here playing jazz'* [3]. Barney did not take the waiter seriously, as he believed Christian was in New York with the Benny Goodman orchestra. However Benny Goodman had broken up his band

19

a few weeks before as he had a slipped disc. So Charlie Christian was in Oklahoma City on a leave of absence. The waiter was true to his word. He telephoned Christian, and the famous guitarist arrived at the Oklahoma City club within an hour. Barney related the story as follows:

So in the middle of the next set I was absolutely astounded and bowled over when I looked down and in front of my very own eyes there was Charlie Christian looking up at me, registering his approval of the music and what we were doing. [4]

When the band leader saw Charlie Christian he asked him to sit in with the band. He agreed and Barney was more than happy to hand over his guitar to his mentor, who went on to play some breathtaking solos.

Barney was then delighted when Christian invited him out to eat after the show. Although only a few years older than Barney, Christian was already regarded as America's finest jazz guitarist. He was happy to answer questions which impressed Barney, as in the past, he had found that whenever he questioned established guitarists in bands visiting Oklahoma about music and technique, they would not answer him. In an interview with Ira Gitler Barney explained;

I used to stop certain professional musicians, and ask them questions. And almost all of them ignored me – they wouldn't give me the time of day. [4]

Barney appreciated Christian's kindness even though with the racial segregation at that time it made it very difficult for the two guitarists to eat together. They finally settled on a restaurant where they were able to eat in the kitchen, as this ended up being the only place they could sit down and get served together.

I spent three days with Charlie, and found him to be a pretty inarticulate person. He didn't have very much of a vocabulary. He didn't even talk hip - he didn't say a lot of hip phrases or cliches. He didn't use a lot of words, and he kind of grunted. When he talked about Benny Goodman or Lionel Hampton, he'd say 'The Benny' or 'The Lionel'. He didn't get into a lot of philosophy or teaching. I had the feeling that he was kind of street-wise.

You know, he was so young at that time, working hard and just scuffling to make a living. Before he joined Benny, he was just working for peanuts.

When I was a kid, I listened to a lot of different musicians. As time has gone on and I listen back to them, many of them don't sound as good as they did at the time. Very few of them sound better to me now, and the reason they do sound better is that the music was actually great all the time. Charlie Christian right now sounds better to me than he did when I was a kid in Muskogee, Oklahoma. It's classic music that weathers the deterioration of time. Time removes fads, while classic music holds up and transcends time in a very graceful manner. Paintings have done this; literature has done this. Shakespeare today is no less than he ever was. So Charlie Christian stands up. His music isn't all that's going on in jazz, but it is the personification of jazz. His contribution represents one of the highest standards of excellence. I don't think of him as a guitar player, but as a person who possessed a great amount of feeling for expressing jazz, and he happened to choose the guitar. [3]

The two guitarists jammed for three full days in Oklahoma City. Charlie Christian was really impressed with Barney Kessel's guitar playing and recommended that he move to California where he would have more opportunity to find work, play and to study with musicians of a high calibre.

BARNEY KESSEL – *A Jazz Legend*
3. Los Angeles and the Chico Marx Orchestra

In November 1941 Abraham Kessel died and this probably gave Barney the impetus to move, with his mother's blessing, to Los Angeles in 1942. Barney recalled in some personal notes his arrival in Los Angeles:

I arrived in Los Angeles early on the morning of 1 July 1942 at the Greyhound Bus Station with my guitar, an amplifier, a suitcase and one nickel in my pocket and didn't know a soul there.

I had several mixed feelings as the bus pulled in at the station at 300 Spring Street. I was glad that the bus ride was over. Glad to finally be in Los Angeles. Very anxious about what I was going to do, I was hungry. I didn't know how I was going to carry off my belongings. Carry them where? I experienced panic contemplating the many unknown factors I was about to face in Los Angeles...but mostly I was hungry.

I got off the bus and walked to the area where all of the bags would be delivered by the driver for the passengers to pick up. On the wall I noticed a sign stating that arriving passengers were allowed to leave their bags in storage free for 24 hours.

I knew that I had to come up with a strategy for survival and I quickly began to go over all of the options that I did not have. As I was getting more hungry I decided to leave all of my belongings at the bus station and try to find a job in a restaurant where they would give me a meal first.

I had the name and address of the Shunkey family, the people that my brother knew from Muskogee, and knew that they lived in an area of Los Angeles called Montebello. I asked someone which direction it was from where I was standing and proceeded to walk in that direction, not realizing that Montebello was eight miles away!

As I was walking I kept looking for any signs in the windows of restaurants and cafes that I passed hoping one of them needed a dishwasher. I even went into some of the places and asked them if I could wash some dishes for a meal but no one accepted my offer. I kept walking and walking and

Chico Marx at the piano.

walking, the sun got hotter and hotter and hotter and I got hungrier and hungrier and weaker...but I kept on walking. [19]

In true Hollywood style he finally managed to get a job as a dishwasher in a local restaurant and he then booked a room at a boarding house that some local musicians had recommended. This house was in fact close to the bus station. As he played jazz guitar in local clubs word soon spread about his outstanding talent. One night he came back to the house and the phone rang in the hall. There was no one else there so Barney answered. The caller said he was looking for the guitar player. Barney quickly replied, *'I am the guitar player'*. Barney went down for an audition and got the job. He was hired by drummer Ben Pollack to take the guitar chair in an all-star orchestra fronted by comedian Chico Marx. Barney related the details of the job in a magazine article:

I knew, even at the age of 14, that if I was going to be really serious about playing, I would have to leave Oklahoma and move to either Los Angeles or New York. And I finally decided upon Los Angeles, where I have spent the greater part of my professional life.

Actually, my first engagement away from the local scene was in a road band headed by Chico Marx of the Marx Brothers, whose musical director was Ben Pollack. There were many traditional musicians in there. Marty Marsala played trumpet and Marty Napoleon (who is now with Louis Armstrong) was the pianist. Mel Torme was my room mate; he sang on the band and played relief drums. The drummer was George Wettling. It was a combination of several older musicians and a few younger ones; not many in the middle-age bracket.

This was how I started. Chico Marx was a comedian, of course, and he presented a show; the orchestra was a backdrop for him. He responded to the direction of Ben Pollack, who shaped the band. [1]

Maxine Marx, the comedian's daughter, described her father's role with the band in her biography of her father:

Band life attracted Chico. The schedule was tough, of course, being reminiscent of the old vaudeville one-night stands, but Chico found that his name packed the house every night. The band was a good vehicle for his talents. He would come on stage, tell a joke or two, and then introduce the show. During the course of the program, he would shuffle toward the center spotlight, pretend to conduct the band, tell a few more jokes, take out a banana and start to eat it, and wind up with a solo number. The solo was what the audience generally waited around for, and they loved it: ten unadulterated minutes of Chico shooting the keys and singing the old songs. [6]

An interesting history of Chico Marx's orchestra is described by Mikael Uhlin's on the website Marxology @ marx-brothers.org. Here are extracts of some facts relevant to Barney's period with the orchestra:

Chico had been making plans for an own band since the winter of 1940. Having linked up with jazz band manager Ben Pollack, he launched his solo career in January 1942. Pollack was the head but Chico had name recognition and fronted the band at the piano. They assembled a group of sixteen solid musicians including eight brass (three trombones), six saxophones plus a vocal group.

Postcard advertising the Chico Marx Orchestra at the Blackhawk in Chicago.

The band was planned under the name Chico Marx and his Ravellies (or Ravellis) and was to follow a short series of solo radio sketches to be called Chico's Barber Shop. Apart from a pilot, the radio sketches never materialized but mutated later as TV-show College Bowl. Variety once referred to the band as Chico Marx and the Chicolets, but there is no other reference to them under this title. By mid-February 1942 billing had been amended to Chico Marx and his Orchestra or Chico Marx, his piano, and orchestra or - simply - Chico Marx Orchestra. All along, the music-stands and the drumskin sported a cartoon of Chico's head. [7]

Uhlin goes on to details the band's first engagements:

The band opened in Flatbush, Brooklyn, on 15 January 1942, moving on to the Windsor, Bronx and the Central, Passaic, New Jersey. In March, the band appeared in Cleveland, accompanying harmonica-player Larry Adler. On 13 March 1942 the Chico Marx Orchestra performed at the Stanley Theater in Pittsburgh, a show which was broadcast locally over radio station WCAE as Stargazer Programme, hosted by Ray Spencer. A nine-minute segment of this show has survived but Chico is not heard on it. Vocalists at the time included Bobby Clark and Cpl. Ziggy Lane. Three days later, 16 March 1942, the band again performed at the Stanley Theater in Pittsburgh, this time in Keep 'Em Smiling, a public service broadcast for Defense Stamps.

From Ohio the tour continued to the west with one-night stands in Sheboygan, Oshkosh, Kenosha, Cedar Rapids and Sioux City and then Los Angeles.

In August 1942, just before turning 17, Mel Tormé joined the band as singer and vocal arranger, and eventually replaced George Wettling as the band's drummer. They headed back east during the autumn of 1942.

In October, the band opened a two-month engagement at the Blackhawk Café in Chicago, broadcasting hightlights on a local radio show and drawing a crowd of 4000 to a venue supposed to hold 500 persons. Fuel rationing forced the band to remain in Chicago for two more months. Several of the band members were born in Chicago and of course Chico was no stranger to the town either, having lived there with the rest of the Marxes from 1909 to 1920 More broadcasts followed after Tormé had joined the band, like a show for KLZ, Lake Side Park, in Denver (also featuring Elisse Cooper, Johnny Frigo and Bobby Clark as vocalists) and the Fitch Bandwagon on 20 December 1942, hosted by Toby Reed and eventually available on record. [7]

Barney told me one aspect that he really enjoyed with the Marx band was Mel Torme's innovative big band arrangements of Glen Miller's biggest hits. Barney said these were so expertly written they sounded great but bore no resemblance to the original sound of the Glenn Miller orchestra. Barney also admired the excellent arrangements for the orchestra by Paul Villepigue.

After Barney had been with the band for four months he got word that he was soon to be drafted into the army. He went back home to Muskogee to stay with his mother until he was called up. However he did not make the necessary health grade for army service and was able to rejoin the Chico Marx band, at the Roxy, in New York. He liked New York so much he decided to leave the Marx band in early 1943 and auditioned for the Les Brown Orchestra at the Glen Island Casino, New Rochelle, NY. However, even though Barney had been playing professionally with the Marx band for several months, he was so nervous that he perspired heavily. When Brown asked him to play a solo on *These Foolish Things*, a song Barney knew really well, he could not hold a pick in his hand. With the heavy perspiration, his pick dropped onto the floor and the audition became a disaster. On this occasion, even though he had made a good impression on playing the rhythm parts Barney did not get the job. However, within a few years, Barney did eventually work with Les Brown several times.

A few weeks later he was able to rejoin the Marx band which was on its way to California.

Barney's old friend, studio guitarist Bob Bain, told Jim LaDiana in an interview how he first met Barney at that time in Los Angeles:

I first met Barney at a rehearsal hall in this big building on Vermont Avenue and Beverly Boulevard in Los Angeles called Bimini Baths. It was a bath house. In those days they had a lot of them around. It was strictly a therapeutic type place but they had a big hall on the second floor. It was a huge rehearsal hall and bands used to rehearse there. And they had smaller rooms that had a piano in them. They were renting it out - University of Southern California wasn't to far from there and City College wasn't to far. So if they needed extra rehearsal space they could come over there and rent that stuff. Freddy Slack rehearsed there once a week when he was putting the band together. That's where I first met Barney Kessel.

All of a sudden I'm in there rehearsing and I hear this other band down the hall and I went down and there's Barney Kessel. He was rehearsing with Chico Marx. So I waited around for them to break and I walked over and we started talking. I told him I was gonna be working with Freddy and we were going to be opening that weekend with Slack at a place called Casa Manana in Culver City - big ballroom, held a couple of thousand people.

We started playing Friday night and I think Barney came in maybe Sunday night. A couple of the guys in the band knew him.

Freddy had a pretty good band. It was a pickup band from L.A. but he had good brass players. Howard Rumsey was the bass player I remember. I had a Charlie Christian guitar - that was my electric guitar, and I had an old L-5 cutaway, blonde model - big, big guitar. So I played rhythm guitar and electric. Barney was there and I said, "Hey, do you want to sit in?" He said, "Sure." So I went up to Freddy and I said, "This guy's a great guitar player." And he said, "Sure, let him sit in".

Well, when Freddy would conduct the band, he'd get up from the piano and stand in front of the band so it would just be bass, guitar and drums in the rhythm section. Barney just used my guitar. He sat in and when it came time for him to play a solo it was just like, "What happened?" Everybody just turned around and looked. He got grooving and played about four, five or six choruses. From then on, I mean every time they changed a tune, Freddy would add a guitar solo to the chart - you know, he'd point to Barney. It was just great. He just knocked everybody out with the style he was play-

ing. Those records of Goodman's had just come out with Charlie Christian on electric guitar. Everybody was still listening to 'Seven Come Eleven', 'Airmail Special' and all those tunes. He played exactly like Charlie Christian. He really played so well. And then, of course, I would keep seeing him around town because he stayed in town then and worked a bunch of clubs with his own trio or with somebody else. [8]

BARNEY KESSEL – *A Jazz Legend*
4. Back in Los Angeles

The job with the Chico Marx Orchestra lasted around a year. In the summer of 1944 he joined the Charlie Barnet orchestra. On 3 August 1944 the band recorded their big hit number *Skyliner*. However whenever Barney was in Los Angeles he also played almost daily in jam sessions. Norman Granz, who early on recognized the young guitarist's emerging jazz talent, booked him to play at his Sunday afternoon jam sessions with Lester Young, Nat King Cole and Illinois Jacquet. Granz had originally tried to book Oscar Moore (the star guitarist with the Nat King Cole trio), but Moore turned him down.

As Barney told Ira Gitler;

I'd just gotten active playing in L.A. I just went to a lot of jam sessions. I would go because there were no guitar players that were making the jam sessions. Norman Granz really wanted Oscar Moore all the time, because Nat Cole used to work a lot of these jam sessions. He wanted Oscar because Oscar was already known and worked so well with Nat, but Oscar didn't want to go to these jam sessions. He did not attend them nor did he play them. He just wanted his free time. I was playing around town, and Norman asked me to play, so I began to play. Years ago I was playing in black clubs in L.A. with Nat Cole, J. C. Heard, Shad Collins, Al Killian, and then, later, many, many times played with people like Sonny Criss, Teddy Edwards, Wardell Gray. We'd be playing every night. Zoot Sims was there - Zoot and I, at one time, were on the scene playing all the time and most of the musicians were black. Jimmy Rowles was right there, too. There was a feeling of not only acceptance, but where you really felt they looked at you as an equal and that you had something to say. [4]

Norman Granz booked Barney to play in his award winning short film *Jammin The Blues*. As the only white musician in the film Warner Brothers were concerned that they would not get distribution in some parts of the USA. Granz refused to replace Barney with a black guitarist so a compromise was reached when Barney agreed to have his hands dyed, and sit in the

Barney Kessel c.1945.

shadows, to make it look like he was black. Barney told the story to Ira Gitler in his book *Swing to Bop*:

Norman asked me to be part of that and I was and we got into some problems because Warner Brothers, at that time, thought there would be a great problem in distributing that picture in the South, and not only would people boycott it but also the feature picture that would be shown with it - this picture was a short - they went into all sorts of things. They went into having me in the shadows. They did get to a point where we all - now it seems ridiculous - but we finally thought that the big, big compromise, which today would be out of the question, that they stain my hands with berry juice. I recall one time there is a picture of Lester Young and I sitting next to each other on the set, it's around somewhere - I think it appeared in a national magazine once - he was so white-skinned and he was sitting under a light, and I'm in the shadows, and he looked so much lighter than me. I said about Lester to all the other musicians, 'I don't know if he should be here with us.' [4]

This recording was to be the start of a long working relationship, and friendship, over very many years between Barney Kessel and Norman Granz.

Barney explained to Les Tomkins in a 1969 Crescendo (UK) magazine article:

Later, having moved to Los Angeles and become a regular member there, I worked on radio shows and did radio commercials, phonograph records, motion picture calls. Occasionally a band would come through and what I would do, for the most part was just play or record with them while they were in Los Angeles; I would not leave. I worked with Hal McIntyre and Les Brown that way. [1]

In late 1944 Barney was hired by Artie Shaw. This was regarded as the best big band of the day and its records sold in large numbers. As the guitarist with this famed outfit Barney, at the age of 21, now became known internationally. He had a contract for one year and appeared with the band at concerts, and on many live broadcasts and recordings. In the same magazine interview Barney told of his admiration for Artie Shaw:

The first time I moved away was when I went with Artie Shaw, committing myself for a year.

On the road with the Artie Show band, it was under very different circumstances from the way it had been with Chico Marx. It paid a lot more money; there was a lot more prestige, personally and for the band itself.

I thought Artie was really exemplary as a leader. Many people rebelled at his strictness; they thought he was a task-master. But actually, he wanted a good band, and he knew, that it took rehearsals. And he probably put forth a little more effort than most people do put, or want to put, or expect to put. He was an excellent musician, also.

I don't think he related to the people very well: he just didn't feel their vibrations. He never really gave of himself in the way that they wanted: I think he wanted to give them something that they didn't want from him. So there wasn't any great communication that way. [1]

In the autumn of the 1944 Barney made his first recordings with the Artie Shaw Orchestra. He recorded more than 70 sides with Artie Shaw in 1945 and the first part of 1946. The excellence of his jazz guitar playing can be heard on the tracks of the 1945 Shaw small band (a band within a band) called the *Gramercy Five*. On tracks such as *Scuttlebut*, *The Grabtown Apple*, *The Gentle Grifter*, and *Hop Skip And Jump*, Barney's impressive guitar solos, at times, reflect the early influence of Charlie Christian.

December 1945 saw Barney on more recordings and live dates with the Charlie Barnet big band. For much of the following year a good portion of his recorded output was divided between the big bands of Barnet, Shaw, and Goodman. In the autumn and winter of 1946 Barney worked mainly for Goodman. His first record performances with the clarinetist/bandleader were in early October on an Armed Forces Radio Services

Barney Kessel with members of the Artie Shaw Orchestra c.1944.

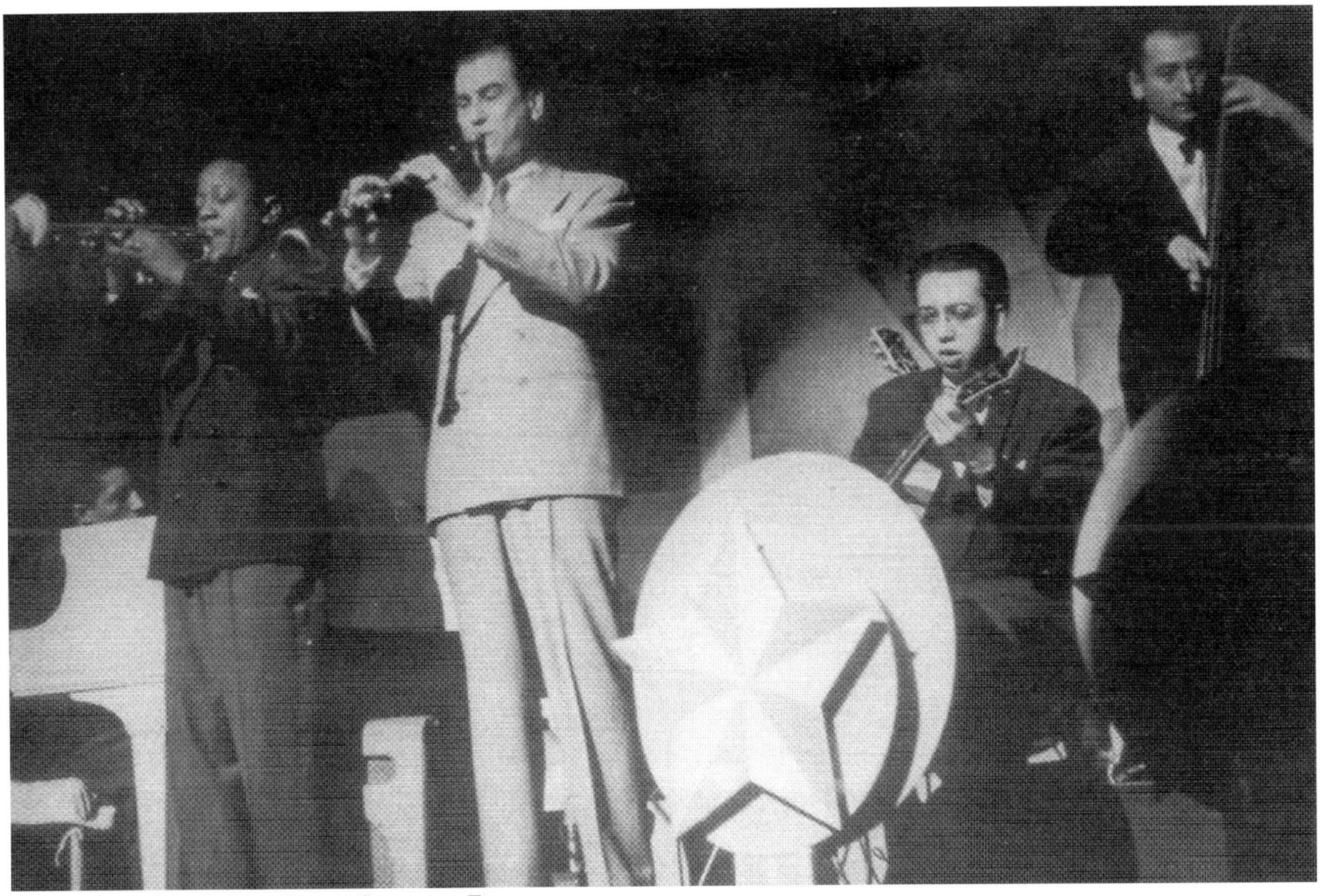

PHOTO: MAURICE J. SUMMERFIELD COLLECTION

Barney Kessel with Artie Shaw's Gramercy Five.

Magic Carpet broadcast from Culver City, California.

Barney confirmed in an August 1987 Cadence magazine interview that he was active in the Central Avenue jazz scene:

I left Oklahoma for the last time in the spring of 1942 and was living in Los Angeles most of the time since then. Where these people now are doing studio work, I was doing it since 1943. There wasn't even television yet. I left there a few times to go out on the road. Those Norman Granz things. I came back and stayed there doing dog food commercials, etc. I would work in the film studios and doing jingles all day then I would go out at night and jam on Central Avenue and several other places that were predominately Black. Usually three or four times a week, sometimes every night. There was also a place in Hollywood called 'The Hangover' which had a lot of musicians come in there. I jammed there so much I left an amplifier there. It reminds me of Charlie Christian's deal because I read later that he left an amp at Minton's. Those amplifiers were heavy in those days and I was in there so much I just left one there. People like Hampton Hawes, Dexter Gordon, Wardell Gray, to name a few, were on the scene then.[17]

On 7 October 1946 Norman Granz featured Barney in a *Jazz at the Philharmonic* (JATP) concert at the Shrine Auditorium in Los Angeles in a group supporting singer Billie Holiday.

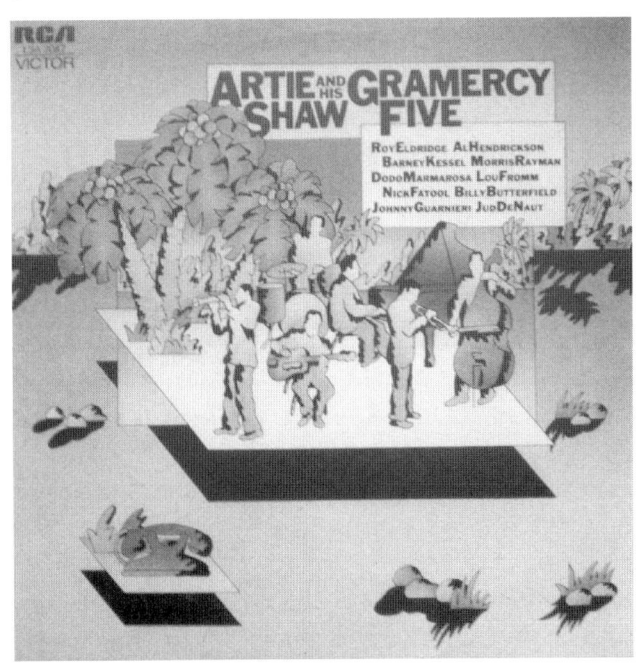

Norman Granz (1918-2001), of Ukranian-Jewish descent, had worked as a film editor at MGM after leaving the army at the end of World War II. He was passionate about jazz, and this led him to persuade Billy Berg, a well-known Los Angeles club owner, to let him present a weekly jam session on Sunday nights at Berg's night club, *The Trouville*. Granz insisted, however, that the club's whites-only audience policy was abandoned. The weekly jam session was a great success and this set the pattern for most of Granz's jazz concerts. In July 1944 Granz booked the Philharmonic Hall for a concert which was another great success. The management of this venue, the home of the Los Angeles Philharmonic, was not happy with the noise level of the loud jam session and would not accept further bookings from Granz. However Norman Granz kept the name, *Jazz at the Philharmonic* (JATP) for what was certainly the most successful jazz touring show of the age. His JATP All-Star concerts crossed America for over ten years, coming to an end with the arrival of the rock and roll era in 1957. Granz continued to promote his JATP concert tours in Europe and the Far East until the late-1970s.

Granz recognized from the late 1940s there would be a relatively large demand for live concert recordings of the JATP All-Stars. After some initial recordings in early 1946 for Asch Records, Granz began his own record label, Clef, later that year. In 1953 he started a second jazz record label, Norgran. Then, in 1956, he joined the two jazz record labels into the highly successful Verve Records. Arguably the most important jazz record producer of all time Granz recorded the great jazz musicians of the day, including Ella Fitzgerald, Duke Ellington, Louis Armstrong, Count Basie, Charlie Parker, Billie Holiday, Oscar Peterson, Stan Getz, Art Tatum, Dizzy Gillespie, Lester Young, Roy Eldridge, Coleman Hawkins, Illinois Jacquet, Barney Kessel, Ray Brown, Harry Edison, Ben Webster, Anita O'Day and many more.

In January 1947 Barney played on his last Benny Goodman Radio Show performance to be issued on record. In a few weeks Barney went on from playing with the *King of Swing* to backing the master of Be Bop. In February 1947 Barney Kessel was a member of the Charlie Parker All Stars recording four songs for Dial Records

Centre of Barney Kessel's first recording as leader, 1945.

including *Carvin' The Bird* and *Relaxin' At Camarillo*. Barney explained to Ira Gitler:

I jammed in different places with Charlie Parker a lot. In fact, once he carried my amplifier into the club from my car. You know, we never sat around and talked. I never saw him except on the bandstand. I really think I had my hands full just trying to learn the music. And I was doing a lot of studio work. During the day. When they were jamming at night, I had already finished a whole day's work, working in the studios.

I remember he wrote out the melodies to these things like 'Relaxin' at Camarillo', which were hard to read for me. They were very syncopated. I was not the reader that I finally developed into, and it was difficult, and they were written on sort of a very coarse-grained paper, like when we were little kids going to school they would have Big Chief tablet paper. If you made one erasure, and you take the whole page, and it makes a very black mark. It's just cheap pulp paper. And this manuscript paper was like that, and he wrote in a very hard leaded pencil, so you could hardly see it, and if the light hit it a certain way you would swear that there was not a mark on that paper. I remember that one of the things - not only could I not read it, except with great difficulty, I had trouble seeing the notes on the page. I recall that really in truth the mixture of that date, not everybody was really into bebop. I don't know why. At that particular time, for some reason, I recall, when Dodo

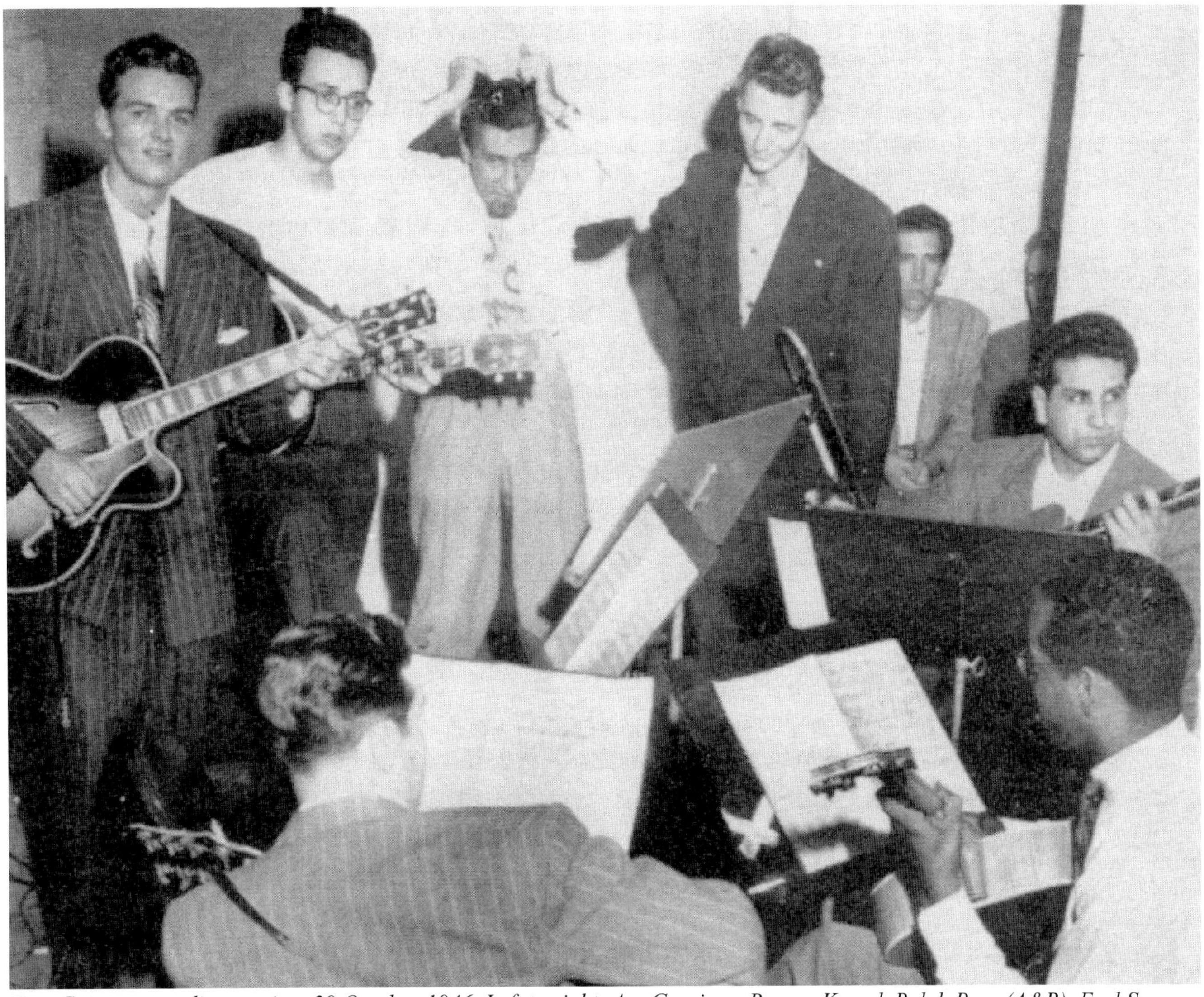

PHOTO: MAURICE J. SUMMERFIELD COLLECTION

Five Guitars recording session, 29 October 1946. Left to right: Arv Garrison, Barney Kessel, Ralph Bass (A&R), Earl Spencer (band leader), Tony Rizzi, Irving Ashby and Gene Sargent.

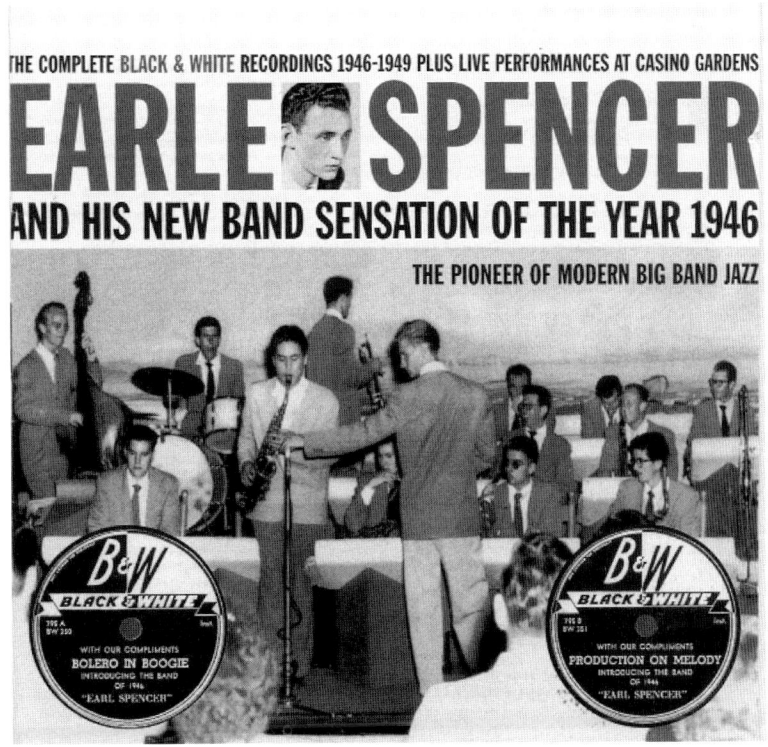

[Marmarosa] played, he played a boom-chick rhythm, which is just the opposite - he never ever did that - that time he did it. It wasn't the appropriate thing for that, nor did he ever do that before or after that.

I recall on one of the tunes - I don't know what it was - Charlie Parker asked him [Don Lamond] to play a four-measure drum break to start. And he played this thing, and I recall that on one of these tunes, when he finished, no one knew where to come in. They asked him to do it again, he did it again, and he did it differently, and they still didn't know. Finally, he did it, and they came in. But it ended up that every time he was absolutely right, and he wasn't trying to be far out; it reminded me of Elvin Jones today; it was very creative and very different and right. It's just that we were used to hearing more of a tap-dance approach - but he was right. He just played an introduction, and we, being used to not counting, but rather to just pick up the traditional metric feel of a typical rhythmic drum solo, we did not bother to count. As a result it went right by us, and we didn't come in right. [4]

When asked if Charlie Parker or producer Ross Russell booked him to play for this historic *Dial* recording session, Barney confirmed:

Ross Russell called me but it was because Charlie Parker asked for me. Unlike Wes Montgomery, who you mentioned, I knew Charlie Parker very well and saw him a lot. Only from the standpoint of music. We never went to dinner together or shot pool but we jammed a lot. When he was in California with Dizzy and after he got out of Camarillo I jammed with him a lot. The whole time he was on the West Coast. When I say a lot, I mean like many nights and many, many hours each night, sometimes until daylight. [17]

Gene Norman was another Californian jazz promoter who was a great fan of Barney Kessel. In the 1940s Norman's radio programmes were very popular in the Los Angeles area. In 1947 he started a successful concert series called *Just Jazz*. For a while he was the principle jazz promoter in Southern California. Norman asked Barney to play in many of his concerts that year. A historic concert was held on 4 August at the Pasadena Civic Auditorium. This featured the *Lionel Hampton Just Jazz All Stars*, which included

Barney on guitar. In 1947 Barney Kessel played on a recording titled *From Dixieland To Bop*, with a group led by saxophonist Lucky Thompson that also featured Benny Carter. Barney also wrote his famous composition *Swedish Pastry* that year for a Capitol Jazz recording session led by his friend Swedish clarinetist Stan Hasselgard. They were supported by Red Norvo on vibraphone and Arnold Ross on piano.

Barney told me that once he had settled in Los Angeles he decided to expand his musical knowledge particularly with arranging, composing and orchestration. From 1935-1943 he had been self-taught using tuition and music books by George Van Eps, Eddie Lang, and Allan Reuss. He also played clarinet studies and exercises, by Hyacinthe Eleanore Klose, to improve his sight-reading. In 1943 he had private classes in counterpoint with Wesley Kuhnle (1898-1962) a well-known recitalist and teacher. In 1948-1949 he studied arranging with Roy Plumb a respected studio recording arranger. In 1951 he studied orchestration with the famous classical composer Mario Castelnuovo-Tedesco (1895-1968). In 1939 Castelnuovo-Tedesco had escaped to the USA from Nazi anti-semitic persecution in Italy and had become a leading Hollywood film composer. From 1951-1953 and then in 1957 Barney studied orchestration with Albert Harris. Before World War II Harris had been one of the UK's top jazz guitarists (and accordionists) playing in a guitar duo with Ivor Mairants. However he gave this up to become a classical music composer, teach orchestration and write music scores for Hollywood films. Both Castelnuovo-Tedesco and Harris wrote classical guitar works for Andrés Segovia.

Barney went on to study music in film technique at night classes with Leith Stevens (1909-1970) a leading composer for Paramount Pictures and a lecturer at the UCLA in Westwood, Los Angeles. Barney also studied conducting with Victor Bay (1901-1988) a former conductor of the Cleveland Symphony Orchestra.

These 15 years of advanced study ensured that Barney was very much in demand in the Hollywood studios for many years not only as a guitar soloist but as a composer, arranger and orchestrator.

From 1948 to early in 1951 Barney worked mainly as a studio musician. He worked for Capitol Records in Hollywood and played on many of their most successful recordings including some by Mel Torme and Billy May. During this time he also played on the recordings of many stars of stage and screen including Gene Autry, Tex Ritter, Tony Martin, Dinah Shore, Jo Stafford, Spike Jones, Mario Lanza, Jane Powell, Fess Parker, The Bell Sisters, Liberace, Frankie Laine, Mario Lanza, Mahalia Jackson, Marlene Dietrich, Barbra Streisand, Frank Sinatra, Dean Martin, Doris Day and Maurice Chevalier. Barney was also very active in the motion picture studios of Paramount, M.G.M, 20th Century-Fox, R.K.O., Columbia and Universal-International. He worked often with the leading Hollywood band leaders and arrangers

Charlie Barnet and his orchestra leaving for Hawaii in 1947. Barney Kessel is third down, top left on the airplane steps.

including Frank DeVol, Paul Weston, Henry Mancini, Elmer Bernstein, Carmen Dragon, Van Alexander, Lawrence Welk and Bob Crosby on their recordings, television and radio programmes.

Jazz at the Philharmonic Concert c.1946. Left to Right; Barney Kessel, Corky Concoran, Illinois Jacquet, Jack McVea. Al Killian and Sammy Yates.

Oscar Peterson Trio.

BARNEY KESSEL – *A Jazz Legend*
5. The Oscar Peterson Trio

Publicity photograph of Barney Kessel used in the 1952/1953 JATP concert tour programme.

In 1952 Barney Kessel, now one of Hollywood's leading studio musicians, was asked by Norman Granz to make up the Oscar Peterson Trio with Ray Brown on bass.

Barney explained to Les Tomkins in a 1969 Crescendo (UK) magazine article;

Then in 1952 I left for a year with the Oscar Peterson Trio. Which was very much of an exposure for me. It was demanding, it involved much fun and growth, and it was financially rewarding. I feel that that particular experience was a real breakaway. There've been several I guess you could call them small or large rungs up a ladder. I'd say that the Peterson Trio was a pretty large rung. It lifted me into another area not only in terms of achieving what needed to be done with the group.

It showed people a different side of my playing. People can only respond to what they see and hear, and they might have thought of me as a good soloist, but in a big band. In a trio you're much more exposed, and able to show your frailties as well as your positive contributions. Of course, Oscar and Ray are both beyond belief as far as technical prowess goes, just dynamic musicians; so it demanded a lot from me.

I was with them ten months in all, and we did a tour for Norman Granz, when we had the pleasure of being the first American musicians in a long time to play in London. That was on the Flood Relief Fund concert.

There was nothing set as to how long I should stay with the trio. I stayed as long as I felt it was the experience I wanted. But I had two young children, and with the normal complexities that come up when a father's been away for a while, it seemed to me that my place was at home. Not from a musical standpoint, but for many other considerations, I felt that I had absorbed about as much out of it as was there for me. In many ways it was a reluctant decision, but nevertheless I had to accept that it was time to move on. [1]

The late Oscar Peterson gave a vivid description of Barney's entry into his trio on his web site history:

Once when we arrived at a club in Los Angeles for a two week engagement, Ray walked in carrying his bass as usual, and upon passing the owner at the door was asked, "Where's the rest of the group?" "Right behind me," replied Ray without stopping. As I came through the door, the owner put his hand out to stop me and said, "What is this, a joke? Where's the rest of the band?" "This is it," I answered and headed for the dressing room. He followed me, ranting and raving about how the booking office was crazy if they thought he was going to pay this kind of money for two guys, regardless of how much music they made. This was precisely the attitude that Norman was referring to when he advised me to consider changing to a trio format.

I finally decided to take the step, and brought in a guitarist who had worked with one of my idols — Irving Ashby from the Nat King Cole Trio. This was only a temporary step, however, lasting until we brought in Barney Kessel. Prior to his stint with us, Barney had been doing a lot of studio work and recording in Los Angeles and hadn't really planned on coming out on the road. He agreed to join us for the period of one year, which would allow us to establish the trio as an operational group in our listeners' minds. I will always remember his entry into the trio: we were playing a little club in Cincinnatti, and he came in 'smoking'. Our very first tune together was Charlie Christian's 'Seven Come Eleven' which has remained in my group's staple library right up to the present time. We opened up by playing the melody chorus in unison, after which I nodded to Barney to take his solo. Kess proceeded to take control of the solo spot for the rest of the evening. How I abdicated this role is still a mystery to me; the only conclusion I was able to come to was that Kess was looking at playing in the trio in the same way 'that a Great Dane looks at a meat counter,' to quote Harry Edison. He continued roasting me on every tune that I called and I could not find any means of opening the door that would allow me back in solo-wise. I have since realized that Kess, constricted in the way that bedevils so many talented studio musicians, was really starving for this kind of jazz improvisation. Brown, of course, enjoyed every moment of my musical consternation, and regularly punctuated the evening by looking over at me with a grin on his face, waiting until Kess had ripped off twelve choruses of something and then asking, 'What are you going to do with that?' Or, 'This is still your trio, isn't it?' I never did get myself together and as the end of the evening arrived, I gave up trying, fully realizing that I had gotten my ass resoundedly kicked.

The marvellous thing about Jazz is that such rude awakenings can pay dividends in your life as an improvising soloist. Thus I went home vowing, as Major Holley would have said, 'to open the vast doors of devastation and destruction' upon Kess at my earliest opportunity. Arriving for work the next night I was immediately serenaded by Ray Brown's carping about whom he was working for in the trio, so struck was he by the difference between the two soloists. I resolved that somehow, somewhere this evening I was going to have to make Barney reckon with me.

As we got ready to play, I decided to retrace our steps of the previous night and once again called for 'Seven Come Eleven'. Brown chuckled and asked, 'Oh? Are we looking for another head-whipping?' Ignoring him, I counted off the tune and we roared into the first chorus, after which I decided to take the first solo. Knowing that Kess was a great Charlie Parker fan and steeped in the Be-Bop era, I geared my solo approach in that direction, quoting segments of Bird's phrases and reshaping others while linking them to phrases of my own. The strategy worked. Kess took another line of approach, and I realized that he was still subconsciously listening to some of the things that I had played, forcing him to go around them musically and change his linear structures. From then on, it became a virtual head-to-head battle between the two of us, punctuated by Ray's solos which we used to separate the two combatants. At the end of the night, Kess walked up to me and said, 'Lord, Oscar, I just came here to play with you, not to make you mad at me. You got terrible on me!' I still remember my reply which was made with loving antagonism, 'It's my trio, Barney.'

Having Barney Kessel in the group opened up new avenues of sound for us. His prodigious technique and harmonic sense allowed me to write arrangements which not only facilitated long flowing lines together, but also contrapuntal lines, accompanied by Ray's big sound and rock-steady time. To add more impetus, we would sometimes have Ray join us in the linear playing, thereby giving tremendous depth and impact to the already exciting effect of three instruments joining forces.

Working with a trio such as this, with Ray's legendary bass foundation and Barney's marvelous harmonic twists, curls and 'shouts' behind me, was something akin to pure heaven. To be in nightly competition with these two great soloists served not only to inspire me but also made me hone my own improvisational efforts. This group did accomplish exactly what its original intent was; the initiation and establishment of the first totally integrated — both musically and racially — Oscar Peterson Trio. [9]

In 1969 Barney described to Alun Morgan his great admiration for Oscar Peterson and Ray Brown:

Let me say that Oscar and Ray Brown are two of the finest human beings that anyone could wish to be associated with. At every level it was a wonderful relationship. They kept me on my toes whenever we played. It was as if I joined the trio at a time when I was just about capable of driving a sports car at sixty miles per hour, but straight away Ray and Oscar kept pushing that pedal down and I found I was trying to control a car at eighty! We got lots of things going with the trio. I learned to recognise Oscar's signals. If he played, say, a little figure in the treble it meant I could go into a chorus of two-part invention! I never had the least trouble over things like passing chords with Oscar, there were no clashes. But nowadays I like to listen to pianists rather than play with them. There are too many problems when you have two instruments capable of playing chords. And the piano can be such a dominant voice too. [5]

When Oscar Peterson heard of Barney's death, in May 2004, he posted the following moving tribute on his web site:

To say that I am saddened by the untimely passing of Barney Kessel would have to be the

Barney Kessel with Oscar Peterson and Ray Brown backing Fred Astaire on his historic Verve recording session.

understatement of mine of 2004. I have been aware of Barney's fight to survive from a major stroke, only to be shackled by cancer of his brain. To me his loss is monumental in the Jazz world.

I was first and foremost a fan and admirer of his from his earlier recordings with various West Coast groups. It was an unbelievable and inspiring occasion for me when he took his place in my trio. To this day I vividly remember his joining the group and on the first night, laying waste to me. Ray Brown loved the occasion of me getting wasted on our first night as a trio, and immediately started a campaign of fear by continually asking me throughout the evening what I was going to do about this new threat that now occupied the guitar chair in our group. After each of Barney's solos in various tunes throughout our first night, Ray would look at me and hit me with queries such as, "What are you going to do with that, Pete?" Or, "Looks like you're going to be in deep water every night." I immediately realized that there was an awful lot of ominous truth in what Raymond was using as his points of musical instigation. All I can remember, at the end of the first night together, is

35

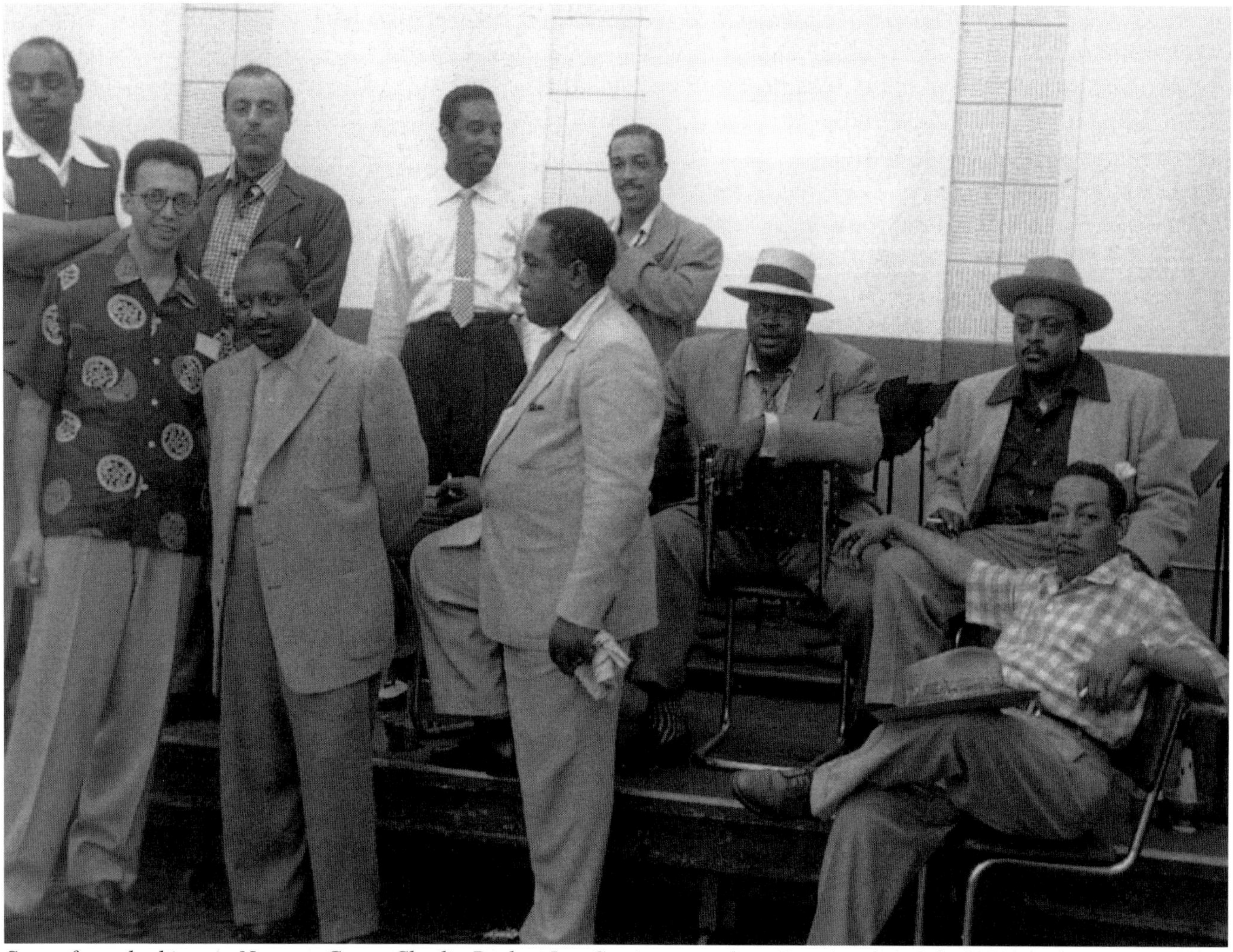

PHOTO: ESTHER BUBLEY. COURTESY: VERVE RECORDS

Scene from the historic Norman Granz Charlie Parker Jam Session recording, Los Angeles, July 1952. Left to Right: Benny Carter, Barney Kessel, Flip Phillips, Charlie Shavers, Ray Brown, Charlie Parker, J.C. Heard, Oscar Peterson, Ben Webster and Johnny Hodges.

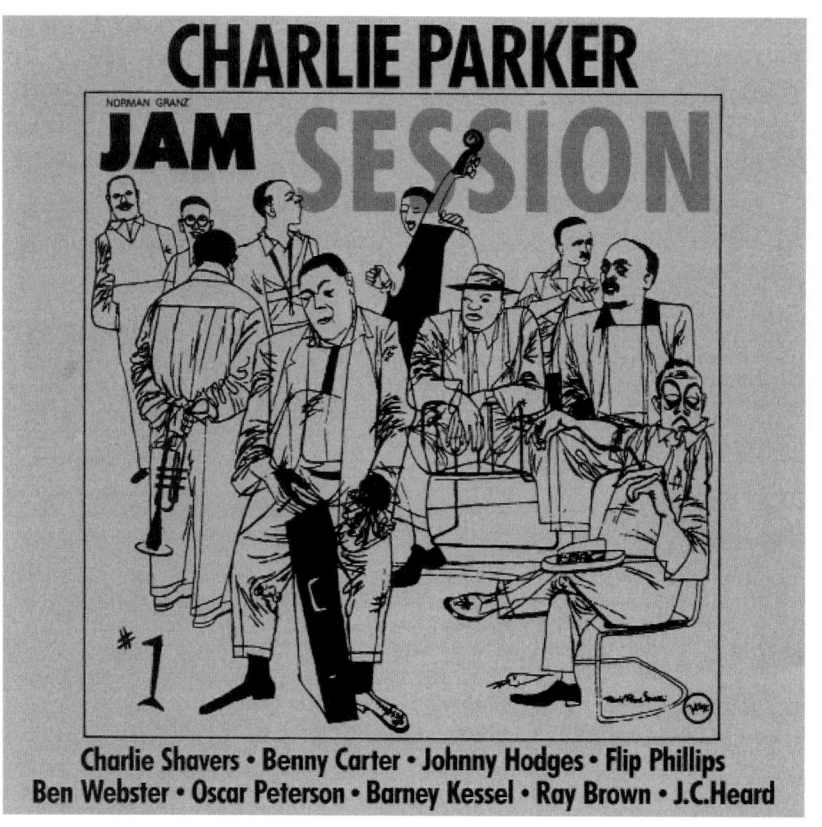

Barney's joyous facial expression when he jubilantly said to me (with that Oklahoma accent), "Oscar, this was better than sex!" Needless to say, I realized at the end of that evening that I was facing an exuberant, overjoyed and caged member of my group. In truth, Barney's fervor and musical talent served to continuously spur my group on to a different and higher level, so to speak, due to his musical presence. When he left the group, needless to say, we felt a tremendous loss. Not only of his musical and inspiring solos, but also his most exuberant guitar "shouts" that he would use behind me at various times during my solos. To say that we missed Barney on his departure from the group would be a tremendous understatement. Barney had a type of almost childlike innocence on various matters that arose from time to time in discussion. We missed this gentle musical genius when he returned to L.A. We shall miss him even more now that he has left our planet for a place beyond our human reach at this moment.

God bless you, Barney, and I hope that you and Ray (Brown died 2 July 2002) *have great fun and musical pleasure together.* [9]

On his return in 1953 to Los Angeles Barney was appointed as Composer, Arranger and Musical Director of the Bob Crosby television show. This networked half-hour programme was broadcast five times a week.

Barney confirmed on the cover of the 1958 *The Poll Winners Ride Again* album that in fact he had wanted to be a composer and arranger for many years:

In small groups today, the amplified guitar is hardly ever used as a rhythm instrument. It's used either to supplement the function of the piano, or to work sometimes instead of a piano, serving as the harmonic basis. Or it's used as an improvised voice in solos. With some guitarists there is a tendency to identify themselves, as far as improvising goes, mainly with what has been created on their own instrument. But I think once you are improvising, being the prominent solo voice, then it's a matter of having a particular idea, or something to say which is within you, and then whatever instrument you play simply becomes your vehicle for expression. All such things as basic techniques, what picking you use, what fingering you use, these are all means to an end. There has been a misconception about me, for example, about Charlie Christian being my sole influence on guitar. Up to a certain point he was, but that doesn't mean I didn't listen to Charlie Parker, or Lester Young, or others. As for my own thoughts: I feel everything I play is actually a combination of all my years of experience and exposure to various types of music that I've played. I think that anything I have done can't help but come out in my playing at some time, and the fact I was playing Count Basie arrangements when I was fourteen years old would by this time serve to be a very natural and instinctive thing. I've wanted to be an arranger and composer for many years, and in the last couple of years I have actually seriously studied and worked on this to try to make what was a boyhood dream come true, and to be writing with all the freedom that I have in playing. It is in a stage of development as is everything else about my music, but the things I have learned about composition find their way into my playing so that there are things, as a result of having studied, that I no longer do, and many things I do now that I was not aware of before. [12]

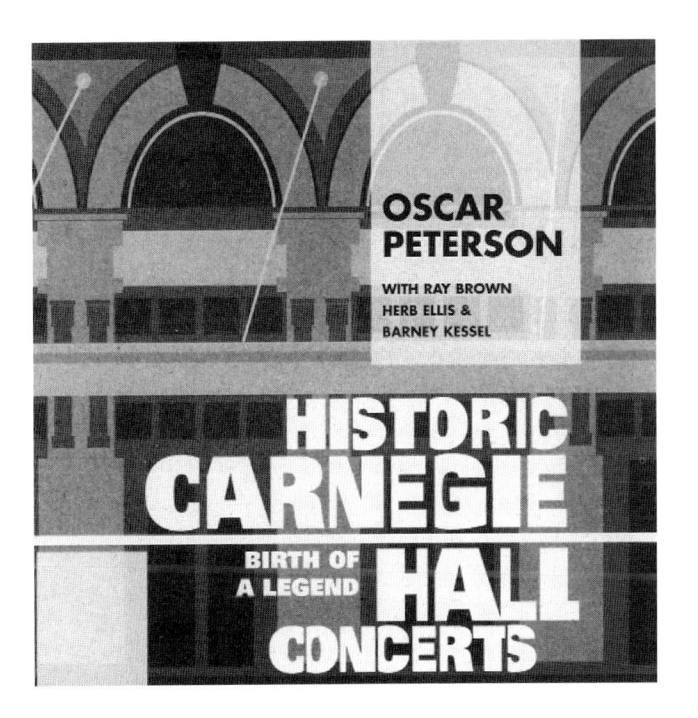

BARNEY KESSEL – *A Jazz Legend*
6. Contemporary Records

Lester Koenig (1917-1977), initially a traditional/classic jazz lover, founded the Good Time Jazz label in 1949 in Los Angeles. His first releases for this label were by the Firehouse Five Plus Two. Koenig went on to record Jelly Roll Morton, Burt Bales, Wally Rose, Lucky Roberts, Willie 'The Lion Smith, Lu Watters, Bob Scobey, Bunk Johnson, Kid Ory, George Lewis, Johnny Wiggs, Sharkey Bonano, and Don Ewell.

Contemporary Records was founded by Lester Koenig in 1951 to record contemporary classical music. However as Koenig became passionate about modern jazz he used his Contemporary label to release recordings by the best modern jazz musicians resident on the West Coast including Sonny Rollins, Ornette Coleman, Curtis Counce, Harold Land, Jack Sheldon, Carl Perkins Ben Webster, Art Pepper, Ray Brown, Shelly Manne, Hampton Hawes, Leroy Vinegar and in particular Barney Kessel. Koenig, like Norman Granz and Gene Norman, recognised Barney's great jazz artistry early on, and over the next few years released some of Barney's finest recordings, including five historic *The Poll Winners* recordings.

Koenig's eventually amalgamated Good Time Records into Contemporary Records, After Koenig's early death in 1977, the Contemporary catalogue was sold to Fantasy Records, who in 2004 sold out to the Concord Music Group. Virtually all of Barney's original Contemporary recordings are fortunately now available on CD.

Barney had a great regard for Lester Koenig, as did all the other musicians who recorded for him. Barney explained to Les Tomkins how Koenig helped his career in a magazine interview:

Yes, about then was the beginning of the era of West Coast Jazz. They were starting to have the Lighthouse concerts, Shorty Rogers was doing a lot of writing, and musicians like Bud Shank and Bob Cooper began to evolve. And Bob Enevoldsen, Frank Rosolino, Hampton Hawes, Teddy Edwards - I worked with all of them through the mushrooming period. It was a kind of a quiet, dainty, precise way of swinging, but it was still different; it was not Dixieland, traditional or bebop. I would say it was a diminutive emotion, yet a pleasant one.

My direct benefit from this phase of activity was in the jazz recording field. I had been unable to have anyone sign me to record until I met Les Koenig of Contemporary Records. Not only would he sign me, but he was very enthusiastic about what could be done.

He just gave me so much freedom: we weren't really concerned with whether the records were a hit, but that they were done well. And Les is so meticulous and immaculate in what he wants on the record; he really has very high standards about the production of them. It was a complete pleasure to work with him. [1]

In December 1953 Barney Kessel recorded *Easy Like*, his first recording for Contemporary. Barney was backed by saxophonist Bud Shank, pianist Arnold Ross, Harry Babasin on bass and Shelly Manne on drums. Of the eight tracks originally released, four were Barney Kessel originals: including *Vicky's Dream* named after Koenig's daughter Vicky, *Bernardo* a reminder of his real first name, and *Salute to Charlie*

Christian – a fantastic tribute to his original jazz guitar inspiration. This first Contemporary recording did very well and in June and July 1954 Barney recorded his *Barney Kessel Plays Standards* quintet album for Contemporary. Shelly Manne is once again on drums, but the other members of the quintet included Claude Williamson (piano), Monte Budwig (bass). with Bob Cooper (playing both tenor saxophone and oboe). It is generally accepted this is the first jazz recording of an oboe playing jazz. This historic recording enjoyed excellent sales and in 1955 Barney recorded for Contemporary his stunning septet album *To Swing or Not To Swing*, and then a further quintet album.

By now Barney Kessel was one of Contemporary's most successful artists winning several leading jazz polls. On 23 February 1956, Barney recorded another album with a quintet that included Claude Williamson (piano), Red Mitchell (bass), Shelly Manne (drums) and Buddy Collette (doubling on alto saxophone and flute).

The continuing sales success of Barney's recordings led to further Contemporary Records releases including *Music to Listen to Barney Kessel By* recorded in in October and December 1956. This recording featured a larger group, including the clarinet, oboe, bassoon. August and December 1957 saw the recording of *Lets Cook'*, and in December 1958 Barney's marvelous jazz arrangement of Bizet's opera *Carmen* was recorded. March 1959 saw Barney's septet recording the music from the film *Some Like It Hot*. Barney had played on the film studio's soundtrack and this had given him the inspiration to produce this album.

Some of Barney's most successful recordings for Contemporary were his five *The Poll Winners* albums. *The Poll Winners*, Barney Kessel, Shelly Manne, and Ray Brown recorded their first album in March 1957. All three musicians, at that time, had won the three respective 1956 and 1957 popularity polls in Downbeat, Metronome and Playboy magazines. This first *The Poll Winners* album was the first jazz recording to have a line up of only electric guitar, bass and drums. With this recording Barney Kessel changed the course of jazz guitar history by giving the guitar a prominence it had never previously enjoyed in jazz.

The Poll Winners in the Contemporary recording studios.

Barney confirmed the idea of this historic trio was his in an interview with Larry Hollis and Eddie Ferguson. When asked how did the Poll Winners trio come about. Was it Lester Koenig's idea or did all three musicians get together and present him with the idea? Barney confirmed:

Well, I'm very happy to say modestly that it was my idea. First of all, each of us were associated with Les Koenig (Contemporary Records) in different ways. Shelly Manne and I both had recording contracts with him to do records on our own. Ray Brown did not have a contract but he did a lot of dates for him. I got the idea of naming the group 'The Poll Winners' since we all, at the time, happened to be winning music polls. It just came to me and I thought it was a good name but I got the idea to play together before I had the idea for the name. Ever since I had left Oscar Peterson I had been experimenting in playing without a piano. No reflection on him or any other piano player. I just wanted to have a group just like a piano player has a group. I played a little around Hollywood trying to bring it together. In order to play that way you have to use a little different psychology and thoughts to make it work out. You have to

The author had a standing order for every Barney Kessel recording at Jeavons record store 1956-1976.

carry the ball and it requires a new orientation. It became apparent to me that in order to make that real good I would have to play with some very wonderful, capable and heavy musicians because there's no weight and I needed a bass and drums that really covered the scene. I really wanted to record in this manner so that's how this came about. Les was always after me to record more. In those days there was every chance to do it and I wish I had recorded more. When I first started recording for Lester Koenig I didn't want to use the same instrumentation for every record because I wasn't trying to be like a Dave Brubeck or George Shearing and have every record sound the same. That's why I used different musicians and different instruments. I purposely wanted them to be different because, in the end I wanted to sell myself rather than have the thought of when you say 'Barney Kessel' you have the idea of a certain instrumentation or sound as George Shearing's quintet was for many years. I came to Les with the idea of the guitar, bass and drums trio, told him the players I wanted to use and said I even have a name for it. He liked the whole idea so we did it. Les gave me a chance to record as a leader when hardly no one else would. To them I was just a good sideman. [17]

Barney's admiration for Ray Brown and Shelly Manne is revealed in an interview at the Contemporary Record company offices on 10 February 1960;

Ray's the best bass player in the world. He's got everything - tone, time, choice of notes. I'm afraid we take him for granted, the way we do Shelly. Besides being a good drummer, Shelly listens to what other people are playing. It's not that other drummers can't play the same things - he just plays them at the right time because he's listening. He's always different, depending on what's being played, and he can do anything from swinging hard to the most delicate lyrical things.

We don't sound exactly the same in any other group as we do on the Poll Winners albums. We have complete freedom, and yet all three are playing together. We listen to each other. It's not a guitar with bass and drum accompaniment - it's a trio in every sense of the word. [12]

Over the years several more excellent and innovative Barney Kessel-led group recordings were made for the Contemporary label – and full details of these can be found in my extensive discography at the end of this book. Koenig also chose Barney as a featured soloist on several of his recordings with groups led by other great jazz musicians including Sonny Rollins, Red Norvo and Hampton Hawes.

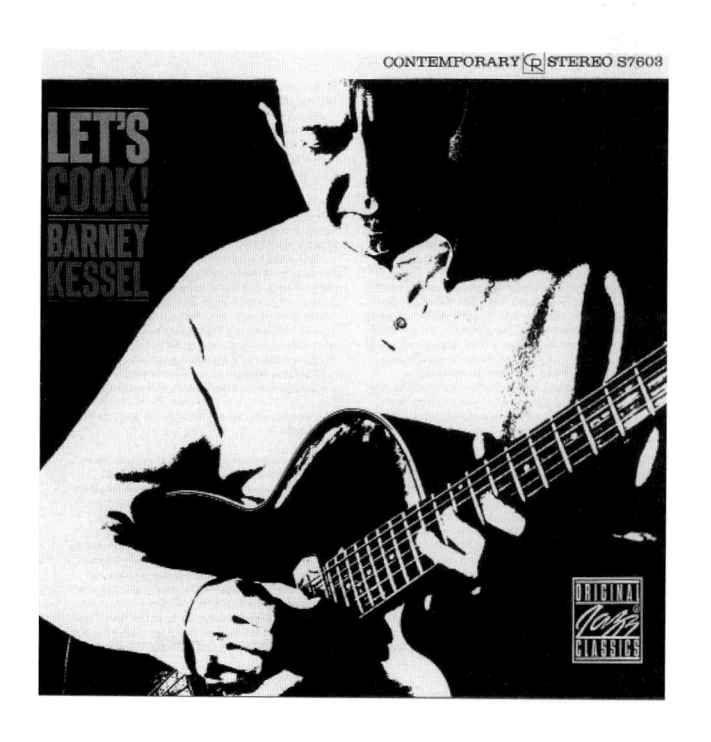

Gibson Guitar Company advertisement celebrating Barney Kessel's 25th Downbeat jazz poll.

guitar

1.	Barney Kessel	1195
2.	Herb Ellis	372
3.	Charlie Byrd	358
4.	Kenny Burrell	319
5.	Jim Hall	288
6.	Freddie Green	262
7.	Johnny Smith	253
8.	Tal Farlow	148
9.	Mundell Lowe	88
10.	Wes Montgomery	84
11.	Jimmy Raney	61
12.	Sal Salvador	60
13.	Barry Galbraith	49
14.	Eddie Condon	43
14.	Howard Roberts	43
15.	John Pisano	37
16.	George Van Eps	36
17.	Chuck Wayne	34
18.	Billy Bauer	25
19.	Al Viola	24
20.	Les Paul	22

Downbeat magazine's 1959 Jazz Poll results.

GUITAR

1.	Barney Kessel (1)	1675
2.	Wes Montgomery (10)	1301
3.	Kenny Burrell (4)	1129
4.	Charlie Byrd (3)	761
5.	Jim Hall (5)	442
6.	Herb Ellis (2)	439
7.	Johnny Smith (7)	363
8.	Freddie Green (6)	250
9.	Sal Salvador (12)	216
10.	Tal Farlow (8)	207
11.	Laurindo Almeida (-)	112
12.	Mundell Lowe (9)	103
13.	Jimmy Raney (11)	81
14.	Les Spann (-)	65
15.	Howard Roberts (14)	50

(None under 50 listed)

Downbeat magazine's 1960 Jazz Poll results.

BARNEY KESSEL – *A Jazz Legend*
7. Julie is Her Name

In August 1956 the Liberty LP recording *Julie is Her Name* was recorded featuring vocalist Julie London backed only by Barney Kessel's guitar and Ray Leatherwood on bass. This historic recording brought to jazz a new line up for vocalists.

Julie London was born 26 September 1926, in Santa Rosa, California, as Gayle Peck the daughter of the vaudeville song-and-dance act Jack and Josephine Peck. At the age of 14 London's family moved to Los Angeles. And, not long after, she began getting some small film parts in the Hollywood studios. During World War II Julie London was one of the GIs' favourite pin ups.

In July 1947 London married actor Jack Webb who would become internationally known through the *Dragnet* television series. The marriage was not a good one and they divorced in November 1953. The one thing they did have in common, however, was a love of jazz.

In 1954, having become a bit reclusive following her divorce from Webb, London met jazz pianist Bobby Troup at a club on La Brea Blvd in Los Angeles. Troup, whom she eventually married, recognised her singing talents. In 1955 he got London hired for a ten week booking at the 881 Club on the Sunset Strip in Los Angeles. Barney Kessel wrote all the arrangements and the sell-out audiences were stunned by the musical completeness of his guitar backings with the support of Ralph Pena on bass.

Troup tried several record companies to sign London up. Finally he managed to persuade Sy Waronker, President of Liberty Records to hear the trio at the club. Waronker, impressed, immediately contracted London to record for Liberty. At first he wanted Bobby Troup's Quartet to back her but Troup insisted that Barney (with Ray Leatherwood on bass) would accompany her on the first *Julie is Her Name* recording. The big hit on the LP recording was the song *Cry Me a River* written by London's high school classmate Arthur Hamilton. After its release as a single in April 1957 *Cry Me A River* sold over one million copies. It was also featured in the 1956 film *The Girl Can't Help It*. The song continues to retain it popularity to this day and was featured in the films *Passion of Mind* (2000) and *V for Vendetta* (2006).

As an actress Julie London starred in more than 20 films. As a singer she made 32 albums from 1956 to 1981. Liberty released *Julie is Her Name Volume 2* in 1958. They wanted Barney to back the singer again on this recording. However the terms of the contract Liberty offered were not acceptable to Barney in light of the fact that most critics agreed it was his guitar backing that had made the first volume such a big success. As a result Liberty hired guitarist Howard Roberts, who had taken some private guitar lessons with Barney, to play the backing (in the Kessel style) with bass player Red Mitchell on this second Julie London recording.

As fate would have it the last recording Julie London made was the song *My Funny Valentine* for the soundtrack of the 1981 Burt Reynolds film *Sharky's Machine*. On this recording she was reunited with Barney on guitar supported, this time, by Ray Brown on bass and Shelly Manne on drums.

Julie London died in October 2000.

Bossa Nova
Barney's guitar backing on *Julie is Her Name* also helped formulate the jazz harmonies of the founders

of the new Bossa Nova movement a few thousand miles south in Brazil. It is well documented that in 1965 one of the founders of this new movement, Roberto Menescal, – spent hours listening to the record *Julie is Her Name*. Not because of the sensual voice of Julie London, or the beautiful pin up picture on the LP album cover, but for the guitar accompaniment of Barney Kessel. Menescal was not alone. Many of the young Brazilian musicians regarded Barney Kessel as one of their main 'influencia do jazz ' in the early development of Bossa Nova. They loved the harmony of Barney's chords and began to incorporate these into their own harmonies. In the 2008 DVD film *Bossa Brasil – The Birth of Bossa Nova (Warner 5061442-806328)* Roberto Menescal explains in detail, with some musical examples played on his guitar, the importance of Barney Kessel's influence on the jazz harmonies incorporated into the original sounds of Bossa Nova. Barney once told me, that when he was playing some concerts in Brazil, he met Antonio Carlos Jobim who surprised Barney by shaking him by the hand and thanking him for giving him so many ideas, from his Contemporary and Liberty recordings, for the harmonisation of some of his bossa nova hit songs.

Copy of 1 June 1967 amendment to Barney Kessel's birth certificate legally changing his first name from Bernard (Bernout) to Barney.

BARNEY KESSEL – *A Jazz Legend*
8. Studio Musician

The purpose of this book is to document the life in jazz of Barney Kessel. However as he was such an important figure in the Hollywood studios a brief mention of his great contribution to this field of popular music is in order.

From 1956-1960 Barney Kessel was head of A&R for Verve Records in Beverly Hills. Verve President, Norman Granz, asked Barney to find him some 'rock 'n' roll product' because his record distributors were asking for it after Elvis Presley hit the scene. Barney, years earlier, had played in a band with Ozzie Nelson on the Red Skelton show. He saw Ricky Nelson on a *The Adventures of Ozzie and Harriet* show on television and saw great potential in the young singer. Nelson's talent agency, MCA, had sent a demo tape of Nelson singing *I'm Walkin'* (written by Fats Domino and Dave Bartholomew and originally a hit for Domino on Imperial Records) out to more than 20 record labels. Each one turned it down. When Barney heard the tape he realized that Ricky had already had a large following through his appearances on Ozzie Nelson's weekly television shows. Barney quickly made a contract with Nelson for one three hour recording session for Verve. Three songs *I'm Walkin* (which would be the first A side), *A Teenager's Romance*, and *You're My One and Only Love* were completed. Barney recorded Ricky Nelson's version of *I'm Walking* for Verve, against, the protests of Ozzie Nelson, and Norman Granz. They thought Ricky shouldn't cover a recent hit. But Barney had already decided that Ricky gave his best performance on that song and he liked the combination of Ricky Nelson with the R&B Fats Domino inspired sound. He decided not only would they record the song but Verve would make it Ricky Nelson's debut release. Barney wrote the arrangements, hired the musicians (including himself on guitar) and produced all the sessions. It went quickly to number #4 in the charts.

After *I'm Walkin* peaked, the radio stations began to play the B-side *A Teenager's Romance* and this soon reached Number #2 on the charts. Barney then wrote (along with Jack Marshall) *You're My One And Only Love* for Ricky's next A-side release. Barney again produced, arranged the recording and played guitar in the backing band. The song shot up the charts to hit number #4. In an innovative move (which set an example for his protégé, Phil Spector) Barney claimed he wrote the instrumental B-side *Honey Rock* in less than one minute and then recorded it in one take. It was Barney Kessel and his band (playing a solid riff support backing with a young girl singer chorusing *Oh, Honey*) that made this record into such a popular record hit.

Such was Nelson's success that Verve could not keep up the supply for the volume of incoming orders and they delayed in pressing new singles by Nelson. Ozzie Nelson also claimed they were slow in paying his son royalties. Lew Chudd of Imperial Records contacted Ozzie Nelson about signing up his Ricky. He had heard that Ozzie was unhappy with Verve and that they only had an agreement for only the one session. Chudd and Ozzie Nelson quickly agreed a five-year contract for Ricky, with Imperial Records, guaranteeing $50,000 against royalties.

Barney Kessel was also impressed when he heard jazz ukulele player Lyle Ritz playing live and quickly signed him for Verve. They released Ritz's albums *How About Uke?* in 1957 and *50th State Jazz in 1959*. These albums sold very well in Hawaii but did not achieve any real success in the USA itself. Ritz eventually gave up playing the ukulele professionally for many years and switched to playing the double bass.

Betty (B.J. Baker) Kessel, Barney's second wife, was a leading studio background singer (she was also a talented jazz singer who had been classically trained) and a vocal contractor for records, films and TV. She had sung on many hit Frank Sinatra recordings including *That's Life*. She also sang on several hit recordings of Elvis Presley, Lloyd Price, Dean Martin, Ray Charles, the Beach Boys, Sam Cooke, Willie Nelson and many others. Barney often played guitar on the same recordings – and sometimes bass guitar.

Barney Kessel performed on many Beach Boys hits such as *I Get Around*, *California Girls* and *Dance, Dance, Dance.* He was also in the backing group for Brian Wilson's historic productions

Phonograph Recording Contract Blank
AMERICAN FEDERATION OF MUSICIANS
OF THE UNITED STATES AND CANADA

Employer's name: **Capitol Records, Inc.**

N° 195427

Local Union No. **47**

THIS CONTRACT for the personal services of musicians, made this **22** day of **January**, 19**66** between the undersigned employer (hereinafter called the "employer") and **16** musicians (including the leader) (hereinafter called "employees").

WITNESSETH, That the employer hires the employees as musicians severally on the terms and conditions below, **and as further specified on reverse side**. The leader represents that the employees already designated have agreed to be bound by said terms and conditions. Each employee yet to be chosen shall be so bound by said terms and conditions upon agreeing to accept his employment. Each employee may enforce this agreement. The employees severally agree to render collectively to the employer services as musicians in the orchestra under the leadership of **Hal Blaine** as follows:

Name and Address of Place of Engagement: **Gold Star Recorders, 6252 Santa Monica Blvd, Los Angeles, Calif.**

Date(s) and Hours of Employment: **January 22, 1966 7: P.M. to 11:30 P.M.**

Type of Engagement: Recording for phonograph records only.

WAGE AGREED UPON $ **Union Scale** (Terms and amount)

Plus pension contributions as specified on reverse side hereof.

This wage includes expenses agreed to be reimbursed by the employer in accordance with the attached schedule, or a schedule to be furnished the employer on or before the date of engagement.

To be paid **Within 14 Days** (Specify when payments are to be made)

Upon request by the American Federation of Musicians of the United States and Canada (herein called the "Federation") or the local in whose jurisdiction the employees shall perform hereunder, the employer either shall make advance payment hereunder or shall post an appropriate bond.

Employer's name and authorized signature: **Capitol Records, Inc.**
Street address: **1750 N. Vine St.**
City/State: **Hollywood 28, Calif.** Phone: **HO-26252**

Leader's name: **Hal Blaine** Local No. **47**
Leader's signature: /s/ Hal Blaine
Street address: **2441 Castilian Dr.**
City/State: **Hollywood 28, Calif.**

(1) Label Name: **Capitol Records, Inc.**

Master No.	No. of Minutes	TITLES OF TUNES
	2:32	WOULDN'T IT BE NICE

(2) Employee's Name (Last, First, Initial)	(3) Home Address	(4) Local Union No.	(5) Social Security Number	(6) Scale Wages	(7) Pension Contribution
(Leader) Blaine, Hal	2441 Castilian Dr., Hollywood, 28, Calif.	47	047-20-5900	284.72	22.78
Kreisman, Steven Douglas	6950 Chisholm Ave., Van Nuys, Calif.	47	556-46-1005	284.72	22.78
Capp, Frank, 2-Dbls bells,tympani,percussion	3017 Dona Nenita Pl., Studio City, Calif.	47	013-24-7193	172.87	13.83
Caton, Roy V.	3760 Willowcrest Ave., No. Hollywood, Calif.	47	192-20-7730	142.36	11.39
DeLory, Alfred V.	5524 Ruthwood Dr., Calabasas, Calif.	47	559-36-9796	142.36	11.39
Fortina, Carl	838 N. Orange Dr., Hollywood 38, Calif.	47	554-32-8082	142.36	11.39
Johnson, Plas	4120 W. 59th St., Los Angeles 43, Calif.	47	434-44-2284	142.36	11.39
Kaye, Carol	4905 Forman, No. Hollywood, Calif.	47	555-46-5389	142.36	11.39
Knechtel, Lawrence W.	4847 Van Noord, Sherman Oaks, Calif.	47	553-54-6386	142.36	11.39
Kessel, Barney	1727 Las Flores Dr., Glendale 7, Calif.	47	447-12-3334	142.36	11.39
Kolbrak, Jerry	4121 Oak St., Burbank, Calif.	47	394-36-7847	142.36	11.39
Marocco, Frank	7063 Whitaker Ave., Van Nuys, Calif.	47	329-22-0203	142.36	11.39
Migliori, Jay	1701 N. Lincoln, Burbank, Calif.	47	208-24-6118	142.36	11.39
Pitman, William	9124 Nagle Ave., Pacoima, Calif.	47	068-16-6762	142.36	11.39

SEE ATTACHED CONTINUATION SHEET****************************

(8) Total Pension Contributions (Sum of Column (7)) $ **207.46**
Make check payable in this amount to "AFM & EPW Fund."

FOR FUND USE ONLY:
Date pay't rec'd _____ Amt. paid _____ to posted _____ By _____

Form B-4 Rev. 4-59

Copy of the American Federation of Musicians contract for the musicians taking part in a Beach Boys recording session. Barney Kessel's rate was $142.36.

Barney Kessel in the recording studio, May 1955, Los Angeles with Chico Hamilton (drums), Curtis Counce (bass) and Gerald Wiggins (piano).

of *Pet Sounds, Good Vibrations* and *Smile*. It is documented that Brian Wilson sent Barney a letter thanking him for his important contribution to the production and ultimate success of *Pet Sounds*.

Barney became first call on guitar for many pop and rock record dates. Leading artists and producers in Los Angeles realised that Barney's musical talent could help make a hit for them by including one of his catchy instrumental hooks. One example is Jimmy Gilmer's number # 1 hit *Sugar Shack* on Dot Records. It was five weeks in the charts in the 1963 record sales, second only to the Beatles' *She Loves You*. Barney also wrote a simple but effective bass line for this hit song which he played on a distinctive sounding Danelectro bass guitar. He also played on several Sonny and Cher's hits including *I Got You Babe* and *The Beat Goes On*. Sonny and Cher gave Barney the nickname *The Professor*!

Barney was the guitarist, along with keyboardist Jack Nitzsche on Marty Balin's 1962 solo debut recording for the Challenge label, *I Specialize In Love.* Balin went on to form the famous group *Jefferson Airplane*. Barney also played with Spencer Davis at the *Troubadour Club* in Los Angeles where they also made a live recording.

Barney and Betty Kessel had several business ventures. In 1964 they founded Emerald Records which, in 1965, released Barney's *On Fire* album. This great recording was distributed by Phil Spector. In 1967 they formed the Windsor Music Company which published Barney's critically acclaimed basic guitar tutor *The Guitar*. Then, in 1967, they opened a retail music store *Barney Kessel's Music World*. This was on Vine St. in Hollywood and was furnished and decorated to a high standard by Betty. They attracted many famous names as customers including John Lennon, George Harrison, Buffalo Springfield, Chris Darrow, Bobby Darin, Sandra Dee, Frank Zappa and the Beach Boys. In 1969 Barney helped Bernardo Ricco (B.C. Rich Guitars) to start his career by letting him one of the two upper lofts in the store, next to Los Angeles' top guitar repair man (at that time) Milt Owen. *Barney Kessel's Music World* traded for only three years.

Barney appeared often on television and can be seen playing in a jazz group in *Shop of The Four Winds,* episode four (first broadcast on 8 October 1959) of the popular late 1950s early 1960s *Johnny Staccato* television series. He also appeared in *The Naked Truth*, the pilot episode (first broadcast 10 September 1959). Barney played the part of a jazz guitarist (called Barney) in the episode *The Case of the Missing Melody* (first broadcast 30 September 1961) in the very popular Perry Mason television series. In this programme he plays opposite pianist/composer Bobby Troup. Barney also composed and conducted all the music for this programme.

The founder of the USA magazine *Guitar Player*, Jim Crockett, was a very great fan of Barney Kessel. In fact Crockett named his son Kessel to mark his admiration for Barney. He invited Barney in 1967, when the magazine was first published, to write a regular column for *Guitar Player* – which Barney did for several of the earlier issues.

Barney Kessel continued working in the film and television studios. He was the guitarist in the orchestra on the soundtrack of the Orson Welles

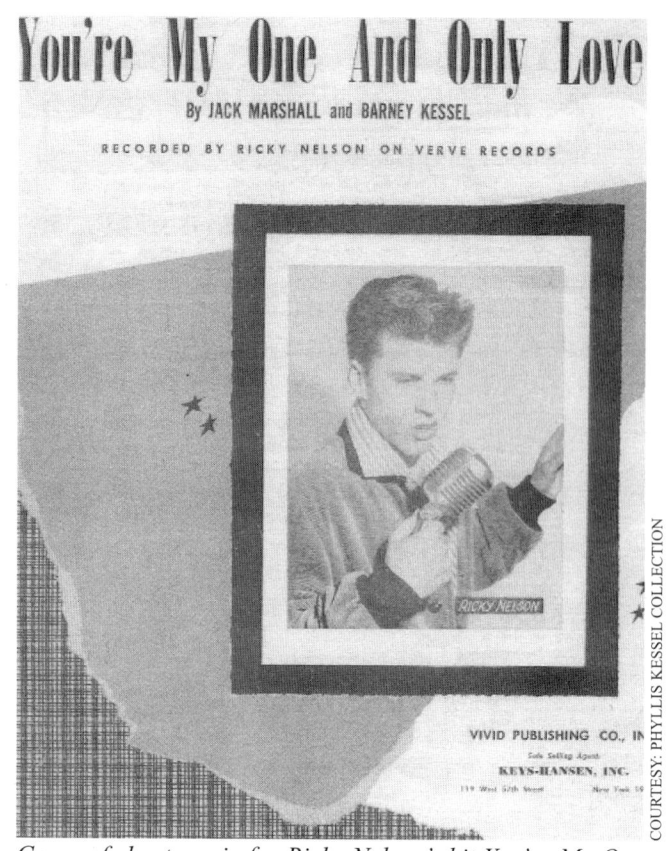

Cover of sheet music for Ricky Nelson's hit You're My One and Only Love.

48

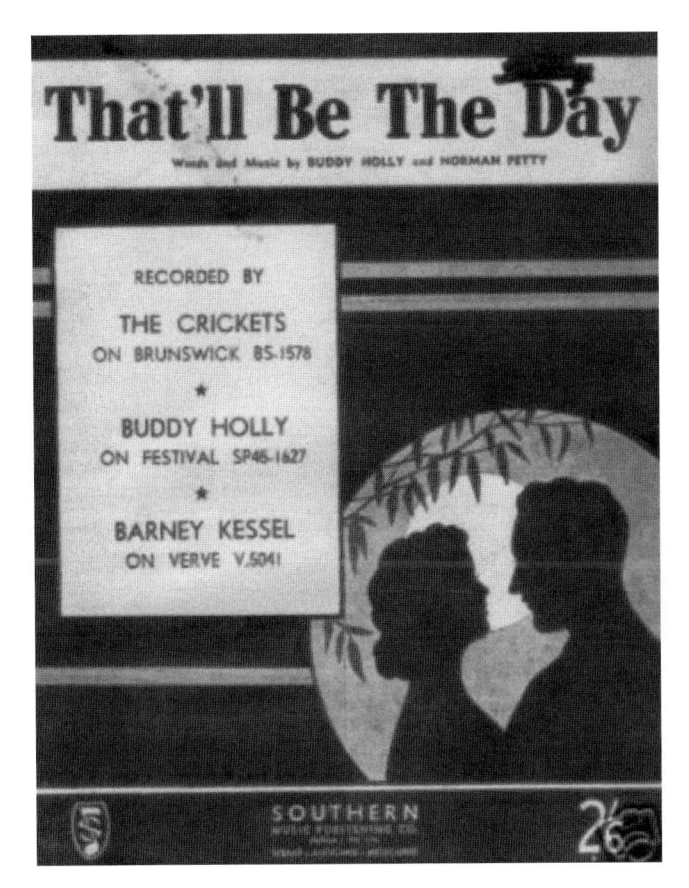

film *A Touch Of Evil* and Billy Wilder's comedy classic *Some Like It Hot* which starred Tony Curtis, Jack Lemmon and Marilyn Monroe. Barney also pre-recorded the guitar for John Saxon in the film *Rock, Pretty Baby* and was in the band that played David Raksin's jazz score on the soundtrack of *Too Late Blues* with Bobby Darin and Stella Stevens.

Barney Kessel can be heard on the soundtrack of four Elvis Presley films – *Girls, Girls Girls* (1962), *Fun in Aculpulco* (January 1963), *It Happened at the World Fair* (April 1963) and *Paradise Hawaiian Style* (1966).

Phil Spector

Phil Spector is one of the great popular music record producers of all time. His historic *Wall of Sound* concept changed the face of rock n' roll and popular music for all time. Barney Kessel was instrumental in setting Spector on his historic career as a record producer, Mick Brown in his excellent book on Phil Spector's life and music explains how Spector's mother and sister first took Phil to see Barney in concert – which led to their long association;

On Phil's fifteenth birthday, Bertha and Shirley took him to see Ella Fitzgerald performing a concert in Hollywood. Playing in her backing group was the guitarist Barney Kessel, and Spector watched transfixed as his fingers flew effortlessly over the frets.

Phil had found a new hero. He collected every Kessel recording he could find, and in an act of homage pinned a photograph of the guitarist on his bedroom wall, alongside the pictures of Albert Einstein and Abraham Lincoln. (When Kessel died in 2004, Spector would describe him as 'the Quintessential. The greatest musician I've ever known; the greatest guitarist that ever lived — well ahead of Segovia whom many, wrongfully, think was the greatest.')

So impassioned was Spector about Kessel's playing that when the jazz magazine Downbeat *ran an interview with Sal Salvador, the guitarist in the Stan Kenton band, in which Salvador singled out his favourite guitarists but omitted to mention Kessel's name, Spector wrote a letter in defence of his hero.* [10]

It appeared as the lead on Downbeat magazine's letter page in the issue dated 14 November 1956:

Just finished reading your article entitled 'Garrulous Sal' in the Oct. 3 issue and am a little disappointed that when naming his favorite guitarists Salvador left out the name of Barney Kessel, who in my opinion holds the title of the greatest guitarist. Salvador mentioned Howard Roberts, a very fine jazz guitarist from the West Coast, and also mentioned the state of California, where Kessel is most well known, yet he failed to say a word about

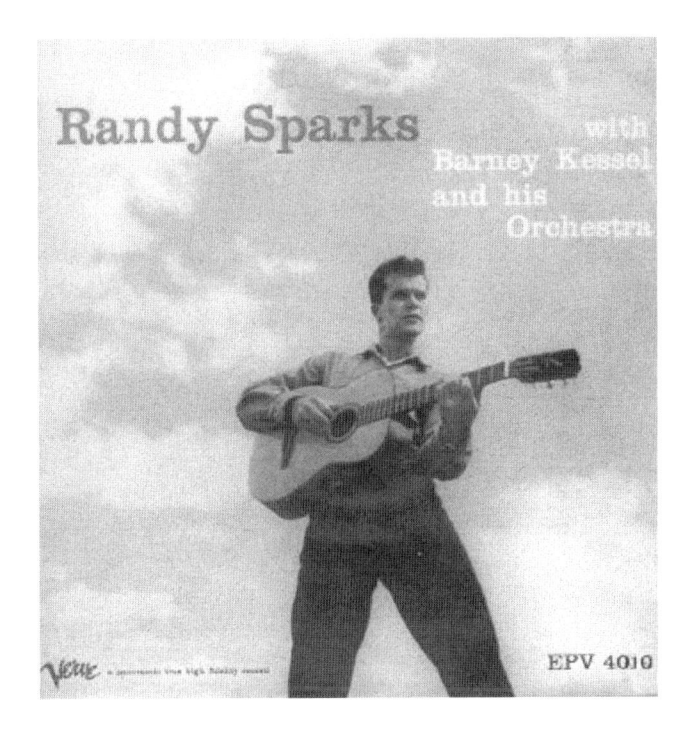

The Big TNT Show, November 1966. Phil Spector conducting his orchestra with Barney Kessel, far left and Herb Ellis to the right of the four guitarists.

the man whose style of guitar is copied so much but never equaled and is a favorite among jazz fans everywhere. This I cannot understand. Maybe you could ask Salvador, who I think is also a fine guitarist, just why Kessel does not rate. Sure wish you would ease my pain and have a story about Barney in one of your future issues.

Phil Spector

Brown confirmed:

The publication of the letter not only thrilled Spector, but also inspired his sister Shirley to act on his behalf. Tracking down Barney Kessel at the Contemporary recording studios in Hollywood, she explained that it was her younger brother who had written the letter to Down Beat, that he worshipped the guitarist and dreamed of following in his footsteps; would Kessel meet him to pass on some advice? Astonished to learn that the correspondent who had championed him so eloquently in Down Beat was just fifteen years old, Kessel readily agreed.

A few days later Phil, Bertha and Shirley presented themselves at Du-par's, a coffee shop on Vine Street, close by the Capitol building and much favoured by musicians on a break from recording sessions, where Kessel was waiting. Spector spent most of the meeting dumb-struck in the presence of his idol, while his mother and sister belaboured Kessel with questions about their son's career prospects in the music industry.

Kessel offered some surprising advice. It was one thing to love jazz and to play it, he told them, but he would not recommend a career as a jazz musician. Phillip should look at the big picture. Fashions in music were cyclical, and jazz was on the downswing; it was rock and roll that people wanted to listen to now. If Phillip wanted to make a career in music he should be thinking of becoming a songwriter or a record producer. [10]

Barney was eventually part of the original *Phil Spector Wrecking Crew*, a group of the best session musicians in Hollywood which recorded at the Gold Star Studios. Phil Spector, by that time, already knew Barney well and asked arranger Jack Nitzsche to select the other musicians to make up the *Wrecking Crew* to support his recordings of the Paris Sisters, the Crystals, the Ronettes, Bob B. Soxx and the Blue Jeans, Darlene Love, the Righteous Brothers and Ike & Tina Turner. Barney was a member of the *Wrecking Crew* musicians in the stage band for Phil Spector's seminal pop music 1966 television event *The Big TNT Show.*

It is also generally accepted that Barney Kessel was the first to introduce the 12-string guitar to rock and pop music recording. He first played a 12-string guitar on the Crystals' recording of *Then He Kissed Me,* one of Phil Spector's most successful recordings. John Lennon said that Barney's playing on this record persuaded him to use a 12-string guitar on some of the Beatles' records. Jack Nitzsche also went on to use a 12-string guitar on the very successful Crystals recording of the hit *Needles And Pins* a song he had written with Sonny Bono.

Reprise Records

Reprise Records was founded in 1961 by Frank Sinatra and lawyer Micky Rudin. Frank Sinatra wanted more artistic freedom for his own recordings. He had left Capitol/EMI Records and then tried to buy Verve Reords without success. Through Reprise, Sinatra, who was chief executive officer (Chairman of the Board) of the company, was able to release 30 records of himself and many other recordings by Sammy Davis Jr., Dean Martin, Rosemary Clooney, Duke Ellington, Count Basie, Errol Garner and Ella Fitzgerald. One of Reprise's first executives was the former Verve Records controller Mo Ostin. He became Executive Vice President of Reprise in 1961. Sinatra was a great admirer of Barney Kessel and persuaded Barney to sign up as a Reprise artist. Barney recorded three LP recordings for Reprise (*Bossa Nova - Barney Kessel plus Big Band, Breakfast at Tiffany's and Contemporary Latin Rhythms*) and several commercial singles. However the Reprise company did not manage to achieve enough profits and, in 1963, the label was sold to Warner Bros. The sales contract for the business included an agreement that Frank Sinatra would star in three Warner Bros. films. Reprise's Dean Martin recording *Dream With Dean* featured Barney Kessel's quartet as the backing group. One track on this LP recording, *Everybody Loves Somebody,* became a big hit.

A 1970 Atlantic album *T-Bone Blues* has Barney sharing solos with T-Bone Walker. This coupling surprised many jazz enthusiasts. However Barney knew, and had played with, T. Bone Walker in the early 1940s:

When I first came to LA I would run into him at after-hours clubs. He was already well-known and I was just fresh from Oklahoma. This was around 1942. We would play together and he would sing but I never saw him again until we did that album. He seemed to be a nice guy, loved to sing and play the blues and that's what he did.[17]

BARNEY KESSEL – *A Jazz Legend*
9. Europe

In November 1967 Barney was booked to play at the Berlin Jazz Festival as part of a Guitar Workshop with Jim Hall, Baden Powell and other guitarists. The Guitar Workshop also played at the Paris Jazz Festival in November. October and November 1968 saw Barney make several recordings for the Black Lion (UK) label. In 1968 and 1969 George Wein booked Barney to be a member of his *Newport Jazz All Stars* for concerts in the USA and then overseas. The other members of the group were Ruby Braff (cornet), Red Norvo (vibraphone), Tal Farlow (guitar), Larry Ridley (bass), Don Lamond (drums) and Wein on piano. After touring Europe with Wein's Newport All-Stars (1968), Barney decided to live in London for a time. Our mutual friend, guitarist Ike Isaacs (1919-1996), had a spare apartment in London and he rented this to Barney who used it as his base for just over a year. Ike was a leading session guitarist originally from Burma who settled in London after World War II. He had played in many small UK jazz groups including the Stephane Grappelli - Diz Disley Quintet and in the big bands of Ted Heath and BBC Radio Show Band. Barney loved Ike's musicality and guitar playing and told me, more than once, that he had never met any guitarist who knew the guitar fingerboard so well. Ike was also a great teacher and became a great inspiration and mentor to jazz guitar virtuoso Martin Taylor. Barney played a few times at London's top jazz club Ronnie Scott's in Soho. His appearances there attracted top jazz, rock and classical guitarists alike. May 1969 saw Barney in Italy where he stayed with another guitarist friend Carlo Pes (1927-1995). He made three recordings in Rome. Barney then moved to Paris in June where he made some historic recordings with Stephane Grappelli for the Black Lion and RCA labels. In early October 1969 Barney travelled to Tokyo, Japan where he appeared in concert and recorded with George Wein's *Newport Festival Jazz All Stars*. Joe Venuti (vio-

Copy of the 1974 UK work permit for Barney Kessel.

lin) replaced guitarist Tal Farlow, and drummer Cliff Leeman replaced Don Lamond. At the end of October the *Newport Jazz All Stars* musicians were in Paris. Two more recordings were made, one under the leadership of Braff and Norvo with Venuti dropping out and Don Lamond back in the drum seat. The second recording was called *Venuppelli Blues*, with Joe Venuti back in the group and violinist Stephane Grappelli replacing Braff. At the end of the month The *Newport Jazz All Stars* regrouped this time with Kenny Burrell joining the lineup. They also played and recorded concerts in Basle and Berlin.

Barney returned to live in the USA in 1970 but the next few years saw him spending several months of each year touring the world playing with his trio, sometimes in a duo with Herb Ellis, sometimes as solo artist – and, from 1974, often as a member of *The Great Guitars*.

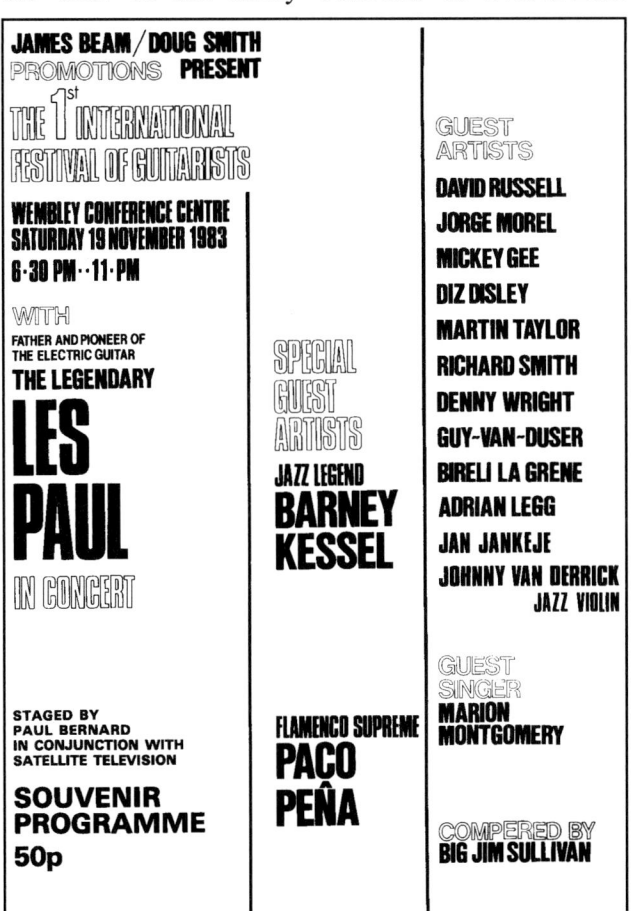

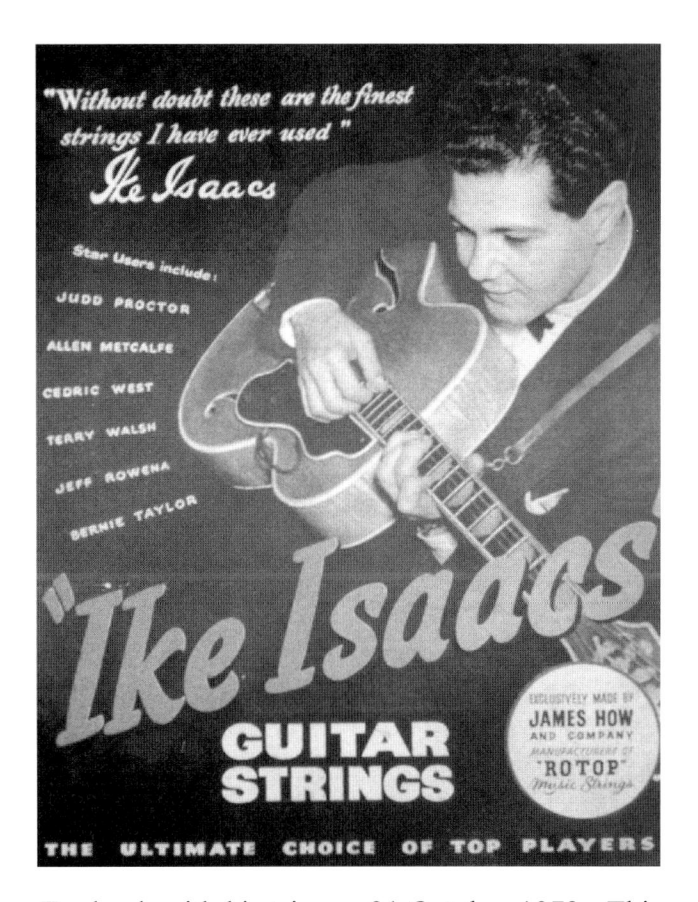

Although I had corresponded with Barney in 1957 to 1959 I actually only first met him, face-to-face, in 1972. Ike Isaacs arranged for us to meet and we finally shook hands over dinner at a London restaurant. Soon after this I booked Barney to play the first of his many concerts in North-East England, with his trio, on 21 October 1973. This was held in conjunction with JNE (Jazz North East). JNE was (and is) run by Chris Yates a great jazz lover and enthusiast who for over 35 years has presented many of the world's great jazz guitarists (and many other great jazz instrumentalists and bands) in concert in the North East of England. In those days it was very hard to get work permits for USA musicians to play in the UK. I was advised to try the Kennedy/Masters Agency in London for this purpose. There I met Robert Masters who quickly arranged the permits, for Barney's trio, for a reasonable fee. After the Kennedy/Masters business closed Robert began his own jazz artists management agency. From my early introduction he signed Barney up as one of his major USA jazz artists, and then represented Barney right through until 1992. Robert is almost certainly one of the best jazz managers I have ever met. Efficient and ethical at all times. We worked a lot together, as he had several good jazz guitarists on his books. He promoted the marvelous *International Festival of Guitarists* concert at Wembley in London on 19 November 1983. This spectacular event featured Barney Kessel and several other of the world's finest guitarists including Martin Taylor, Bireli Lagrene, classical maestro David Russell, South American virtuoso Jorge Morel, flamenco giant Paco Peña and, as a special guest artist, jazz singer Marion Montgomery. Les Paul was also booked to play at the festival but did not arrive due to ill health. Robert remains a friend to this day. In 1996 he arranged a successful benefit concert for Barney at London's 100 Club.

It was over that dinner in 1972 that Barney told me about his seminar *The Effective Guitarist*, and in October 1973 my company presented what was to be the first of twelve annual Barney Kessel seminars in Newcastle upon Tyne. Over the years almost 350 guitarists had the great privilege of studying with Barney, a naturally gifted teacher, on this very special four-day course. Barney's regular visits to the UK over the 21 year period from 1971 gave us the opportunity to socialize with a wide circle of friends, and also listen to a lot of music. During this time I learned to appreciate Barney's ability as a raconteur, and his great sense of humour. My two sons Ashley and Mark, as toddlers then, also much appreciated his fabulous card tricks. He had taught himself these card tricks on the band bus, while travelling from one city to the another, to keep himself amused - and to exercise his fingers.

I invited my friend, the Finnish guitarist and leading guitar personality, Ole Halen, to attend one of Barney's UK seminars in Newcastle upon Tyne. Ole was so impressed that he invited Barney to teach and play at his 1988 *Hot Guitars Festival* in Ikaalinen, Finland.

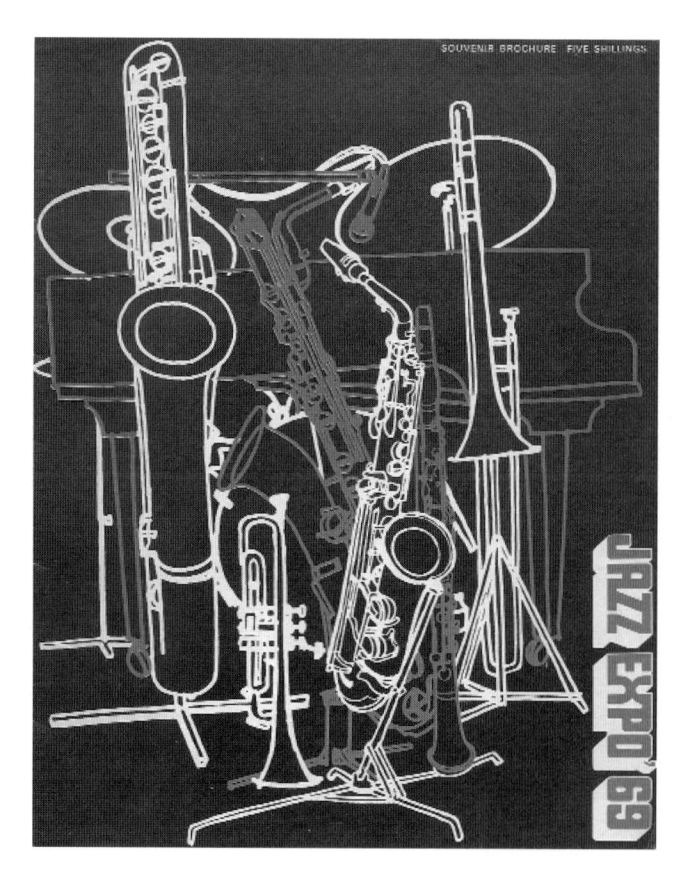

BARNEY KESSEL – *A Jazz Legend*
10. The Great Guitars

The Great Guitars in concert, Newcastle upon Tyne, UK, 1976. Left to right: Joe Byrd, Wayne Phillips, Charlie Byrd, Barney Kessel and Herb Ellis.

It was the Australian concert promoter and jazz enthusiast Kim Bonython who came up with the idea that Barney Kessel, Herb Ellis and Charlie Byrd should form a guitar trio with bass and drums – and that it should be called *The Great Guitars*.

Bonython, who was from Adelaide, originally planned a nine concert tour for the Charlie Byrd trio to tour Australia and New Zealand in 1973. He then asked Barney to come along, and suggested it would be nice if Barney would perform in a duo with another guitarist before Byrd's trio began their set. Barney asked his old friend Herb Ellis to come on the tour as he knew they already played very well together, and they also got along socially. Barney only met Charlie Byrd for the first time when the guitarists arrived in Los Angeles prior to the start of their Australian tour. The first concerts began with a set by the Kessel/Ellis Duo and this was followed by the Charlie Byrd trio. In the middle of the concert tour, someone suggested that the guitarists play a few songs as trio. They did and the audience loved the trio and asked for encore after encore. At the end of the Australian tour *The Great Guitars* had come into being and soon became one of jazz's most popular new groups.

The Great Guitars group first appeared in the USA in March 1974 at the Carnegie Hall, New York. Once again this concert was a great success and the group was booked in July 1973 to headline the Concord Summer Jazz Festival in California. Their concert attracted the largest audience ever for the festival, and a recording of the concert was released soon after on the Concord record label. *The Great Guitars* made five albums in the original Kessel, Byrd, and Ellis line-up, three studio recordings and then two live sessions. In July 1974, the three guitarists were supported by Charlie Byrd's brother Joe Byrd on bass and drummer Johnny Rae in a New York recording studio for their first Concord album. In August 1976 their second Concord album was recorded in San Francisco with Joe Byrd again on bass and Wayne Phillips on drums. In 1978 *Straight Tracks*, another studio recording was released featuring the same lineup as in 1976. *The Great Guitars at the Winery* album, a live concert, was recorded in 1980 with drummer Jimmie Smith taking over from Wayne Phillips. This live session was recorded at the Paul Masson Mountain Winery in Saratoga, California. August 1982 saw the last Great Guitars album recorded with the Kessel, Ellis, Byrd lineup. Titled *The Great Guitars at Charlie's Georgetown* the three guitarists were backed by Joe Byrd on bass and Chuck Redd on drums. Again this was a live recording and it was made in Washington DC. *The Great Guitars* group continued to give concerts even when one of the original trio was indisposed. When Herb Ellis returned to play with Oscar Peterson in 1989, Tal Farlow and then Martin Taylor took his place.

After Barney had a massive stroke in May 1992 his place was taken by Tal Farlow.

In 1981 Barney moved to Oklahoma City to live with his new wife Jo Ann Dodson who had taught at the University of Oklahoma. Barney used his new home there as his base for his international concert engagements. When he was in Oklahoma he taught at the Central State University, part of the Oklahoma University System. He also had a regular Sunday morning jazz radio programme which broadcasted from the University. In all he made 60 one-hour shows on the history of jazz called *Inside Jazz*. Within a few years this marriage broke down and Barney decided to move back to California.

BARNEY KESSEL – *A Jazz Legend*
11. The End of a Legendary Career

Barney Kessel moved to San Diego in December 1989, living for a time in a motel on El Cajon Boulevard. He had met Phyllis Van Doren, a longtime senior editor for San Diego Home & Garden magazine, and they had soon fallen in love. He decided to move to San Diego to be close to her home on Madison Avenue. On 24 January 1992 they were married. On 20 May 1992 Barney, at the age of 68, suffered the devastating stoke that brought an end to one of the most historic careers in music. He had been looking forward to coming to London in June to play in a reunion concert of the Artie Shaw Orchestra.

In a 10 July 1996 San Diego Reader interview Barney talked to Philip Dawdy about the stroke and its effect on his life with his typical fortitude of character:

I don't know why I had a stroke. Neither do the doctors. I didn't smoke and my blood pressure and cholesterol were always good. It did a lot of damage. No one knows how far back you can come from the crippling effects. I've come back in small increments. I still have all the tunes in my head. I'm going to start writing music again, but my eyes are not good. I don't need to play guitar again. From 16 to 68 I only missed 17 days of practice." He pauses, then points to his head and his heart. This is where it all is. The music is all there, not in the guitar. [14]

When asked did he miss playing the guitar he answered *'No'*. He then drew the numbers 12 and 68 in the air, the ages when he began and stopped playing guitar and said - *It was good.*

In 1994 Barney Kessel was flown to Turin, Italy for a huge tribute concert and after that there were several benefit concerts in England, Germany and Los Angeles to honour him. He was also a guest at Flip Phillips' 80th birthday jazz party in Florida in 1995. At the July 1995 memorial concert for Carl Jefferson (Concord Records' founder), Barney walked out on to the stage (with a walking stick) for the first time since his stroke and took a bow. In May 1996, Barney flew to Oklahoma and was given an honorary doctoral degree by the University of Oklahoma for his lifetime contribution to music.

On 25 June 1997 Charles Carlini produced a special tribute concert – *To Barney Kessel – With Love From Your Friends* – as part of the JVC Jazz Festival in New York. Over 15 of the world's finest jazz guitarists played in this historic concert, in front of the special guests Barney and Phyllis Kessel, who had flown in from San Diego.

In the autumn of 2003 Barney was diagnosed with an inoperable brain tumour. Over the next months Barney's health deteriorated quite rapidly and he died on 6 May 2004 in San Diego.

Family

Barney always said that once he began to play the guitar his relationship with his father became strained. This is not surprising as there was 54 years age difference between them. Abraham could not comprehend that a successful life for his son could be achieved through playing the guitar. At the same time his father's health was not good, with failing eye sight and other problems. All of this did not help Barney's father have any sympathy towards his son's musical aspirations. Barney loved his mother very deeply, and she became very supportive of him. Some time after Abraham's death Ruth Kessel moved back to live in St Louis to be near to her (Raisher) family. She died there on 3 January 1968. Barney was fond of his brother Lester. Lester also moved to St Louis where he died, from a brain tumour, on 29 May 1992. Barney was also very close to his step-sister Lee. She died in Florida on 10 June 1996.

Barney married Gail Sexton-Farmer in 1949. Born 5 October 1927, Sexton-Farmer was originally from Texas. When she first came to Hollywood she was a model and later an artist/sculptress. At university in Los Angeles she was a Dean's List Scholar. They had two sons Dan (1951-) and David (1954-). They also had a daughter, Alice, who died prematurely at only 22 days in January 1956. Barney and Gail divorced in 1958. Gail currently lives in Glendale, California.

In 1961 Barney married Betty Jane Baker. Born Betty Jane Phillips in Birmingham, Alabama, Betty sang in big bands and had her own local radio show at age 14. She was also a beauty queen and, as Betty Jane Rase, represented Alabama in the 1944 *Miss America* contest - and came fourth. She met film star Mickey Rooney at the contest and they were married later that year. They had two sons, Mickey Jnr (1945-) and Tim (1947-2006). They divorced in 1949.

In 1950 Betty married Buddy Baker, who was a composer and head of the Walt Disney Studios' music department from 1955 to 2003. She divorced Baker in 1957. Among the best-selling records Baker sang on were Elvis Presley's *I Can't Help Falling in Love With You*, Lloyd Price's *Stagger Lee*, Sam Cooke's *You Send Me,* Jackie Wilson's *Baby Workout*, Frank Sinatra's *That's Life*, Bobby Darin's *Dream Lover* and the Righteous Brothers' *You've Lost That Lovin' Feeling*. Betty also dubbed the vocal parts for actress Nancy Kwan on the hit song *I Enjoy Being a Girl* in the musical film *Flower Drum Song.* she also appeared regularly on the Dean Martin and the Judy Garland television shows. Barney played in the support band for many of these sessions.

Barney and Betty Kessel brought up Dan, David, Mickey Jnr. and Tim in what was a very musical household. They were married 19 years, and divorced in 1980. Betty died of complications following a stroke, aged 74, on 2 April 2002, in Rancho Mirage, California.

Dan and David Kessel

Dan Kessel was born 7 February 1951. He has never married. David Kessel was born 17 March 1954. He is married. David and his wife Jan have no children.

As toddlers Dan and David aspired to emulate Desi Arnaz by forming a rhumba band with some neighbourhood kids. Barney allowed them to use a variety of the Latin percussion instruments he had brought back with him from South America. Some of their earliest memories are of Oscar Peterson and Ray Brown practicing with their father in their home with their mother, Gail, providing some delicious Texas style home cooking for everyone.

Dan and David Kessel attended many recording sessions with their father and also with their step mother, B. J. Baker. They kept their eyes and ears open and their mouths shut during various jazz sessions with Lester Koenig and Roy Dunnan at Contemporary Records as well as rock and pop sessions in different studios with Elvis Presley, Ricky Nelson, Duane Eddy, Doris Day, Judy Garland and Frank Sinatra. Sometimes they got into the act, such as when they performed hand claps (Dan was eleven and David eight) during the recording of *He's A Rebel*, with Phil Spector at Gold Star Studios.

Another activity they pursued whenever possible was spending time watching and learning inside the sound stages of Hollywood's film studios, accompanying their step brothers, Mickey Jr. and Tim and their father, Mickey Rooney. Dan and David Kessel received a valuable education observing many great actors, directors, singers, musicians, orchestra leaders and producers, at work.

All the while, they kept at their music. Barney had advised them to always continue to love and appreciate jazz but to focus on the pop and rock field. Especially song writing and production, as this would be a sound basis for a safe career choice. When they were teenagers Dan and David became multi-instrumentalists and formed various rock 'n' roll bands. One such band, *Stars in the Sky*, played at the Teenage Fair at the Hollywood Palladium on the same show as Jimi Hendrix. They had already met Hendrix earlier that year at the *Bag o' Nails* club in London. They kept getting better and occasionally Barney had one or the other, or both of them, perform with him on stage, as they had not neglected their jazz sensibilities.

After graduating from high school, Dan majored in Cinematography in college, and then began working in the local film industry. David went away to college to study business and practice the guitar in the mountainous region of Utah, where he also excelled as a rescuer in the ski patrol.

While growing up, they maintained friendships with Oscar Peterson, Ray Brown, Shelly Manne and Lester Koenig, whom they much admired. Koenig, at one point, offered them free reign of his recording studio to try out some things, even knowing that it would be rock 'n' roll and not jazz.

Dan Kessel with a Gibson Barney Kessel guitar.

As young adults Dan and David Kessel entered the international charts with their band, *Stars in the Sky*, with a recording made on their own label, which they manufactured and shipped out. Their success continued with more record releases, as songwriter-publishers, and with other artists who recorded songs they had written. Barney also recorded one of their compositions. Next, they began branching out, producing themselves and other artists, such as The Ramones, Blondie, Annette Funicello and The Ventures. They produced these artists, and others, for their own label, as well as licensing their independent productions to major labels. In addition they co-produced recordings with the *Beach Boys* leader, Brian Wilson, for the girl group, *American Spring*.

At the same time, Dan and David were much in demand as session musicians and back up vocalists on recordings, with Phil Spector, John Lennon, Cher, Leonard Cohen, Bob Dylan, The Ramones, Celine Dion and many other notable artists. They also did some writing and recording for several independent films.

In recent times they have been pioneers in the digital realm, with David serving on the board of directors of I.U.M.A. (Internet Underground Music Archive), where he spearheaded, the release of the very first multi-media CD ever (Crunchy Smacks) on the company's label, Offline Records, with Dan working as co-executive producer on that release.

Dan Kessel is co-executive producer of the award winning stage show, *Shag With A Twist*, which had a successful two year run in both Los Angeles and Las Vegas. The show is based on the artwork and characters of the internationally acclaimed 'low brow' artist, Shag, (joSH AGle). It's currently being re-vamped for future openings in San Francisco, and New York. David Kessel is an associate producer on the show.

For over 10 years, Barney's sons, along with record mogul, Jerry Moss, have owned the successful *Backstage Café* night club in Beverly Hills, with senior partners Ian and Stewart Copeland. As they continue their work into the future, the brothers are encompassing full media, and multi-platform integration with music, theatre and film.

Dan and David Kessel told me they acknowledge their father for his genius but more importantly, they will always cherish his memory for his love and inspiration.

In 1981 Barney married Jo Ann Dodson who had taught at Oklahoma University. Dodson had grown up in Muskogee (from the age of 12) but

David Kessel with Oscar Peterson, Jazz Alley, Seattle.

they never met there. They actually only met for the first time in 1980 at a jazz club where Barney had been playing. Barney, after their marriage, decided to move from Los Angeles to live in Oklahoma City. They divorced in 1991.

On 24 January 1992 Barney married Phyllis Van Doren (born Phyllis Ann Magary in Canandaigua, NY, 19 December 1933) and moved permanently to San Diego where she was (and still is) senior editor of San Diego Home & Garden Lifestyles magazine. Phyllis, a knowledgeable and enthusiastic jazz lover, has two married daughters, a son and five grandchildren. Barney and Phyllis met for the first at one of his concerts, even though Phyllis had been a great fan of his music ever since she had been at university in Los Angeles. She explained that she first met Barney in late 1980's when she went to interview him for her magazine:

I knew who he was. I was at a jazz festival and I knew who all the other players were. and I interviewed everybody, just for fun. I had been a jazz fan in the '50s and had seen Barney and a lot of other people play. I can remember Charlie Parker, Nat King Cole, Red Norvo, Tal Farlow, Dinah Washington, all those people, in Los Angeles when I was in college in the `50's. Barney was well-known at that time. I just happened to be at a jazz festival and met him through an interview, and then ran into him later again and interviewed him some more. I am a writer and an editor and so it was of interest to me that these retirement age musicians were going strong and sounding better than ever. I didn't know what I was going to do with it, but it looked like a story. And he loved to talk. Barney was a good interview, for anybody. He was really a good interview. [8]

Phyllis recalled she was able to attend Barney's last recording session:

I happened to be in the Bay Area and he was making 'Red, Hot and Blues' (Contemporary Records 1988) and I asked if I could see a record being made. He said, "Of course!"

From the time I met him, when I had the opportunity, I never missed a set he played. If I was on the road with him and he was playing three sets, I didn't watch the first one, and then go to bed for the other two. I stayed there and watched every single note. And I'm so glad I did. You know, you never know. I was fascinated. I mean, he was incredible. [8]

Barney Kessel spent the last few years of his life in San Diego, California. With incredible care and devotion from his wife Phyllis, and with his own unique strength of character, he was able to enjoy a relatively high quality of life for most of the last twelve years of his life.

Religion, Faith and Lifestyle

Barney was brought up in a traditional Jewish household. He told me that in early 1936, when he was twelve, his parents arranged for a rabbi to come weekly from Oklahoma City to teach him to sing the blessings in Hebrew at the synagogue service for his barmitzvah. The service took place at the end of 1936 in Muskogee. Barney surprised me one evening in my house when he suddenly sang these blessings in perfect Hebrew - over 40 years after his barmitzvah. He also told me that his mother only gave him two bits of advice when he left Muskogee in 1942 for Los Angeles. One - *Don't eat hamburgers, Jews don't eat ham* and Two - *Don't marry a non-Jewish girl - because every time you have a row she will call you 'a lousy Jew'*. Barney laughed when he remembered her advice because he said it turned out she was wrong on both counts. He discovered hamburgers are not made of ham - and although he had been married (at that time) to three non-Jewish girls, and had rows, none had ever referred to his Jewish background.

Once he got to Los Angeles it seems, by the time he was 20 years old he began to take an interest, in both the Old and New testaments. He enjoyed and respected the teachings of Jesus in the latter. He never really talked about his Jewish background. This was not unusual in the entertainment business, as in Hollywood, in the 1940s and 1950s particularly, being Jewish could sometimes prove an impediment to getting a valuable booking. There is the famous story of Artie Shaw, when asked by some wealthy person interested in booking his band if he was Jewish, he responded - *'Not necessarily so!'*

Phyllis Kessel summed up Barney's approach to life very clearly:

Barney had a very strong spiritual life. Considering the multitude of daily distractions that occur during any given day, it sometimes seems next to impossible, given the situation, to adhere to a schedule, let alone one's ethics. In addition to these complications, those individuals involved in the entertainment business face additional pressures, stressors and alluring stimulants. Maintaining a long successful and respectful career is not an easy task, and depends greatly on morality - how one lives. Regardless of the guitar and of music, Barney Kessel was an individual of principles.

He was a very moral person. He really stuck to his principles, from the time he was a little boy. Most of us I don't think do that. He never smoked dope. He never touched any hard liquor. It didn't appeal to him and he saw all these musicians, from the time he was a little boy, destroying themselves with alcohol and drugs so he didn't go near it.

He was a nervous, high energy hyper-active person. He told me that, when he was around 40 - I don't know whether he was having trouble sleeping or what, but he was going to a doctor, and the doctor suggested maybe it would help him if he'd have a glass of wine with dinner. And that's when he started drinking wine. He never drank more than one or one and a half glasses, and never before he played. It was always afterwards when we had dinner. He did enjoy a glass of wine with dinner. He'd write down what he had discovered in Europe teaching himself to be a wine connoisseur. [8]

She stressed he was a very disciplined person;

Barney was an extremely disciplined person. You'd be in awe if you could have seen him on a daily basis. It didn't matter whether he was on the road, whether he was at home with a couple weeks off. It didn't matter where he was - how uncomfortable a situation was, he'd find a way to do these things. He would get up in the morning and he would do these exercises - jumping up and down, pushups, situps, etc. He could be in the tiniest hotel room in the world - I've seen him do this. He'd put down a bath towel and he'd do his exercises. He had a tiny notebook where he wrote how many to do each day of each thing and sometimes he'd write how many he did do and he'd keep track of it. This went on for decades. I think they were those Canadian Air Force exercises. I think they came into the trend during the Kennedy administration or before that, but I kind of think it was in the '60s. But, he did those every single day until he had his stroke. He also walked a great deal. While on the road, he did not drive a car, so a lot of his life was walking around the cities where he was playing. [8]

Phyllis also confirmed that Barney always maintained a very healthy diet:

Barney liked a regular breakfast, lunch and dinner and did not eat in between meals, did not snack, while I knew him. He did not miss meals. He did not overeat. He clearly was interested in maintaining a reasonable weight, which he did, and being healthy. He always said I was a great cook and so his foods were my foods and he really seemed to appreciate that. Obviously, he ate out all the time on the road. French food was a favorite but so was the food in Italy and what I cooked at home. Mexican food was a favorite, in England he ate a lot of Indian food, he loved Chinese food. He could hardly wait to introduce me to favorite dishes in Austria. He just seemed to enjoy good food wherever he was. [8]

Barney Kessel loved good literature. He loved Shakespeare, and had read all of the Sherlock Holmes mysteries written by Sir Arthur Conan Doyle. He found great inspiration in the work of Frank Lloyd Wright. Over the years he also developed a deep interest in psychology. He had read many books by Freud, Jung and Adler, and books on the Gestalt Theory and Transactional Analysis. For several years he had made copious notes in order to write two books on psychology but unfortunately these were never completed. As Phyllis confirmed:

Oh, he had a huge library. He didn't read fiction - never did. Although he had read all of Shakespeare when he was about 30 years old. He only went to the ninth grade and he was self-educated. So one of the things he did after he got into Los Angeles and made something of a name for himself was - he did things like; read all of

Shakespeare. He had read the Bible several times so he knew all of those stories. He was attracted to books like; 'How To Make the Best Use of Your Time' and things like that. [8]

I know Barney had a firm belief in God throughout his life. He would have been happy to know that his committal service on 18 May 2004 at Woodlawn Cemetery, Canandaigua, NY was conducted by the Rev. Dr. P. Joseph Barth with readings from both the Old and New testaments. Barth, appropriately, is a long time jazz guitar enthusiast and great fan of Barney Kessel.

Barney Kessel summed up the priorities of his life at the age of 75, in a March/April 1998 edition of Marge Hofacre's *Jazz News* paper, as follows:

Of first importance is my relationship to God, this above all drives my life.

Second is my relationship with Phyllis, my wife. She is so loving and good, there for me all the time, and is the single most important person in my life.

Next come all my friends and relatives.

Fourth, all the other people living in the world.

Then comes my country, the USA, (the ideals and principles embodied in the Constitution and Declaration of Independence).

Sixth, comes jazz and classical music.

And seventh comes the guitar.

Woodlawn Cemetery, Canandaigua, NY.

Honours & Awards
received by Barney Kessel in his lifetime

Winner Jazz Poll - Downbeat magazine (USA) - Best Guitarist – 1957, 1959 and 1960.

Winner Jazz Poll - Metronome magazine (USA) Best Guitarist 1956.

Winner Jazz Poll - Esquire magazine (USA) Best Guitarist 1947.

Winner All Stars Jazz Poll Playboy magazine (USA) Best Guitarist 1957, 1958, 1959 (also All Star's All Star), 1960, 1961 (also All Star's All Star) and 1962.

1972 - Artist at the Inaugural reception for President Richard Nixon.

1979/1980 - Appointed Cultural Ambassador for the United States, Department of State in Asia, Egypt, South America, and East European countries including Yugoslavia, Romania and East Germany.

1981 - Performance at the White House for U.S. President Jimmy Carter.

1988 - Performance at the White House for U.S. President Ronald Reagan.

1991 - Induction into the Oklahoma Jazz Hall of Fame along with Chet Baker.

1996 - An Honorary Doctorate from the University of Oklahoma.

1997 - JVC Jazz Festival – Tribute to Barney Kessel – June, New York, USA.

1997 - Just Jazz Guitar magazine publish a special Barney Kessel Collectors' Edition in September.

1997 - Lifetime Music Award, San Diego, California, USA.

1998 - Lifetime Music Award, San Diego, California, USA.

1999 - Inducted into the Oklahoma Music Hall of Fame, on stage together with Vince Gill.

1999 - Inducted into the Big Band and Jazz Hall of Fame, along with Sonny Rollins, Les Brown and Nancy Wilson.

2003 - In October, to commemorate Barney Kessel's 80th birthday, Contemporary Records released the compilation *Barney Kessel Plays For Lovers* (CCD-6022-2).

A COMPREHENSIVE LIST OF ORIGINAL BARNEY KESSEL COMPOSITIONS RECORDED BY BARNEY KESSEL

64 Bars on Wilshire Boulevard
A Playboy In Love
Almost The Blues
Amelia
Army Rocks And Navy Rolls
Atom Buster
B J's Samba
Barney's Blues
Be Deedle Dee Do
Begin The Blues
Bernardo
Blue Boy
Blue Fountain
Blue Grass
Blue Soul
Blues A La Carte
Blues All Night Long
Blues For A Playboy
Blues For Bird
Blues For George
Blues For Space Travellers
Blues Up, Down And All Around
Bluesy
Brazilian Beat
Bridging The Blues
Caliente Blues
Carlo's Dream
Chez Roger
Comin' Home
Contemporary Blues
Contrary-Ness
Cool Groove
Copa Cola
Crisis
Criss Cross
Down in the Swamp
Easy Like
Every Time I Hear This Song
For My Love
Foreign Intrigue
Free Wheeling
Freeway
From My Heart
Going Thru Some Changes
Happy Feeling
Happy Little Song
Here's That Sunny Day
Holiday In Rio
I Remember Django
I'm Fallin' In Love
I'm On My Way
In The Garden Of Love
Jelly Beans
Juarez After Dark

Kingston Cutie
Latin Dance Band No. 1
Latin Groove
Let's Cook
Lison
Little Star
Love of My Life
Malibu
Mermaid
Messin' With The Blues
Meu Irmao
Minor Major Mode
Minor Mode
Minor Mood
Monsieur Armand
Moonlight Walk
Moving Up
Mysterioso Impromptu
North of the Border
On The Riviera
One Foot Off The Curb
Pedal Point
Quail Beat
Red Sails
Reflections In Rome
Rio
Salute to Charlie Christian
Sea Miner
Seagull
Shufflin
Shufflin' The Blues
Slick Chick
Slow Burn
Spanish Scenery
Star Fire
Stumblin' Around
Swedish Pastry
Sweet Baby
Swing Samba
The ABC Blues
The Fourth Way
The Opener
True Blues
Twilight In Acapulco
Two Note Samba
Two Way Conversation
Vicky's Dream
Wail Street
Walkin' And Talkin'
Waltz In Spingtime
Watch The Birds Go By
You're The One For Me

A SELECTED LISTING OF JAZZ AND BIG BAND MUSICIANS WHO RECORDED with BARNEY KESSEL – 1942-1988

Accordion
Tommy Gumina
Gene Garf

Alto Saxophone & Flute
Dick Paladino
Buddy Collette
Herb Geller
Benny Carter
Lou Prisby
Ray DeGeer
Plas Johnson
Paul Horn
Paul Desmond
Mel Flory
Marshal Royal
Vi Redd
Les Robinson
Les Clarke
Lennie Niehaus
Lee Robinson
Riley Weston
Matt Utal
Ronnie Lang
Rudy Tanza
Shelly Gold
Skeets Herfurt
Sonny Criss
Ted Nash
Jules Jacobs
Vernon Yokum
Johnny Hodges
Wilbur Schwartz
Willie Smith
Tommy Mace
Larry Molinelli
Earl Bostic
Dick Paladino
Clint Neagley
Clint Bellew
Charlie Parker
Eddie Rosa
Charles Kennedy
Charlie Barnet
Bud Shank
Bob Hardaway
Bill Shine
Bill Gillette
Benny Carter
Abe Most
Joe Meisner
Gabe Gelinas
Gene Kinsey
Gus Bivona
Gus McReynolds
Hal McKusick
Harold Herzon
Harry Klee
Herb Geller
Herbert Stewart
Jack Dumont
Buddy Collette
Jimmy Giuffre
Frank Pappalardo
Art Pepper
Dale Brown
Paul Horn

Arranger & Conductor
Johnny Thompson
Harry Fields
Russ Garcia
Pete Rugolo
Don Redman
Benny Carter
Sonnie Burke
Belford C. Hendricks
Billy May
Buddy Bregman
Frank De Vol
Hal Mooney
Harry Geller
Lincoln Mayorga
Paul Weston
Ralph Burns

Baritone Saxophone
William Ulyate
Don Davidson
Harry Sopp
Leo Anthony
Justin Gordon
John Rotella
Joe Maini
Jimmy Giuffre
Irving Roth
Fred Falensby
Bill Hood
Dale Issenhuth
Jewell Grant
Chuck Gentry
Dave Pell
Butch Stone
Bob Poland
Bob Lawson
Bob Gordon
Bob Dawes

Double Bass
John Heard
Larry Wooten
Michel Gaudry
Max Bennett
Marty Corb
Monty Budwig
Lucas Lindholm
Morris Rayman
Leroy Vinnegar
Leroy Gray
Mike Rubin
Larry Ridley
Larry Breen
Kunimitsu Inaba
Kenny Napper
John Simmons
Joe Mondragon
John Frigo
John Clayton
John "Shifty" Henry
Kenny Baldock
Robert West
Joe Comfort
William Plummer
Tony Campo
Sture Nordin
Slam Stewart
Scott LeFaro
Rufus Reid
Rolly Bundock
Thomas Moultrie
Percy Heath
Red Wooten
Red Mitchell
Red Callender
Ray Pohlman
Ray Leatherwood
Ray Brown
Ralph Pena
Phil Stephens
Rollo Gaberg
Bob Stone
Dan Whitaker
Curtis Counce
Clifford Hills
Chuck Domanico
Chuck Berghofer
Charlie Drayton
Buddy Clark
Bruce Lawrence
Dave Sperling
Bob West
Arnold Fishkind
Bob Maize
Bob Magnusson
Bob Bates
Billy Hadnott
Bill Woodson
Arthur Netzel
Joe Byrd
Albert Stinson
Ben Tucker
Al McKibbon
Bobby Haynes
Howard Rumsey
Jerry Scheff
Jerry Good
James Bond
Jack Smalley
Jim Hughart
Don Simpson
Jack Lesberg
Herb Mickman
Harry Babasin
Hank Wayland
Guy Pettersen
Earl May
Jack Ryan
Don Whitaker
Giovanni Tommaso
Ed Garland
Ed Mihelich
Eddie Sanfranski
Frank Clarke
Gary Peacock
Gene Englund

George Tucker

Clarinet
Paul Horn
George Smith
Howard Terry
Jimmy Giuffre
Matty Matlock
Don Bonnie
Stan Hasselgard
Justin Gordon
Art Pepper
George Probert
Abe Most
Artie Shaw
Barney Bigard
Benny Goodman
Bill Smith
Buddy DeFranco
Matty Matlock

Conductor
Russ Garcia
John Williams
Judd Conlon
Henry Mancini
Buddy Bregman
Henri Rene
Ralph Burns
Frank DeVol
Jack Marshall
Nelson Riddle
Rene Hall

Cornet
Red Nichols
Ruby Braff

Drums
Joe Dodge
Louis Fromm
Nick Fatool
Minor Hall
Milt Holland
Mel Lewis
Mel Lee
Marcel BlancLouis Singer
Louis Bellson
Leroy Harrison
Lee Young
Larry Bunker
Johnny Richardson
Jo Jones
Jimmy Pratt
John Marshall
Sid Balkin
Wayne Phillips
Vincenzo Restuccia
Tony Inzalaco
Tommy Romersa
Tim Kennedy
Tetsujiroh Obara
Stan Pepper
Ron Lunberg
Sid Catlett
Pelle Hulten
Sherman Ferguson
Shelly Manne

Ken Kennedy
Roy Harte
Jimmie Smith
Remo Belli
Rabon Tarrant
Pierre-Alain Dahan
Percy Brice
Stan Levey
Chico Hamilton
Ed Carr
Earl Palmer
Don Lamond
Dick Shanahan
Daniel Humair
Connie Kay
Cliff Leeman
Ciro Cicco
Chuck Thompson
Edward Hall
Chester Jones
Jeff Hamilton
Charles Blackwell
Lawrence Marable
Buddy Rich
Bobby White
Bob Neal
Billy Higgins
Ben Riley
Barry Morgan
Alvin Stoller
Chuck Redd
Irv Cottler
Jake Hanna
Jackie Mills
Jack Sperling
Jack Mills
J.C. Heard
Carl Maus
Elvin Jones
Harold Hahn
George Wettling
George Jenkins
Gene Krupa
Gene Gammage
Frankie Capp
Frank Severino
Frank Carlson
Frank Butler
Frank Bode
Irv Kluger

Guitar
Tommy Tedesco
Joe Gibbons
Joe Pass
John Gray
John Pisano
Kenny Burrell
Jimmy Wyble
T-Bone Walker
Ulysees Livingstone
Tony Rizzi
Jim Hall
Al Hendrickson
Arv Garrison
Bill Pitman
Bob Bain
Charlie Byrd

Gene Sargent
Herb Ellis
Jack Marshall
Howard Roberts
Irving Ashby
Ike Isaacs
Carlo Pes
Tal Farlow

Piano & Keyboard
Jackie Davis
George Wein
Joe Zawinul
Don Ewell
Eddie Beal
Ernie Freeman
Don Abney
Frank Patchen
Garland Finney
Gene Garf
Dodo Marmarosa
George Greeley
Hampton Hawes
Geoff Clarkson
Dave Grusin
Claude Williamson
Carl Perkins
Buddy Cole
Billy Miller
Art Tatum
Arnold Ross
André Previn
Al Haig
Hank Jones
Brian Lemon
Russ Freeman
Milt Rogers
Monty Alexander
Murray Arnold
Oscar Peterson
Page Cavanagh
Paul Smith
Pete Johnson
Ray Johnson
Milt Raskin
Roy Kral
Pete Jolly
Sonny White
Stan Wrightsman
Victor Feldman
Gerald Wiggins
Ronnell Bright
Jess Stacy
Harry Fields
Ray Sherman
Jeff Clarkson
Milt Buckner
Jimmy Rowles
Joe Bushkin
Joe Harnell
John Williams
Ken Kersey
Ken Lane
Marty Napoleon
Kenny Barron
Michael Lang
Maurice Vander
Jack Wilson

Marty Paich
Lou Levy
Mildred Falls
Kenny Drew
Marvin Jenkins

Tenor Saxophone
Teddy Edwards
John Lowe
Walter Benton
Skeets Herfurt
Marty Berman
Jewell Grant
Harold Land
Carrington Visor
Bill Robinson
Jim Horn
George Auld
Ted Nash
Ronnie Lang
Plas Johnson
Paul Horn
Justin Gordon
Julie Jacob
Harry Klee
Abe Most
George Smith
Don Raffell
Dave Pell
Chuck Gentry
Butch Stone
Bob Lawson
Babe Russin
Illinois Jacquet
Joe Howard
Jimmy Giuffre
Jack Schwarz
Jack Montrose
Justin Gordon
Jack Chaney
Plas Johnson
Howard Dietterman
Herbie Steward
Herbie Haymer
Herb Geller
Jack McVea
Stan Getz
Zoot Sims
Willie Schwartz
William Green
Wardell Gray
Vido Musso
Tom Makagon
Lucky Thompson
Ted Nash
Kurt Bloom
Richie Kamuca
Ralph Roselund
Ray Norman
Maxwell Davis
Harold Land
Lester Young
Teddy Edwards
Bill Holman
Bumps Myers
Buddy Collette
Bud Shank
Bob Hardaway

Bob Cooper
Bill Trujillo
Carey Visor
Bill Moore
Arthur Herfurt
Benny Golson
Ben Webster
Babe Russin
Al Cohn
George Auld
Sonny Rollins
Bill Perkins
Eddie Miller
Gene Cipriani
Freddie Simon
Gene Montgomery
Fred Falensby
Carter Englund
Emmett Carls
Ed Pripps
Don Raeffel
Dexter Gordon
Dave Pell
Dave Harris
Danny Moss
Corky Corcoran
Cliff Strickland
Charlie Ventura
Flip Phillips

Trombone
Lou Blackburn
Owen Marshall
Oliver Wilson
Murray McEarchern
Moe Schneider
Milt Bernhardt
Marshall Cram
Lloyd Ulyate
Lloyd Elliott
Leon Cox
King Jackson
Kid Ory
Ken Shroyer
Pat McNaughton
Karl De Karske
Mike Barone
Russ Bown
Juan Tizol
William Schaefer
Walter Benson
Trummy Young
Tommy Pederson
Tom Shepard
Wilbur Schwartz
Si Zentner
Pete Myers
Robert Swift
Richard Nash
Ray Sims
Ray Coniff
Ray Anderson
Randall Miller
Quentin Anderson
Phil Washburne
Porky Cohen
Simon Zentner
Bob Fitzpatrick

John Halliburton
Dick Nash
Dick Kenny
Dave Hallett
Cutty Cutshall
Chuck Maxon
Charles Coolidge
Dick Noel
Burton Johnson
Bob Edmondson
Bob Burgess
Bill Harris
Bill Haller
Barrett O'Hara
Babe Bowman
Albert Anderson
Pullman Pederson
Cappy Lewis
Harry Betts
Joe Howard
Bob Enevoldsen
Dicky Wells
Joe Cadeno
Jimmy Priddy
Hoyt Bohannon
Harry Rodgers
Gus Dixon
Gerald Foster
Earle Spencer
Ed Fromm
Herbie Harper
Ed Kusby
George Roberts
Ernest Tack
Francis Howard
Frank Rosolino
Gene Foster
George Arus
Frank Bradley

Trumpet
Maynard Ferguson
Lee Katzman
Lyman Vunk
Manny Klein
Marty Marsala
Melvin Moore
Maurice Harris
Nate Kazebier
Joe Dolney
Neal Hefti
Klein Sherock
Ken Hanna
Jules Chaiken
Johnny Martel
Johnny Coles
John Best
John Audino
John Anderson
Joe Gordon
Neil Hefti
Whitey Thomas
Joe Triscari
Shorty Rogers
Ziggy Elman
Zeke Zarchey
Ed Kusby
Vito Mangano

Jimmy Zito
Tony Terran
Tony Faso
Tony Facciuto
Tom Patton
Stu Williamson
Uan Rasey
Shorty Sherock
Oliver Mitchell
Rubin Zarchy
Roy Eldridge
Red Rodney
Ray Triscari
Ray Linn
Ray Anthony
Pete Candoli
Peanuts Holland
Paul Geil
Paul Cohen
Ollie Mitchell
Stan Fishelson
Bobby Bryant
Conte Candoli
Conrad Gozzo
Chico Alvarez
Chet Baker
Charlie Teagarden
Charlie Shavers
Carroll Lewis
Carmell Jones
Jimmy Pupa
Dick Catheart
Bob Scobey
Bill Stean
Bill Castagino
Bernie Glow
Art Robey
Anthony Terran
Alvin Alcorn
Al Porcini
Al Killian
Carlton McBeath
George Seaburg
Jim Zito
Jack Sheldon
Jack Mootz
Jack Millman
Irving Lewis
Irving Goodman
Irv Lewis
Howard McGhee
Harry 'Sweets' Edison
Dale Pierce
George Werth
Dick Mains
George Schwartz
Gene Duerneyer
Freddie Hill
Frank Beach
Everett McDonald
Ernie Royal
Don Fagerquist
Diz Mullins
Dick Sherman

Vibraphone
Milt Jackson
Lionel Hampton

Victor Feldman
Roy Ayers
Red Norvo
Larry Bunker
Bobby Hutcherson
Johnny White
Gene Estes
Frank Flynn
Charles Garble
Ralph Hansell
Emil Richards

Violin
Stuff Smith
Joe Venuti
Stephane Grappelli

Vocalist
Buddy Mel
Junko Mine
Mahalia Jackson
Loulie Jean Norman
Lou Rawls
Liz Tilton
Lena Horne
Kitty White
Kim Kimberly
Kay Brown
Mel Torme
June Christy
Julie London
Woody Herman
Josephine Premice
Johnny Mercer
Johnny Holiday
Kay Starr
Skip Nelson
Jeri Simpson
Vicky Lane
Tommy Traynor
Thelma Gracen
The Skylarks
Marie Bryant
Sue Allen
Mary Ann McCall
Sarah Vaughan
Roy Clark
Roselle Gayle
Rod McKuen
Phil Barton
Peggy Lee
Fred Astaire
Sylvia Telles
Bill Thompson
Charlie Cochran
Cathy Hayes
Buddy Greco
Buddy Anderson
Bobby Darin
Bing Crosby
Claire Austin
Ann Richards
Bill Henderson
Billie Holiday

Bill Brown
Betty Bennett
Bernie Parkie

Jackie Cain
Anita O'Day
Hal Stevens
Billy Eckstine
Ernie Andrews
The Four Freshmen
Imogene Lynn
Helen Humes
Helen Grayco
Gloria Wood
Claudia Thompson
Eve Young
Ella Mae Morse
Ella Fitzgerald
Dinah Washington
Fran Warren
Dean Martin
Earl Grant
Doris Day
Dorothy Allen
Dorothy Carless
Dorothy Collins
Dory Previn
Gogi Grant
Nellie Lutcher
Rose Murphy

Vocal (and Trumpet)
Art Robey
Wingy Manone
Roy Eldridge
Peanuts Holland

Barney Kessel

A Jazz Legend

GUITARS & EQUIPMENT

Early 1950s Gibson Guitar advertisement featuring Barney Kessel with a Blonde ES350T.

BARNEY KESSEL – *A Jazz Legend*
GUITARS & EQUIPMENT

During his long professional career Barney Kessel owned many guitars. From 1942-1947 he played on two Gibson ES300 guitars. This is confirmed by the various photographs of him playing at that time with the Artie Shaw and Charlie Barnet orchestras.

In 1947 the Gibson Guitar company introduced a new ES 350 model. Barney purchased one of the first of these. Gibson's December 1947 price list offers two versions of the ES 350 *Premier*. A sunburst finish model at $325.00 and a natural finish model at $340.00. The first ES 350 guitars featured only one pick-up placed at the end of the fingerboard and two controls. In 1948 the ES 350 was upgraded to feature two pick-ups and three controls. The fingerboard featured the 'double parallelogram' position markers and the peg head was inlaid with the distinctive Gibson crown. The distinctive Gibson trapeze shaped tailpiece with pointed ends had three raised parallelograms reflecting the fingerboard inlays.

It was this guitar that Barney was to play on virtually every jazz performance until 1992. He soon upgraded the original guitar replacing the standard Alnico pickup with a 1939 Charlie Christian (sometimes called Oscar Moore) straight bar pick-up. Barney always claimed that the amplified sound from this 1939s pick up was superior to anything else he had played. He eventually replaced the original rosewood fingerboard with a Nigerian ebony one stating that it was less porous and therefore less likely to capture dust and dirt to cause premature wear on the strings. The original position markers were replaced with simple small dot pearl markers. He replaced the standard Gibson bridge with one especially made for him. Barney also replaced Gibson's standard round plastic control knobs with two knobs taken from an old record player. He said that as these controls had pointers he could feel – without having to look – exactly where the controls were set.

Over the years the tuning pegs of his Gibson ES350 were replaced several times. In a February 1973 issue of Guitar magazine (UK) Barney described to guitarist Ike Isaacs other features of his equipment and famous guitar. His picks (plectrums), were specially made from pick guards, and were very stiff:

I reached a critical point the last time I was here, in 1970. I was down to one pick, which had been made for me by someone here in London out of a plastic material. The problem with me is that I like it to have absolutely no flexibility at all. It tends to have a rounded edge on it, more than a sharp point, because there's a greater chance of accuracy. I don't use tortoiseshell, I don't like the sound. My picks are made out of pick guards, and are very, very stiff. [10]

Ike Isaacs in this article confirmed the action on Barney's guitar was low — not as low as on most rock guitars but (according to Barney) *'400% lower'* than when he made his first records. He used to play with a high action, but now sets the strings merely high enough to allow him to play vigorously without distortion. Ike confirmed that the ES 350 was made of plywood! The sound on

1950's Gibson Guitar advertisement featuring Barney Kessel with his 1947 Sunburst ES350.

an electric guitar comes from the pickup, and therefore the wood was not an important ingredient. Nevertheless, Barney admitted to Ike to not feeling too comfortable when playing some plywood guitars:

I like to feel the vibration against my stomach from the back of the instrument. Some sort of response. This guitar does have some acoustic properties in it, so that there is a resonance. I feel this. [10]

Ike pointed out that the fret wire on Barney's guitar was wider than normal and asked why he changed it? Barney confirmed:

I wanted a larger, rounder sound. I want a high note to sound more like a trombone than a trumpet. But in the beginning it was purely experimental, like transplanting the Charlie Christian pickup: When I took this pick-up out of a Charlie Christian guitar, the repair man was quite concerned and didn't know whether it would work. But I was willing to take a chance and we did it.

Ike confirmed that thicker guitar strings also helped Barney in his search for the ideal sound: *'While you can't bend the strings as much, you have to assess the matter and compromise. I don't need or want to bend strings to the degree that rock people bend their strings, but I do want the sound. So I choose the string that is consistent with my mental image of how I want the music to sound.* [10]

Barney went on to explain that his frets, though thicker, were no higher than normal, but added that frets alone would not make a significant difference in the sound:

It's like adding weight in a scale; you just add another nail, and then another nail, and finally it tips the scale down. All these things I've done to the guitar over a period of time — changing the bridge, changing the nut, using the strings I use, the pickup I use — all these combined make a complete difference in sound.[10]

Ike then queried if a thicker fret meant more force was needed to hold the string down, and therefore this helped Barney achieve a 'fatter' sound? Barney responded:

I think it's a matter of setting up the instrument so that it will allow you to stress the musical values that you want to stress. The stiff pick also gives it a rounder sound, a sharper attack. A thinner pick allows you to play with more speed, but if you're playing with as much speed as you want, then you've got it! [10]

In the mid 1940s Barney used a Gibson BR-3 amplifier. It had a 10inch speaker, circa 10 watts output with three channels, one for vocal mic and two for instruments. This was the amplifier he used when he played with Charlie Parker in 1947. He stopped using this as his main amplifier in the early 1950s but occasionally he would use it when he was working on certain jazz, rhythm and blues or rock'n'roll recording sessions.

Barney Kessel's main amplifier in the 1950s and 1960s was a Gibson GA50. This tube amplifier, circa 22 watts, was first introduced in 1948 and was a combo featuring one 12" and one 18" speakers, two volume controls, two channels and two volume (bass and treble) controls. Gibson sold 114 GA50s in 1948, 277 in 1949, 233 in 1950, 168 in 1951, 133 in 1952, 92 in 1953 and 35 in 1954.

In a 1967 Guitar Player (USA) magazine article Barney confirmed he used two Gibson GA 50 amplifiers at that time but that he had altered everything in them, in some way, to produce a sound that satisfied him personally

The GA50 is the amplifier that Barney used on all his early historic Contemporary recordings. However the amplifier he was using in the 1970's had been greatly modified over the years. Barney confirmed in the Guitar (UK) magazine article:

Each new improvement has added a little weight, but it's still not fantastically heavy. Teddy Wallace, here in London, is a good friend, and he's done a lot of good work for me with my amplifiers. He's arranged it so that I can take the amplifier out of the cabinet and leave the speaker in the cabinet. It doesn't get a lot of highs; it doesn't have any echo built in, no vibrato built in, no fuzz. It's just a heavy-duty amplifier. Nevertheless, it's not a powerful amp by modern standards. The whole premise is different today. Most of the volume comes from the amplifier, not the pickup. It's mostly the amplifier boost. This old pickup I have seems to be more powerful than the new pickups, and therefore I don't have to use a lot of volume. [10]

1948 Gibson GA50 amplifier.

In the same article, Barney gave his opinion on the fact that most modern guitars have twin pickups:

They are arranged so that sound will be picked up in different places on the guitar. Near the bridge, it's brittle and nasal; near the fingerboard the sound is more mellow and round and sweet. My single pickup is at this mellow position. But in today's music, when they want a harsh, biting, percussive sound, they will pick it up near the bridge. You can also arrange a middle position, both pickups at the same time. I have a guitar like that. I have 25 guitars, and most of them are geared that way, with two pickups. It's to be able to use them in freelance work, to offer a variety of sounds. I have certain guitars that sound very ordinary. You could not recognise who was playing, because it's a very nondescript sort of sound. What you might hear on the radio at teatime, you know; music for conversation. A little guitar comes through, and it plays eight measures of something, and it could be one of ten thousand people, because there's nothing distinctive. You need these guitars when you want to be non-distinctive. [10]

Barney Kessel's thousands of fans all over the world, in the late 1940's and early 1950's, were aware that Barney had played Gibson guitars virtually exclusively since 1944. He had been featured in some Gibson adverts up to the mid 1950's as a Gibson player but by 1956 he had no agreement with Gibson. The Kay Guitar company, in the mid-1950's, was endeavouring to take a larger share of the electric guitar market from the Gibson and Epiphone companies. To this end the Kay company's president Sydney Katz decided that if he could get Barney Kessel, voted by several jazz magazines at that time as the world's best jazz guitarist, as a Kay endorsee – Barney could do for Kay what Les Paul was doing for Gibson. In 1956 Kay made a special edition of their Kay Pro archtop electric guitar and took it to the Chicago jazz club where Barney was playing. During the interval they showed him the guitar and made him an offer, to become a Kay endorsee, that was financially very attractive. Barney signed up and in late 1956 Kay introduced three Barney Kessel models as part of their '57 Gold 'K' line – the *Jazz Special*, the *Artist* and the *Pro*.

Introducing

THE SUPERLATIVE NEW KAY LINE

- **ONLY KAY** offers you so complete a line—ranging from a $24.50 student model to a $400 professional electric
- **ONLY KAY** boasts slim, steel-reinforced necks on every guitar
- **ONLY KAY** gives you life time laminated construction on every guitar

The Ultimate in Professional Electric Guitars...
...The Gold "K" Line

Sensitive instruments with action... sound... and style for the fine guitarist.

The Gold "K" guitars feature "planned electronics". Power, balance, sensitivity and style are perfectly united. Separate tone and volume controls. Each string has its own output adjusting post.

The Gold "K" guitar necks are perfect in their slimness... steel reinforced, adjustable, too... and fully guaranteed.

The Gold "K" guitars feature highly figured curly maple and super-selected seasoned spruce... and the luxurious, hand finish you deserve.

KESSEL JAZZ SPECIAL. Barney's choice features a Melita bridge for absolutely perfect intonation. Maximum Fidelity sound reproduction assured by new Gold "K" pickups. Pearl inlaid Ebony fingerboard. New style THIN master size — the finest strings, hardware and styling.

8700S	Double pickup, shaded finish, sunburst	$400.00
8700B	Double pickup, gleaming natural blonde	400.00
8701S	Single pickup, shaded finish, sunburst	350.00
8701B	Single pickup, gleaming natural blonde	350.00
8000C	Hard-shell, plush-lined case for above	52.50

KAY
MUSICAL INSTRUMENT COMPANY
1640 WALNUT ST., CHICAGO 12, ILL.

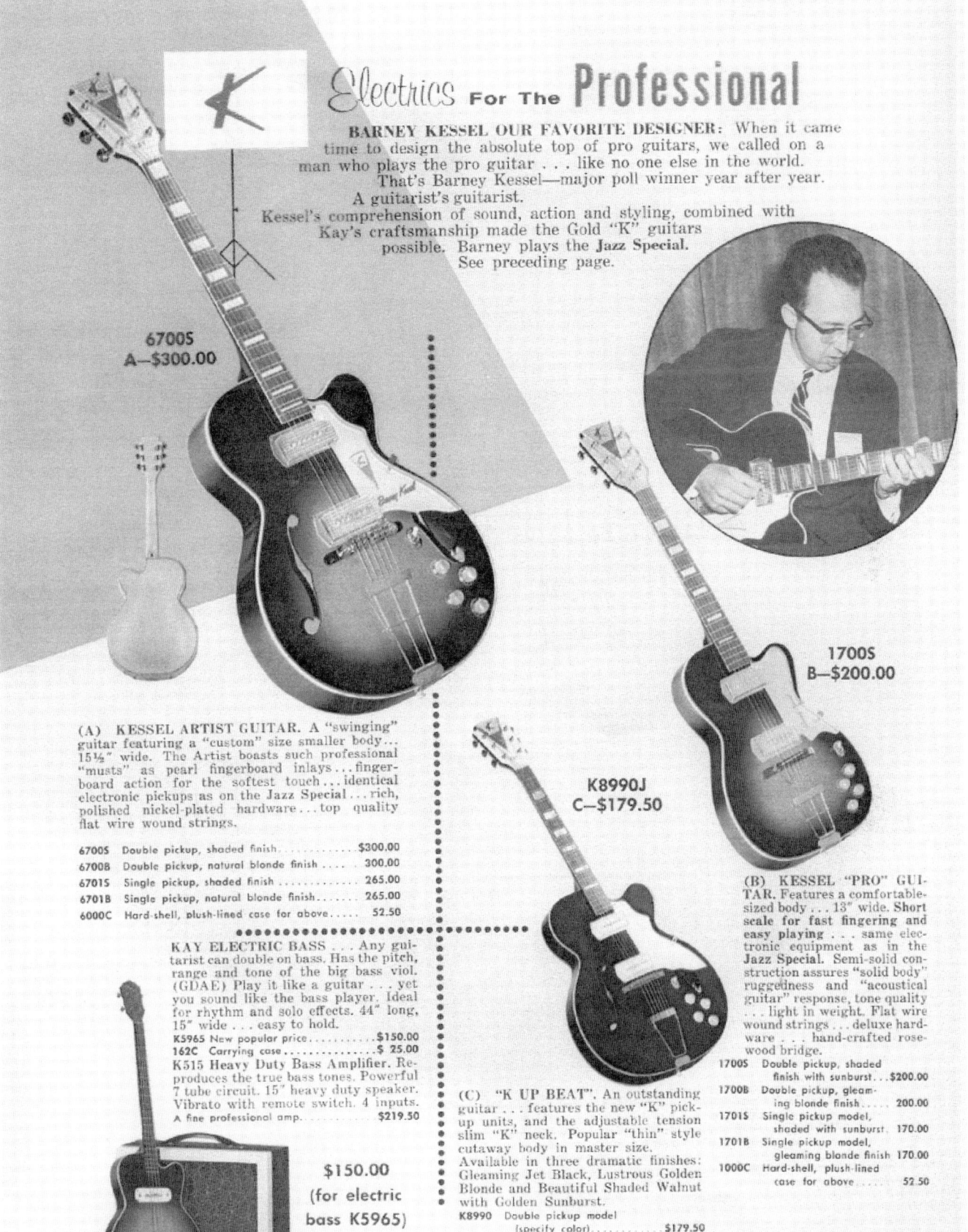

Electrics For The Professional

BARNEY KESSEL OUR FAVORITE DESIGNER: When it came time to design the absolute top of pro guitars, we called on a man who plays the pro guitar ... like no one else in the world. That's Barney Kessel—major poll winner year after year. A guitarist's guitarist.
Kessel's comprehension of sound, action and styling, combined with Kay's craftsmanship made the Gold "K" guitars possible. Barney plays the Jazz Special. See preceding page.

6700S
A—$300.00

1700S
B—$200.00

K8990J
C—$179.50

(A) KESSEL ARTIST GUITAR. A "swinging" guitar featuring a "custom" size smaller body... 15½" wide. The Artist boasts such professional "musts" as pearl fingerboard inlays ... fingerboard action for the softest touch ... identical electronic pickups as on the Jazz Special ... rich, polished nickel-plated hardware ... top quality flat wire wound strings.

6700S	Double pickup, shaded finish	$300.00
6700B	Double pickup, natural blonde finish	300.00
6701S	Single pickup, shaded finish	265.00
6701B	Single pickup, natural blonde finish	265.00
6000C	Hard-shell, plush-lined case for above	52.50

KAY ELECTRIC BASS ... Any guitarist can double on bass. Has the pitch, range and tone of the big bass viol. (GDAE) Play it like a guitar ... yet you sound like the bass player. Ideal for rhythm and solo effects. 44" long, 15" wide ... easy to hold.
K5965 New popular price $150.00
162C Carrying case .... $ 25.00
K515 Heavy Duty Bass Amplifier. Reproduces the true bass tones. Powerful 7 tube circuit. 15" heavy duty speaker. Vibrato with remote switch. 4 inputs. A fine professional amp. $219.50

$150.00
(for electric bass K5965)

(C) "K UP BEAT". An outstanding guitar ... features the new "K" pickup units, and the adjustable tension slim "K" neck. Popular "thin" style cutaway body in master size.
Available in three dramatic finishes: Gleaming Jet Black, Lustrous Golden Blonde and Beautiful Shaded Walnut with Golden Sunburst.
K8990 Double pickup model (specify color) $179.50
K8980 Single pickup model (specify color) 145.00

(B) KESSEL "PRO" GUITAR. Features a comfortable-sized body ... 13" wide. Short scale for fast fingering and easy playing ... same electronic equipment as in the Jazz Special. Semi-solid construction assures "solid body" ruggedness and "acoustical guitar" response, tone quality ... light in weight. Flat wire wound strings ... deluxe hardware ... hand-crafted rosewood bridge.

1700S	Double pickup, shaded finish with sunburst	$200.00
1700B	Double pickup, gleaming blonde finish	200.00
1701S	Single pickup model, shaded with sunburst	170.00
1701B	Single pickup model, gleaming blonde finish	170.00
1000C	Hard-shell, plush-lined case for above	52.50

COURTESY: KAY MUSICAL INSTRUMENT COMPANY

LOVE MATCH   KAY/KESSEL

It's no mere flirtation. The new "K" Professional guitar line has won the heart of the country's most accomplished guitar artist—Barney Kessel. And when the object of his affection is the stunning Kessel Jazz Special it's the beginning of making sweet music together.

Winner of the Down Beat, Metronome, Playboy and other leading magazine polls, Barney is shown here playing the "K" Kessel Jazz Special, model BK8700, priced at $400. Write for free catalog.

KAY MUSICAL INSTRUMENT CO. 1640 WALNUT ST, CHICAGO 12

ACTION

SOUND

STYLE

IT'S THE YEAR FOR K !

COURTESY: KAY MUSICAL INSTRUMENT COMPANY

The Barney Kessel Kay *Jazz Special*

This was full-sized (17 inch) single-cutaway jazz archtop guitar. With one Kay Gold K 8701 pickup it retailed in the USA for $350. The two K7801 pickup version retailed for $400. These pickups had patterned plastic covers. The guitar had an unusual shaped pickguard and this was engraved with the Barney Kessel name. These guitars had *Melitta* adjuastable bridge, bound ebony fingerboards inlaid with block and oval pearl position markers, Grover Imperial tuning pegs and an original design tailpiece. The large headstock had a unique design, made in extruded plastic that soon received the nickname 'Kelvinator'. The fitted case for these guitars retailed at $32.50.

The Barney Kessel Kay *Artist*

This was a smaller guitar than the *Jazz Special*. It had a 15 1/2inch lower bout. A bound rosewood fingerboard, with pearl block markers, had a shorter neck length of 24 inches and had the same 'Kelvinator' headstock as the *Jazz Special*. There was a single-pickup K6701 model retailing at $265 and a two-pickup version K6700 retailing for $300.

The Barney Kessel *Pro*

These smaller bodied guitars were based on an earlier Kay *Pro* range. Featuring a 13 inch body with the Kelvinator headstock, Gold K pickups, Grover tuning pegs and a the Barney Kessel engraved pick guard. The single pickup model (K1701) retailed for $170 and the two-pick up model (K1700) retailed for $200.

All three guitars could be purchased in either sunburst or blonde finishes. Barney Kessel's endorsee agreement with Kay guitars ended sometime in 1959. The guitars were still offered by Kay in early 1960 – but without the Barney Kessel name.

Despite the extensive advertising campaign for Kay's Barney Kessel guitar line from 1957-1960 Barney continued to play his Gibson ES350 virtually exclusively in concert and on record during that time. However, in episode four of the Johnny Staccato television series, *Shop of the Four Winds* Barney is featured in a jazz group, (with Pete Candoli, Red Mitchell and Shelly Manne) playing a Barney Kessel Kay guitar with its distinctive headstock.

The Gibson Barney Kessel Guitar

In early 1960 Ted McCarty, who had taken over the running of the Gibson Guitar company in 1948, heard that Barney was not happy with the Kay company's instruments and that Barney had finished, or was about, to finish, his endorsee agreement with them. He met Barney in New York and assured Barney that Gibson would make him a top line jazz guitar bearing his name – and the financial deal would be at least as good as Kay's. Barney is reported as saying that he would like such a deal with Gibson but the guitar *'has got to be an instrument I can play and that I will enjoy playing'* – *'I don't play that Kay, it's a terrible guitar'*.[23]

The Gibson *Barney Kessel* guitar was introduced in late 1960. It is instantly recognisable by its double Florentine cutaways and a large peghead. It had a 17-inch body with similar dimensions to the popular Gibson L-5 model. Except it had a narrower 3 inch rim. The guitar's body was made with a laminated spruce top and laminated maple back and sides. The first *Barney Kessel* guitars had an awkward neck heel as a result of a neck-to-body junction at the 14th fret. In 1965 this junction was moved to the 17th fret that gave the player a much improved access to the upper register of the fingerboard.

The Barney Kessel Custom (BK-C)

This guitar was made with a two-piece maple neck, a distinctive quaver inlay on the headstock, bow-tie shaped pearl fingerboard markers and bound f-holes. Standard hardware included Grover *Rotomatic* tuners, a Gibson *Tune-O-Matic* bridge, all gold-plated. The guitar was supplied in shaded cherry sunburst finish and was fitted with Gibson's standard twin humbucker assembly. The tailpiece had a rosewood shield fitted with a plastic plate featuring the Barney Kessel name. In 1961 this guitar retailed for $560. About 250 BK-C guitars were produced between 1962-1966.

The Barney Kessel Regular (BK-R)

This Gibson guitar was very similar in construction to the Custom model but was fitted with mahogany neck. The headstock had a crown, instead of a quaver, inlay. The fingerboard had Gibson's popular double parallelogram pearl inlays and the f-holes were unbound. The tuners were Kluson Deluxe and

BARNEY KESSEL Guitar

Barney Kessel means guitar to a great many people. A jazz guitar... a guitar with individual sounds... a guitar with a highly personal technique... a guitar that makes you feel you've experienced something very special after you've heard it played. It's the magic of this guitar which gives Barney his perennial position at the top of the popularity polls. Barney is one of the most inventive and vital musicians in jazz... as a soloist, in a combo, with a big-name band. Whether he's playing a concert in Paris or Venezuela, packing them in at Chicago's London House and Hollywood's Sanbah, or working (and directing) a network TV show, Barney's breathtaking creativity on the guitar produces reverent awe and loud acclaim. The sudden chord changes, distinctive tones and dramatically varied harmonics are uniquely Barney Kessel guitar. And by the way, did you know that there are now available two Barney Kessel Model instruments... created by *Gibson*

Gibson, Inc., Kalamazoo, Michigan

COURTESY: GIBSON GUITAR CORPORATION

the guitar was fitted with a preset rosewood Gibson bridge. The hardware was nickel-plated. And, like the Custom model, the tailpiece also had a rosewood shield with the fitted plastic plate featuring the name - Barney Kessel. About 750 BK-R guitars were produced between 1962-1966.

Gibson Guitars featured their Barney Kessel models in extensive press advertising. Both models remained in production until 1972. Barney Kessel made up the trio of big jazz name endorsees for Gibson's jazz guitar range at that time. The other two jazz guitarists were Johnny Smith and Tal Farlow. Whereas Smith and Farlow played their Gibson model guitars almost exclusively Barney continued to play his modified ES350 in almost all his concert and club dates, and on all his jazz recordings.

As one of the world's busiest studio musicians Barney Kessel needed a wide range of guitars so that he could supply the right sound for any particular recording, film sound track, radio and television show. He also had banjos and mandolins in his collection which he could play to an acceptable standard when required. However he did have two rare and very special Gibson L5 guitars originally owned by the famous studio guitarist George M. Smith (1912-1993). One had been made in 1933 and the other was made in 1937. Barney purchased both guitars on 10 July 1948 from Smith who had owned them since they were made. As one of the leading staff musicians in the 1930's and 1940's in Los Angeles Smith had played extensively with the 20th Century Fox film studios in Hollywood.

After purchasing the guitars in 1948. Barney Kessel played them from July 1948 to March 1969 for all his studio work. This included films for all the major Hollywood studios including four Elvis Presley films, Barbara Streisand's *On a Clear Day You Can See Forever*, two films with Dean Martin and Jerry Lewis and another with Jerry Lewis alone. He played these L5 guitars on numerous recordings including those of the Righteous Brothers, Sarah Vaughan, Ella Fitzgerald, Billie Holiday, Sonny & Cher, The Beach Boys and on many recordings produced by Phil Spector.

Kessel also played his Gibson L5 guitars on many television shows including *Hollywood Palace*, the *Judy Garland Show*, a *Bing Crosby Christmas Special* (with the Paul Weston Orchestra) and the *Bob Crosby Show*, He played them on many radio shows including Bob Crosby's (five days a week for a year) and Jack Smith's radio show (five days a week for two years).

Barney made some interesting comments about playing rhythm guitar in a 1958 Metronome (USA) magazine interview:

I have played rhythm guitar and still do on many record dates where it is required. I enjoy this type of playing very much, especially with a large string orchestra, or a band playing in a Basie groove. There is a particular resonance I have noticed in rhythm guitar that pleases me when only the rhythm section and brass in straight mutes are playing. I enjoy the approach to rhythm guitar playing by Freddie Green, Herb Ellis, and Barry Galbraith.

I don't feel that rhythm guitar helps much in other fields of playing, except to develop the ability to keep time, and this one thing could be utilized in any other musical endeavor. Many young players I have heard lately, while having great technique, have great difficulty in keeping time on their solos. Regardless of what instrument it is, the inability to keep time is the one great flaw that most youngsters share even though they play all the right notes.

Most orchestras today have economic problems which force them to get by with as few men as possible. In a ballroom, if the acoustics aren't good and the band isn't balanced properly with microphones in the right places, the guitar won't be heard. If it is heard, it won't be under the best possible conditions and will therefore make only a minor contribution. Even at best, the guitar makes a very subtle, though very important contribution to an orchestra playing in a ballroom. Sometimes you can't hear it loudly, but you can feel it. If it starts playing and then drops out, you certainly will register the feeling of a great loss. Irving Ashby once put it this way, "Rhythm guitar is like the vanilla in a cake. You can't taste it, but you know when its been left out."

Orchestra leaders feel many times that they can do without guitar and have less problems than if other instruments are eliminated. Most guitarists today, who want to make a good living, must be able to play amplified guitar and so they spend most of their time developing this skill. The only guitarists I have found that do take rhythm guitar seriously are

Two rare Gibson L-5 guitars owned by Barney Kessel. One was made in 1933. The other in 1937. Barney purchased both guitars on 10 July 1948 from the American guitarist George M.Smith who had owned them since they were made. As a staff musician at the time Smith played with 20th Century Fox movie studio in Hollywood in the 1930's and 1940's.

Features Exclusive to the Master Model

"F" sound holes; Larger sounding board of finest spruce; Fingerboard elevated from top; Neck and body join at fifteenth fret; Tuned sound chamber; Richly finished in Cremona brown; Gold trimmings.

The GIBSON Master Guitar

- Style L-5 Professional Model

Just as the mighty organ of the great theatre fills every nook and corner with it's majestic tones, so does the Gibson Master Guitar bring the lovely coloring of the guitar voice **surging** forth to thrill the ear of both player and listener with it's **new power and grandeur.**

You will find the Gibson stamp of **Master** applied only to that model of the individual families which embodies every known feature, representing the utmost which Gibson skill, knowledge, design, selection of material and Master - Craftsmanship can build into one **superb instrument.**

Gibson L-5 guitars details from a 1928 Gibson Guitar catalogue.

the ones that do not play amplified guitar. When a orchestra has a guitarist, the charts almost always have amplified parts to play, and the leaders are more insistent that the guitarist be able to play these parts than be an extraordinary rhythm man. Most guitarists in dance bands today are primarily amplified guitarists, who have to play rhythm as part of the job and make an effort at it. A player of this sort, while being a good amplified player, would not make the kind of rhymthic contribution needed from a rhythm guitar.' [Metronome Editor's note: One notable exception to this comment was Barry Galbraith, a great rhythm guitarist and a great soloist.] [20]

By the time I first met Barney Kessel in person (in 1972) my UK distribution company, Summerfield Music, was already established as one of the UK's leading musical instrument distributors. As a result, over the years, Barney and I talked about several joint music accessory and other business projects. Some of these came to fruition with varying success.

BARNEY KESSEL STRINGS by DARCO

The *BARNEY KESSEL* guitar string line was produced for my Summerfield Musical Instrument distribution company by the Darco string company in 1972. I have had a close business and personal relationship with the D'Addario family (the original owners of the Darco string company) for almost 40 years. Barney had never been associated with any particular music string company, and used many different brands over the years. He really liked the quality of the Darco company's sample string sets that I supplied him to test. He soon agreed to recommend and endorse a jazz guitar string range, bearing his name, with a selection of the gauges he preferred for playing jazz. With the help of my good friends John D'Addario Jnr and his brother Jim, an attractive package was put together, and the range enjoyed very good sales for several years.

THE BARNEY KESSEL AMPLIFLIER by MERSON

In 1976 Barney told me about the U.4100 Minimax amplifier, made by the Merson company in the USA, that he had discovered and was using.. He believed, with a few small modifications, this lightweight amplifier was ideal for jazz guitarists. He

---

DARCO

BARNEY KESSEL GUITAR STRINGS

Since 1944, Barney Kessel has been recognized as one of the world's leading figures in Jazz, and today is accepted in every corner of the globe as the world's finest exponent of the electric guitar. He has been associated with many world famous artists such as: Charlie Parker, Mahalia Jackson, Maurice Chevalier, Tex Ritter, Frank Sinatra, Bing Crosby, Ella Fitzgerald, Benny Goodman, Artie Shaw, Charlie Barnet, Elvis Presley, Sonny & Cher, The Righteous Brothers, The Beach Boys, Rick Nelson and Phil Spector. He has been a guitarist, arranger, composer, orchestrator and conductor in dance bands, radio, recordings, motion pictures and television. He has won awards presented by such magazines as: Down Beat, Esquire, Metronome, Melody Maker and Playboy, acknowledging him as the world's best Jazz guitarist. He has always been as demanding in his choice of strings as he has for his instruments and music. As a result he got together with Darco Strings to produce a range of strings that would be superior to anything previously marketed and so you now have available this outstanding new range of electric guitar strings.

The Barney Kessel String by DARCO Unconditionally Guaranteed
BK000   Extra Light   BK200   Medium
BK100   Light   BK300   Heavy

Made in U.S.A.

AVAILABLE FROM GOOD MUSIC SHOPS EVERYWHERE

EXCLUSIVE WORLD DISTRIBUTION:
CSL SUMMERFIELD
SALTMEADOWS ROAD, GATESHEAD, NE8 3AJ. TEL. (0632) 770431

HAPPINESS...
...is Barney Kessel and his 4100 AMPLIFIER BY MERSON

Famed guitarist Barney Kessel currently touring the world with his famous jazz trio exclusively uses a Merson 4100 amplifier which gives him that pure uncluttered sound he wants. The 4100 is a no nonsense amplifier for the jazz guitar player who wants a warm undistorted sound so typical of Barney Kessel and other top jazz artists. Its nice to know that in a world of amplifiers so orientated to the rock and beat market that an amplifier is now available for the player who wants quality and warmth of sound above all.

THE MERSON U4100 BARNEY KESSEL AMPLIFIER, 105 WATTS RMS (4 OHMS)

Distributed to Good Music shops throughout Great Britain by Summerfield, Gateshead NE8 3AJ

"The effective Guitarist" — world famous guitar seminar

This seminar "THE EFFECTIVE GUITARIST" was created and is directed by BARNEY KESSEL in person. It is a 4-day course designed for *anyone* who spends time with the guitar pursuing musical goals. It doesn't matter how long you have been playing or whether you play professionally or just for fun.

This seminar takes into consideration your *needs* — what *you* want to know — and offers techniques that will require less of your power (time, money, effort) and still allow you to be more effective.

For the first time, here is a concentrated, concise, information-packed course for guitarists, utilizing the most recent discoveries in cybernetics and other related sciences.

Barney Kessel with the outstanding jazz pianist Errol Garner.

These concepts have been used in the development of missiles and have greatly contributed to men landing on the moon. These principles have been taught to executives and professional men and women and have been proven to be effective in their lives by helping them increase their earnings; do more in less time; improve the quality of their work; integrate their work into their total life pattern to produce more fulfilment and serenity.

This seminar is designed to show you:

- How To Determine Your Musical Goals
- How To Improve Your Playing and Musicianship
- How To Avoid Working In Unrelated, Non-Functional and Minimum Effective Areas and How to Effectively Progress in Top-Priority Areas
- How To Practise
- How To Develop A Complete Comprehension Of The Fingerboard Through The "Structure Concept"
- How To Read and Sight Read
- How To Refine and Improve Your Technique
- How To Play Faster With Less Effort
- Harmony – Effective Voicings – Chord Substitutions – Harmonic Super – Imposition
- How To Play Melodies Using Chords
- How To Improvise Using Chords
- How To Set Up A Work and Practice Schedule
- How To Form Concepts To Escalate Your Career, Earn Money Through Music and Continue Increasing Your Earnings

This new concept for musicians includes and utilizes principles designed to increase effectiveness in every area of your musical thoughts and activities. The purpose of this seminar is to help you be more effective right now, right where you are in your musical development with the least expenditure of your resources.

For Full Details of This Year's Seminars Write To:

U.S.A.	GREAT BRITAIN
MUSIC DYNAMICS SEMINARS BOX 2629 Hollywood, Ca. 90028 U.S.A.	SUMMERFIELD SALTMEADOWS ROAD, GATESHEAD NE8 3AJ

Details of Barney Kessel's Seminar Programme – 'The Effective Guitarist'.

Scenes from the 4th annual British Guitar Seminar 'The Effective Guitarist' – October 1976 – Newcastle upon Tyne.

made several suggestions to the Merson company and within a short time we were distributing in the UK the new *Barney Kessel Amplifier* by Merson. It proved quite popular with many jazz guitarists. The amplifier had 11 silicon transistors with an output power of 105 watts RMS. It weighed 31 pounds. The Barney Kessel amplifier had a limited production over a short period of time in 1976-1977. However during that time Barney used it almost exclusively.

THE BARNEY KESSEL GUITAR by IBANEZ

One project that never came to fruition was the *Barney Kessel* model guitar by Ibanez. My instrument company distributed with great success Ibanez products in the UK from 1964 to 1988. During that time I introduced Joe Pass to the Ibanez company, and also provided them with basic plans and ideas for a Joe Pass guitar. Joe and I had worked out the special features of this guitar in 1978 when he was playing at Ronnie Scott's jazz club in London. I then confirmed the terms of the Ibanez endorsee agreement with Joe's manager Norman Granz – and he quickly gave me his go ahead for the project. This guitar eventually became Ibanez's very successful *Joe Pass JP 20* model.

The quality of the Joe Pass guitar was excellent and I believed that I could achieve similar success for a jazz guitar made to Barney's specifications.. Three prototype guitars were produced, and Barney really liked the third one. He used it on a European concert tour in 1979. However, in the end, no agreement was finalised and the guitar was never commercially produced. I recognised Barney had decided he still preferred to play his modified 1947 Gibson ES350 guitar because he felt more comfortable with it and because of the special quality of the sound obtained from it's 1939 bar pick-up.

SEMINARS and PUBLICATIONS

In 1972, over dinner one night in London, Barney told me about his recently developed seminar *The Effective Guitarist*. I was really impressed by the content of his seminar programme and in October 1973 my company presented what was to be the first of twelve annual Barney Kessel seminars in Newcastle upon Tyne, in the North-East of England. Over the years almost 350 guitarists had the great privilege of studying with Barney on this very special four-day course. It was through these seminars that I discovered what a great teacher Barney was. He had a rare and special ability to communicate the essence of how to study music, develop instrumental technique, and so eventually become a good musician.

As Barney explained to Bill Lee:

What I have attempted to do is base these seminars on psycho-cybernetic techniques and various executive efficiency techniques that have been used by all sorts of industries and professions other than music. I've decided to work it from a standpoint that the guitarist should learn abstract things and that he also should define his goals. He may not have known what his goals were, or how to go about reaching them. My course should give people techniques to help them reach and establish their goals. It isn't necessary to have played a long time. What is necessary is that the individual is very involved with the guitar. They don't have to want to be a professional, but when they find that they are attached to the guitar, this course is for them. [16]

Over the years many of the UK's best guitarists, including Adrian Ingram, Ron Moore, Roy Sainsbury and Jim Birkett, attended the seminars. Through these, and two master classes, Barney Kessel made a great contribution to the quality of jazz guitar playing in the UK. He also held his *The Effective Guitarist* and other seminars in parts of the USA, Europe, Australia and Sweden.

In 1967 Barney completed writing his critically acclaimed basic guitar tutor *The Guitar* and a series of technical exercises. These were all published through his Windsor Music Company based in Los Angeles. These works achieved acceptable sales levels through his various international printed music distributors.

For many, years I tried to persuade Barney to let me publish some of his original compositions - as recorded by him for the Contemporary and Concord record companies. He finally agreed to the project and in 1986 we published two volumes, of a selection of his compositions, under the title *The Jazz Guitar Artistry of Barney Kessel*. These two volumes were then published in 1992 in one volume under the same title (Hal Leonard

ELECTRIC *Spanish Guitars*

The true artist is more than a technician or a stereotyped showman. He is true master of all that is necessary to his performance, including a fine instrument. And he requires more of his instrument than the ordinary performer.

It is natural then that Gibson turns to such outstanding artists as Barney Kessel, Tal Farlow and Johnny Smith for recommendation and counsel.

With pride we present this series of artist's instruments. Each is designed to the specifications of the renowned guitarist and created by the finest of craftsmen to satisfy every demand of each critical artist.

These fine guitars differ, as does individual taste, but each is a jewel of perfection, a tribute to the artist and the Gibson craftsmen. They are constructed to afford every player the best instrument available for exacting and brilliant execution. Try each of them—there's one that will suit your style of playing and your most critical inspection.

JOHNNY SMITH

BARNEY KESSEL

TAL FARLOW

BARNEY KESSEL GUITAR

A Gibson guitar designed by the great jazz guitarist himself, with musical capability to match his tremendous technique and vital, inventive playing. It offers the purest tone over the entire range with a special magnetic field in the bridge pickup to emphasize the highs.

FEATURES: Laminated spruce arched top and laminated maple back. Slim, fast, low-action neck joins body at 14th fret. Three-piece curly maple neck, adjustable truss rod. 20 fret rosewood fingerboard with "bow-tie" pearl inlays. Gold-plated adjustable Tune-O-Matic bridge. Powerful twin humbucking pickups . . . separate tone and volume controls can be pre-set. Three-position toggle switch to activate either or both pickups. Gold-plated metal parts. 17" wide, 21" long, 3" thin, 25½" scale, 20 frets.

Custom Model
BK-C Cherry sunburst finish
Regular Model
BK-R Cherry sunburst finish
Like the custom model with these differences: mahogany neck with pearl inlaid peghead, rosewood fingerboard with rectangular pearl inlays, rosewood bridge, nickel-plated metal parts.
600   Faultless plush-lined case
ZC-6 Deluxe zipper case cover

COURTESY: GIBSON GUITAR CORPORATION

85

000699350/ AM1305). A further two volumes (Volume 2 in 1997 - HL00699350 /AM2183) and Volume 3 in 2000 - HL00330588/AM2851) were published. Despite his initial reservation in publishing these note-for-note collections, of some of his best compositions and improvised solos, Barney was very happy with all three volumes. The books have enjoyed good sales all over the world for many years.

MODULAR CASSETTE COURSE

In 1978 Barney became very enthusiastic about a modular cassette tuition course for guitarists that he had developed with Sonny Gray of ITTI Studios in Tulsa and jazz promoter Dino Economos. Gray's company had produced tapes for several years teaching everything from foreign languages to flight training for pilots. Barney called it a modular course as he said his tapes could be bought as a package or individually. As he explained:

You don't go from one specific tape to another. Each tape can be utilised according to the player's own goals and needs, without a need of the other.[21]

Ten tapes were actually produced and covered various topics including self concepts and goals, using the hands, improvisation and the blues. Barney said that with this tape course:

I hope to impart the psychological and professional information that makes an artist an artist......What I want to teach is a total lifestyle, how to achieve the perspective and attitudes that make a person a musician rather than an instrumentalist.[21]

However, despite Barney's enormous enthusiasm, the sales programme never really got going for the modular cassette course and very few units were actually sold.

TUITION VIDEOS

Barney Kessel was a natural teacher, and teaching was something he really enjoyed doing. So he agreed to let Mark Helman of Rumark Video Inc. in Winnipeg, Canada produce three jazz guitar improvisation tutorial videos in 1986. These are still available in VHS format. The first is a 90-minute video called *Jazz Guitar Improvisation*. It includes ten lessons including how to play what you hear, fills, turnarounds, the building blocks of improvisation and the blues. The second video is 53 minutes long and is called *Jazz Guitar Improvisation – Progressive Concepts*. It deals with chord formations and sequence playing in six prepared lessons. The third video is called *Jazz Guitar Improvisation – Chord Melody Style*. It is 45 minutes long contains seven lessons on how to harmonise a melody. On all three videos Barney is accompanied by the excellent jazz bass player, Dave Young.

Barney also made an *Elementary Guitar* VHS video Tutorial for beginners. This was distributed, until recently, by the Kultur company in the USA. As at September 2008 none of these VHS videos had been made into DVDs.

STEINWAY PIANO

Barney Kessel also played the piano (what he called arranger's piano) for composing and arranging for records, films and television. For many years he had a 1925 Steinway grand piano that he loved to play for this purpose.

BARNEY KESSEL
Jazz Guitar improvisation
"CHORD-MELODY STYLE"

A QUALITY PROFESSIONAL SERIES — RUMARK VIDEO

THE BARNEY KESSEL
PERSONAL MANUSCRIPT SERIES
#105
THE VERY FIRST WARM UPS
THIS HELPS THE GUITARIST PREPARE FOR DAILY PRACTICE AND PLAYING SESSIONS

PRICE $1.00
WINDSOR MUSIC CO.

SOLE SELLING AGENT:
CRITERION MUSIC CORP.   17 WEST 60TH ST.   NEW YORK, N.Y. 10023
ALL RIGHTS RESERVED   INTERNATIONAL COPYRIGHT SECURED   MADE IN U.S.A.

WINDSOR MUSIC JAZZ SERIES FOR GUITAR

JAZZ GUITAR ARTISTRY OF BARNEY KESSEL
9 ORIGINAL GUITAR SOLOS

NOTE-FOR-NOTE TRANSCRIPTIONS FROM BARNEY KESSEL'S CONTEMPORARY & CONCORD RECORDINGS

I'M ON MY WAY • HERE'S THAT SUNNY DAY
HOLIDAY IN RIO • LOVE OF MY LIFE • BLUES FOR BIRD
MOONLIGHT WALK • BLUESY
STAR FIRE • JUAREZ AFTER DARK

WINDSOR MUSIC CO.
1136 Madison Avenue · San Diego · CA92116 · USA

In conjunction with
ASHLEY MARK PUBLISHING CO.
1 & 2 Vance Court, Trans Britannia Enterprise Park,
Blaydon on Tyne NE21 5NH, United Kingdom.

Volume 3
USA $16.95

KULTUR
LEARN TO PLAY WITH "THE GRAND MASTER OF THE GUITAR"

ELEMENTARY GUITAR
with BARNEY KESSEL

MUSIC INSTRUCTIONAL

87

Gibson, the workingman's guitar.

Barney Kessel & Gibson at work for Contemporary Records.

Barney Kessel

A Jazz Legend

THOUGHTS on Music & Life

BARNEY KESSEL – *A Jazz Legend*
Thoughts on Music & Life

Music

Barney often related how he learnt some important lessons in life quite unexpectedly.

The first was after he had played with Charlie Christian for three days in 1939. It dawned upon him that all he had played was a copy of Christian's guitar solos, and that this really had no value. Barney recognised that he must find his own musical voice and be himself. Christian also told Barney that he never took his guitar out of the case unless he was getting paid, learning something, or having fun. This became Barney's philosophy throughout his professional career. The second affected his approach to playing music and occurred during his time with the Chico Marx orchestra. He described how this happened to Ira Gitler:

When I was playing with Chico Marx, at the Black Hawk for four months, I had a lot of solos to play and every time I played I didn't think a thing about it. I just sort of closed my eyes and played whatever came to me, freely, whatever it was. At one point somebody in the band just happened to mention that we had a very large listening audience. He said, "Do you know how many people are listening to us? Millions!"

Something happened to me at that point. I started thinking in a particular way. I said to myself, there are millions of people listening when I play a solo, and I'm a professional, and the thing that a professional should do is never make a mistake. Therefore, I should memorize my solos so that I don't.

For one thing, the solos that had been free, that represented a kind of a breathing thing within these arrangements, were now set, so it offered no really fresh kind of an interjection from me, because the band had been playing written parts, and now I came into my solos, and they were all set and the band could sing them with me. Not only did I not change them, but it even got worse because if I made a mistake, everyone knew it, whereas before, if I hadn't played exactly what I thought and it wasn't wrong, nobody knew. And I didn't realize that I'm sort of limiting myself in developing my own ability to improvise. I hadn't been to a jam session in about two months, and I went to a jam session in Chicago, after doing this for a number of weeks, playing this way and memorizing my chords because I didn't want to make a mistake on the radio. When I sat down to play, I realized that my reflexes weren't there, that if I thought of something it didn't come out right away; so something within me told me that I must get back to the way I was before and dare to make a mistake and dare to play freely, and that's the only way to get good at playing. The only way of getting good at making things up on the spot is to constantly make things up on the spot. That was an insight to me. Since that time, it wouldn't matter which show I've been on, I've been on radio shows, TV shows, when it comes time to blow, I just blow, and I could care less about the mistakes.[4]

When asked what he looks for in a song that makes him want to play it Barney confirmed:

First, a beautiful melody. There are only three elements in music: melody, rhythm, and harmony. If it's rich in all three qualities, usually I'll like it. Today, I don't hear many songs that I like. First of all, many of the songs that come to us come as a result of being recorded; and when they're recorded, they're not recorded because they're good. They're recorded because they can be sold as a product. Therefore, the writers are writing so they can get a hit record and get royalties. Everybody's caught up in the game of producing products that will sell—not necessarily creative and artistic output. So every-body, whether capable of putting out artistic material or not, isn't producing artistically; it's just what they can draw from themselves that's a marketable product. So, I'm not interested in a marketable product; I'm interested in what I know from my life experience to be standards of excellence. It's like this: I can't get excited about a tinny, junky car that's being made now just to compete with other tinny, junky cars when I know that a Rolls Royce exists. Whether or not I have a Rolls Royce is not important; I know it exists, and it's a standard of excellence.[2]

Barney was then asked if uses the original chords for the song or did he harmonize a lot – to which he replied:

I try to learn the song as it is, first. I try to show that much respect to the composer and to get it right. Then, if I get a feeling for the song that way, I'll do it that way. But it's not a matter of thinking, "I am a guitar player who is offering a service to the public, and that service is playing that song for them." I'm not giving them the song, and I'm not giving them the guitar. I'm giving them Barney Kessel. But I'm using the guitar as a tool, and I'm using the song as a vehicle. And if they come away more impressed with the guitar or with the song than with me, then I've missed it. I don't want people to say, "That guy plays a lot of guitar," or "He knows a lot of songs." I want them to say, "Barney Kessel really made me feel good".[2]

In an August 1987 Cadence magazine interview Barney confirmed why he had for many years preferred playing in a guitar, bass and drums trio:

For a number of years I have preferred to work with just bass and drums for any number of reasons. I could probably sit here all night giving you my reasons but just to touch on a few, for one I found myself that the way I play, using a lot of chords as well as single notes, I get greater clarity by not having a piano or another chord instrument. A lot of guitar players, for one reason or another, do not choose to use a lot of chords. They may use some now and then but if you listen to them over a whole night most of what they play is not chords. By not having another chord instrument the guitar comes through more prominent. It shines. Another thing is, as I play I find myself enjoying changing harmonies on things from night to night. I may play a song five nights in a row and each night it will be different and if I don't have another chord instrument on the bandstand I'm not locked in with those chords. I still respect what the bass player's doing and if he's playing certain notes I relate to him but it leaves enormous possibilities for changing things. It gives me a lot of variety. It's not to be far out or weird, it just offers me more pleasure, excitement and keeps it more spontaneous. I've got to work in an atmosphere that allows me to be fresh and one of those ways is to change the harmonies.

Barney, when asked what his influences were, replied:

Everything has influenced me. Not only jazz. My favourite music in the world is Ravel and Debussy. Paintings influence me as well; and books on architecture by Frank Lloyd Wright. I have taken concepts that I suppose are in architecture and tried to apply them in music. But everything is an influence: Life itself, the Bible, Shakespeare, all these things.

My approach is very simple. So simple that sometimes it deludes people. All I am trying to do is to be myself. When I was very young I worked in theatres as an usher and I saw many movies. I saw Fred Astaire pictures umpteen times, and these songs from the movies, they stay with you. All this is just part of my background. Every little thing gives you insight. You get a better picture of it the more you learn about life; the more you are calm; and the less competitive you are. When you're not competitive in your music you can be more natural, because you are not doing it to impress: you are doing it to express.

When you're trying to impress you are trying to get people to like you, and so you end up doing the kind of things that may not be natural to you. In my case, I've done it long enough that I am more interested in expressing than impressing. I hope that what I express would be that which would impress.

It's what I feel. I love people. I feel secure with people. I feel secure with myself, and I want them to feel the same. I'm not a humorist, but I like to present a mildly humorous atmosphere. That way, people don't feel intimidated because there is an 'artist' out there who demands absolute silence. I just demand that we have fun.

All I've got to do is be the best Barney Kessel I can be and let the world go by because no one can take away from you what you've got. I don't care who comes along. You are you, and if you're original, no one can take that away from you. You see, I don't try to follow trends. If anything, and I say this modestly, I try to set trends. You don't have to worry about competition if you're going to be yourself. I look at music as a lifelong work, and in it you win a few, you lose a few. It's just like a ball-game.

You have to look at it over a lifetime, and when I do I see it has been great. I've been very fortunate. I'm not saying this like I'm Miss Goody Two Shoes, but I've never been involved with the drug situation. I do smoke cigars. I do drink wine with my meals, and I walk on the water with one foot! I feel very fortunate that I have not come under the spell of things that are destructive, as I have seen in other musicians. If I were having a good time, I would want to know it. I wouldn't want someone to tell me about it tomorrow. Also, it's a sense of not losing control, and in playing the guitar it's important not to lose control. Anything which you are doing where you have to be good requires a lot of effort, but if you love it, it doesn't seem like you've put in the effort.[15]

Barney went on to confirm there were several loves in his life greater than the guitar:

I have no real affection for the guitar. It's just a tool. To me, it's what a pencil would be to Shakespeare and a paintbrush to Van Gogh. The music is not in the guitar, and there is no real sentiment about it. The reason I like it is that it allows me to play and sound the way I hear it. The guitar is inanimate, and has nothing to offer unless someone brings it out. So, the music is in the person.[15]

Other Musicians

When asked which of all musicians he had played with or met best personified jazz Barney confirmed:

For me, the most fulfilling experience I've had was listening to Lester Young on saxophone. Without Lester Young, there would have been no Charlie Parker. He had a great tone, a great sense of time, his melodies were inventive, and he didn't run scales and arpeggios - he played ideas. He wasn't an angry young man exploding, going through a lot of technical gyrations; it had lots of warmth, and it just appealed to me.[22]

Barney often expressed to me his highest regard for the Canadian-born composer and arranger Robert Farnon (1917-2005). Robert Farnon was also revered as an arranger of quality popular songs and influenced many top writers on both sides of the Atlantic. He also wrote some memorable film scores. For 46 years Farnon lived on the Channel Island of Guernsey and worked mainly in the UK. He continued to compose and arrange until his death.

Other Guitarists

Barney told me the guitar players he listened to as a boy, and admired, were Eddie Lang, Dick McDonough and Carl Kress. In the late 1930s he listened to Tony Mottola five days a week, fifteen minutes a day, on the radio. It was at this time he became interested in jazz and discovered George Van Eps, Allan Reuss, Bus Etri and Charlie Christian. When he was in New York City in 1944, with the Artie Shaw band, he heard for the first time Remo Palmier and Chuck Wayne. He said he rated both these guitarists very highly.

When asked in a 1958 Metronome magazine (USA) interview who were his favourite guitarists Barney confirmed;

My favorite guitarists are truly too numerous to mention and I admire each for a different thing. They are: Tal Farlow. George Van Eps, Barry Galbraith. Herb Ellis, Chuck Wayne. Jimmy Raney, Laurindo Almeida, and Charlie Christian and Django Reinhardt, though deceased, continue to be my favorites. Also, among the comparatively new guitarists, I like Howard Roberts, Jim Hall and Kenny Burrell.

I have an especial affection for Andrés Segovia that I'm sure all the other guitarists would join me in. He not only is a great, great artist truly dedicated to music and his instrument, but has enlarged the scope of the instrument, helped bring about a greater acceptance of it and raised its stature by giving concerts in great concert halls and also by playing the guitar with concert and symphony orchestras.

On another occasion he was asked by Bill Lee if he had ever played with Django Reinhardt. Barney responded:

No, I never played with him. We met in Europe in 1953. I couldn't speak French and he couldn't speak English so we sort of smiled at each other. He was backstage listening. Recently, when I was in Paris I was given one of the guitars that he owned. This guitar* has a round sound hole and a funny cutaway look. It's not an all-around guitar. Django's relatives gave me this guitar. I met Django's son, and many in the clan of gypsies. They all play guitar. They live in caravans and they don't have indoor plumbing, but they know and are aware of John Coltrane, Herbie Hancock and what's going on.

*Barney thought this guitar was an original Selmer/Maccaferri guitar, however a recent appraisal confirmed it was a Maccaferri style guitar made by the French luthier Jacques Favino.

A two part interview that appeared in Guitar (UK) magazine (December 1972/January 1973) gives a good overall picture of Barney's thoughts on music and life. Therefore I am pleased to reprint this in full on the next five pages.

Barney Kessel

In conversation with Ike Isaacs

BARNEY KESSEL: It's more critical in improvising that the sound pleases the player, because the player must be inspired. If I hear the music I am making and I don't like the sound of it, I really don't want to make music. Yet I'm caught in a web there, because I'm producing a sound that it appals me to listen to. So I am the cause and the effect at the same time; it tends to turn off any creative incentive, and I tend to go through the motions. There is some small area perhaps where a guitarist could perhaps use a little more treble than is comfortable and not quite as much as to have the person out in the 50th row hearing every note — I mean, I wish they could hear every note, but at the same time there's more to it than just the sound. There's also the spirit of the thing that you play.

IKE ISAACS: *Don't you think there'd be an advantage if some form of PA system was introduced so that the sound you played was perfect within your own hearing? In other words you play within the limits of your own hearing, and you don't have to play too loud to project to the man in the 50th row.*

BK: That would be the thing to do. Ordinarily what I do is play only at the volume that is comfortable for me; it is picked up by a microphone that is fed into the house system, and then they have speakers mounted in the walls, and that sound comes to the people, it doesn't come from my amplifier, it comes through there. It's not distorted, and it's been monitored, so that it's at the right volume and the right setting. Therefore they're hearing it the right way for them, and I'm hearing it the right way from my angle.

Teaching

I teach beginners. I wouldn't want to, but I do. I teach people who are already professionals. I teach people who may be very well equipped in certain areas but who want to work in other areas. I can even teach them in areas that I do not play in myself, because I know what techniques to tell them in order to be effective. I know what books to work on — sometimes I go through books they already have, and I say 'Do this page, skip the next five, and then go on' — because the books are not always written in a sequential manner.

You've tried and tested these things?

Yes, not only in terms of music books that I've read and books I've read by great violin teachers and piano teachers and conductors, but in availing myself of data about what the human body can stand, how long it can sit, when it should rise, how you should breathe, how you should relax, the amount of time you should be able to practice. All this put into the context of music, so it's not just a matter of my opinions, it's the data I've acquired plus my own experience.

There are various ways to go about playing scales and playing fast. Let's say that you're playing a passage with eight notes in it. Many people down through the ages have thought of how to play this, and in order to play it faster they simply start very slowly and begin to play faster and faster. Now another way of thinking about this — and it can apply to any instrument — is to play the first two notes as quickly as possible, thinking of all the motor skills and all that's invci(bed in playing these two notes. When you can play them at a rapid-fire speed, add the third note, and again play only three notes as rapidly as possible. And then the fourth note, and then the fifth note. This is another way to arrive at speed. What happens is that you're starting by handling units of two, and when you've handled that unit of two as quickly as possible, then you add on, and you're handling a unit of three.

The other way, there's always eight notes, no matter whether you play slowly or fast. It's always eight units. Now that kind of in-formation could apply to any instrument. I'm not saying there isn't benefit to be derived from playing it both ways. There is no answer, but there are many answers.

You have a particular way of picking which expresses your musical phraseology. In other words you might not adopt up and down picking for the whole passage. What do you advocate?
I would suggest to anyone that they become adept at all the various known ways of picking. In my estimation the best sound you can get is down picking. There is no better sound and there is no better control. But when the situation calls for more speed than down picking will make possible, then you have to go into various kinds of alternate picking.

There is up and down picking, which is called alternate picking, strict alternate picking where you consistently pick up and down, and then just up and down picking that may vary; it may be that in an eight to ten note passage there will be some that are up and some that are down, but they don't follow a consistent series of alternate pickings.

So there's that kind of picking, and then there is consistent up picking. In addition there are notes that are not picked at all but are simply hammer-ons, you hammer these notes on. There are also slide notes like glissandos or slurs that are taken by the finger.

Having learned these various ways of picking, it then behoves you to use the picking which is appropriate to the occasion.

Left hand fingering
When you find that it's difficult to play something, or that it doesn't flow well, or it seems clumsy and you can't play it up to speed, you might try to simply reduce the number of strings involved by one string, and see where you play it in that manner.

I think of two ways of using my fingers. One way is for anything that's of a legitimate nature, or where you want straight-edge notes; for something that's what I call legit, it would be with the finger-tips. But if it's jazz, or if it's something that sounds in the idiom of jazz, it's better to play it flat-fingered, not on the fingertips. When it's on the flat of the finger, it sounds like some drunk walking down the street with one foot on the kerb and one foot in the street. It has a happy, raucous sort of an undisciplined sound.

One of the characteristics of jazz is that it has a primitive, jagged feeling; it has an unmeasured element to it. It does not sound like someone from a conservatory who's been drinking. It sounds trained, but at the same time it sounds primitive. It's controlled primitivism. Elvin Jones had this in his drumming. The drum rolls — they're there, but it doesn't sound like a Scottish band, it doesn't sound like a marching band, it isn't so clearly measured. At the same time, if it's too ragged and too jagged and too primitive, it is too inarticulate and actually comes off being so inarticulate that it's not really interesting.

In other words the charm of jazz is that there is reckless abandon still within a boundary. Even in avant-garde music it's very interesting, and many musicians lose sight of this. In the States it's called free form — but it is a form, it says form. If it said no form, then we would have to call it simply free — that's not free form!

This means, then, that in jazz you can use any of the training that you've received and somehow modify it so that it sounds primitive. It's asking a trained person to sound primitive, or a primitive person to increase his training so that he sounds a little more trained. You want this kind of element.

Would we be right in calling it a dialect? English language, for example, if spoken in a proper way is very cut and dried, but you do have people from the country who speak beautifully and convey that thing with their own accent. So isn't jazz a dialect of music?
It is — as indeed anything else is. They're all dialects. Johann Sebastian Bach is a dialect, if you stop and think about it, because in any music there is the introduction of certain characteristics and values that are stressed. Others are either not stressed or simply eliminated.

Deck of cards
Each musician has a particular musical capacity, and I think about it as a deck of cards. A deck has 52 cards. No matter how they're shuffled and dealt, there's always 52 cards. But they come in different sequences.

Now, it is necessary for a player to continue to grow, to add to his card collection so that his sequences will come out and there will be more. The only difference between for instance me playing and someone who's been playing jazz for a year is that I'm playing with a larger deck of cards. I have more things at my disposal. I am aware of more principles, more devices, more formulae and all of this.

Yet, after you get to a point where you have absorbed many formulae and devices and all of this superimposition, you're finally forced back almost to the very beginning, which is simply to make music. To make music and to be inspired, creative, innovative, not extrapolative. And it's like everything else you've learned, all the devices, all the formulae; they do not come to life and they do not live unless you also inject your own life experience into the music. So you can't be like a trained chimpanzee that's just sitting there, going through one cliche after another, stringing them together as if it were a set of beads, you know, because there's no creativitity, there's no individuality. And even in mixing up various players' styles, in playing four bars of Chet Atkins, four bars of Johnny Smith and four of Wes Montgomery, or playing Chet Atkins licks with a pick or Wes Montgomery's licks with all the fingers, or Johnny Smith passages with the fingers, it's still extrapolation and it doesn't call on you. In the end, those jazz players that continue to live are people who have really said their own thing.

No one is free of influences. No one. I was very heavily influenced. And I've been influenced by many things, not only the guitar but things I've learned in orchestration, things I've learned from piano players and in looking at sheets of music. But there comes a time when the influence must be met and actually enlarged with your own self.

I don't think parroting — copying — is a bad thing in the early stages. It's like going into the field of invention; you would certainly want to know what had already been invented so that you don't spend ten years trying to invent a light bulb only to have someone tell you that it's already been done. You'd want to find out what's gone on. And you grow, and you use what's gone on as a point of departure, to build upon.

Each generation takes what the entire civilisation has given them up to this point. They take it and they go on and they make their own contribution. We should in our time make our contribution for posterity, as we have borrowed from all that has come before us.

I've been influenced, coupled with my life experience, with everything I've learned in the past, so that I have gone on and said a few things that weren't said before. Someone will take what I've done, use that as a point of departure, and go on. This is the way we grow.

There are very few fountainheads in plectrum (pick) guitar. What's happening now seems to be just an offshoot. There are not many innovators.

They're a sort of splinter school; they're taking a certain thing that one of the fountainheads did and they're sort of enlarging on it.

It takes courage to be different. It takes an open mind to consider that there may be another way, or there should be another way. People always get the feeling that it's all been done. But you mustn't forget that before Django played that way, no one was playing that way. And before Charlie Christian played his way he was influenced by several others, and he played like they did.

I notice one thing that happens quite often is that there will be a period of time in which several individuals are all groping and playing little things within a certain school of thought, and each one has a different portion of the entire picture. Then someone will come along in time and absorb all of this, put it together in a neat little package plus his own thing, and he will come out as a new giant because he represents the epitome of this. It's the culmination, it's what everybody was trying to get going, and this fellow's done it; he's captured Mr A's tone and Mr B's speed and Mr C's swing, and he's coupled it all together so that when you finally go and see this one person he is the embodiment of all his predecessors.

Benny Goodman did this, he was heavily influenced by Jimmy Noone, Barney Bigard — he was influenced by many old clarinet players in various ways, plus his legitimate training, plus his own genius. He was also influenced by Pee Wee Russell. And when I hear Benny Goodman's records, it's always Benny Goodman, but I can hear he's hammering away at stressing a great number of the values that PeeWee Russell was stressing.

I enjoy doing this at times. Some nights one or two songs will awaken a spirit in me in which I want to hear Charlie Christian, and I will play this way. It's almost nostalgia. I know that Django did this. And I was surprised to read in a biography of Charlie Christian that he knew most of Django Reinhardt's solos note tbr note. I don't think he played them with Django's sound, and I don't think he did that little vibrato, but he liked them. He was amused by them, he thought they were cute. He was pleased, and pleased with himself for being able to do this, but it still did not reflect his own nature. Even today I can play an old-time chord solo like, you know, Eddie Lang and this kind of thing, because I grew up that way. And you like these things, they're part of your early life. It's like seeing an old movie.

You are utilising accepted ingredients. Isn't it a tragedy that today, in the ingredients being utilised by many of the younger people — single notes, very little chord playing, electronic sound — they are limiting themselves?

I feel that most younger players are simply not aware of these things. I think they would become fascinated by them — any young people that I know who have heard a lot of the old guitar players have become fascinated with them, taking it for what it is: 'Oh I didn't know people did this, Gee that's fantastic, I didn't know this could be done'.

In my estimation, when you are expressing yourself, when you sit there and you play a song, you can only express what has been in your life.

You see, I am enormously curious about my musical ancestors. I'd like to know who did what with the guitar before I was alive. I'd like to know how they were playing; I'd like to know what was the standard, what was considered to be the standard of good jazz playing in 1920. Not that I want to do that or be that, but just because I'm as curious about that as people going back to their ancestral country, seeing where their grandfathers or great-grandfathers came from.

It's just a curiosity, because I love music and all the aspects of music.

Barney Kessel and Ike Isaacs continue their conversation in next month's Guitar.

Barney Kessel

The best thing to be into is life...

part II In conversation

IKE ISAACS: *Do you agree that the current preoccupation with sound is a valid one? If one's going to use an amplifier, then to do research and get as much variation as possible seems to me a perfectly good thing to do.*

BARNEY KESSEL: I've talked to young people who play the guitar, and they consider it as an electronic instrument, and they want to do things, they want to portray what they feel, stressing the electronic values. Well, that's their choice. There ate people who would be completely absorbed in the electronic aspect of it; there are others who would not be concerned at all with it; there are others somewhere in the middle. That is up to the individual.

I do think this, though: if I play an electronic instrument, it behoves me to learn something of the characteristics of an amplitier, to know what it does, what it cannot do, to know that I must not touch a microphone while I play the guitar because it might electrocute me, to know what it means when there's a certain spluttering in the amplifier.

On the other side of the coin, if a person is in music they should know something about music, and so people who play music and don't know how to read a note, they don't know how to interpret, they don't know the names of chords, they don't know how to articulate and communicate in musical terminology — I think there's something grossly wrong there.

But didn't King Oliver and early Louis Armstrong produce some of their best music when they were really very ill-educated as far as music was concerned? Wasn't the problem that those old musicians couldn't join the union because they couldn't read music, and therefore had to cheat their way in?

I think King Oliver and Louis could read, but I don't think they read in such a way that they could play a show somewhere. I don't think they were fast readers, but they certainly knew terminology, they knew the names of the notes, they knew a half note from a whole note, they could see it on the staff, and they did learn, they did know; it's just that they weren't good studio men.

An enormous number of young people, especially on the guitar, don't know one note from another. They're not concerned with the music because they're looking for something else. They are by nature very impatient. They want instant success, just like you fix some instant coffee. They don't want to pay the dues, they're looking for short cuts.

Well, I don't mind a short cut when I find it, but when you come to a situation where there is no short cut and it simply demands work, then there's no way to work. You can work in a skilful manner, but you still have to put in the time.

With older people there's a tendency to become rigid, set in your ways, not to have an open mind. If the young people could become less impatient and older people less rigid, it would be an even more marvellous world than it is.

Sitar School

I'll give you an interesting example of what I mean by impatience. Ravi Shankar opened a school in Los Angeles for the sitar, and when he opened it the sitar was at the height of its popularity because of his association with the Beatles and because of the fad that had caught on with the sitar in the States.

There were a lot of people enrolling. After the first week most of them dropped out. And after a very short time almost all of them dropped out, and they closed the school. What happened was that all these people were studying the sitar because it was posh, it was the thing to do, it was a conversation piece. When they met at night they could tell each other what they were doing: What are you doing darling? Well I'm going to Switzerland to ski. Really? Well I've enrolled at the sitar school. Oh how splendid!

But when they get in these little cubby holes and start practising, there's no one around, there's no one there to bring them things, there's no one there to talk, it's just a matter of hard work. Then it becomes very unglamorous and they simply didn't want to pay the price. So they did the honest thing: they quit. But they wanted instant success, they wanted to come out, get a little piece of carpet, take their shoes off, sit: down

with Ike Isaacs

and play in a robe, burn some incense anal just have a ball and play. But there's a little more to it, a little work. And they just weren't prepared for the work.

It may he then that with the use of all the appurtenances such as wah-wahs and, fuzz boxes, that this in itself becomes a means of expression. cutting out that kind of work which some people must think is so unnecessary if they can produce what they want to do as regards sound or noise, aided by the electronics industry.

If it becomes an extension of your musical training, then it adds another dimension, but if it is a substitute for learning and studying music, then it's an avoidance mechanism and can be explained psychiatrically. It is avoiding dealing with the realities of the situation. And the reality of the situation is that they must learn music. There is no way of learning to be a skilled cabinet maker without going through the apprenticeship of learning to be a skilled cabinet maker. There's no way!

Open mindedness

As a matter of fact young people have really brought about an enormous amount of open mindedness in saying Well why can't we do this and why can't we do that and why do we have to do this the old way? To that degree youth is always questioning older people. You realise that you don't have to do it the old way, but it still gets back that there is a certain amount of discipline in learning your craft. Not only in rock, but also avant-garde and any of these forms.

I don't question these forms and I don't question the people, but I have a greater respect for those people in rock and jazz who have taken the time to learn their craft and go on to do these things. If someone is playing avant-garde now and says 'Look, I've been playing since 1930 and I've gone through all the phases, I've played swing, I've played Benny Goodman style, I've played bebop, I've played this and this, and I just feel that I must continue to progress, I must go on and on and I just can't be hack where I was years ago' — well and good! If that's what they want to do. But quite often there are many avant-garde musicians who can't play a C scale, they can't play in tune, they can't play a Rodgers and Hart song. Whenever they make a record they never record a standard, it's always an original, it's a modal thing. it's something in one.

Music is a science. You learn a chord, you learn that this is called a quaver. this is called the key of D, this means that you slur the note — after you learn these things you go off on your own. There's no quarrel. But at least you understand your terminology, and you understand your craft. That's all.

You see, what happens is that people without training start playing music for people who are not sophisticated enough to understand music. So you have untrained people playing for untrained listeners. I mean, as far as I'm concerned they are entitled to it, because they're human beings and they're alive. But because I have studied it, it is my duty to tell them: enjoy yourselves, have a good time, make a lot of money, have some fun! But it really isn't quite as profound as you think it is.

I can't look at someone's financial success and equate that with musical accomplishment. I can applaud their success. I can applaud that they came from some small city and after playing the guitar for only three months they made a record that sold a million. I mean, I think that's tremendous, but that doesn't make it music. I do feel that they're very fortunate, and I hope they use the money to good effect — you know, they take care of their parents and get their teeth fixed and send their children to university. But it still is not music.

You see, that's only one kind of success; they've had no success in learning to play. They've had success in making money. Now if I wanted to make money I would never just play music. If I want to make money, I invest my money. Because the only way to make money is to deal in money, not to deal in music.

It's a beautiful thing when as a result of making music one of the secondary things that happens is you make some money. But making music and making money do not always happen simultaneously.

If a man has devoted time and effort, I respect him. But many of the younger people brush aside capabilities for players of our generation and say it's not valid. A case in point is a young player who said 'Well, you older people have lost sight of the ethnic quality of the guitar. This is the ethnic quality of the guitar — an E major chord! That is the guitar!'

Well, I would have to regard it much more seriously if that person were capable of doing these other things. Even so, all music is based on value judgements, it cannot be measured. It's not like running a race in which the winner is the one who breaks the tape at the end. Music, literature, art, poetry, painting — all these are expressions of the human mind, and they are things we learn more about people from than anything else. When archaeologists are looking for old ruins, they look for these artistic expressions, because they are more the indicator, the barometer of' what people were like, than anything else. But these things are not to be measured.

But no person has the right to limit the guitar?

I've been playing music for 35 years, I've studied my craft. If I were to engage in conversation with someone who's been playing for three, it doesn't mean that he couldn't show me something or teach me something or that he hasn't uncovered a certain thing that is valid and that I've never thought of, because the mind is infinite, the concepts are infinite. But it does mean that because I've played for 35 years and he's played for three, I'm going to expect him to speak from his frame of reference and I'm going to speak from mine. And there's a wide distance there.

I prefer certain things in rock to certain things in jazz. I've heard things in rock that I thought were quite good, and things in jazz that are quite bad. I've heard things in avant-garde music that I think are very good. There is imagination, spontaneity, creativity in every art form. Sometimes I have not liked certain rock musicians while I may have liked the song. Or I may not have liked anything in it except the production of the record. Sometimes I just admire the success of it. But I think it is a very limiting thing to be, as they say. 'into' Zen Buddhism, 'into' macrobiotics or 'into' avant-garde. The best thing to be 'into' is life.

BARNEY KESSEL Blues For A Playboy
1952-56 recordings as leader and with
BILLIE HOLIDAY ART TATUM LESTER YOUNG ANITA O'DAY

FiveFour

A Tribute to Barney Kessel Vol.1

Stuttgarter Gitarren Trio

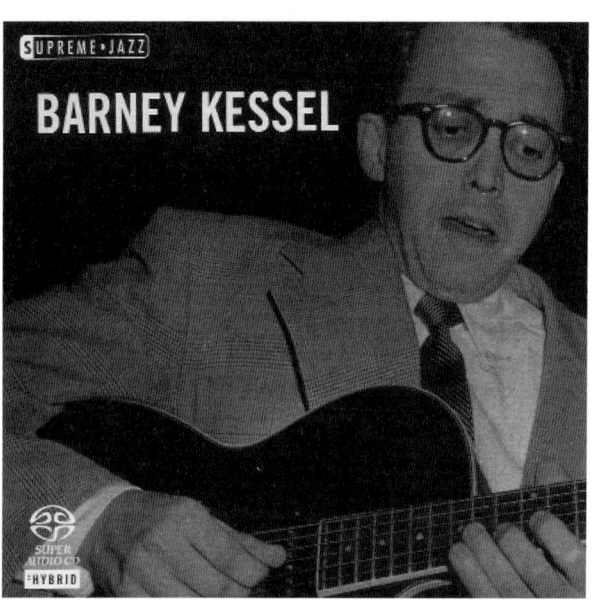

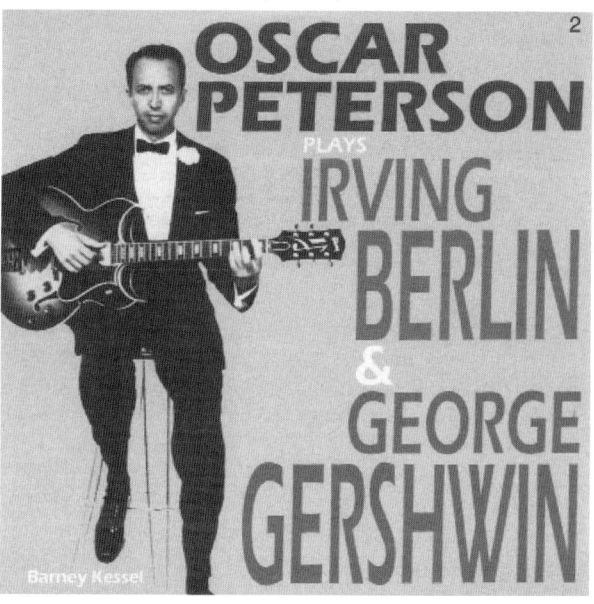

SUPREME • JAZZ

BARNEY KESSEL

OSCAR PETERSON PLAYS IRVING BERLIN & GEORGE GERSHWIN

Barney Kessel

BARNEY KESSEL TRIO LIVE IN LOS ANGELES AT P.J.'S CLUB

THE SONET JAZZ STORY

BARNEY KESSEL & RED MITCHELL TWO WAY CONVERSATION

RECORDED IN STOCKHOLM IN 1973

98

BIBLIOGRAPHY

Magazine Articles

Title	Author	Publication
Jazz Guitar – Front & Center		Metronome (USA) June 1958
Barney Kessel Looks Back at Django	Tynan	Downbeat (USA) 25 June 1959
Barney's Tune	Tynan	Downbeat (USA) 24 July 1958
Barney Kessel	Discus (John W. Duarte)	B.M.G. (UK) August 1959
Barney Kessel - Why He is Back on the Road	Lees	Downbeat (USA) 5 January 1961
Kessel '66		Downbeat (USA) July 1966
Barney Kessel		Guitar Player (USA) 1967
Barney Kessel talks to Alun Morgan	Morgan	Jazz Monthly (UK) June 1969
Barney Kessel The Formative Years	Tomkins	Crescendo (UK) 1969
At the Barney Kessel Guitar Clinic 1	Tomkins	Crescendo (UK) 1969
At the Barney Kessel Guitar Clinic 2	Tomkins	Crescendo (UK) 1969
Barney Kessel Blindfold Test	Feather	Downbeat (USA) 1970
Barney Kessel	Lee	Guitar Player (USA) October 1970
Barney Kessel – The Way He Sees It	Tomkins	Crescendo (UK) November 1972
Barney Kessel In conversation w/ Ike Isaacs Part 1		Guitar (UK) December 1972
Barney Kessel In conversation w/ Ike Isaacs Part 2		Guitar (UK) January 1973
Barney Kessel Speaks His Mind	Tomkins	Crescendo (UK) 1976
The Barney Kessel Viewpoint	Tomkins	Crescendo (UK) 1976
Guitarists Talking Barney Kessel with Ike Isaacs and Judd Proctor		Crescendo (UK) 1969
The Practice Methods of Barney Kessel	Isaacs	Crescendo (UK) March 1969
Barney Kessel's Gear	Achard/Bradley	Guitar (UK) February 1973
Kessel at Concord	Bangerter/Cassady	Guitar Player (USA) Jan/Feb 1973
Historic Jazz Guitar Trio	Yelin	Guitar Player (USA) October 1974
Master Guitarist Kessel	Butler	Tulsa World (US) 16 June 1978
Barney Kessel Speaks Out	Berle	Guitar Player (USA) March 1982
On Charlie Christian	Obrecht	Guitar Player (USA) May 1982
Barney Kessel – Interview	Hollis & Ferguson	Cadence (USA) August 1987
Barney Kessel - Quintessential Jazz	Batey	Guitarist (UK) September 1990
A Nickel, A Guitar and Amplifier	Dawdy	San Diego Reader (USA) 10 July 1996
The Rhythms of His Life	Varga	San Diego Union-Tribune (USA) 14 July 1996
Barney Kessel Collectors' Edition		Just Jazz Guitar (USA) September 1997
Giant of Jazz Coming Home		Muskogee Neighbours (USA) September 1969
Tribute to Barney Kessel #1	Forte	Vintage Guitar (USA) November 2002
Tribute to Barney Kessel #2	Forte	Vintage Guitar (USA) December 2002
The Gentleman Guitarist	Laurie	Jazz Review February 2003

Books

Title	Author	Publisher
Growing up with Chico	Maxine Marx	Prentice Hall (USA) 1980
Singing Cowboys & All That Jazz	Savage Jnr	University of Oklahoma Press (USA) 1983
Great Guitarists	Kienzle	Facts On File (USA) 1985
Swing to Bop	Gitler	Oxford University Press (USA) 1985
Kay Guitars 50's Cool	Scott	Seventh String Press (USA) 1992
Guitar Stories Vol. 2	Wright	Vintage Guitar Books (USA) 2000
Gibson Electrics – The Classic Years	Duchossoir	Hal Leonard (USA) 1994
Bossa Nova – The Brazilian Music That Seduced The World	Castro	a Capella (USA) 2000
Contemporary Records Story Booklet & 4 CD set	Ginell	Contemporary Records 1994
The Jazz Guitar – Its Evolution, Players and Personalities since 1900	Maurice J. Summerfield 4th Edition	Ashley Mark Publishing Company (UK) 1998
Masters of Jazz Guitar	Alexander/Bacon	Balafon (UK) 1999
Oklahoma Music Guide	Carney/Foley	New Forums Press (USA) 2003
Tearing Down the Wall of Sound – The Rise and Fall of Phil Spector	Brown	Bloomsbury (UK) 2007

Web Sites
Jim LaDiana – www.classicjazzguitar.com
Oscar Peterson – www.oscarpeterson.com
Marxology - www.marx-brothers.org/marxology
Spectropop – www.spectropop.com

SOURCES FOR QUOTATIONS IN THE TEXT

(1) Barney Kessel - The Formative Years. Les Tomkins — Crecendo Magazine (UK) 1969

(2) Barney Kessel Speaks Out — Arnie Berle — Guitar Player Magazine (USA) March 1982

(3) Barney Kessel on Charlie Christian — Jas Obrecht — Guitar Player Magazine (USA) May 1982

(4) Swing to Bop — Ira Gitler — Oxford University Press (USA) 1985

(5) Barney Kessel Talks — Alun Morgan — Jazz Monthly (UK) June 1969

(6) Growing up with Chico — Maxine Marx — Prentice Hall (USA) 1980

(7) Marxology Web Site — www.marx-brothers.org/marxology

(8) Jim LaDiana Web Site — www.classicjazzguitar.com

(9) Oscar Peterson Web Site — www.oscarpeterson.com

(10) Tearing Down the Wall of Sound – The Rise and Fall of Phil Spector – Mick Brown — Bloomsbury (UK) 2007

(11) Barney Kessel's Gear – Achard/Bradley — Guitar (UK) February 1973

(12) The Poll Winners Ride Again — Contemporary OJCCD 607-2 (sleeve notes)

(13) Andre Previn - Music to Listen to Barney Kessel By — Contemporary OJCCD 746-2 (sleeve notes)

(14) A Nickel, A Guitar and Amplifier — Dawdy — San Diego Reader (USA) 10 July 1996

(15) The Gentleman Guitarist — Jennifer Laurie — Jazz Review (UK) February 2003

(16) Barney Kessel — Bill Lee — Guitar Player (USA) October 1970

(17) Barney Kessel — Hollis/Ferguson — Cadence (USA) August 1987

(18) Giant of Jazz Coming Home — Muskogee Neighbours September 1969

(19) Personal Notes – Barney Kessel — Courtesy: Phyllis Kessel Collection

(20) Jazz Guitar – Front & Center — Metronome (USA) June 1958

(21) Master Guitarist Kessel — RonaldButler — Tulsa World (US) 16 June 1978

(22) Barney Kessel – Quintessential Jazz — Rick Batey — Guitarist (UK) September 1990

(23) Gibson Electrics – The Classic Years — Duchossoir — Hal Leonard (USA) 1994

Friends of Oklahoma Music

presents

The 3rd Annual

OKLAHOMA MUSIC
HALL OF FAME

CONCERT
& INDUCTION CEREMONY

Vince Gill

Barney Kessel

Byron Berline

THURSDAY - 8 PM
OCTOBER 14TH, 1999
MUSKOGEE CIVIC CENTER

TICKETS AVAILABLE AT:
MUSKOGEE CIVIC CENTER • SOUNDWORLD • NSU SEQUOYAH INSTITUTE • CARSON ATTRACTIONS
INTERNET: carsonattractions.com • CALL 918.584.2000 • TICKETS: $15 PER PERSON

BANK OF OKLAHOMA   OG+E   KJRH 2

Barney Kessel with Bob Cooper (oboe) in the Contemporary Records studio June 1954 during the recording of 'Barney Kessel Plays Standards'.

Barney Kessel

A Jazz Legend

PHOTO GALLERY

Abraham Kessel (1869-1941), Barney Kessel's father.

Ruth (nee Raisher) Kessel (1890-1968), Barney Kessel's mother, c. 1940s.

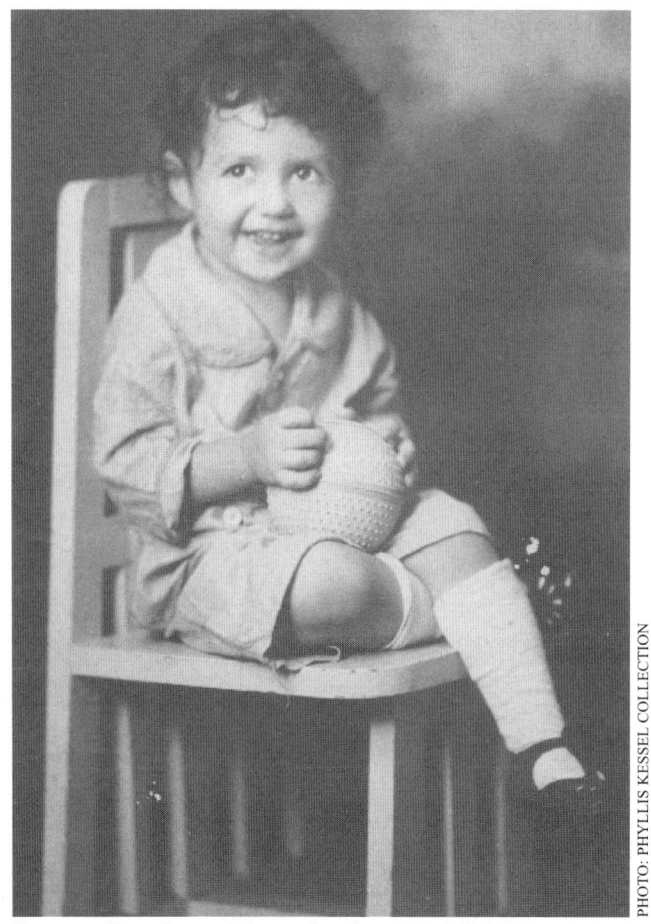

Barney Kessel, age 20 months, June 17, 1925.

Brother Lester Kessel, 4 years (left) and Barney Kessel, 5 ½ years, March 28, 1929. Muskogee, Oklahoma.

A copy of Barney Kessel's birth certificate obtained in September 1981.

Tombstone of Abraham Kessel, Barney's father, in Muskogee, Oklahoma.

Barney Kessel mother, Ruth Raisher, was only naturalized as an US citizen in 1943 after her husband died.

Barney Kessel, aged 15 years, February 23, 1939, with his first electric guitar, a National.

Barney Kessel in 1940.

Summer of 1940 in Siloam Springs, Arkansas. Joe Hayes of Texas on trumpet; Barney Kessel on guitar, age 16.

Barney Kessel playing at The Jade club in Hollywood, Los Angeles in the mid-1940s.

Varsity Club Band, 1941-42. Leader was Dub Parsons. Barney Kessel on guitar. This band was in Norman, Oklahoma. The college was called OU, Oklahoma University at the time. Now it's University of Oklahoma and where Barney Kessel received an honorary doctorate in May 1996.

Varsitonians Band, Oklahoma A&M College. Later called OSU, Oklahoma State University.
Front row: leader, Hal Price; piano, Rev Mullins; Barney Kessel, guitar; Jack Cole, tenor sax; Paul Knox, alto sax; Erskine Hill, alto sax; Harrison Peak, tenor sax.
Back row: Jimmie Reid, drums; Jerry Poole, trumpet; Max Hamilton, trumpet; Glenn Floyd, trumpet; Jimmie James, trombone This picture taken on a gig in an Oklahoma City ballroom, 1940 while Barney Kessel was still 16. This is where Charlie Christian came to see him play and where they then spent three days together.

Barney Kessel, late 1940s, location unknown.

Barney Kessel performing at the Jazz Mill in Arizona c.1951. He is using his Gibson BR3 amplifier (under the piano). Pete Jolly is on piano.

Django Reinhardt with Barney Kessel after the Jazz at the Philharmonic concert in Paris in 1953.

Jazz at the Philharmonic All Stars. This is an army photo taken at the Honolulu Airport shortly after they arrived there for a series of engagements c. 1952. Top row left to right - Ray Brown. Oscar Peterson, Barney Kessel, Norman Granz. Unidentified. Roy Eldridge. Hank Jones, Lester Young. Bottom row left to right: Willie Smith, Flip Phillips. Ella Fitzgerald, Buddy Rich, Gene Krupa. Unidentified. On Floor: Charlie Shavers.

Oscar Peterson Trio with Barney Kessel and Ray Brown, 1952.

Barney and Gail Kessel c.1950.

Barney Kessel with (left) David Kessel and (right) Dan Kessel c.1965.

Betty Kessel c.1950.

Betty Kessel c.1965 at a Hollywood recording session.

Barney Kessel playing the Kay Barney Kessel guitar in concert.

Barney Kessel playing the Kay Barney Kessel guitar in concert.

Contact Sheet of Barney Kessel from a Hollywood photo shoot for the Barney Kessel Gibson guitar c.1961.

Contact Sheet of Barney Kessel from a Hollywood photo shoot for the Barney Kessel Gibson guitar c.1961.

PHOTO: STANLEY LEVEY. COURTESY: PHYLLIS KESSEL COLLECTION

115

Barney Kessel c.1955.

Barney Kessel with Johnny Smith, c.1950.

Barney Kessel with Sonny Rollins in the Contemporary Records studio, 1958.

Barney Kessel with John Magnus, radio station KGFJ. c.1957.

Barney Kessel on the Parade Television show, Toronto, Canada. c.1963. Background, Left to right: Charlie Byrd, Laurindo Almeida, Juan Serrano.

Barney Kessel. c.1963.

Barney Kessel in the recording studio, at Polydor Records, London, November 3, 1968.

Barney Kessel presenting an in-store clinic at the Ivor Mairants Musicentre in London c.1969. Ivor Mairants is in the background.

Barney Kessel and Red Mitchell, Sweden, 1972

The Concord Music Camp, June 1972. Barney Kessel, right, the musical director of the camp. Milt Hinton on bass and Louis Bellson on drums.

Barney Kessel with Maurice Summerfield in the author's home, Newcastle upon Tyne, UK, c.1973.

Holiday Inn, Chicago, July 1978. Left to right: Maurice Summerfield, Bill Bay, Herb Ellis, Barney Kessel, Ivor Mairants and George Van Eps.

Barney Kessel Trio in concert, Jim Richardson (bass) and Tony Mann (drums) October 1979, Newcastle upon Tyne, UK.

The launch of the first edition of Maurice Summerfield's book, The Jazz Guitar - Its Evolution and Its Players since 1900 at the Britannia Hotel, Grosvenor Square, London, October 1978. Left to Right; Charlie Byrd, Joe Pass, Herb Ellis, Barney Kessel and Maurice Summerfield.

Top table at the last night dinner, 1981 Barney Kessel seminar 'The Effective Guitarist', Newcastle upon Tyne, UK. Left to right: Charles Smith, Adrian Ingram, Barney Kessel, Maurice Summerfield and Melville Summerfield.

THE PRESIDENT AND MRS. CARTER
welcome you to
THE WHITE HOUSE
Wednesday, January 7, 1981

ETHEL ENNIS

is a native Baltimore singer who achieved international prominence in 1958 after a European tour with an all-star Benny Goodman band. Since that time she has recorded ten albums on major labels. Miss Ennis has appeared on many major network shows and she continues to sing in clubs and concerts throughout the United States and overseas.

BARNEY KESSEL

has played with Benny Goodman and Artie Shaw and has worked with Barbra Streisand, Frank Sinatra, Marlene Dietrich and Maurice Chevalier. He has also done motion pictures and recorded with Elvis Presley and the Beach Boys. Mr. Kessel has recorded over forty albums and still tours the United States and overseas.

BARNEY KESSEL

Gene Byrd
bass

Charles Redd
drums

ETHEL ENNIS

Charles Covington
piano

John Nazdin
bass

Wiley Porter
bass

Marolin Hitchye
guitar

Gaynell Colburn
percussion

COURTESY: PHYLLIS KESSEL COLLECTION

White House Invitation for an evening where Barney Kessel and his Trio played for President and Mrs. Carter their guests who were governors of all the United States.

124

Best Wishes to Barney Kessel,
Rosalynn Carter   Jimmy Carter

White House concert. Top - Left to right, Joe Byrd, Barney Kessel, Rosalynn Carter, Jimmy Carter, Chuck Redd. Bottom The Barney Kessel Trio playing for President and Mrs. Carter, 7 January 1981.

Barney Kessel rehearsing the Harry James Band, November 12, 1982, at the Oklahoma 75th Anniversary of Statehood Diamond Jubilee celebration in Oklahoma City.

Barney Kessel was the guest soloist at the Oklahoma 75th Anniversary of Statehood Diamond Jubilee celebration, Oklahoma City. Harry James Band. November 1982.

Barney Kessel featured on the cover of 'The Oklahomans' magazine, 6 September 1981.

Barney Kessel in concert with Tal Farlow.

Barney Kessel in concert with Herb Ellis.

Arundel Castle, UK, Nov 1979. Left to right: Herb Ellis, Bryan Braban, Ian Macgregor, Charlie Byrd and Barney Kessel.

Barney Kessel Trio with Tony Mann (drums) and Jim Richardson (bass), at the Red Barn, Blindley Heath, Sussex, UK, November 1980.

Barney Kessel c. 1975.

Barney Kessel c. 1975.

The Great Guitars at the Winery July 1980. Charlie Byrd, Barney Kessel, Joe Byrd and Herb Ellis.

Barney Kessel accompanying Marion Montgomery, Wembley, London 19 November 1983.

Barney Kessel Quartet in the recording studio, Los Angeles, February 1987. Barney Kessel with John Clayton (bass), Monty Alexander (piano) and Jeff Hamilton (drums).

Left to right: John Knowles, Arlen Roth, Barney Kessel, Ole Halen, Jim Ferguson, Jorge Morel, Maurice Summerfield and Philip Catherine. Hot Guitars Festival, Ikaalinen, Finland, June 1988.

Barney Kessel and Philip Catherine in concert at the Midnight Sun Guitar Festival, Ikaalinen, Finland, 1988.

Leroy Vinegar and Barney Kessel at the Rose City Jazz Party in Portland, Oregon, 1988.

The Great Guitars 1989 Tour. Charlie Byrd, Martin Taylor and Barney Kessel. Martin had taken the place of Herb Ellis who had left the group to rejoin the Oscar Peterson Trio

Barney Kessel at the 1991 Cascais, Estoril Jazz Festival in Portugal. The group includes Hal Galper (piano), Terence Blanchard (trumpet), Billy Pierce (tenor saxophone) and Alan Dawson (drums).

Fujitsu Concord Japan '91 programme cover.

Barney Kessel practicing back stage in Japan, 1991. Buddy de Franco in the background. Fujitsu Concord 1991 fall tour of Japan.

Fujitsu Concord 1991 fall tour of Japan. Left to right: Milt Jackson, Phyllis Kessel and Barney Kessel.

135

Phyllis and Barney Kessel in Japan, 1991, during the 1991 Fujitsu Concord tour of Japan.

Barney Kessel and Buddy de Franco c.1989.

Phyllis and Barney Kessel, Turin, Italy. Late 1980's.

Barney Kessel in Rome, Italy 1990. He was playing at Big Mama's jazz club for a week.

Barney Kessel c.1990.

Barney and Phyllis Kessel. Thanksgiving Day, 1996, on the beach in Coronado, California.

Barney Kessel giving private tuition in 1996.

The Barney Kessel Tribute Concert
Danny and Sylvia Kaye Playhouse, New York City, 25 June 1997

Back row: Peter Leitch, Bill Wurtzel, Vic Juris, Howie Collins, Ray Gogarty,

4th row: Frank Vignola, John Pizzarelli, Jack Wilkins, Ron Affif, John Abercrombie,
            Howard Alden, Jimmy Bruno, Randall Kremer (Smithsonian Institution)

3rd row: Gene Bertoncini, Billy Bauer, Bucky Pizzarelli, Don Arnone,
            Wayne Wright, Tony Mottola, Sal Salvador, Larry Lucie;

2nd row: Charles Carlini, Remo Palmier, Joe Puma

Front row: Mundell Lowe, Charlie Byrd, Barney Kessel,
            Herb Ellis, Tal Farlow and Bob Benedetto.

Not shown: Kenny Burrell.

Back stage at the Barney Kessel Tribute Concert, New York City 25 June 1997. Left to Right: Back Row: Peter Leitch, Ed Benson, John Pizzarelli Jnr., Bucky Pizzarelli and Bob Benedetto. Middle Row: Jimmy Bruno, Rich Raezer and Howard Alden. Front: Phyllis Kessel, Barney Kessel and Frank Forte.

Barney Kessel's grave and headstone. He is buried in Woodlawn Cemetery in Canandaigua, New York which is in the Finger Lakes region of western New York near Rochester.

Copy of Barney Kessel's death certificate.

IMAGINE YOURSELF IN SUNNY SAN DIEGO LISTENING TO CLASSIC JAZZ...
CHECK OUT OUR NEW WEBSITE: WWW.SDJP.ORG

SAN DIEGO JAZZ PARTY

FEBRUARY 25TH–27TH, 2005
DEL MAR HILTON
IN HONOR OF BARNEY KESSEL

YOUR HOSTS:
DAVE & JOANNE COOPER,
PHIL MOODY & DAVE NUFFER

THREE GREAT GUITARS

Our 2005 three-day festival of mainstream jazz will be dedicated in honor of master jazz guitarist Barney Kessel, who died in San Diego on May 6. Bucky Pizzarelli and Howard Alden are in our lineup of great musicians honoring Barney. They will be joined Sunday by another guitar all-star, Mundell Lowe of San Diego, for an incredible three-guitar jam session. Attendance is limited, so make your reservations early to assure seating. Dress is casual.

For more information:
(858) 453-0846 or
dcooper4@hotmail.com

TRUMPET
Ed Polcer
Joe Wilder

REEDS
Harry Allen
Ken Peplowski
Houston Person
Dan Block

TROMBONE
Dan Barrett

PIANO
John Sheridan
Johnny Varro

VIBES
John Cocuzzi

BASS
Richard Simon
Frank Tate

GUITAR
Bucky Pizzarelli
Howard Alden
Mundell Lowe

DRUMS
Joe Ascione
Jake Hanna

VOCALS
Barbara Morrison

JAZZ PARTY SCHEDULE

FRI. 5 - 6 P.M. Patron Cocktail Reception
7:30 - 11 P.M. San Diego Jazz Party

SAT. 10:30 A.M. - NOON Jazz Brunch
1 P.M. - 5 P.M. San Diego Jazz Party
7 P.M. - 11 P.M. San Diego Jazz Party

SUN. 11 A.M. - 4 P.M. San Diego Jazz Party

Special Jazz Party Rates at the Del Mar Hilton:

$112 (+ tax) Based on availability.

Reservations must be made before January 24, 2005.

Mention San Diego Jazz Party when you make your reservation. Free parking. Lots of great dining within minutes.

For hotel reservations call:
800-833-7904 or 858-792-5200

DAY	DESCRIPTION	QTY.	PRICE
Patron	All Events *Brunch included. Reserved seating based on receipt of order.*		$200
Friday	Beginning Session		$55
Saturday	Three Sessions *Brunch included.*		$110
Sunday	One Session		$55
	Order Total		$

As a 501c(3) non-profit organization, SDJP accepts and welcomes tax-deductible contributions to assure continuation of this festival. Revenues exceeding expenses will be used to help fund youth jazz programs at the high school or college level.

Name
Address
Phone

Method of Payment
☐ Check (enclosed)   ☐ MasterCard   ☐ Visa
Credit Card No.
Exp. Date ____ Signature

MAIL TO: SAN DIEGO JAZZ PARTY
8959 CAMINITO FRESCO
LA JOLLA, CA 92037
OR CALL (858) 453-0846

PHOTO: PHYLLIS KESSEL COLLECTION

Barney Kessel

A Jazz Legend

JAZZ DISCOGRAPHY

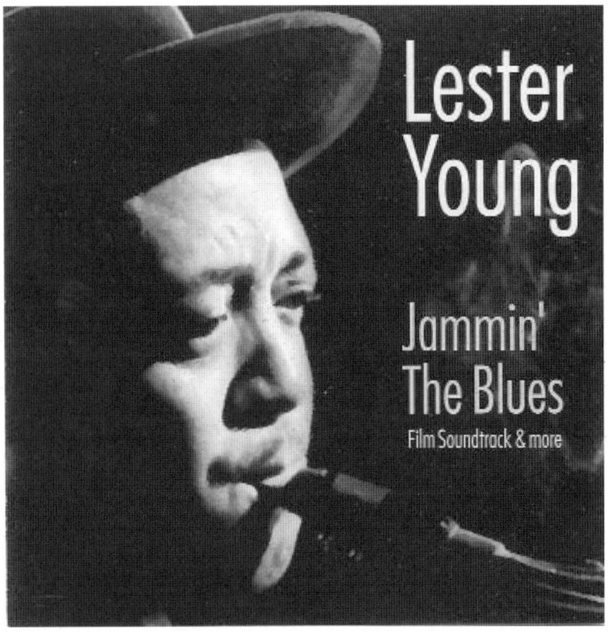
Lester
Young
Jammin'
The Blues
Film Soundtrack & more

THE METRONOME SERIES
Artie Shaw
AND HIS ORCHESTRA
1944-45

CHARLIE BARNET
AND HIS ORCHESTRA
SHOWCASE
FEATURING
DODO MARMAROSA
BARNEY KESSEL
SHORTY ROGERS
LENA HORNE
PEANUTS HUCKO

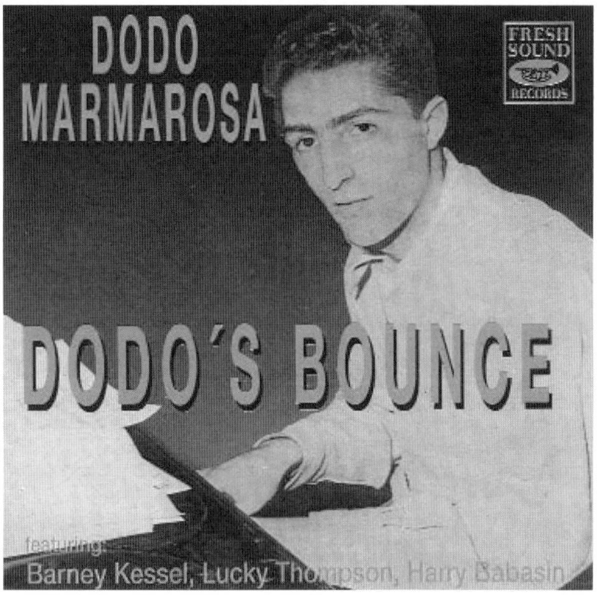
DODO
MARMAROSA
FRESH SOUND RECORDS
DODO'S BOUNCE
featuring:
Barney Kessel, Lucky Thompson, Harry Babasin

WARDELL
GRAY
featuring:

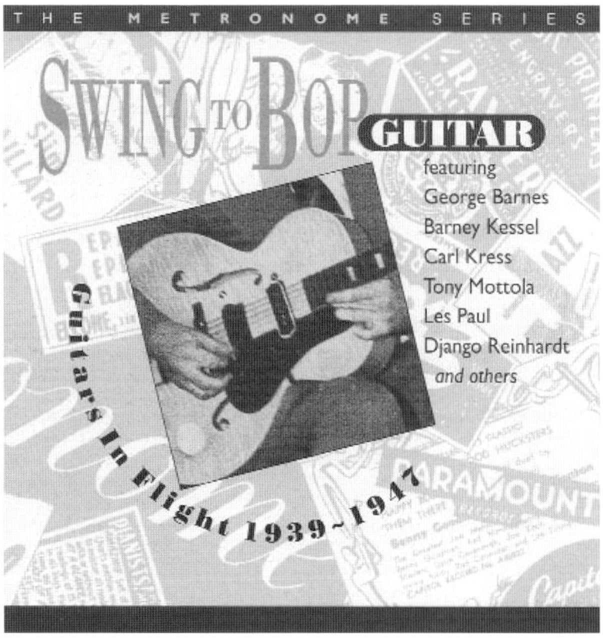
THE METRONOME SERIES
SWING TO BOP
GUITAR
featuring
George Barnes
Barney Kessel
Carl Kress
Tony Mottola
Les Paul
Django Reinhardt
and others
Guitars In Flight 1939~1947

Barney Kessel Jazz Discography

20 December 1942   Chicago, USA

Chico Marx Orchestra

Desi Arnez and Chico Marx Big Bands Of Hollywood [CD, Laser Light, 15 767]

[Musicians: Barney Kessel: Guitar, Marty Marsala: Trumpet, Irving Goodman: Trumpet, Chuck Maxon: Trombone, Elmer Schneider: Trombone, Gabe Gelinas: Alto Saxophone, Vernon Yokum: Alto Saxophone, Howard Dietterman: Tenor Saxophone, Emmett Carls: Tenor Saxophone, Harry Sopp: Baritone Saxophone, Marty Napoleon: Piano, John Frigo: Bass, George Wettling: Drums, Skip Nelson: Vocals, Kim Kimberly: Vocals, Mel Torme: Vocals.]

- Abraham (Berlin)
- Beer Barrel Polka (Brown)
- Chicago Strut (Anonymous)
- Mr. Five By Five (Raye)
- Padliacci (Leoncavallo)
- Swing Stuff (Anonymous)
- Velvet Moon (DeLange)

08 March 1944 [Estimated]   Los Angeles, USA

Jack McVea

Open The Door, Richard [LP, Solid Sender, SOL 507]

[Musicians: Barney Kessel: Guitar, Jack McVea: Tenor Saxophone, Unknown: Piano, Frank Clarke: Bass, Rabon Tarrant: Drums.]

- Tea For Two (Youmans/Caesar)

03 August 1944   Los Angeles, USA

Charlie Barnet

Big Band Bounce & Boogie [LP, Affinity, AFS 1012]

[Musicians: Barney Kessel: Guitar, Peanuts Holland: Trumpet, Lyman Vunk: Trumpet, Johnny Martel: Trumpet, Jack Mootz: Trumpet, Charles Coolidge: Trombone, Gerald Foster: Trombone, Dave Hallett: Trombone, Burt Johnson: Trombone, Charlie Barnet: Alto & Soprano Saxophones, Harold Herzon: Alto Saxophone, Joe Meisner: Alto Saxophone, Kurt Bloom: Tenor Saxophone, Ed Pripps: Tenor Saxophone, Bob Poland: Baritone Saxophone, Dodo Marmarosa: Piano, Howard Rumsey: Bass, Harold Hahn: Drums, Kay Starr: Vocals.]

- Sharecroppin' Blues (Robinson/Mayer)

Charlie Barnet

Drop Me Off In Harlem [CD, MCA, GRP 16122]
Big Band Bounce & Boogie [LP, Affinity, AFS 1012]

[Musicians: Barney Kessel: Guitar, Peanuts Holland: Trumpet, Lyman Vunk: Trumpet, Johnny Martel: Trumpet, Jack Mootz: Trumpet, Charles Coolidge: Trombone, Gerald Foster: Trombone, Dave Hallett: Trombone, Burt Johnson: Trombone, Charlie Barnet: Saxophones, Harold Herzon: Alto Saxophone, Joe Meisner: Alto Saxophone, Kurt Bloom: Tenor Saxophone, Ed Pripps: Tenor Saxophone, Bob Poland: Baritone Saxophone, Dodo Marmarosa: Piano, Howard Rumsey: Bass, Harold Hahn: Drums, Kay Starr: Vocals.]

- Skyliner (Barnet)

01 September 1944 — New York, USA

Charlie Barnet

Showcase - Charlie Barnet Orchestra [LP, First Heard, FH44]

[Musicians: Barney Kessel: Guitar, Peanuts Holland: Trumpet, Lyman Vunk: Trumpet, Johnny Martel: Trumpet, Jack Mootz: Trumpet, Charles Coolidge: Trombone, Gerald Foster: Trombone, Dave Hallett: Trombone, Burt Johnson: Trombone, Charlie Barnet: Alto & Soprano Saxophones, Harold Herzon: Alto Saxophone, Joe Meisner: Alto Saxophone, Kurt Bloom: Tenor Saxophone, Ed Pripps: Tenor Saxophone, Bob Poland: Baritone Saxophone, Dodo Marmarosa: Piano, Howard Rumsey: Bass, Harold Hahn: Drums.]

- Pompton Turnpike (Barnet)

---

11 September 1944 — Los Angeles, USA

Charlie Barnet

Charlie Barnet And His Orchestra [LP, Joyce, LP2012]

[Musicians: Barney Kessel: Guitar, Peanuts Holland: Trumpet, Lyman Vunk: Trumpet, Johnny Martel: Trumpet, Jack Mootz: Trumpet, Charles Coolidge: Trombone, Gerald Foster: Trombone, Dave Hallett: Trombone, Burt Johnson: Trombone, Charlie Barnet: Saxophones, Harold Herzon: Alto Saxophone, Joe Meisner: Alto Saxophone, Kurt Bloom: Tenor Saxophone, Ed Pripps: Tenor Saxophone, Bob Poland: Baritone Saxophone, Dodo Marmarosa: Piano, Howard Rumsey: Bass, Harold Hahn: Drums, Kay Starr: Vocals.]

- I Can't Get Started (Duke/Gershwin)
- I Like To Riff (Cole)
- Nobody Knows What Trouble I've Seen (Traditional)
- Pompton Turnpike (Rogers/Osbourne)
- Smiles (Callaghan/Roberts)

---

01 October 1944 — Los Angeles, USA

Lester Young

Jammin' The Blues [CD, Definitive Records, DRCD11117]
Jammin' The Blues [LP, Musidisc, 30 JA 5110]

[Musicians: Barney Kessel: Guitar, Harry Edison: Trumpet, Garland Finney: Piano, Red Callender: Bass, Sid Catlett: Drums, Illinois Jacquet: Tenor Saxophone.]

- Sweet Georgia Brown (Pinkard/Bernie/Casey)

[Musicians: Barney Kessel: Guitar, Harry Edison: Trumpet, Marlowe Morris: Piano, John Simmons: Bass, Sid Catlett: Drums, Illinois Jacquet: Tenor Saxophone, Jo Jones: Drums.]

- Jammin' The Blues (Ad Lib)

[Musicians: Barney Kessel: Guitar, Harry Edison: Trumpet, Marlowe Morris: Piano, Red Callender: Bass, Sid Catlett: Drums, Illinois Jacquet: Tenor Saxophone, Dicky Wells: Trombone, Marie Bryant: Vocals.]

- If I Could Be With You One Hour Tonight (Creamer)

[Musicians: Barney Kessel: Guitar, Harry Edison: Trumpet, Marlowe Morris: Piano, Red Callender: Bass, Sid Catlett: Drums, Illinois Jacquet: Tenor Saxophone, Dicky Wells: Trombone.]

- Blues For Marvin (Ad Lib)

[Musicians: Barney Kessel: Guitar, Harry Edison: Trumpet, Marlowe Morris: Piano, Red Callender: Bass, Sid Catlett: Drums.]

- Midnight Symphony (Ad Lib)

[Musicians: Barney Kessel: Guitar, Marie Bryant: Vocals, Marlowe Morris: Piano, Red Callender: Bass, Sid Catlett: Drums.]

- On The Sunny Side Of The Street (McHugh/Fields)

22 November 1944   Los Angeles, USA

Artie Shaw

Artie Shaw 1944-1945 [CD, Hep Records, CD 70(3)]

[Musicians: Barney Kessel: Guitar, Artie Shaw: Clarinet, Ray Linn: Trumpet, Jimmy Pupa: Trumpet, Roy Eldridge: Trumpet, George Schwartz: Trumpet, Harry Rodgers: Trombone, Pat McNaughton: Trombone, Charles Coolidge: Trombone, Ray Coniff: Trombone, Les Clarke: Alto Saxophone, Tommy Mace: Alto Saxophone, Jon Walton: Tenor Saxophone, Herbie Steward: Tenor Saxophone, Chuck Gentry: Baritone Saxophone, Dodo Marmarosa: Piano, Morris Rayman: Bass, Lou Fromm: Drums, Imogene Lynn: Vocals.]

- Ac-Cen-Tchu-Ate The Positive (Arlen/Mercer)
- Let's Take The Long Way Home (Arlen/Mercer)

Artie Shaw

The Indispensable Artie Shaw Vol5/6 [LP, Black & White/RCA, NL89914(2)]
Artie Shaw 1944-1945 [CD, Hep Records, CD 70(3)]

[Musicians: Barney Kessel: Guitar, Artie Shaw: Clarinet, Ray Linn: Trumpet, Jimmy Pupa: Trumpet, Roy Eldridge: Trumpet, George Schwartz: Trumpet, Harry Rodgers: Trombone, Pat McNaughton: Trombone, Charles Coolidge: Trombone, Ray Coniff: Trombone, Les Clarke: Alto Saxophone, Tommy Mace: Alto Saxophone, Jon Walton: Tenor Saxophone, Herbie Steward: Tenor Saxophone, Chuck Gentry: Baritone Saxophone, Dodo Marmarosa: Piano, Morris Rayman: Bass, Lou Fromm: Drums, Imogene Lynn: Vocals.]

- Jumpin' On the Merry-Go-Round (Conniff)
- Lady Day (Mundy)

---

01 January 1945 [Estimated]   Los Angeles, USA

Timmie Rogers

That's Where The Jive Goes [CD, P-Vine (Japan), PCD 5779]

[Musicians: Barney Kessel: Guitar, Timmie Rogers: Vocals/Ukulele, Maxwell Davis: Tenor Saxophone, Jimmy Rowles: Piano, Red Callender: Bass, Lee Young: Drums.]

- Bring Enough Clothes For Three Days (Rogers)

---

09 January 1945   New York, USA

Artie Shaw

Artie Shaw 1944-1945 [CD, Hep Records, CD 70(3)]

[Musicians: Barney Kessel: Guitar, Artie Shaw: Clarinet, Paul Cohen: Trumpet, Tony Faso: Trumpet, Roy Eldridge: Trumpet, George Schwartz: Trumpet, Harry Rodgers: Trombone, Pat McNaughton: Trombone, Charles Coolidge: Trombone, Ray Coniff: Trombone, Les Clarke: Alto Saxophone, Tommy Mace: Alto Saxophone, Jon Walton: Tenor Saxophone, Herbie Steward: Tenor Saxophone, Chuck Gentry: Baritone Saxophone, Dodo Marmarosa: Piano, Morris Rayman: Bass, Lou Fromm: Drums, Imogene Lynn: Vocals.]

- Can't Help Lovin' That Man (Kern/Hammerstein)

Artie Shaw

The Complete Gramercy Five Sessions [CD, Bluebird, ND87637]
Artie Shaw 1944-1945 [LP, Black & White, NL89914(2)]
Artie Shaw 1944-1945 [CD, Hep Records, CD 70(3)]

[Musicians: Barney Kessel: Guitar, Artie Shaw: Clarinet, Roy Eldridge: Trumpet, Dodo Marmarosa: Piano, Morris Rayman: Bass, Lou Fromm: Drums.]

- The Grabtown Grapple (Shaw)
- The Sad Sack (Shaw)

Artie Shaw

The Indispensable Artie Shaw Vol5/6 [LP, Black & White/RCA, NL89914(2)]
Artie Shaw 1944-1945 [CD, Hep Records, CD 70(3)]

[Musicians: Barney Kessel: Guitar, Artie Shaw: Clarinet, Paul Cohen: Trumpet, Tony Faso: Trumpet, Roy Eldridge: Trumpet, George Schwartz: Trumpet, Harry Rodgers: Trombone, Pat McNaughton: Trombone, Charles Coolidge: Trombone, Ray Coniff: Trombone, Les Clarke: Alto Saxophone, Tommy Mace: Alto Saxophone, Jon Walton: Tenor Saxophone, Herbie Steward: Tenor Saxophone, Chuck Gentry: Baritone Saxophone, Dodo Marmarosa: Piano, Morris Rayman: Bass, Lou Fromm: Drums, Imogene Lynn: Vocals.]

- Bedford Drive (Harding)

I'll Never Be the Same (Kahn/Malneck/Signorelli)

'S Wonderful (Gershwin/Gershwin)

05 April 1945   New York, USA

Artie Shaw

The Indispensable Artie Shaw Vol5/6 [LP, Black & White/RCA, NL89914(2)]

Artie Shaw 1944-1945 [CD, Hep Records, CD 70(3)]

[Musicians: Barney Kessel: Guitar, Artie Shaw: Clarinet, Paul Cohen: Trumpet, Bernie Glow: Trumpet, Roy Eldridge: Trumpet, George Schwartz: Trumpet, Harry Rodgers: Trombone, Robert Swift: Trombone, Ollie Wilson: Trombone, Gus Dixon: Trombone, Rudy Tanza: Alto Saxophone, Lou Prisby: Alto Saxophone, Jon Walton: Tenor Saxophone, Herbie Steward: Tenor Saxophone, Chuck Gentry: Baritone Saxophone, Dodo Marmarosa: Piano, Morris Rayman: Bass, Lou Fromm: Drums.]

    Little Jazz (Harding)

    September Song (Weill/Anderson)

17 April 1945   New York, USA

Artie Shaw

Artie Shaw 1944-1945 [CD, Hep Records, CD 70(3)]

[Musicians: Barney Kessel: Guitar, Artie Shaw: Clarinet, Paul Cohen: Trumpet, Bernie Glow: Trumpet, Roy Eldridge: Trumpet, George Schwartz: Trumpet, Harry Rodgers: Trombone, Robert Swift: Trombone, Ollie Wilson: Trombone, Gus Dixon: Trombone, Rudy Tanza: Alto Saxophone, Lou Prisby: Alto Saxophone, Jon Walton: Tenor Saxophone, Ralph Roselund: Tenor Saxophone, Chuck Gentry: Baritone Saxophone, Dodo Marmarosa: Piano, Morris Rayman: Bass, Lou Fromm: Drums.]

    But Not for Me (Gershwin/Gershwin)

    Summertime (Take 2) (Gershwin/Gershwin)

Artie Shaw

The Indispensable Artie Shaw Vol5/6 [LP, Black & White/RCA, NL89914(2)]

Artie Shaw 1944-1945 [CD, Hep Records, CD 70(3)]

[Musicians: Barney Kessel: Guitar, Artie Shaw: Clarinet, Paul Cohen: Trumpet, Bernie Glow: Trumpet, Roy Eldridge: Trumpet, George Schwartz: Trumpet, Harry Rodgers: Trombone, Robert Swift: Trombone, Ollie Wilson: Trombone, Gus Dixon: Trombone, Rudy Tanza: Alto Saxophone, Lou Prisby: Alto Saxophone, Jon Walton: Tenor Saxophone, Ralph Roselund: Tenor Saxophone, Chuck Gentry: Baritone Saxophone, Dodo Marmarosa: Piano, Morris Rayman: Bass, Lou Fromm: Drums.]

    Summertime (Gershwin/Gershwin)

    Tea for Two (Youmans/Caesar)

07 June 1945   Los Angeles, USA

Artie Shaw

Artie Shaw 1944-1945 [CD, Hep Records, CD 70(3)]

[Musicians: Barney Kessel: Guitar, Artie Shaw: Clarinet, Stan Fishelson: Trumpet, Bernie Glow: Trumpet, Roy Eldridge: Trumpet, George Schwartz: Trumpet, Harry Rodgers: Trombone, Robert Swift: Trombone, Ollie Wilson: Trombone, Gus Dixon: Trombone, Rudy Tanza: Alto Saxophone, Lou Prisby: Alto Saxophone, Jon Walton: Tenor Saxophone, Ralph Roselund: Tenor Saxophone, Chuck Gentry: Baritone Saxophone, Dodo Marmarosa: Piano, Morris Rayman: Bass, Lou Fromm: Drums.]

    Easy to Love (Porter)

    Tabu (Lecuona)

Barney Kessel

Barney Kessel's All Stars * [LP, Onyx, ORI215]

Dodo Marmarosa 1945-1950 [CD, Classics Jazz, 1165]

[Musicians: Barney Kessel: Guitar, Dodo Marmarosa: Piano, Morris Rayman: Bass, Louis Fromm: Drums, Herbie Steward: Clarinet, Johnny White: Vibraphone.]

    Slick Chick (Kessel)

    The Man I Love (Gershwin/Geshwin)

    What Is This Thing Called Love (Porter)

Barney Kessel

Barney Kessel's All Stars [LP, Onyx, ORI215]
California Boppin' [CD, ABM, ABMMCD1065]
Dodo Marmarosa 1945-1950 [CD, Classics Jazz, 1165]

[Musicians: Barney Kessel: Guitar, Dodo Marmarosa: Piano, Morris Rayman: Bass, Louis Fromm: Drums, Herbie Steward: Clarinet, Johnny White: Vibraphone.]

    Atom Buster (Kessel)

Artie Shaw

The Indispensable Artie Shaw Vol5/6 [LP, Black & White/RCA, NL89914(2)]
Artie Shaw 1944-1945 [CD, Hep Records, CD 70(3)]

[Musicians: Barney Kessel: Guitar, Artie Shaw: Clarinet, Stan Fishelson: Trumpet, Bernie Glow: Trumpet, Roy Eldridge: Trumpet, George Schwartz: Trumpet, Harry Rodgers: Trombone, Robert Swift: Trombone, Ollie Wilson: Trombone, Gus Dixon: Trombone, Rudy Tanza: Alto Saxophone, Lou Prisby: Alto Saxophone, Jon Walton: Tenor Saxophone, Ralph Roselund: Tenor Saxophone, Chuck Gentry: Baritone Saxophone, Dodo Marmarosa: Piano, Morris Rayman: Bass, Lou Fromm: Drums.]

    Time on my Hands (Youmans/Adamson/Gordon)

---

09 June 1945   Los Angeles, USA

Artie Shaw

Artie Shaw 1944-1945 [CD, Hep Records, CD 70(3)]

[Musicians: Barney Kessel: Guitar, Artie Shaw: Clarinet, Stan Fishelson: Trumpet, Bernie Glow: Trumpet, Roy Eldridge: Trumpet, George Schwartz: Trumpet, Harry Rodgers: Trombone, Robert Swift: Trombone, Ollie Wilson: Trombone, Gus Dixon: Trombone, Rudy Tanza: Alto Saxophone, Lou Prisby: Alto Saxophone, Jon Walton: Tenor Saxophone, Ralph Roselund: Tenor Saxophone, Chuck Gentry: Baritone Saxophone, Dodo Marmarosa: Piano, Morris Rayman: Bass, Lou Fromm: Drums.]

    These Foolish Things (Strachey/Marvell/Link)

Artie Shaw

The Indispensable Artie Shaw Vol5/6 [LP, Black & White/RCA, NL89914(2)]
Artie Shaw 1944-1945 [CD, Hep Records, CD 70(3)]

[Musicians: Barney Kessel: Guitar, Artie Shaw: Clarinet, Stan Fishelson: Trumpet, Bernie Glow: Trumpet, Roy Eldridge: Trumpet, George Schwartz: Trumpet, Harry Rodgers: Trombone, Robert Swift: Trombone, Ollie Wilson: Trombone, Gus Dixon: Trombone, Rudy Tanza: Alto Saxophone, Lou Prisby: Alto Saxophone, Jon Walton: Tenor Saxophone, Ralph Roselund: Tenor Saxophone, Chuck Gentry: Baritone Saxophone, Dodo Marmarosa: Piano, Morris Rayman: Bass, Lou Fromm: Drums.]

    A Foggy Day (Gershwin/Gershwin)

---

12 June 1945   Los Angeles, USA

Artie Shaw

Artie Shaw 1944-1945 [CD, Hep Records, CD 70(3)]

[Musicians: Barney Kessel: Guitar, Artie Shaw: Clarinet, Stan Fishelson: Trumpet, Bernie Glow: Trumpet, Roy Eldridge: Trumpet, George Schwartz: Trumpet, Harry Rodgers: Trombone, Robert Swift: Trombone, Ollie Wilson: Trombone, Gus Dixon: Trombone, Rudy Tanza: Alto Saxophone, Lou Prisby: Alto Saxophone, Jon Walton: Tenor Saxophone, Ralph Roselund: Tenor Saxophone, Chuck Gentry: Baritone Saxophone, Dodo Marmarosa: Piano, Morris Rayman: Bass, Lou Fromm: Drums, Dorothy Allen: Vocals.]

    You Go To My Head (Gillespie/Cootes)

Artie Shaw

The Indispensable Artie Shaw Vol5/6 [LP, Black & White/RCA, NL89914(2)]
Artie Shaw 1944-1945 [CD, Hep Records, CD 70(3)]

[Musicians: Barney Kessel: Guitar, Artie Shaw: Clarinet, Stan Fishelson: Trumpet, Bernie Glow: Trumpet, Roy Eldridge: Trumpet, George Schwartz: Trumpet, Harry Rodgers: Trombone, Robert Swift: Trombone, Ollie Wilson: Trombone, Gus Dixon: Trombone, Rudy Tanza: Alto Saxophone, Lou Prisby: Alto Saxophone, Jon Walton: Tenor Saxophone, Ralph Roselund: Tenor Saxophone, Chuck Gentry: Baritone Saxophone, Dodo Marmarosa: Piano, Morris Rayman: Bass, Lou Fromm: Drums.]

    Lucky Number (Coniff)

13 June 1945 — Los Angeles, USA

Artie Shaw

The Indispensable Artie Shaw Vol5/6 [LP, Black & White/RCA, NL89914(2)]

[Musicians: Barney Kessel: Guitar, Artie Shaw: Clarinet, Stan Fishelson: Trumpet, Bernie Glow: Trumpet, Roy Eldridge: Trumpet, George Schwartz: Trumpet, Harry Rodgers: Trombone, Robert Swift: Trombone, Ollie Wilson: Trombone, Gus Dixon: Trombone, Rudy Tanza: Alto Saxophone, Lou Prisby: Alto Saxophone, Jon Walton: Tenor Saxophone, Ralph Roselund: Tenor Saxophone, Chuck Gentry: Baritone Saxophone, Dodo Marmarosa: Piano, Morris Rayman: Bass, Lou Fromm: Drums.]

    I Could Write a Book (Rodgers/Hart)

    The Man I Love (Gershwin/Gershwin)

---

14 June 1945 — Los Angeles, USA

Artie Shaw

Artie Shaw 1944-1945 [CD, Hep Records, CD 70(3)]

[Musicians: Barney Kessel: Guitar, Artie Shaw: Clarinet, Stan Fishelson: Trumpet, Bernie Glow: Trumpet, Roy Eldridge: Trumpet, George Schwartz: Trumpet, Harry Rodgers: Trombone, Robert Swift: Trombone, Ollie Wilson: Trombone, Gus Dixon: Trombone, Rudy Tanza: Alto Saxophone, Lou Prisby: Alto Saxophone, Jon Walton: Tenor Saxophone, Ralph Roselund: Tenor Saxophone, Chuck Gentry: Baritone Saxophone, Dodo Marmarosa: Piano, Morris Rayman: Bass, Lou Fromm: Drums.]

    Kasbah (Coniff)

    Lament (Coniff)

Artie Shaw

The Indispensable Artie Shaw Vol5/6 [LP, Black & White/RCA, NL89914(2)]
Artie Shaw 1944-1945 [CD, Hep Records, CD 70(3)]

[Musicians: Barney Kessel: Guitar, Artie Shaw: Clarinet, Stan Fishelson: Trumpet, Bernie Glow: Trumpet, Roy Eldridge: Trumpet, George Schwartz: Trumpet, Harry Rodgers: Trombone, Robert Swift: Trombone, Ollie Wilson: Trombone, Gus Dixon: Trombone, Rudy Tanza: Alto Saxophone, Lou Prisby: Alto Saxophone, Jon Walton: Tenor Saxophone, Ralph Roselund: Tenor Saxophone, Chuck Gentry: Baritone Saxophone, Dodo Marmarosa: Piano, Morris Rayman: Bass, Lou Fromm: Drums.]

    Thrill of a Lifetime (Hollander/Coslow/Lombardo)

---

03 July 1945 — Los Angeles, USA

Artie Shaw

The Indispensable Artie Shaw Vol5/6 [LP, Black & White/RCA, NL89914(2)]
Artie Shaw 1944-1945 [CD, Hep Records, CD 70(3)]

[Musicians: Barney Kessel: Guitar, Artie Shaw: Clarinet, Stan Fishelson: Trumpet, Bernie Glow: Trumpet, Roy Eldridge: Trumpet, George Schwartz: Trumpet, Harry Rodgers: Trombone, Robert Swift: Trombone, Ollie Wilson: Trombone, Gus Dixon: Trombone, Rudy Tanza: Alto Saxophone, Lou Prisby: Alto Saxophone, Jon Walton: Tenor Saxophone, Ralph Roselund: Tenor Saxophone, Chuck Gentry: Baritone Saxophone, Dodo Marmarosa: Piano, Morris Rayman: Bass, Lou Fromm: Drums.]

    Love Walked In (Gershwin/Gershwin)

    Soon (Gershwin/Gershwin)

---

06 July 1945 — Los Angeles, USA

Artie Shaw

Artie Shaw 1944-1945 [CD, Hep Records, CD 70(3)]

[Musicians: Barney Kessel: Guitar, Artie Shaw: Clarinet, Stan Fishelson: Trumpet, Bernie Glow: Trumpet, Roy Eldridge: Trumpet, George Schwartz: Trumpet, Harry Rodgers: Trombone, Robert Swift: Trombone, Ollie Wilson: Trombone, Gus Dixon: Trombone, Rudy Tanza: Alto Saxophone, Lou Prisby: Alto Saxophone, Jon Walton: Tenor Saxophone, Ralph Roselund: Tenor Saxophone, Chuck Gentry: Baritone Saxophone, Dodo Marmarosa: Piano, Morris Rayman: Bass, Lou Fromm: Drums.]

    Keepin' Myself For You (Youmans/Clare)

    No One But You (Leslie/Siravo/Shaw)

Artie Shaw

The Indispensable Artie Shaw Vol5/6 [LP, Black & White/RCA, NL89914(2)]
Artie Shaw 1944-1945 [CD, Hep Records, CD 70(3)]
[Musicians: Barney Kessel: Guitar, Artie Shaw: Clarinet, Stan Fishelson: Trumpet, Bernie Glow: Trumpet, Roy Eldridge: Trumpet/Vocal, George Schwartz: Trumpet, Harry Rodgers: Trombone, Robert Swift: Trombone, Ollie Wilson: Trombone, Gus Dixon: Trombone, Rudy Tanza: Alto Saxophone, Lou Prisby: Alto Saxophone, Jon Walton: Tenor Saxophone, Ralph Roselund: Tenor Saxophone, Chuck Gentry: Baritone Saxophone, Dodo Marmarosa: Piano, Morris Rayman: Bass, Lou Fromm: Drums.]

    Natch (Leslie/Shaw)

---

11 July 1945   Los Angeles, USA

Artie Shaw

The Indispensable Artie Shaw Vol5/6 [LP, Black & White/RCA, NL89914(2)]
Artie Shaw 1944-1945 [CD, Hep Records, CD 70(3)]
[Musicians: Barney Kessel: Guitar, Artie Shaw: Clarinet, Stan Fishelson: Trumpet, Bernie Glow: Trumpet, Roy Eldridge: Trumpet, George Schwartz: Trumpet, Harry Rodgers: Trombone, Robert Swift: Trombone, Ollie Wilson: Trombone, Gus Dixon: Trombone, Rudy Tanza: Alto Saxophone, Lou Prisby: Alto Saxophone, Jon Walton: Tenor Saxophone, Ralph Roselund: Tenor Saxophone, Chuck Gentry: Baritone Saxophone, Dodo Marmarosa: Piano, Morris Rayman: Bass, Lou Fromm: Drums.]

    That's for Me (Rodgers/Hammerstein)

    They Can't Take That Away From Me (Gershwin/Gershwin)

---

14 July 1945   Los Angeles, USA

Artie Shaw

Artie Shaw 1944-1945 [CD, Hep Records, CD 70(3)]
[Musicians: Barney Kessel: Guitar, Artie Shaw: Clarinet, Stan Fishelson: Trumpet, Bernie Glow: Trumpet, Roy Eldridge: Trumpet, George Schwartz: Trumpet, Harry Rodgers: Trombone, Robert Swift: Trombone, Ollie Wilson: Trombone, Gus Dixon: Trombone, Rudy Tanza: Alto Saxophone, Lou Prisby: Alto Saxophone, Jon Walton: Tenor Saxophone, Ralph Roselund: Tenor Saxophone, Chuck Gentry: Baritone Saxophone, Dodo Marmarosa: Piano, Morris Rayman: Bass, Lou Fromm: Drums.]

    I Was Doing Alright (Gershwin/Gershwin)

    Our Love Is Here To Stay (Gershwin/Gershwin)

    They Can't Take That away From Me (Gershwin/Gershwin)

---

17 July 1945   Los Angeles, USA

Artie Shaw

The Indispensable Artie Shaw Vol5/6 [LP, Black & White/RCA, NL89914(2)]
Artie Shaw 1944-1945 [CD, Hep Records, CD 70(3)]
[Musicians: Barney Kessel: Guitar, Artie Shaw: Clarinet, Stan Fishelson: Trumpet, Bernie Glow: Trumpet, Roy Eldridge: Trumpet, George Schwartz: Trumpet, Harry Rodgers: Trombone, Robert Swift: Trombone, Ollie Wilson: Trombone, Gus Dixon: Trombone, Rudy Tanza: Alto Saxophone, Lou Prisby: Alto Saxophone, Jon Walton: Tenor Saxophone, Ralph Roselund: Tenor Saxophone, Chuck Gentry: Baritone Saxophone, Dodo Marmarosa: Piano, Morris Rayman: Bass, Lou Fromm: Drums.]

    Someone To Watch Over Me (Gershwin/Gershwin)

    Things Are Looking Up (Gershwin/Gershwin)

19 July 1945 Los Angeles, USA

Artie Shaw

The Indispensable Artie Shaw Vol5/6 [LP, Black & White/RCA, NL89914(2)]
Artie Shaw 1944-1945 [CD, Hep Records, CD 70(3)]

[Musicians: Barney Kessel: Guitar, Artie Shaw: Clarinet, Stan Fishelson: Trumpet, Bernie Glow: Trumpet, Roy Eldridge: Trumpet, George Schwartz: Trumpet, Harry Rodgers: Trombone, Robert Swift: Trombone, Ollie Wilson: Trombone, Gus Dixon: Trombone, Rudy Tanza: Alto Saxophone, Lou Prisby: Alto Saxophone, Jon Walton: Tenor Saxophone, Ralph Roselund: Tenor Saxophone, Chuck Gentry: Baritone Saxophone, Dodo Marmarosa: Piano, Morris Rayman: Bass, Lou Fromm: Drums.]

    The Maid with the Flaccid Hair (Sauter)

---

21 July 1945 Los Angeles, USA

Artie Shaw

Artie Shaw 1944-1945 [CD, Hep Records, CD 70(3)]

[Musicians: Barney Kessel: Guitar, Artie Shaw: Clarinet, Stan Fishelson: Trumpet, Bernie Glow: Trumpet, Roy Eldridge: Trumpet, George Schwartz: Trumpet, Harry Rodgers: Trombone, Robert Swift: Trombone, Ollie Wilson: Trombone, Gus Dixon: Trombone, Rudy Tanza: Alto Saxophone, Lou Prisby: Alto Saxophone, Jon Walton: Tenor Saxophone, Ralph Roselund: Tenor Saxophone, Chuck Gentry: Baritone Saxophone, Dodo Marmarosa: Piano, Morris Rayman: Bass, Lou Fromm: Drums.]

    No One But You (Leslie/Siravo/Shaw)
    They Didn't Believe Me (Kern/Reynolds)

---

24 July 1945 Los Angeles, USA

Artie Shaw

The Indispensable Artie Shaw Vol5/6 [LP, Black & White/RCA, NL89914(2)]
Artie Shaw 1944-1945 [CD, Hep Records, CD 70(3)]

[Musicians: Barney Kessel: Guitar, Artie Shaw: Clarinet, Stan Fishelson: Trumpet, Bernie Glow: Trumpet, Roy Eldridge: Trumpet, George Schwartz: Trumpet, Harry Rodgers: Trombone, Robert Swift: Trombone, Ollie Wilson: Trombone, Gus Dixon: Trombone, Rudy Tanza: Alto Saxophone, Lou Prisby: Alto Saxophone, Jon Walton: Tenor Saxophone, Ralph Roselund: Tenor Saxophone, Chuck Gentry: Baritone Saxophone, Dodo Marmarosa: Piano, Morris Rayman: Bass, Lou Fromm: Drums.]

    Dancing on the Ceiling (Rodgers/Hart)
    I Can't Get Started with You (Gershwin/Duke)

---

26 July 1945 Los Angeles, USA

Artie Shaw

The Indispensable Artie Shaw Vol5/6 [LP, Black & White/RCA, NL89914(2)]
Artie Shaw 1944-1945 [CD, Hep Records, CD 70(3)]

[Musicians: Barney Kessel: Guitar, Artie Shaw: Clarinet, Stan Fishelson: Trumpet, Bernie Glow: Trumpet, Roy Eldridge: Trumpet, George Schwartz: Trumpet, Harry Rodgers: Trombone, Robert Swift: Trombone, Ollie Wilson: Trombone, Gus Dixon: Trombone, Rudy Tanza: Alto Saxophone, Lou Prisby: Alto Saxophone, Jon Walton: Tenor Saxophone, Ralph Roselund: Tenor Saxophone, Chuck Gentry: Baritone Saxophone, Dodo Marmarosa: Piano, Morris Rayman: Bass, Lou Fromm: Drums.]

    Just Floatin' Along (Siravo/Shaw)

28 July 1945 — Los Angeles, USA

Artie Shaw

Artie Shaw 1944-1945 [CD, Hep Records, CD 70(3)]

[Musicians: Barney Kessel: Guitar, Artie Shaw: Clarinet, Stan Fishelson: Trumpet, Bernie Glow: Trumpet, Roy Eldridge: Trumpet, George Schwartz: Trumpet, Harry Rodgers: Trombone, Robert Swift: Trombone, Ollie Wilson: Trombone, Gus Dixon: Trombone, Rudy Tanza: Alto Saxophone, Lou Prisby: Alto Saxophone, Jon Walton: Tenor Saxophone, Ralph Roselund: Tenor Saxophone, Chuck Gentry: Baritone Saxophone, Dodo Marmarosa: Piano, Morris Rayman: Bass, Lou Fromm: Drums.]

- Don't Blame Me (Fields/McHugh)
- Yolanda (Freed/Warren)

30 July 1945 — Los Angeles, USA

Artie Shaw

The Indispensable Artie Shaw Vol5/6 [LP, Black & White/RCA, NL89914(2)]
Artie Shaw 1944-1945 [CD, Hep Records, CD 70(3)]

[Musicians: Barney Kessel: Guitar, Artie Shaw: Clarinet, Stan Fishelson: Trumpet, Bernie Glow: Trumpet, Roy Eldridge: Trumpet, George Schwartz: Trumpet, Harry Rodgers: Trombone, Robert Swift: Trombone, Ollie Wilson: Trombone, Gus Dixon: Trombone, Rudy Tanza: Alto Saxophone, Lou Prisby: Alto Saxophone, Jon Walton: Tenor Saxophone, Ralph Roselund: Tenor Saxophone, Chuck Gentry: Baritone Saxophone, Dodo Marmarosa: Piano, Morris Rayman: Bass, Lou Fromm: Drums.]

- I Can't Escape From You (Robin/Whiting)

31 July 1945 — New York, USA

Artie Shaw

The Complete Gramercy Five Sessions [CD, Bluebird, ND87637]
The Indispensable Artie Shaw Vol5/6 [LP, Black & White, NL89914(2)]
Artie Shaw 1944-1945 [CD, Hep Records, CD 70(3)]

[Musicians: Barney Kessel: Guitar, Artie Shaw: Clarinet, Roy Eldridge: Trumpet, Dodo Marmarosa: Piano, Morris Rayman: Bass, Lou Fromm: Drums.]

- Scuttlebutt (Shaw)

02 August 1945 — New York, USA

Artie Shaw

The Complete Gramercy Five Sessions [CD, Bluebird, ND87637]
The Indispensable Artie Shaw Vol5/6 [LP, Black & White, NL89914(2)]
Artie Shaw 1944-1945 [CD, Hep Records, CD 70(3)]

[Musicians: Barney Kessel: Guitar, Artie Shaw: Clarinet, Roy Eldridge: Trumpet, Dodo Marmarosa: Piano, Morris Rayman: Bass, Lou Fromm: Drums.]

- Hop, Skip And Jump (Shaw)
- Mysterioso (take 1) (Shaw)
- Mysterioso (take 2) (Shaw)
- The Gentle Grifter (Shaw)

12 September 1945 — San Diego, USA

Artie Shaw

Artie Shaw 1945 Spotlight Bands [CD, Jazz Unlimited, 201 2088]

[Musicians: Barney Kessel: Guitar, Artie Shaw: Clarinet, Roy Eldridge: Trumpet, Dodo Marmarosa: Piano, Morris Rayman: Bass, Lou Fromm: Drums.]

- Summit Ridge Drive (Shaw)

[Musicians: Barney Kessel: Guitar, Artie Shaw: Clarinet, Stan Fishelson: Trumpet, Bernie Glow: Trumpet, Roy Eldridge: Trumpet, George Schwartz: Trumpet, Harry Rodgers: Trombone, Robert Swift: Trombone, Ollie Wilson: Trombone, Gus Dixon: Trombone, Rudy Tanza: Alto Saxophone, Lou Prisby: Alto Saxophone, Jon Walton: Tenor Saxophone, Ralph Roselund: Tenor Saxophone, Chuck Gentry: Baritone Saxophone, Dodo Marmarosa: Piano, Morris Rayman: Bass, Lou Fromm: Drums.]

- Begin The Beguine (Porter)
- Little Jazz (Harding)
- Lucky Number (Conniff)
- Nightmare (Shaw)
- Tabu (Lecuona)

---

19 September 1945   Fort Ord, California, USA

Artie Shaw

Artie Shaw 1945 Spotlight Bands [CD, Jazz Unlimited, 201 2088]

[Musicians: Barney Kessel: Guitar, Artie Shaw: Clarinet, Roy Eldridge: Trumpet, Dodo Marmarosa: Piano, Morris Rayman: Bass, Lou Fromm: Drums.]

- Scuttlebutt (Carleton/Shaw)

[Musicians: Barney Kessel: Guitar, Artie Shaw: Clarinet, Stan Fishelson: Trumpet, Bernie Glow: Trumpet, Roy Eldridge: Trumpet, George Schwartz: Trumpet, Harry Rodgers: Trombone, Robert Swift: Trombone, Ollie Wilson: Trombone, Gus Dixon: Trombone, Rudy Tanza: Alto Saxophone, Lou Prisby: Alto Saxophone, Jon Walton: Tenor Saxophone, Ralph Roselund: Tenor Saxophone, Chuck Gentry: Baritone Saxophone, Dodo Marmarosa: Piano, Morris Rayman: Bass, Lou Fromm: Drums.]

- Gotta Be This Or That (Skylar)
- Just Floating Along (Siravo/Shaw)
- My Heart Stood Still (Rodgers/Hart)
- Nightmare (Shaw)
- On The Atcheson, Topeka And Santa Fe (Mercer/Warren)

---

26 September 1945   Obispo, California, USA

Artie Shaw

Artie Shaw 1945 Spotlight Bands [CD, Jazz Unlimited, 201 2088]

[Musicians: Barney Kessel: Guitar, Artie Shaw: Clarinet, Ray Linn: Trumpet, Dodo Marmarosa: Piano, Morris Rayman: Bass, Lou Fromm: Drums.]

- Hop, Skip And Jump (Shaw/Carleton)
- The Sad Sack (Carleton/Shaw)

[Musicians: Barney Kessel: Guitar, Artie Shaw: Clarinet, Stan Fishelson: Trumpet, Bernie Glow: Trumpet, Ray Linn: Trumpet, George Schwartz: Trumpet, Harry Rodgers: Trombone, Robert Swift: Trombone, Ollie Wilson: Trombone, Gus Dixon: Trombone, Rudy Tanza: Alto Saxophone, Lou Prisby: Alto Saxophone, Jon Walton: Tenor Saxophone, Ralph Roselund: Tenor Saxophone, Chuck Gentry: Baritone Saxophone, Dodo Marmarosa: Piano, Morris Rayman: Bass, Lou Fromm: Drums.]

- Blue Skies (Berlin)
- Jumpin' On The Merry-Go-Round (Conniff)
- Nightmare (Shaw)
- On The Sunny Side Of The Street (Fields/McHugh)

---

03 October 1945   Santa Ana, California, USA

Artie Shaw

Artie Shaw 1945 Spotlight Bands [CD, Jazz Unlimited, 201 2088]

[Musicians: Barney Kessel: Guitar, Artie Shaw: Clarinet, Stan Fishelson: Trumpet, Bernie Glow: Trumpet, Ray Linn: Trumpet, George Schwartz: Trumpet, Harry Rodgers: Trombone, Robert Swift: Trombone, Ollie Wilson: Trombone, Gus Dixon: Trombone, Rudy Tanza: Alto Saxophone, Lou Prisby: Alto Saxophone, Jon Walton: Tenor Saxophone, Ralph Roselund: Tenor Saxophone, Chuck Gentry: Baritone Saxophone, Dodo Marmarosa: Piano, Morris Rayman: Bass, Lou Fromm: Drums.]

- Along The Navajo Trail (Charles/De Lange/Markes)
- Bedford Drive (Harding)
- Nightmare (Shaw)

S'Wonderful (Gershwin/Gershwin)

10 October 1945 — Santa Barbara, California,

Artie Shaw

Artie Shaw 1945 Spotlight Bands [CD, Jazz Unlimited, 201 2088]

[Musicians: Barney Kessel: Guitar, Artie Shaw: Clarinet, Stan Fishelson: Trumpet, Bernie Glow: Trumpet, Ray Linn: Trumpet, George Schwartz: Trumpet, Harry Rodgers: Trombone, Robert Swift: Trombone, Ollie Wilson: Trombone, Gus Dixon: Trombone, Rudy Tanza: Alto Saxophone, Lou Prisby: Alto Saxophone, Jon Walton: Tenor Saxophone, Ralph Roselund: Tenor Saxophone, Chuck Gentry: Baritone Saxophone, Dodo Marmarosa: Piano, Morris Rayman: Bass, Lou Fromm: Drums.]

Can't You Read Between The Lines? (Cahn/Styne)
Hindustan (Wallace/Weeks)
Love Walked In (Gershwin/Gershwin)
Nightmare (Shaw)
The Glider (Harding)

14 November 1945 — Los Angeles, USA

Artie Shaw

Artie Shaw [LP, Everest, FS-248]
Artie Shaw 1944-1945 [CD, Hep Records, CD 70(3)]

[Musicians: Barney Kessel: Guitar, Artie Shaw: Clarinet, Stan Fishelson: Trumpet, Bernie Glow: Trumpet, Ray Linn: Trumpet, George Schwartz: Trumpet, Harry Rodgers: Trombone, Robert Swift: Trombone, Ollie Wilson: Trombone, Gus Dixon: Trombone, Rudy Tanza: Alto Saxophone, Lou Prisby: Alto Saxophone, Herbie Steward: Tenor Saxophone, Ralph Roselund: Tenor Saxophone, Chuck Gentry: Baritone Saxophone, Dodo Marmarosa: Piano, Morris Rayman: Bass, Lou Fromm: Drums.]

How Deep Is The Ocean (Berlin)
Let's Walk (Siravo)
Love of My Life (Shaw/Mercer)

Artie Shaw

Artie Shaw 1944-1945 [CD, Hep Records, CD 70(3)]

[Musicians: Barney Kessel: Guitar, Artie Shaw: Clarinet, Stan Fishelson: Trumpet, Bernie Glow: Trumpet, Ray Linn: Trumpet, George Schwartz: Trumpet, Harry Rodgers: Trombone, Robert Swift: Trombone, Ollie Wilson: Trombone, Gus Dixon: Trombone, Rudy Tanza: Alto Saxophone, Lou Prisby: Alto Saxophone, Herbie Steward: Tenor Saxophone, Ralph Roselund: Tenor Saxophone, Chuck Gentry: Baritone Saxophone, Dodo Marmarosa: Piano, Morris Rayman: Bass, Lou Fromm: Drums, Hal Stevens: Vocals.]

Ghost Of A Chance (Young/Washington)
The Glider (Harding)
The Hornet (Harding)

01 December 1945 [Estimated] — Los Angeles, USA

Charlie Barnet

Showcase - Charlie Barnet Orchestra [LP, First Heard, FH44]

[Musicians: Barney Kessel: Guitar, Peanuts Holland: Trumpet, Lyman Vunk: Trumpet, Johnny Martel: Trumpet, Jack Mootz: Trumpet, Tommy Pederson: Trombone, Porky Cohen: Trombone, Bill Haller: Trombone, Ed Fromm: Trombone, Charlie Barnet: Alto & Soprano Saxophones, Les Robinson: Alto Saxophone, Gene Kinsey: Alto Saxophone, Kurt Bloom: Tenor Saxophone, Ed Pripps: Tenor Saxophone, Bob Dawes: Baritone Saxophone, Al Haig: Piano, Morris Rayman: Bass, Harold Hahn: Drums.]

Haunted Town
Zamboanga

02 December 1945 [Estimated] Los Angeles, USA

Charlie Barnet

Big Band Bounce & Boogie [LP, Affinity, AFS 1012]
[Musicians: Barney Kessel: Guitar, Peanuts Holland: Trumpet/Vocal, Al Killian: Trumpet, Everett McDonald: Trumpet, George Seaburg: Trumpet, Ed Fromm: Trombone, Bill Haller: Trombone, Tommy Pederson: Trombone, Porky Cohen: Trombone, Charlie Barnet: Alto & Soprano Saxophones, Gene Kinsey: Alto Saxophone, Les Robinson: Alto Saxophone, Kurt Bloom: Tenor Saxophone, Ed Pripps: Tenor Saxophone, Bob Dawes: Baritone Saxophone, Al Haig: Piano, Morris Rayman: Bass, Harold Hahn: Drums.]

    Xango (Gibson)

---

06 December 1945 Los Angeles, USA

Charlie Barnet

Charlie Barnet And His Orchestra [LP, Ajax, 155]
[Musicians: Barney Kessel: Guitar, Peanuts Holland: Trumpet/Vocal, Al Killian: Trumpet, Everett McDonald: Trumpet, George Seaburg: Trumpet, Porky Cohen: Trombone, Ed Fromm: Trombone, Bill Haller: Trombone, Tommy Pederson: Trombone, Charlie Barnet: Saxophones, Gene Kinsey: Alto Saxophone, Les Robinson: Alto Saxophone, Kurt Bloom: Tenor Saxophone, Ed Pripps: Tenor Saxophone, Bob Dawes: Baritone Saxophone, Al Haig: Piano, Morris Rayman: Bass, Harold Hahn: Drums, Kay Starr: Vocals, Phil Barton: Vocals.]

    E-Bob-O-Lee-Bob
    Madame Butterball
    When The One You Love

---

27 January 1946 Los Angeles, USA

Charlie Barnet

Charlie Barnet Orchestra [LP, Joyce, 1001]
[Musicians: Barney Kessel: Guitar, Peanuts Holland: Trumpet/Vocal, Everett McDonald: Trumpet, George Seaburg: Trumpet, Al Killian: Trumpet, Porky Cohen: Trombone, Tommy Pederson: Trombone, Bill Haller: Trombone, Ed Fromm: Trombone, Charlie Barnet: Alto and Tenor Saxophone, Ray DeGeer: Alto Saxophone, Gene Kinsey: Alto Saxophone, Ed Pripps: Tenor Saxophone, Kurt Bloom: Tenor Saxophone, Bob Dawes: Baritone Saxophone, Sheldon Smith: Piano, Morris Rayman: Bass, Harold Hahn: Drums, Phil Barton: Vocals, Fran Warren: Vocals.]

    C Jam Blues (Ellington)
    Day by Day (Stordahl/Cahn/Weston)
    Medley: A Door Will Open
        Gee, Its Good to Hold You
        Nancy (Silvers/Van Heusen)
    Shady Lady
    Symphony
    Take the "A" Train (Strayhorn)
    The Seargent Was Sky
    Theme
    Theme 2
    When The One You Love

Charlie Ventura

Charlie Boy [LP, Phoenix Records, LP-6]
Charlie Ventura 1945-1946 [CD, Classics, 1044]
[Musicians: Barney Kessel: Guitar, Barney Bigard: Clarinet, Ray DeGeer: Alto Saxophone, Charlie Ventura: Tenor Saxophone, Harry Fields: Piano, Red Callender: Bass, Nick Fatool: Drums.]

    Stompin' At The Savoy Parts 1 & 2 (Goodman)
    The Man I Love Parts 1 & 2 (Gershwin/Gershwin)

30 January 1946   Ocean Park, California, US

Charlie Barnet

One Night Stand Volume 2 [LP, Joyce, 1031]

[Musicians: Barney Kessel: Guitar, Peanuts Holland: Trumpet, Everett MacDonald: Trumpet, George Seaburg: Trumpet, Al Killian: Trumpet, Tommy Pederson: Trombone, Porky Cohen: Trombone, Bill Haller: Trombone, Ed Fromm: Trombone, Charlie Barnet: Alto & Soprano Saxophones, Les Robinson: Alto Saxophone, Gene Kinsey: Alto Saxophone, Kurt Bloom: Tenor Saxophone, Ed Pripps: Tenor Saxophone, Bob Dawes: Baritone Saxophone, Al Haig: Piano, Morris Rayman: Bass, Harold Hahn: Drums.]

     Give Me The Simple Life (Ruby/Bloom)

     More And More (Kern)

     More Than Yesterday

     Tchaikovsky Medley

     When The One You Love (Fisher/Roberts)

     Yalta

Charlie Barnet

Showcase - Charlie Barnet Orchestra [LP, First Heard, FH44]

[Musicians: Barney Kessel: Guitar, Peanuts Holland: Trumpet, Everett MacDonald: Trumpet, George Seaburg: Trumpet, Al Killian: Trumpet, Tommy Pederson: Trombone, Porky Cohen: Trombone, Bill Haller: Trombone, Ed Fromm: Trombone, Charlie Barnet: Alto & Soprano Saxophones, Les Robinson: Alto Saxophone, Gene Kinsey: Alto Saxophone, Kurt Bloom: Tenor Saxophone, Ed Pripps: Tenor Saxophone, Bob Dawes: Baritone Saxophone, Al Haig: Piano, Morris Rayman: Bass, Harold Hahn: Drums.]

     Poor Little Rich Girl (Coward/Braham)

[Musicians: Barney Kessel: Guitar, Peanuts Holland: Trumpet, Everett McDonald: Trumpet, George Seaburg: Trumpet, Al Killian: Trumpet, Tommy Pederson: Trombone, Porky Cohen: Trombone, Bill Haller: Trombone, Ed Fromm: Trombone, Charlie Barnet: Alto & Soprano Saxophones, Les Robinson: Alto Saxophone, Gene Kinsey: Alto Saxophone, Kurt Bloom: Tenor Saxophone, Ed Pripps: Tenor Saxophone, Bob Dawes: Baritone Saxophone, Al Haig: Piano, Morris Rayman: Bass, Harold Hahn: Drums.]

     Strolling

     The Sergeant Was Shy/Theme - Redskin Rhumba (Barnet)

---

01 February 1946 [Estimated]   Ocean Park, California, US

Charlie Barnet

Charlie Barnet Orchestra [LP, Joyce, 5004]

[Musicians: Barney Kessel: Guitar, Peanuts Holland: Trumpet, Everett McDonald: Trumpet, George Seaburg: Trumpet, Al Killian: Trumpet, Tommy Pederson: Trombone, Porky Cohen: Trombone, Bill Haller: Trombone, Ed Fromm: Trombone, Charlie Barnet: Alto & Soprano Saxophones, Les Robinson: Alto Saxophone, Gene Kinsey: Alto Saxophone, Kurt Bloom: Tenor Saxophone, Ed Pripps: Tenor Saxophone, Bob Dawes: Baritone Saxophone, Al Haig: Piano, Morris Rayman: Bass, Harold Hahn: Drums.]

     Come To Baby, Do (James/Miller)

     Cuban Jam

     E-Bob-O-Lee-Bop

     Haunted Town

     Jubilee Jump

     Redskin Rhumba (Theme) (Barnet)

     Xango

---

01 March 1946 [Estimated]   Los Angeles, USA

Charlie Ventura

Charlie Boy [LP, Phoenix Records, LP-6]
Charlie Ventura 1945-1946 [CD, Classics, 1044]

[Musicians: Barney Kessel: Guitar, Barney Bigard: Clarinet, Willie Smith: Alto Saxophone, Charlie Ventura: Tenor Saxophone, Arnold Ross: Piano, Billy Hadnott: Bass, Nick Fatool: Drums, Red Rodney: Trumpet.]

     Nobody Knows The Trouble I've Seen (Cox)

     'S Wonderful (Gershwin/Gershwin)

The Man I Love (Gershwin/Gershwin)

Who's Sorry Now (Kalmer/Ruby/Snyder)

---

04 March 1946   California, USA

Charlie Barnet

Charlie Barnet Orchestra [LP, First Heard, FH44]

[Musicians: Barney Kessel: Guitar, Peanuts Holland: Trumpet, Everett McDonald: Trumpet, George Seaburg: Trumpet, Al Killian: Trumpet, Tommy Pederson: Trombone, Porky Cohen: Trombone, Bill Haller: Trombone, Ed Fromm: Trombone, Charlie Barnet: Alto & Soprano Saxophones, Les Robinson: Alto Saxophone, Gene Kinsey: Alto Saxophone, Kurt Bloom: Tenor Saxophone, Ed Pripps: Tenor Saxophone, Bob Dawes: Baritone Saxophone, Al Haig: Piano, Morris Rayman: Bass, Harold Hahn: Drums, Lena Horne: Vocals.]

    Everything But You (Ellington/George/James)

    Zamboanga

---

01 April 1946 [Estimated]   Los Angeles, USA

Clifford Lang

Clifford Lang's All Star Orchestra [78rp, Pan American, 141]

[Musicians: Barney Kessel: Guitar, Ray Linn: Trumpet, Chuck Gentry: Baritone Saxophone, Camille Howard: Piano/Vocals, Gene Foster: Trombone, Other Musicians: Unknown.]

    Let's Try Again

    Widow Jenkins Blues

Clifford Lang

Clifford Lang's All Star Orchestra [78rp, Pan American, 142]

[Musicians: Barney Kessel: Guitar, Ray Linn: Trumpet, Chuck Gentry: Baritone Saxophone, Camille Howard: Piano/Vocals, Gene Foster: Trombone, Other Musicians: Unknown.]

    Exactly Like You (Fields/McHugh)

    These Foolish Things (Marvell/Strachey/Link)

---

01 May 1946 [Estimated]   Los Angeles, USA

Wingy Manone

Wingy Manone [LP, Audio-Lab, AL 1558]

[Musicians: Barney Kessel: Guitar, Wingy Manone: Trumpet/Vocal, King Jackson: Trombone, Matty Matlock: Clarinet/Alto Saxophone, Jack Dumont: Alto Saxophone, Jack Chaney: Tenor Saxophone, Stan Wrightsman: Piano, Hank Wayland: Bass, Nick Fatool: Drums.]

    Route 66 (Troup)

    Sugar (Mitchell/Alexander/Pinkard)

---

01 July 1946 [Estimated]   Los Angeles, USA

Barney Kessel

Swing To Bop Guitar [CD, HEP CD, 66]

[Musicians: Barney Kessel: Guitar, Sonny White: Piano, Thomas Moultrie: Bass, Percy Brice: Drums.]

    Medley: Cherokee (Noble)

            Honeysuckle Rose (Waller)

            How High The Moon (Hamilton)

            I Got Rhythm (Gershwin/Gershwin)

14 August 1946　　　　　　　　**Los Angeles, USA**

Ella Mae Morse

The Morse Code [CD, Jasmine, JASCD 418]

[Musicians: Barney Kessel: Guitar, Ella Mae Morse: Vocals, Ray Linn: Trumpet, Charles Gentry: Baritone Saxophone, Arthur Herfurt: Tenor Saxophone, Herbert Stewart: Alto Saxophone, Oliver Wilson: Trombone, Dodo Marmarosa: Piano, Harry Babasin: Bass, Jack Mills: Drums.]

　　The Merry Ha-Ha

---

01 September 1946 [Estimated]　　　**Los Angeles, USA**

Joe Bushkin

Jazz Keyboards-Bushkin/McPartland/Scott/Tristano [CD, Savoy, SV 0224]
Jazz Keyboards-Bushkin/McPartland/Scott/Tristano [LP, Savoy, MG 12043]
Joe Bushkin 1940-1948 [CD, Classics, 1434]

[Musicians: Barney Kessel: Guitar, Joe Bushkin: Piano, Harry Babasin: Bass.]

　　Boogie Woogie Platter (Bushkin)
　　Indian Summer (Herbert/Dubin)
　　Indiana (Hanley/Macdonald)
　　Mean To Me (Turk/Ahlert)

---

23 September 1946　　　　　　　　**Los Angeles, USA**

Dodo Marmarosa

Dodo Marmarosa 1945-1950 [CD, Classic Records, 1165]

[Musicians: Barney Kessel: Guitar, Dodo Marmarosa: Piano, Gene Englund: Bass.]

　　I've Got News For You (Easton)

Dodo Marmarosa

Dodo's Bounce [CD, Fresh Sound, FSCD-1019]

[Musicians: Barney Kessel: Guitar, Dodo Marmarosa: Piano, Gene Englund: Bass.]

　　Bopmatism (Marmarosa)
　　Compadoo (Marmarosa)
　　Dodo's Bounce (Marmarosa)
　　Escape (Marmarosa)
　　I'm In Love (Kreisler)
　　Lover Come Back To Me (Romberg)
　　Opus # 5 (Marmarosa)
　　Raindrops (Marmarosa)
　　Smoke Gets In Your Eyes (Kern)
　　You Thrill Me (Marmarosa)

---

01 October 1946 [Estimated]　　　**Culver City, California, USA**

Benny Goodman

AFRS Magic Carpet 514 [LP, Sunbeam, 156]

[Musicians: Barney Kessel: Guitar, Benny Goodman: Clarinet, John Best: Trumpet, Nate Kazebier: Trumpet, Dick Mains: Trumpet, Dale Pierce: Trumpet, Cutty Cutshall: Trombone, Leon Cox: Trombone, Addison Collins: French Horn, John Rotella: Baritone Saxophone, Bill Shine: Alto Saxophone, Larry Molinelli: Alto Saxophone, Cliff Strickland: Tenor Saxophone, Zoot Sims: Tenor Saxophone, Joe Bushkin: Piano, Harry Babasin: Bass, Louis Bellson: Drums.]

　　Rattle And Roll

[Musicians: Barney Kessel: Guitar, Benny Goodman: Clarinet, Johnny White: Vibraphone, Joe Bushkin: Piano, Harry Babasin: Bass, Louis Bellson: Drums.]

　　Just One Of Those Things (Porter)

07 October 1946 — Los Angeles, USA

Benny Goodman

Benny Goodman Vol.1 - Live Performances [LP, Giants of Jazz, GOJLP-1005]
[Musicians: Barney Kessel: Guitar, Benny Goodman: Clarinet, Johnny White: Vibraphone, Joe Bushkin: Piano, Harry Babasin: Bass, Louis Bellson: Drums.]

    St. Louis Blues (Handy)

Billie Holiday

Jazz At The Philharmonic [LP, Verve, 314 521 642-2]
[Musicians: Barney Kessel: Guitar, Howard McGhee: Trumpet, Trummy Young: Trombone, Illinois Jacquet: Tenor Saxophone, Ken Kersey: Piano, Charlie Drayton: Bass, Jackie Mills: Drums.]

    He's Funny That Way (Whiting)

    Trav'lin Light (Mundy)

14 October 1946 — Los Angeles, USA

Benny Goodman

Benny Goodman AFRS Show [LP, First Heard, FH37]
[Musicians: Barney Kessel: Guitar, Benny Goodman: Clarinet, John Best: Trumpet, Nate Kazebier: Trumpet, Dick Mains: Trumpet, Dale Pierce: Trumpet, Cutty Cutshall: Trombone, Leon Cox: Trombone, Addison Collins: French Horn, John Rotella: Baritone Saxophone, Bill Shine: Alto Saxophone, Larry Molinelli: Alto Saxophone, Cliff Strickland: Tenor Saxophone, Zoot Sims: Tenor Saxophone, Joe Bushkin: Piano, Harry Babasin: Bass, Louis Bellson: Drums.]

    King Porter Stomp (Morton)

Benny Goodman

Benny Goodman AFRS Show [LP, Swing House, SWH 3]
[Musicians: Barney Kessel: Guitar, Benny Goodman: Clarinet, Johnny White: Vibraphone, Joe Bushkin: Piano, Harry Babasin: Bass, Louis Bellson: Drums.]

    Honeysuckle Rose (Waller/Razaf)

22 October 1946 — Los Angeles, USA

Benny Goodman

Benny Goodman Small Group Recordings [CD, TIM, 205360-303]
[Musicians: Barney Kessel: Guitar, Benny Goodman: Clarinet, Johnny White: Vibraphone, Joe Bushkin: Piano, Harry Babasin: Bass, Louis Bellson: Drums.]

    Honeysuckle Rose (Razaf/Waller)

    I'll Always Be In Love With You (Stept/Green/Ruby)

28 October 1946 — New York, USA

Benny Goodman

Benny Goodman AFRS Show 18 [LP, Swing House, SWH 3]
[Musicians: Barney Kessel: Guitar, Benny Goodman: Clarinet, Johnny White: Vibraphone, Joe Bushkin: Piano, Harry Babasin: Bass, Louis Bellson: Drums.]

    Flying Home (Hampton/Goodman/DeLange)

29 October 1946 — Los Angeles, USA

Earle Spencer Orchestra

Swing To Bop Guitar [CD, HEP CD, 66]

[Musicians: Barney Kessel: Guitar, Arv Garrison: Guitar, Irving Ashby: Guitar, Tony Rizzi: Guitar, Gene Sargent: Guitar, Earle Spencer: Trombone, John Anderson: Trumpet, Tony Facciuto: Trumpet, Bill Stean: Trumpet, Keith Williams: Trumpet, Chuck Gale:, J.D. Marsh:, Ollie Wilson:, Bill Gillette: Alto Saxophone, Matt Utal: Alto Saxophone, Carter Englund: Tenor Saxophone, Tom Makagon: Tenor Saxophone, Steve Perlow:, Bob Clark: Piano, Dave Sperling: Bass.]

    Five Guitars In Flight (Garrison)

---

01 November 1946 — New York, USA

Benny Goodman

AFRS One Night Stand [CD, Echo, EJCD 11]

[Musicians: Barney Kessel: Guitar, Benny Goodman: Clarinet, John Best: Trumpet, Nate Kazebier: Trumpet, Dick Mains: Trumpet, Dale Pierce: Trumpet, Cutty Cutshall: Trombone, Leon Cox: Trombone, Addison Collins: French Horn, John Rotella: Baritone Saxophone, Clint Bellew: Alto Saxophone, Larry Molinelli: Alto Saxophone, Cliff Strickland: Tenor Saxophone, Zoot Sims: Tenor Saxophone, Joe Bushkin: Piano, Harry Babasin: Bass, Louis Bellson: Drums.]

    A String Of Pearls (Gray/DeLange)
    For You, For Me, For Evermore (Gershwin)
    Hora Staccato
    Put That Kiss Back Where You Found It

---

18 November 1946 — New York, USA

Benny Goodman

The Victor Borge Show with Benny Goodman [LP, Sunbeam, 155]

[Musicians: Barney Kessel: Guitar, Benny Goodman: Clarinet, John Best: Trumpet, Nate Kazebier: Trumpet, Dick Mains: Trumpet, Dale Pierce: Trumpet, Cutty Cutshall: Trombone, Leon Cox: Trombone, Addison Collins: French Horn, John Rotella: Baritone Saxophone, Clint Bellew: Alto Saxophone, Larry Molinelli: Alto Saxophone, Cliff Strickland: Tenor Saxophone, Zoot Sims: Tenor Saxophone, Joe Bushkin: Piano, Harry Babasin: Bass, Louis Bellson: Drums.]

    You Brought A New Kind Of Love To Me (Fain/Kahal/Norman)

---

29 November 1946 — New York, USA

Benny Goodman

Benny Goodman [CD, Laserlight, 15762]

[Musicians: Barney Kessel: Guitar, Benny Goodman: Clarinet, John Best: Trumpet, Nate Kazebier: Trumpet, Dick Mains: Trumpet, Dale Pierce: Trumpet, Cutty Cutshall: Trombone, Leon Cox: Trombone, Addison Collins: French Horn, John Rotella: Baritone Saxophone, Clint Bellew: Alto Saxophone, Larry Molinelli: Alto Saxophone, Cliff Strickland: Tenor Saxophone, Zoot Sims: Tenor Saxophone, Joe Bushkin: Piano, Harry Babasin: Bass, Louis Bellson: Drums.]

    Flying Home (Hampton/Goodman/DeLange)

---

01 December 1946 [Estimated] — Ocean Park, CA, USA

Charlie Barnet

Showcase - Charlie Barnet Orchestra [LP, First Heard, FH44]

[Musicians: Barney Kessel: Guitar, Charlie Barnet: Alto Saxophone, Gus McReynolds: Alto Saxophone, Frank Pappalardo: Alto Saxophone, Kurt Bloom: Tenor Saxophone, Don Raeffel: Tenor Saxophone, Art Robey: Trumpet, Everett McDonald: Trumpet, Irv Lewis: Trumpet, Shorty Rogers: Trumpet, Al Killian: Trumpet, Burt Johnson: Trombone, Tommy Pederson: Trombone, Phil Washburne: Trombone, Frank Bradley: Trombone, Bill Miller: Piano, Ed Mihelich: Bass, Dick Shanahan: Drums.]

    Makin` Whoopee (Donaldson/Kahn)

02 December 1946   **New York, USA**

Benny Goodman Quintet

Benny Goodman AFRS Show 24 [LP, Sunbeam, 155]

[Musicians: Barney Kessel: Guitar, Benny Goodman: Clarinet, Jess Stacy: Piano, Harry Babasin: Bass, Louis Bellson: Drums.]

I've Found A New Baby

---

16 December 1946   **Los Angeles, USA**

Benny Goodman

Victor Borge - Benny Goodman Show [LP, Sunbeam, 156]

[Musicians: Barney Kessel: Guitar, Benny Goodman: Clarinet, Johnny White: Vibraphone, Jess Stacy: Piano, Harry Babasin: Bass, Sam Weiss: Drums.]

Where Or When   (Rodgers/Hart)

---

23 December 1946   **Los Angeles, USA**

Benny Goodman

Victor Borge - Benny Goodman Show [LP, Sunbeam, 156]

[Musicians: Barney Kessel: Guitar, Benny Goodman: Clarinet, Johnny White: Vibraphone, Jess Stacy: Piano, Harry Babasin: Bass, Sam Weiss: Drums.]

The World Is Waiting For A Sunrise (Lockhart/Seltz)

---

06 January 1947   **Los Angeles, USA**

Benny Goodman

Victor Borge - Benny Goodman Show [LP, Sunbeam, 156]

[Musicians: Barney Kessel: Guitar, Benny Goodman: Clarinet, Johnny White: Vibraphone, Jess Stacy: Piano, Harry Babasin: Bass, Sam Weiss: Drums.]

Slipped Disc (Goodman)

---

13 January 1947   **Los Angeles, USA**

Benny Goodman

Victor Borge - Benny Goodman Show [LP, Sunbeam, 156]

[Musicians: Barney Kessel: Guitar, Benny Goodman: Clarinet, Johnny White: Vibraphone, Jess Stacy: Piano, Harry Babasin: Bass, Sam Weiss: Drums.]

I'll Always be In Love With You (Stept/Green/Ruby)

---

03 February 1947   **Los Angeles, USA**

Charlie Barnet

Charlie Barnet and his Orchestra [LP, Ajax, LP 209]
For Dancing Lovers [LP, Verve, MGV-2031]

[Musicians: Barney Kessel: Guitar, Art Robey: Trumpet/Vocal, Everett McDonald: Trumpet, Irving Lewis: Trumpet, Shorty Rogers: Trumpet, Al Killian: Trumpet, Burt Johnson: Trombone, Tommy Pederson: Trombone, Phil Washburne: Trombone, Frank Bradley: Trombone, Charlie Barnet: Alto and Tenor Saxophone, Gus McReynolds: Alto Saxophone, Frank Pappalardo: Alto Saxophone, Kurt Bloom: Tenor Saxophone, Don Raeffel: Tenor Saxophone, Bob Dawes: Baritone Saxophone, Billy Miller: Piano, Ed Mihelich: Bass, George Jenkins: Drums.]

Blue Lou

Caravan (Tizol/Ellington/Mills)

Darktown Strutter's Ball (Brooks)

Juice Head Blues

Power Steering (Killian)

12 February 1947   Los Angeles, USA

Benny Goodman

Benny Goodman Small Group Recordings [CD, TIM, 205360-303]

[Musicians: Barney Kessel: Guitar, Benny Goodman: Clarinet, Jess Stacy: Piano, Harry Babasin: Bass, Tommy Romersa: Drums.]

     I'll Always Be In Love With You (Stept/Green/Ruby)

     Sweet Georgia Brown (Pinkard/Bernie/Casey)

     Sweet Lorraine (Burwell/Parrish)

26 February 1947   Los Angeles, USA

Charlie Parker All Stars

Charlie Parker on Dial Volume 3 [LP, Spotlite, 103]

[Musicians: Barney Kessel: Guitar, Charlie Parker: Alto Saxophone, Howard McGhee: Trumpet, Wardell Gray: Tenor Saxophone, Dodo Marmarosa: Piano, Red Callender: Bass, Don Lamond: Drums.]

     Carvin' The Bird (Take 2) (McGhee)

     Cheers (Take 2) (McGhee)

     Cheers (Take 3) (McGhee)

     Cheers (Take 4) (McGhee)

     Relaxin' at Camarillo (Take 2) (Parker)

     Relaxin' at Camarillo (Take 3) (Parker)

     Relaxin' at Camarillo (Take 4) (Parker)

     Stupendous (Take 2) (McGhee)

Charlie Parker All Stars

In A Soulful Mood [CD, Music Club, MCCD 205]

Charlie Parker on Dial Volume 3 [LP, Spotlite, 103]

[Musicians: Barney Kessel: Guitar, Charlie Parker: Alto Saxophone, Howard McGhee: Trumpet, Wardell Gray: Tenor Saxophone, Dodo Marmarosa: Piano, Red Callender: Bass, Don Lamond: Drums.]

     Carvin' The Bird (McGhee)

     Cheers (McGhee)

     Relaxin' At Camarillo (Parker)

     Stupendous (McGhee)

27 February 1947   Los Angeles, USA

Just Jazz All Stars

Best of Gene Norman's Just Jazz [LP, Vogue, LDE 101]

[Musicians: Barney Kessel: Guitar, Wardell Gray: Tenor Saxophone, Vido Musso: Tenor Saxophone, Ernie Royal: Trumpet, Arnold Ross: Piano, Harry Babasin: Bass, Don Lamond: Drums.]

     California Conquest

     Just Bop

Just Jazz All Stars

Best of Gene Norman's Just Jazz [LP, Vogue, LDE 12001]

[Musicians: Barney Kessel: Guitar, Wardell Gray: Tenor Saxophone, Vido Musso: Tenor Saxophone, Ernie Royal: Trumpet, Arnold Ross: Piano, Harry Babasin: Bass, Don Lamond: Drums.]

     C Jam Blues   (Ellington)

31 March 1947 — Los Angeles, USA

June Christy

Ultimate Jazz Archive [CD, Membran, 222797CD41]

[Musicians: Barney Kessel: Guitar, June Christy: Vocals, Neil Hefti: Trumpet, Rubin Zarchy: Trumpet, Dick Catheart: Trumpet, Ray Linn: Trumpet, Burton Johnson: Trombone, Babe Bowman: Trombone, Juan Tizol: Trombone, Skeets Herfut: Reeds, Jules Kinsler: Reeds, Ted Romersa: Reeds, Jerome Kasper: Reeds, Ronald Perozzi: Reeds, Buddy Cole: Piano, Eddie Sanfranski: Bass, Shelly Manne: Drums, Frank DeVol: Arranger/Leader.]

    I'll Bet You Do (Pack)

    Little Grass Skirt

    Skip Rope (Sylvia/Lippman)

---

01 April 1947 — Los Angeles, USA

Sonny Criss

California Boppin' 1947 [CD, Fresh Sounds, FSR-CD156]

[Musicians: Barney Kessel: Guitar, Sonny Criss: Alto Saxophone, Wardell Gray: Tenor Saxophone, Russ Freeman: Piano, Harry Babasin: Bass, Tim Kennedy: Drums, Al Killian: Trumpet.]

    Backbreaker (Hawkins)

    Blow Blow Blow (Brunner)

---

22 April 1947 — Los Angeles, USA

Lucky Thompson and his Lucky Seven

Esquire's All-American Hot Jazz [LP, RCA Victor, LPV 544]
Lucky Thompson 1944-1947 [CD, Jazz Factory, JFCD 22843]

[Musicians: Barney Kessel: Guitar, Neal Hefti: Trumpet, Benny Carter: Alto Saxophone, Lucky Thompson: Tenor Saxophone, Bob Lawson: Baritone Saxophone, Dodo Marmarosa: Piano, Red Callender: Bass, Jackie Mills: Drums.]

    Boulevard Bounce (Carter)

    From Dixieland To Be-Bop (Lipschitz)

    Just One More Chance (Coslow/Johnston)

Lucky Thompson and his Lucky Seven

Lucky Thompson 1944-1947 [CD, Jazz Factory, JFCD 22843]

[Musicians: Barney Kessel: Guitar, Neal Hefti: Trumpet, Benny Carter: Alto Saxophone, Lucky Thompson: Tenor Saxophone, Bob Lawson: Baritone Saxophone, Dodo Marmarosa: Piano, Red Callender: Bass, Lee Young: Drums.]

    Boppin' The Blues (Thompson)

---

17 June 1947 — Los Angeles, USA

Ernie Andrews Orchestra

Ernie Andrews and his Orchestra [LP, Columbia, 30187]

[Musicians: Barney Kessel: Guitar, Eddie Beal: Piano, Irving Ashby: Guitar, Red Callender: Bass, Edward Hall: Drums, Lucky Thompson: Tenor Saxophone.]

    Bein' in Love

    You Better Be Satisfied

Ernie Andrews Orchestra

Ernie Andrews and his Orchestra [LP, Columbia, 37075]

[Musicians: Barney Kessel: Guitar, Eddie Beal: Piano, Irving Ashby: Guitar, Red Callender: Bass, Edward Hall: Drums, Lucky Thompson: Tenor Saxophone.]

    Hickory Dickory Dock

[Musicians: Barney Kessel: Guitar, Eddie Beal: Piano, Irving Ashby: Guitar, Red Callender: Bass, Edward Hall: Drums.]

    Soothe Me

19 June 1947   Los Angeles, USA

Mary Ann McCall & Ralph Burns Orchestra

   Mary Ann McCall & Ralph Burns Orchestra [LP, Epic, EG 37315]

   Mary Ann McCall 1939-1950 [CD, Hep Records, CD46]

   [Musicians: Barney Kessel: Guitar, Howard McGhee: Trumpet, Willie Smith: Alto Saxophone, Dexter Gordon: Tenor Saxophone, Jimmy Rowles: Piano, Red Callender: Bass, Jackie Mills: Drums, Mary Ann McCall: Vocals, Ralph Burns: Conductor & Arranger.]

      Big Butter and Egg Man (Armstrong/Venable)

      Money Is Honey (Hopkins)

      On Time (Rome)

---

06 July 1947   Los Angeles, USA

Bill Moore

   Bill Moore Sextet Elk's Auditorium [LP, Bop, 103]

   [Musicians: Barney Kessel: Guitar, Bill Moore: Tenor Saxophone, Gene Montgomery: Tenor Saxophone, Russ Freeman: Piano, John "Shifty" Henry: Bass, Ken Kennedy: Drums.]

      Perdido (Tizol/Lenk/Drake)

   [Musicians: Barney Kessel: Guitar, Bill Moore: Tenor Saxophone, Gene Montgomery: Tenor Saxophone, Russ Freeman: Piano, Leroy Gray: Bass, Ken Kennedy: Drums.]

      Wild Bill (Moore)

Bop All Stars

   Elk's Auditorium [CD, Masters Of Jazz, MJCD 176]

   Jazz Concert - West Coast [LP, London, LTZ-C15045]

   [Musicians: Barney Kessel: Guitar, Hampton Hawes: Piano, Howard McGhee: Trumpet, Sonny Criss: Alto Saxophone, Trummy Young: Trombone, Wardell Gray: Tenor Saxophone, Dexter Gordon: Tenor Saxophone, Connie Kay: Drums, Leroy Gray: Bass.]

      Bopera (Disorder At The Border) (Hawkins)

   [Musicians: Barney Kessel: Guitar, Hampton Hawes: Piano, Howard McGhee: Trumpet, Sonny Criss: Alto Saxophone, Trummy Young: Trombone, Wardell Gray: Tenor Saxophone, Dexter Gordon: Tenor Saxophone, Connie Kay: Drums, Red Callender: Bass.]

      Bopland (Byas-A-Drink) (Byas)

      Jeronimo/Cherokee (Noble)

   [Musicians: Barney Kessel: Guitar, Hampton Hawes: Piano, Howard McGhee: Trumpet, Sonny Criss: Alto Saxophone, Trummy Young: Trombone, Wardell Gray: Tenor Saxophone, Dexter Gordon: Tenor Saxophone, Ken Kennedy: Drums, Leroy Gray: Bass.]

      The Hunt (Rocks And Shoals) (Gordon/Gray)

---

04 August 1947   Los Angeles, USA

Lionel Hampton All Stars

   Memorable Concerts [LP, Vogue, VJD 508]

   [Musicians: Barney Kessel: Guitar, Lionel Hampton: Vibraphone, Charlie Shavers: Trumpet, Willie Smith: Alto Saxophone, Corky Corcoran: Tenor Saxophone, Milt Buckner: Piano, Slam Stewart: Bass, Lee Young: Drums.]

      Central Avenue Breakdown (Hampton)

      Flying Home (Hampton/Goodman/DeLange)

      Hamp's Boogie Woogie (Hampton)

      Kaba's Blues (Hampton)

      Perdido (Tizol/Lenk/Drake)

      That's My Desire (Loveday/Kremsa)

Lionel Hampton All Stars

Star Dust [LP, Coral, COP 2451]
Star Dust [CD, Decca, UCCU-5038]
[Musicians: Barney Kessel: Guitar, Lionel Hampton: Vibraphone, Willie Smith: Alto Saxophone, Charlie Shavers: Trumpet, Slam Stewart: Bass, Tommy Todd: Piano, Lee Young: Drums, Corky Corcoran: Tenor Saxophone.]

    Stardust (Carmichael/Parish)

[Musicians: Barney Kessel: Guitar, Willie Smith: Alto Saxophone, Charlie Shavers: Trumpet, Slam Stewart: Bass, Tommy Todd: Piano, Jackie Mills: Drums, Corky Corcoran: Tenor Saxophone, Lionel Hampton: Vibraphone.]

    Oh, Lady Be Good (Gershwin/Gershwin)

    The Man I Love (Gershwin/Gershwin)

[Musicians: Barney Kessel: Guitar, Willie Smith: Alto Saxophone, Charlie Shavers: Trumpet, Slam Stewart: Bass, Tommy Todd: Piano, Lee Young: Drums, Corky Corcoran: Tenor Saxophone, Lionel Hampton: Vibraphone.]

    One O'Clock Jump (Basie/James)

Kay Starr

The Complete Lamplighter Recordings 1945-1946 [CD, Crystalette Records, BJH-305 CD]
[Musicians: Barney Kessel: Guitar, Tommy Todd: Piano, Red Callender: Bass, Lee Young: Drums, Kay Starr: Vocals.]

    If I Could Be With You (Alt) (Creamer)

---

01 November 1947 [Estimated]   Los Angeles, USA

Willie Smith

Alto Saxes [LP, Verve, MGV 8126]
Willie Smith- A Sound of Distinction [CD, Ocium, 0013]
[Musicians: Barney Kessel: Guitar, Willie Smith: Alto Saxophone, Dodo Marmarosa: Piano, Red Callender: Bass, Jo Jones: Drums.]

    Not So Bop Blues (Smith)

    Tea for Two (Youmans/Caesar)

Willie Smith

The Jazz Scene [LP, Verve, MGV 8060]
Willie Smith- A Sound of Distinction [CD, Ocium, 0013]
[Musicians: Barney Kessel: Guitar, Willie Smith: Alto Saxophone, Dodo Marmarosa: Piano, Red Callender: Bass, Jo Jones: Drums.]

    Sophisticated Lady (Ellington/Mills)

---

15 November 1947   Los Angeles, USA

Mills Blue Rhythm Band

Big Bands [LP, Polydor Select, 2344 048]
[Musicians: Barney Kessel: Guitar, Ray Linn: Trumpet, Jimmy Zito: Trumpet, Juan Tizol: Valve Trombone, Willie Smith: Alto Saxophone, Eddie Rosa: Alto Saxophone, Herbie Haymer: Tenor Saxophone, Butch Stone: Baritone Saxophone, Walter Weschler: Piano, Charles Garble: Vibraphone, Arnold Fishkind: Bass, Irv Cottler: Drums.]

    Blue Rhythm Bounce (Van Alexander/Mills)

    Blue Rhythm Chant (Van Alexander/Mills)

    Blue Rhythm Ramble (Van Alexander/Mills)

    Blue Rhythm Serenade (Van Alexander/Mills)

28 November 1947   Los Angeles, USA

Red Norvo Septet

Walking Shoes [LP, Capitol, M-11029]
Norvo [LP, Pausa, PR 9015]
Red Norvo - El Rojo [CD, Definitive, DRCD 11128]
[Musicians: Barney Kessel: Guitar, Red Norvo: Vibraphone, Dexter Gordon: Tenor Saxophone, Jimmy Giuffre: Alto Saxophone, Red Callender: Bass, Jackie Mills: Drums, Ray Linn: Trumpet, Dodo Marmarosa: Piano.]

    Bop! (Norvo)

    I'll Follow You (Turk/Ahlert)

---

01 December 1947 [Estimated]   Los Angeles, USA

Anita O'Day

Anita O'Day [CD, Sony Music, AK39418]
[Musicians: Barney Kessel: Guitar, Anita O'Day: Vocals, Benny Carter: Alto Sax/Arranger/Conductor, Ray Linn: Trumpet, Al Killian: Trumpet, Conrad Gozzo: Trumpet, Dale Pierce (or possibly Harry Edison): Trumpet, Ray Sims: Trombone, Bill Harris: Trombone, Harry Klee: Alto Saxophone, Hal McKusick: Alto Saxophone, Herbie Steward: Tenor Saxophone, Unknown: Baritone Saxophone, Arnold Ross: Piano, Joe Mondragon: Bass, Jimmy Pratt: Drums.]

    Key Largo (Higgins)

[Musicians: Barney Kessel: Guitar, Anita O'Day: Vocals, Benny Carter: Arranger, Ray Linn: Trumpet, Al Killian: Trumpet, Conrad Gozzo: Trumpet, Dale Pierce (or possibly Harry Edison): Trumpet, Ray Sims: Trombone, Bill Harris: Trombone, Harry Klee: Alto Saxophone, Hal McKusick: Alto Saxophone, Herbie Steward: Tenor Saxophone, Unknown: Baritone Saxophone, Arnold Ross: Piano, Joe Mondragon: Bass, Jimmy Pratt: Drums.]

    I Ain't Getting' Any Younger

[Musicians: Barney Kessel: Guitar, Anita O'Day: Vocals, Ralph Burns: Arranger/Conductor, Ray Linn: Trumpet, Al Killian: Trumpet, Conrad Gozzo: Trumpet, Dale Pierce (or possibly Harry Edison): Trumpet, Ray Sims: Trombone, Bill Harris: Trombone, Harry Klee: Alto Saxophone, Hal McKusick: Alto Saxophone, Herbie Steward: Tenor Saxophone, Unknown: Baritone Saxophone, Arnold Ross: Piano, Joe Mondragon: Bass, Jimmy Pratt: Drums.]

    How High The Moon (Hamilton/Lewis)

    I Told Ya I Love Ya, Now Get Out

    Malaguena (Lecuona)

---

18 December 1947   Los Angeles, USA

Red Norvo

Norvo [LP, Pausa, PR 9015]
Red Norvo - El Rojo [CD, Definitive, DRCD 11128]
[Musicians: Barney Kessel: Guitar, Red Norvo: Xylophone, Manny Klein: Trumpet, John Cave: French Horn, Al Berlich: French Horn, Vic Poscella: Flute, Don Bonnie: Clarinet, Jules Kinsler: Bass Clarinet, Bob Lawson: Bass Clarinet, Lloyd Rathburn: Oboe, Art Fleming: Bassoon, Arnold Ross: Piano, Red Callender: Bass, Irv Cottler: Drums, Johnny Thompson: Arranger.]

    Band In Boston (Norvo)

    I Don't Stand A Ghost Of A Chance With You (Young/Crosby/Washington)

    Take The Red Car (Norvo/Thompson)

    Twelfth Street Rag (Bowman)

Stan Hasselgard and His All-Star Six

Walking Shoes [LP, Capitol, M-11029]
Stan Hasselgard and His All-Star Six [EP, Capitol, K 41345]
[Musicians: Barney Kessel: Guitar, Stan Hasselgard: Clarinet, Red Norvo: Vibraphone, Arnold Ross: Piano, Rollo Gaberg: Bass, Frank Bode: Drums.]

    I'll Never Be The Same (Kahn/Malneck)

    Swedish Pastry (Kessel)

    Sweet Hot Mop (White)

    Who Sleeps? (Norvo)

27 December 1947　　　　　Los Angeles, USA

Gene Norman All Stars
Just Jazz Concerts [CD, King Record, K1CJ 116/7CD]
Wardell Gray [CD, Giants of Jazz, CD 53317]
[Musicians: Barney Kessel: Guitar, Howard McGhee: Trumpet, Wardell Gray: Tenor Saxophone, Vido Musso: Tenor Saxophone, Arnold Ross: Piano, Harry Babasin: Bass, Don Lamond: Drums.]

- C Jam Blues (Ellington)
- Just You, Just Me (Just Bop) (Klages)
- Sweet Georgia Brown (Pinkard/Bernie/Casey)

Gene Norman All Stars
Just Jazz Concerts. [CD, King Record, K1CJ 116/7CD]
[Musicians: Barney Kessel: Guitar, Pete Johnson: Piano, Harry Babasin: Bass, Don Lamond: Drums.]

- Just Jazz Boogie (Johnson)
- St. Louis Blues (Handy)
- Swanee River Boogie (Johnson)
- Yancey Special (Lewis)

Kay Starr
The Complete Lamplighter Recordings 1945-1946 [CD, Crystalette Records, EP CR 472]
[Musicians: Barney Kessel: Guitar, Arnold Ross: Piano, Harry Babasin: Bass, Don Lamond: Drums, Kay Starr: Vocals.]

- A Sunday Kind Of Love (Belle)
- Garbage Can Blues (Starr)
- Them There Eyes (Pincard)

---

05 January 1948　　　　　Los Angeles, USA

Stan Hasselgard
Jammin' At Jubilee [LP, Dragon, DRLP 29]
[Musicians: Barney Kessel: Guitar, Jimmy Rowles: Piano, Harry Babasin: Bass, Stan Hasselgard: Clarinet, Jackie Mills: Drums, Gene Norman: M.C.]

- Indiana (Hanley/Macdonald)
- Swedish Pastry (Kessel)

---

06 July 1948　　　　　Los Angeles, USA

The Bop Jam All Stars
Jazz Concert West Coast [CD, Savoy, SV-0166]
[Musicians: Barney Kessel: Guitar, Howard McGhee: Trumpet, Trummy Young: Trombone, Sonny Criss: Alto Saxophone, Wardell Gray: Tenor Saxophone, Dexter Gordon: Tenor Saxophone, Hampton Hawes: Piano, Connie Kay: Drums, Leroy Gray: Bass, Ken Kennedy: Drums.]

- Back Breaker (Rose)
- Blow, Blow, Blow (Gordon)
- What Is This Thing Called Love (Porter)

The Bopland Boys
Jazz Concert West Coast Vol. 2 [CD, Savoy, SV-0165]
[Musicians: Barney Kessel: Guitar, Howard McGhee: Trumpet, Trummy Young: Trombone, Sonny Criss: Alto Saxophone, Wardell Gray: Tenor Saxophone, Dexter Gordon: Tenor Saxophone, Hampton Hawes: Piano, Connie Kay: Drums, Leroy Gray: Bass, Ken Kennedy: Drums.]

- Byas A Drink (Gordon/Gray)
- Cherokee (Noble)

13 January 1949   Los Angeles, USA

Mel Torme

Gentlemen Of Song - Mel Torme [CD, Capitol, CDP0777-7-89941-2]

[Musicians: Barney Kessel: Guitar, Mel Torme: Vocals, Ziggy Elman: Trumpet, Paul Geil: Trumpet, Ray Linn: Trumpet, George Seaburg: Trumpet, Walter Benson: Trombone, Joe Howard: Trombone, Ed Kusby: Trombone, Si Zentner: Trombone, Arthur Herfurt: Saxophones, Harry Klee: Saxophones, Bob Lawson: Saxophones, Don Raffell: Saxophones, Babe Russin: Saxophones, Walter Weschler: Piano, Larry Breen: Bass, Alvin Stoller: Drums, Sonnie Burke: Arranger/Conductor.]

    Careless Hands (Hilliard/Sigman)
    Do,Do,Do (Gershwin/Gershwin)
    Stompin' At The Savoy (Goodman/Sampson/Razaf/Webb)
    You're Getting To Be A Habit With Me (Dubin/Warren)

---

21 May 1949   Los Angeles, USA

Mel Torme

Gentlemen Of Song - Mel Torme [CD, Capitol, CDP0777-7-89941-2]

[Musicians: Barney Kessel: Guitar, Mel Torme: Vocals, Uan Rasey: Trumpet, Joe Triscari: Trumpet, Ray Linn: Trumpet, Tommy Pederson: Trombone, Colin Satterwhite: Trombone, Joe Howard: Trombone, Huntington Burdick: French Horn, June Weiland: Harp, Arthur Herfurt: Woodwind, Jerome Kasper: Woodwind, Jules Kinsler: Woodwind, Roland Pirozzi: Woodwind, Ernest Romersa: Woodwind, Arnold Ross: Celeste, Harry Babasin: Bass, Milt Holland: Percussion, Frank De Vol: Arranger/Conductor, Unknown: Vocal Group.]

    Too Late Now (Lerner/Lane)

---

26 August 1949   Los Angeles, USA

Mel Torme

Gentlemen Of Song - Mel Torme [CD, Capitol, CDP0777-7-89941-2]

[Musicians: Barney Kessel: Guitar, Mel Torme: Vocals, Uan Rasey: Trumpet, Joe Triscari: Trumpet, Ray Linn: Trumpet, Tommy Pederson: Trombone, Colin Satterwhite: Trombone, Joe Howard: Trombone, Huntington Burdick: French Horn, June Weiland: Harp, Arthur Herfurt: Woodwind, Jerome Kasper: Woodwind, Jules Kinsler: Woodwind, Roland Pirozzi: Woodwind, Ernest Romersa: Woodwind, Arnold Ross: Celeste, Harry Babasin: Bass, Milt Holland: Percussion, Frank De Vol: Arranger/Conductor, Unknown: Vocal Group.]

    Oh, You Beautiful Doll (Brown/Ayer)
    Sonny Boy (Sylva/Brown/Henderson/Jolson)

---

25 June 1951   Los Angeles, USA

Billy May And His Orchestra

Billy May Orchestra [LP, Capitol, C80201]
Billy May Orchestra Studio Recordings 1951-1953 [CD, Jasmine, JASCD 399]

[Musicians: Barney Kessel: Guitar, Manny Klein: Trumpet, John Best: Trumpet, Uan Rasey: Trumpet, Conrad Gozzo: Trumpet, Murray McEarchen: Trombone, Ed Kusby: Trombone, Si Zentner: Trombone, Jimmy Priddy: Trombone, Wilbur Schwartz: Alto Saxophone, Skeets Herfurt: Alto Saxophone, Ted Nash: Tenor Saxophone, Fred Falensby: Tenor Saxophone, Chuck Gentry: Baritone Saxophone, Buddy Cole: Piano, Joe Mondragon: Bass, Alvin Stoller: Drums/Vocals, Billy May: Leader/Arranger.]

    All Of Me (Simons/Marks)
    My Silent Love (Suesse/Heyman)

Billy May And His Orchestra

Billy May Orchestra [LP, Capitol, LAC 281]
Billy May Orchestra Studio Recordings 1951-1953 [CD, Jasmine, JASCD 399]

[Musicians: Barney Kessel: Guitar, Manny Klein: Trumpet, John Best: Trumpet, Uan Rasey: Trumpet, Conrad Gozzo: Trumpet, Murray McEarchen: Trombone, Ed Kusby: Trombone, Si Zentner: Trombone, Jimmy Priddy: Trombone, Wilbur Schwartz: Alto Saxophone, Skeets Herfurt: Alto Saxophone, Ted Nash: Tenor Saxophone, Fred Falensby: Tenor Saxophone, Chuck Gentry: Baritone Saxophone, Buddy Cole: Piano, Joe Mondragon: Bass, Alvin Stoller: Drums/Vocals, Billy May: Leader/Arranger.]

    If I Had You (Shapiro/Campbell/Connelly)
    Lulu's Back In Town (Dubin/Warren)

22 August 1951　　　　　　　　Los Angeles, USA

Billy May And His Orchestra

Billy May Orchestra [LP, Capitol, C80216]

Billy May Orchestra Studio Recordings 1951-1953 [CD, Jasmine, JASCD 399]

[Musicians: Barney Kessel: Guitar, Manny Klein: Trumpet, John Best: Trumpet, Uan Rasey: Trumpet, Joe Triscari: Trumpet, Murray McEarchen: Trombone, Ed Kusby: Trombone, Si Zentner: Trombone, Jimmy Priddy: Trombone, Wilbur Schwartz: Alto Saxophone, Skeets Herfurt: Alto Saxophone, Ted Nash: Tenor Saxophone, Fred Falensby: Tenor Saxophone, Chuck Gentry: Baritone Saxophone, Buddy Cole: Piano, Phil Stephens: Bass, Alvin Stoller: Drums/Vocals, Billy May: Leader/Arranger.]

Fat Man Boogie (May)

I Guess I`ll Have To Change My Plans (Dietz/Schwartz)

Lean, Baby (May)

When My Sugar Walks Down The Street (McHugh/Mills/Austin)

04 September 1951　　　　　　　　Los Angeles, USA

Nat King Cole

The Billy May Sessions [CD, Capitol Jazz, CDP 0777 7 89545 2 1]

[Musicians: Barney Kessel: Guitar, Skeets Herfurt: Alto Saxophone, Willie Schwartz: Alto Saxophone, Ted Nash: Tenor Saxophone, Fred Falensby: Tenor Saxophone, Chuck Gentry: Baritone Saxophone, Manny Klein: Trumpet, Conrad Gozzo: Trumpet, Ray Linn: Trumpet, John Best: Trumpet, Ed Kusby: Trombone, Tommy Pederson: Trombone, Murray McEarchen: Trombone, James Priddy: Trombone, Jimmy Rowles: Piano, Phil Stephens: Bass, Alvin Stoller: Drums, Jack Costanzo: Percussion.]

I'm Hurtin (McDonald)

Walkin' (Williams)

Walkin' My Baby Back Home (Turk)

What Does It Take (Burke)

10 September 1951　　　　　　　　Los Angeles, USA

Billy May And His Orchestra

Billy May And His Orchestra [LP, Aero Space, 2043]

[Musicians: Barney Kessel: Guitar, Manny Klein: Trumpet, John Best: Trumpet, Uan Rasey: Trumpet, Conrad Gozzo: Trumpet, Murray McEarchen: Trombone, Joe Howard: Trombone, Si Zentner: Trombone, Dick Nash: Trombone, Willie Schwartz: Alto Saxophone, Skeets Herfurt: Alto Saxophone, Bob Hardaway: Tenor Saxophone, Fred Falensby: Tenor Saxophone, Chuck Gentry: Baritone Saxophone, Buddy Cole: Piano, Joe Mondragon: Bass, Alvin Stoller: Drums/Vocals, Billy May: Arranger/Conductor.]

Cocktails For Two   (Johnston/Coslow)

Top Hat, White Tie And Tails (Berlin)

Billy May And His Orchestra

Billy May And His Orchestra [LP, Capitol, 2227]

[Musicians: Barney Kessel: Guitar, Manny Klein: Trumpet, John Best: Trumpet, Uan Rasey: Trumpet, Conrad Gozzo: Trumpet, Murray McEarchen: Trombone, Joe Howard: Trombone, Si Zentner: Trombone, Dick Nash: Trombone, Willie Schwartz: Alto Saxophone, Skeets Herfurt: Alto Saxophone, Bob Hardaway: Tenor Saxophone, Fred Falensby: Tenor Saxophone, Chuck Gentry: Baritone Saxophone, Buddy Cole: Piano, Joe Mondragon: Bass, Alvin Stoller: Drums/Vocals, Billy May: Arranger/Conductor.]

Fat Man Mambo (May)

11 September 1951   Los Angeles, USA

Billy May And His Orchestra

Billy May And His Orchestra [LP, Aero Space, 2043]

[Musicians: Barney Kessel: Guitar, Manny Klein: Trumpet, John Best: Trumpet, Uan Rasey: Trumpet, Conrad Gozzo: Trumpet, Murray McEarchen: Trombone, Joe Howard: Trombone, Si Zentner: Trombone, Dick Nash: Trombone, Willie Schwartz: Alto Saxophone, Skeets Herfurt: Alto Saxophone, Ted Nash: Tenor Saxophone, Fred Falensby: Tenor Saxophone, Chuck Gentry: Baritone Saxophone, Buddy Cole: Piano, Joe Mondragon: Bass, Alvin Stoller: Drums/Vocals, Billy May: Arranger/Conductor.]

     Little Brown Jug (Traditional)

---

05 October 1951   Los Angeles, USA

Jerry Gray And His Orchestra

Jerry Gray And His Orchestra [78rp, Decca, DE27839]

[Musicians: Barney Kessel: Guitar, John Best: Trumpet, Conrad Gozzo: Trumpet, Charlie Teagarden: Trumpet, Whitey Thomas: Trumpet, Murray McEarchen: Trombone, Jimmy Priddy: Trombone, George Arus: Trombone, Herbie Harper: Trombone, Willie Schwartz: Alto Saxophone/Clarinet, Riley Weston: Alto Saxophone, Ted Nash: Tenor Saxophone, Dave Harris: Tenor Saxophone, John Rotella: Baritone Saxophone, Jimmy Rowles: Piano, Morty Corb: Bass, Alvin Stoller: Drums, Tommy Traynor/Guilda: Vocals, The Skylarks: Vocals, Tony Gray: Vocals/Accordion.]

     I Was Never Loved By Anyone
     Turn Back The Hands Of Time

Jerry Gray And His Orchestra

Jerry Gray And His Orchestra [78rp, Decca, DE28435]

[Musicians: Barney Kessel: Guitar, John Best: Trumpet, Conrad Gozzo: Trumpet, Charlie Teagarden: Trumpet, Whitey Thomas: Trumpet, Murray McEarchen: Trombone, Jimmy Priddy: Trombone, George Arus: Trombone, Herbie Harper: Trombone, Willie Schwartz: Alto Saxophone/Clarinet, Riley Weston: Alto Saxophone, Ted Nash: Tenor Saxophone, Dave Harris: Tenor Saxophone, John Rotella: Baritone Saxophone, Jimmy Rowles: Piano, Morty Corb: Bass, Alvin Stoller: Drums, Tommy Traynor/Guilda: Vocals, The Skylarks: Vocals, Tony Gray: Vocals/Accordion.]

     Bess, You Is My Woman (Gershwin/Gershwin)

---

25 November 1951   Los Angeles, USA

Oscar Peterson

Oscar Peterson Piano Power [CD, Proper Records, Proper Box 94-4CD]
College Album Oscar Peterson [LP, Verve, MGV8341]

[Musicians: Barney Kessel: Guitar, Oscar Peterson: Piano, Ray Brown: Bass.]

     It's Easy To Remember (Rodgers/Hart)
     Love For Sale (Porter)
     Pooper
     Turtle Neck
     Until The Real Thing Comes Along (Chaplin/Cahn/Holiner/Nichols)

---

12 December 1951   Los Angeles, USA

Billy May And His Orchestra

Billy May Orchestra [LP, Capitol, C80216]
Billy May Orchestra Studio Recordings 1951-1953 [CD, Jasmine, JASCD 399]

[Musicians: Barney Kessel: Guitar, Manny Klein: Trumpet, John Best: Trumpet, Uan Rasey: Trumpet, Conrad Gozzo: Trumpet, Murray McEarchen: Trombone, Ed Kusby: Trombone, Si Zentner: Trombone, Jimmy Priddy: Trombone, Wilbur Schwartz: Alto Saxophone, Skeets Herfurt: Alto Saxophone, Ted Nash: Tenor Saxophone, Fred Falensby: Tenor Saxophone, Chuck Gentry: Baritone Saxophone, Buddy Cole: Piano, Phil Stephens: Bass, Alvin Stoller: Drums/Vocals, Billy May: Leader/Arranger, Maytimers: Vocal Group.]

     Charmaine (Rapee/Pollack)
     Orchids In The Moonlight (Youmans/Kahn/Eliscu)
     When I Take My Sugar To Tea (Fain/Kahal/Norman)

07 January 1952   Los Angeles, USA

Billy May And His Orchestra
Billy May Orchestra [LP, Capitol, C80216]
Billy May Orchestra Studio Recordings 1951-1953 [CD, Jasmine, JASCD 399]

[Musicians: Barney Kessel: Guitar, Manny Klein: Trumpet, John Best: Trumpet, Uan Rasey: Trumpet, Conrad Gozzo: Trumpet, Murray McEarchen: Trombone, Ed Kusby: Trombone, Si Zentner: Trombone, Ray Sims: Trombone, Wilbur Schwartz: Alto Saxophone, Skeets Herfurt: Alto Saxophone, Ted Nash: Tenor Saxophone, Fred Falensby: Tenor Saxophone, Chuck Gentry: Baritone Saxophone, Buddy Cole: Piano, Phil Stephens: Bass, Alvin Stoller: Drums/Vocals, Billy May: Leader/Arranger, Ensemble: Vocal Group, Liz Tilton: Vocals.]

- Always (Berlin)
- Silver And Gold (Prichard/Sharbutt/Crosby)
- There Is No Greater Love (Jones/Symes)
- Unforgettable (Gordon)

---

01 February 1952 [Estimated]   New York, USA

Oscar Peterson
Romance [CD, Verve, POCJ-2573]

[Musicians: Barney Kessel: Guitar, Oscar Peterson: Vocals & Piano, Ray Brown: Bass.]

- But Not For Me (Gershwin/Gershwin)
- Too Marvellous For Words (Mercer/Whiting)

---

08 February 1952   Los Angeles, USA

Billy May And His Orchestra
Billy May And His Orchestra [LP, Aero Space, 2043]
Billy May Orchestra Studio Recordings 1951-1953 [CD, Jasmine, JASCD 399]

[Musicians: Barney Kessel: Guitar, Manny Klein: Trumpet, John Best: Trumpet, Uan Rasey: Trumpet, Conrad Gozzo: Trumpet, Murray McEarchen: Trombone, Ed Kusby: Trombone, Si Zentner: Trombone, Joe Howard: Trombone, Wilbur Schwartz: Alto Saxophone, Les Robinson: Alto Saxophone, Ted Nash: Tenor Saxophone, Fred Falensby: Tenor Saxophone, Chuck Gentry: Baritone Saxophone, Buddy Cole: Piano, Don Whitaker: Bass, Remo Belli: Drums, Billy May: Leader/Arranger.]

- My Last Affair

Billy May And His Orchestra
The Best Of Billy May [LP, Capitol, MFP 3609]
Billy May Orchestra Studio Recordings 1951-1953 [CD, Jasmine, JASCD 399]

[Musicians: Barney Kessel: Guitar, Manny Klein: Trumpet, John Best: Trumpet, Uan Rasey: Trumpet, Conrad Gozzo: Trumpet, Murray McEarchen: Trombone, Ed Kusby: Trombone, Si Zentner: Trombone, Joe Howard: Trombone, Wilbur Schwartz: Alto Saxophone, Les Robinson: Alto Saxophone, Ted Nash: Tenor Saxophone, Fred Falensby: Tenor Saxophone, Chuck Gentry: Baritone Saxophone, Buddy Cole: Piano, Don Whitaker: Bass, Remo Belli: Drums, Billy May: Leader/Arranger.]

- Mayhem (May)
- My Last Affair (Johnson)
- Please Be Kind (Cahn/Chaplin)
- When Your Lover Has Gone (Swan)

---

15 February 1952   Los Angeles, USA

Billy May And His Orchestra
The Best Of Billy May [LP, Capitol, MFP 3609]
Billy May Orchestra Studio Recordings 1951-1953 [CD, Jasmine, JASCD 399]

[Musicians: Barney Kessel: Guitar, Manny Klein: Trumpet, John Best: Trumpet, Uan Rasey: Trumpet, Conrad Gozzo: Trumpet, Murray McEarchen: Trombone, Ed Kusby: Trombone, Si Zentner: Trombone, Jimmy Priddy: Trombone, Willie Schwartz: Alto Saxophone, Les Robinson: Alto Saxophone, Ted Nash: Tenor Saxophone, Fred Falensby: Tenor Saxophone, Bob Dawes: Baritone Saxophone, Buddy Cole: Piano, Don Whitaker: Bass, Remo Belli: Drums, Billy May: Leader/Arranger.]

- Diane (Rapee/Pollack)
- Perfidia (Dominguez/Leeds)

Tenderly   (Gross/Lawrence)
You're Driving Me Crazy (Donaldson)

22 February 1952 [Estimated]   Los Angeles, USA

Billy May And His Orchestra

Billy May And His Orchestra [LP, Capitol, 2218]

[Musicians: Barney Kessel: Guitar, Manny Klein: Trumpet, John Best: Trumpet, Uan Rasey: Trumpet, Conrad Gozzo: Trumpet, Murray McEarchen: Trombone, Ed Kusby: Trombone, Si Zentner: Trombone, Francis Howard: Trombone, Willie Schwartz: Alto Saxophone, Les Robinson: Alto Saxophone, Ted Nash: Tenor Saxophone, Fred Falensby: Tenor Saxophone, Bob Dawes: Baritone Saxophone, Buddy Cole: Piano, Dan Whitaker: Bass, Remo Belli: Drums, Billy May: Arranger/Conductor, Johnny Mercer: Vocals.]

   Memphis In June

[Musicians: Barney Kessel: Guitar, Manny Klein: Trumpet, John Best: Trumpet, Uan Rasey: Trumpet, Conrad Gozzo: Trumpet, Murray McEarchen: Trombone, Ed Kusby: Trombone, Si Zentner: Trombone, Joe Howard: Trombone, Wilbur Schwartz: Alto Saxophone, Les Robinson: Alto Saxophone, Ted Nash: Tenor Saxophone, Fred Falensby: Tenor Saxophone, Bob Dawes: Baritone Saxophone, Buddy Cole: Piano, Don Whitaker: Bass, Remo Belli: Drums, Billy May: Leader/Arranger, Johnny Mercer: Vocals.]

   Hello Out There

25 February 1952   Los Angeles, USA

Maynard Ferguson Orchestra

Maynard Ferguson Orchestra [LP, Mercury, 5819]
Maynard Ferguson Orchestra [LP, Mercury, 5863]
Band Ain't Draggin [CD, Fresh Sound, FSRCD 2204]

[Musicians: Barney Kessel: Guitar, Maynard Ferguson: Trumpet, Chico Alvarez: Trumpet, Shorty Rogers: Trumpet, Herbie Harper: Trombone, Milt Bernhart: Trombone, Dick Kenny: Trombone, Abe Most: Alto Saxophone, Bud Shank: Alto Saxophone, Jimmy Giuffre: Tenor Saxophone, Bob Gordon: Baritone Saxophone, Frank Patchen: Piano, Joe Mondragon: Bass, Shelly Manne: Drums, Kay Brown: Vocals, Pete Rugolo: Arranger.]

   And So I Waited Around (Altman/Kaye)
   Homing Pidgeon (Drake/Shirl/Jerome)
   Roses All The Way (Carpenter/Weber)
   Wow! (Rogers)

26 February 1952   Los Angeles, USA

Oscar Peterson

Oscar Peterson Quartet [LP, ARS, G415]

[Musicians: Barney Kessel: Guitar, Oscar Peterson: Piano, Ray Brown: Bass, Alvin Stoller: Drums.]

   Tea for Two (Youmans/Caesar/Harbach)

Oscar Peterson

Oscar Peterson Quartet [LP, Metronome, 0040.198]
Oscar Peterson Quartet [LP, Verve, MGV 8072]

[Musicians: Barney Kessel: Guitar, Oscar Peterson: Piano, Ray Brown: Bass, Alvin Stoller: Drums.]

   Body and Soul (Green/Heyman/Sour/Eyton)
   Oh, Lady Be Good (Gershwin/Gershwin)
   Stompin' At The Savoy (Sampson/Webb/Razof/Goodman)
   The Astaire Blues (Peterson)

Oscar Peterson

Oscar Peterson Quartet [LP, Verve, MG 2032]

[Musicians: Barney Kessel: Guitar, Oscar Peterson: Piano, Ray Brown: Bass, Alvin Stoller: Drums.]

   Rough Ridin' (Peterson)

26 March 1952 Los Angeles, USA

Billie Holiday
Billie Holiday - Solitude [CD, Verve, 519 810-2]
Billie Holiday - Volume 1 [LP, Verve Super, 2304 104]
[Musicians: Barney Kessel: Guitar, Billie Holiday: Vocals, Flip Phillips: Tenor Saxophone, Charlie Shavers: Trumpet, Oscar Peterson: Piano, Ray Brown: Bass, Alvin Stoller: Drums.]

- Blue Moon (Rodgers/Hart)
- East of the Sun (Bowman)
- Easy to Love (Porter)
- I Only Have Eyes for You (Dubin/Warren)
- Solitude (Ellington/Mills/DeLange)
- These Foolish Things (Maschwitz/Strachey/Link)
- You Go to My Head (Coots/Gillespie)
- You Turned the Tables on Me (Mitchell/Alter)

---

28 March 1952 Los Angeles, USA

Jerry Gray And His Orchestra
Jerry Gray And His Orchestra [78rp, Decca, DE28141]
[Musicians: Barney Kessel: Guitar, Frank Beach: Trumpet, Conrad Gozzo: Trumpet, Tom Patton: Trumpet, Whitey Thomas: Trumpet, John Halliburton: Trombone, Jimmy Priddy: Trombone, George Arus: Trombone, Herbie Harper: Trombone, Willie Schwartz: Alto Saxophone/Clarinet, Les Robinson: Alto Saxophone, Ted Nash: Tenor Saxophone, Jules Jacobs: Tenor Saxophone, John Rotella: Baritone Saxophone, Sid Hurwitz: Piano, Harry Babasin: Bass, Alvin Stoller: Drums, Tommy Traynor: Vocals, Tony Gray: Vocals/Accordion.]

- Pittsburgh, Pennsylvania (Merrill)
- Somewhere Along The Way (Gallop/Adams)

Jerry Gray And His Orchestra
Jerry Gray And His Orchestra [LP, Decca, DL8101]
[Musicians: Barney Kessel: Guitar, Frank Beach: Trumpet, Conrad Gozzo: Trumpet, Tom Patton: Trumpet, Whitey Thomas: Trumpet, John Halliburton: Trombone, Jimmy Priddy: Trombone, George Arus: Trombone, Herbie Harper: Trombone, Willie Schwartz: Alto Saxophone/Clarinet, Les Robinson: Alto Saxophone, Ted Nash: Tenor Saxophone, Jules Jacobs: Tenor Saxophone, John Rotella: Baritone Saxophone, Sid Hurwitz: Piano, Harry Babasin: Bass, Alvin Stoller: Drums, Tommy Traynor: Vocals, Tony Gray: Vocals/Accordion.]

- The Darktown Strutter's Ball (Brooks)

---

01 April 1952 Los Angeles, USA

Billie Holiday
Billie Holiday - Solitude [CD, Verve, 519 810-2]
Billie Holiday - Volume 2 [LP, Verve Super, 2304 109]
[Musicians: Barney Kessel: Guitar, Billie Holiday: Vocals, Flip Phillips: Tenor Saxophone, Charlie Shavers: Trumpet, Oscar Peterson: Piano, Ray Brown: Bass, Alvin Stoller: Drums.]

- Autumn in New York (78rpm take) (Duke)
- Autumn in New York (LP take) (Duke)
- Everything I Have is Yours (Adamson/Lane)
- If the Moon Turns Green (Coates/Hanighen)
- Love for Sale (Porter)
- Moonglow (Hudson/DeLange/Mills)
- Remember (Berlin)
- Tenderly (Lawrence/Gross)

10 June 1952   Los Angeles, USA

Flip Phillips and His Orchestra

Swinging with Flip [LP, Contact, ST1019]

[Musicians: Barney Kessel: Guitar, Charlie Shavers: Trumpet, Flip Phillips: Tenor Saxophone, Oscar Peterson: Piano, Ray Brown: Bass, Alvin Stoller: Drums.]

- Blues For The Midgets (Phillips)
- Cottontail (Ellington)
- If I Had You (Campbell)
- What Is This Thing Called Love? (Porter)

---

30 June 1952 [Estimated]   Los Angeles, USA

Ella Fitzgerald

Ella Fitzgerald [LP, Curcio, GJ 96]

[Musicians: Barney Kessel: Guitar, Ella Fitzgerald: Vocals, Flip Phillips: Tenor Saxophone, Oscar Peterson: Piano, Ray Brown: Bass, J.C. Heard: Drums.]

- Lester Leaps In (Young)

---

01 July 1952 [Estimated]   Los Angeles, USA

Charlie Parker

Charlie Parker Jam Session [CD, Verve, 833 564-2]
Norman Granz Jam Session [LP, Verve, MGC 601]
Legendary 1952 Jam Sessions [CD, Definitive, DRCD 11254]

[Musicians: Barney Kessel: Guitar, Charlie Shavers: Trumpet, Benny Carter: Alto Saxophone, Charlie Parker: Alto Saxophone, Johnny Hodges: Alto Saxophone, Flip Phillips: Tenor Saxophone, Ben Webster: Tenor Saxophone, Oscar Peterson: Piano, Ray Brown: Bass, J.C. Heard: Drums.]

- Ballad Medley: All The Things You Are (Kern/Hammerstein)
  - Dearly Beloved (Kern)
  - Everything Happens To Me (Dennis/Adair)
  - I'll Get By (Ahlert/Turk)
  - Isn't It Romantic? (Rodgers/Hart)
  - Someone To Watch Over Me (Gershwin/Gershwin)
  - The Man I Love (Gershwin/Gershwin)
  - The Nearness Of You (Carmichael/Washington)
  - What's New (Haggert/Burke)
- Funky Blues (Hodges)
- Jam Blues (Shrdlu)
- What Is This Thing Called Love (Porter)

---

14 July 1952   Los Angeles, USA

Billy Eckstine

Everything I Have Is Yours [CD, Verve, 819 442-2]

[Musicians: Barney Kessel: Guitar, Bobby Tucker: Piano, Red Callender: Bass, Lee Young: Drums, Billy Eckstine: Vocals.]

- If You Could See Me Now (Dameron/Sigman)
- One for My Baby (and One More for the Road) (Arlen/Mercer)
- Tenderly (Gross/Lawrence)

20 July 1952 [Estimated]   Los Angeles, USA

Charlie Barnet

Charlie Barnet and his Orchestra [LP, World Record Club, TP 303]

[Musicians: Barney Kessel: Guitar, Al Porcino: Trumpet, Dick Sherman: Trumpet, Bill Castagino: Trumpet, Ken Hanna: Trumpet, Charlie Barnet: Alto, Soprano & Tenor Saxophones, Dick Paladino: Alto Saxophone, Shelly Gold: Alto Saxophone, Al Cohn: Tenor Saxophone, Ray Norman: Tenor Saxophone, Don Davidson: Baritone Saxophone, Dick Kenny: Trombone, Owen Marshall: Trombone, Hank Jones: Piano, Ed Sanfranski: Bass, Don Lamond: Drums.]

     Rhubarb (Cohn)
     Swingin' Down The Lane (Kahn/Jones)

---

22 July 1952 [Estimated]   Los Angeles, USA

Billy Eckstine

Billy Eckstine with the Bobby Tucker Quartet [LP, MGM, 2353.122]

[Musicians: Barney Kessel: Guitar, Billy Eckstine: Vocals, Bobby Tucker: Piano, Red Callender: Bass, Lee Young: Drums.]

     Baby Won't You Say You Love Me
     Because You're Mine (Brodszky/Cahn)
     Kiss Of Fire (Allen/Hill)
     More Than You Know (Youmans/Eilscu/Rose)
     Over The Rainbow (Arlen/Harburg)
     People Will Say We're In Love (Rodgers/Hammerstein)
     So Far
     Wonder Why

---

23 July 1952   Los Angeles, USA

Billy Eckstine

Everything I Have Is Yours [CD, Verve, 819 442-2]

[Musicians: Barney Kessel: Guitar, Bobby Tucker: Piano, Red Callender: Bass, Lee Young: Drums, Billy Eckstine: Vocals.]

     April in Paris (Duke/Harburg)
     Ill Wind (You're Blowin' Me No Good) (Arlen/Koehler)
     Laura (Mercer/Raskin)
     Mister You've Gone and Got the Blues (Eckstine/Russell)
     Smoke Gets in Your Eyes (Kern)

---

01 August 1952 [Estimated]   Los Angeles, USA

Benny Carter

Alone Together [LP, Verve, 2304512]
Alone Together [CD, Verve, POCJ 2136]

[Musicians: Barney Kessel: Guitar, Oscar Peterson: Piano, Ray Brown: Bass, Buddy Rich: Drums, Benny Carter: Alto Saxophone, Unknown: String Section.]

     Alone Together (Schwartz/Dietz)
     Bewitched, Bothered And Bewildered (Rodgers/Hart)
     Cocktails For Two (Coslow/Johnston)
     Isn't It Romantic? (Rodgers/Hart)
     Key Largo (Carter/Worth/Suessdorf)
     'Round Midnight (Monk/Hanighen/Williams)
     Some Other Spring (Wilson/Herzog)
     These Things You Left Me (Dickenson/Lippman)

'S WONDERFUL SWING
BENNY GOODMAN AND HIS ORCHESTRA
FEATURING
LOUIS BELLSON
JESS STACY
BARNEY KESSEL
ZOOT SIMS
BERNIE PRIVIN
VICTOR BORGE
AND MANY MORE

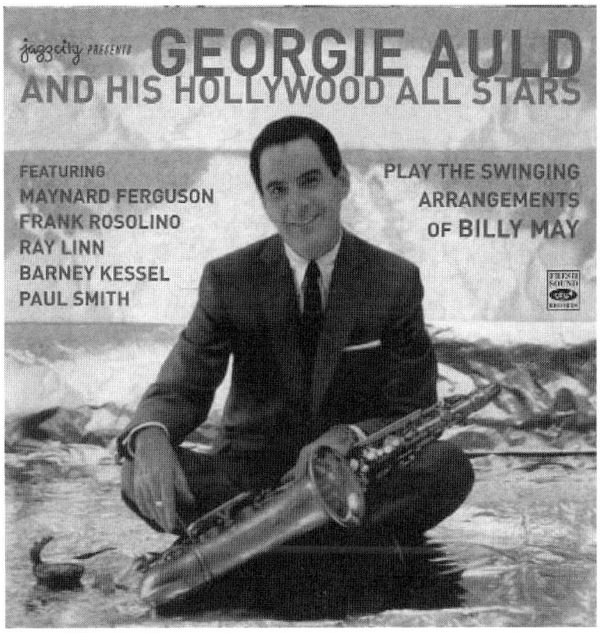
jazzcity PRESENTS
GEORGIE AULD
AND HIS HOLLYWOOD ALL STARS
FEATURING
MAYNARD FERGUSON
FRANK ROSOLINO
RAY LINN
BARNEY KESSEL
PAUL SMITH
PLAY THE SWINGING ARRANGEMENTS OF BILLY MAY

THE CHRONOLOGICAL
JOE BUSHKIN
1940-1946
piano solos
and with Hot Lips Page, Zoot Sims, Cozy Cole,
Specs Powell, Barney Kessel, Al Morgan...
CLASSICS

jazzcity PRESENTS
PETE RUGOLO
AND HIS ORCHESTRA
ADVENTURES IN SOUND
featuring MAYNARD FERGUSON, BUD SHANK
FRANK ROSOLINO, SHELLY MANNE, RAY LINN
DAVE PELL, BARNEY KESSEL, JOHN GRAAS
HOWARD ROBERTS, RUSS FREEMAN
DON FAGERQUIST, MILT BERNHART
ANDRE PREVIN, BOB COOPER

Jack Millman
and his All-Stars
Arrangements by
Shorty Rogers, Jimmy Giuffre,
Johnny Mandel, Bill Holman,
Peter Rugolo, Jack Montrose,
Spud Murphy, Gene Roland,
Gerald Wiggins, Chico Alvarez
and Frank Erickson

The Candoli Brothers Sextet
Jazz Horizons
Featuring
Pete & Conte Candoli, Jimmy Rowles, Barney Kessel, Joe Mondragon

SHORTY ROGERS
featuring: ART PEPPER - JIMMY GIUFFRE - HAMPTON HAWES - SHELLY MANNE
BUD SHANK - JIMMY ROWLES - PETE JOLLY - BOB ENEVOLDSEN - LOU LEVY
HARRY EDISON - BARNEY KESSEL - HERB GELLER - BILL HOLMAN
DON BAGLEY - LEROY VINNEGAR - GENE ENGLUND and others
"Just a Few"
1951
1956
GIANTS OF JAZZ

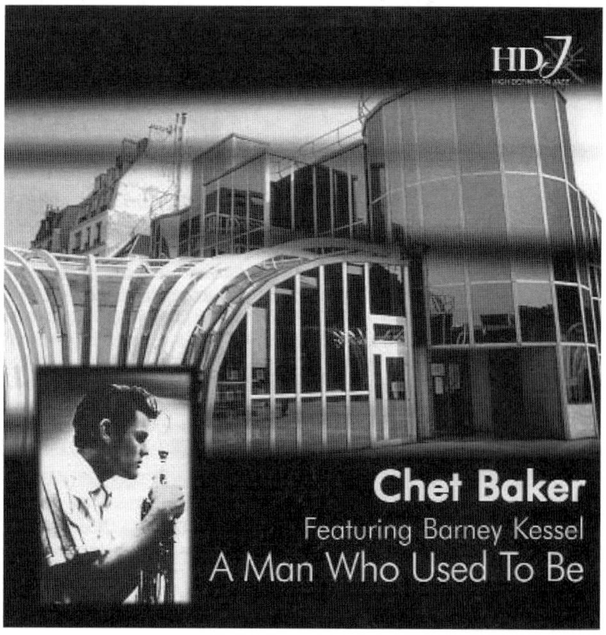
HDJ
Chet Baker
Featuring Barney Kessel
A Man Who Used To Be

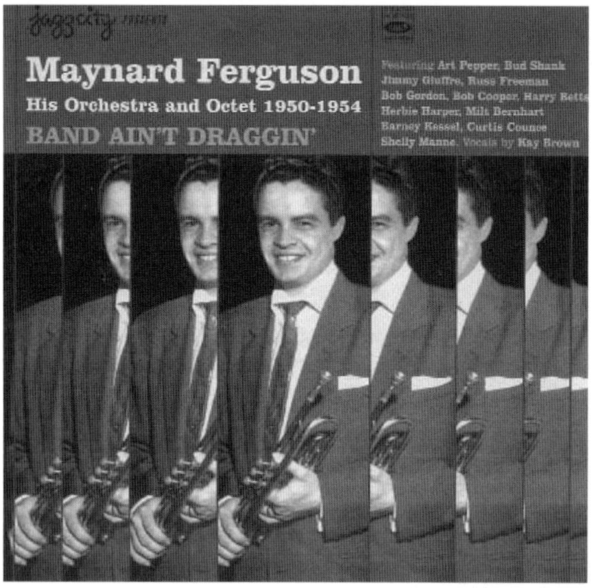
Maynard Ferguson
His Orchestra and Octet 1950-1954
BAND AIN'T DRAGGIN'
Art Pepper, Bud Shank
Jimmy Giuffre, Russ Freeman
Bob Gordon, Bob Cooper, Harry Betts
Herbie Harper, Milt Bernhart
Barney Kessel, Curtis Counce
Shelly Manne. Vocals by Kay Brown

PAUL
SMITH
THE GOOD
LIFE
With Monty Budwig,
Frank Capp
& Barney Kessel

MOOD FOR 12
PAUL WESTON
Two Classic Albums from
PAUL WESTON
SOLO MOOD
collectors' choice
MUSIC

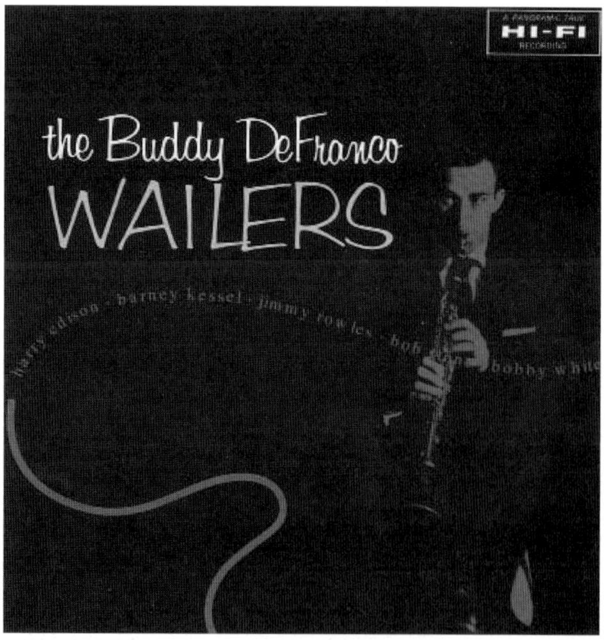
HI-FI
the Buddy DeFranco
WAILERS
harry edison · barney kessel · jimmy rowles · bob
bobby white

13 August 1952   Los Angeles, USA

Jerry Gray And His Orchestra
Jerry Gray And His Orchestra [78rp, Decca, 28382]
[Musicians: Barney Kessel: Guitar, Frank Beach: Trumpet, John Best: Trumpet, Tom Patton: Trumpet, Whitey Thomas: Trumpet, Joe Dolney: Trumpet, Jimmy Priddy: Trombone, George Arus: Trombone, Milt Bernhart: Trombone, John Halliburton: Trombone, Riley Weston: Alto Saxophone, Dale Brown: Alto Saxophone/Clarinet, Bob Cooper: Tenor Saxophone, Dave Harris: Tenor Saxophone, John Rotella: Baritone Saxophone, Jimmy Rowles: Piano, Harry Babasin: Bass, Shelly Manne: Drums, Tony Gray: Vocals/Accordion, The Skylarks: Vocals.]

    On Brave Old Army Team

Jerry Gray And His Orchestra
Jerry Gray And His Orchestra [78rp, Decca, DL8101]
[Musicians: Barney Kessel: Guitar, Frank Beach: Trumpet, John Best: Trumpet, Tom Patton: Trumpet, Whitey Thomas: Trumpet, Joe Dolney: Trumpet, Jimmy Priddy: Trombone, George Arus: Trombone, Milt Bernhart: Trombone, John Halliburton: Trombone, Riley Weston: Alto Saxophone, Dale Brown: Alto Saxophone/Clarinet, Bob Cooper: Tenor Saxophone, Dave Harris: Tenor Saxophone, John Rotella: Baritone Saxophone, Jimmy Rowles: Piano, Harry Babasin: Bass, Shelly Manne: Drums, Tony Gray: Vocals/Accordion, The Skylarks: Vocals.]

    Anchors Aweigh (Traditional)

Jerry Gray And His Orchestra
Jerry Gray And His Orchestra [LP, Decca, DL8101]
[Musicians: Barney Kessel: Guitar, Frank Beach: Trumpet, John Best: Trumpet, Tom Patton: Trumpet, Whitey Thomas: Trumpet, Joe Dolney: Trumpet, Jimmy Priddy: Trombone, George Arus: Trombone, Milt Bernhart: Trombone, John Halliburton: Trombone, Riley Weston: Alto Saxophone, Dale Brown: Alto Saxophone/Clarinet, Bob Cooper: Tenor Saxophone, Dave Harris: Tenor Saxophone, John Rotella: Baritone Saxophone, Jimmy Rowles: Piano, Harry Babasin: Bass, Shelly Manne: Drums, Tony Gray: Vocals/Accordion, The Skylarks: Vocals.]

    Jurame

---

13 September 1952   New York, USA

JATP Jam Session
JATP Carnegie Hall Concert [LP, Columbia, 33CX10010]
[Musicians: Barney Kessel: Guitar, Roy Eldridge: Trumpet, Charlie Shavers: Trumpet, Benny Carter: Alto Saxophone, Flip Phillips: Tenor Saxophone, Lester Young: Tenor Saxophone, Oscar Peterson: Piano, Ray Brown: Bass, Buddy Rich: Drums.]

    Cottontail (Ellington)

Oscar Peterson
JATP Carnegie Hall Concert [LP, Verve, 2683063]
JATP Carnegie Hall Concert [CD, Giant Steps/Cherry Red, GSCR011]
[Musicians: Barney Kessel: Guitar, Oscar Peterson: Piano, Ray Brown: Bass.]

    C Jam Blues (Ellington)
    Cheek to Cheek (Berlin)
    Seven Come Eleven (Christian/Goodman)
    Sweet Georgia Brown (Pinkard/Bernie/Casey)
    Tenderly (Lawrence/Gross)

Gene Krupa and Buddy Rich
The Drum Battle At JATP [CD, Verve, 559 810-2]
[Musicians: Barney Kessel: Guitar, Gene Krupa: Drums, Buddy Rich: Drums, Roy Eldridge: Trumpet, Charlie Shavers: Trumpet, Benny Carter: Alto Saxophone, Flip Phillips: Tenor Saxophone, Lester Young: Tenor Saxophone, Oscar Peterson: Piano, Ray Brown: Bass, Ella Fitzgerald: Vocals.]

    Perdido (Tizol)

Benny Carter - Roy Eldridge - Charlie Shavers
The Trumpet Battle at JATP 1952 [LP, Verve, VRV 2]
[Musicians: Barney Kessel: Guitar, Roy Eldridge: Trumpet, Charlie Shavers: Trumpet, Benny Carter: Alto Saxophone, Flip Phillips: Tenor Saxophone, Lester Young: Tenor Saxophone, Oscar Peterson: Piano, Ray Brown: Bass, Buddy Rich: Drums.]

    Jam Session Blues (Ad Lib)
    The Ballad Medley: Cocktails For Two (Coslow/Johnston)

I Can't Get Started (Duke/Gershwin)
It's The Talk Of The Town (Symes/Neiburg/Livingston)
Summertime (Gershwin)
Sweet Lorraine (Burwell/Parrish)
The Trumpet Battle (Ad Lib)

18 September 1952   New York, USA

Benny Carter

Alone Together [LP, Verve, 2304512]
Alone Together [CD, Verve, POCJ 2136]
Benny Carter Cosmopolite [CD, Verve, 314-521673-2]
[Musicians: Barney Kessel: Guitar, Oscar Peterson: Piano, Ray Brown: Bass, Buddy Rich: Drums, Benny Carter: Alto Saxophone.]

Gone With The Wind (Magidson/Wrubel)
I Got It Bad And That Ain't Good (Ellington/Webster)
I've Got The World On A String (Arlen/Koehler)
Long Ago And Far Away (Kern/Gershwin)

Benny Carter

Benny Carter Cosmopolite [CD, Verve, 314-521673-2]
[Musicians: Barney Kessel: Guitar, Oscar Peterson: Piano, Ray Brown: Bass, Buddy Rich: Drums, Benny Carter: Alto Saxophone.]

Gone With The Wind (Alt) (Magidson/Wrubel)
I Got It Bad (and That Ain't Good) (Alt) (Kennedy/Webster)
I've Got The World On A String (Alt) (Arlen/Koehler)
Long Ago (And Far Away) (Alt) (Kern/Gershwin)

01 November 1952 [Estimated]   Los Angeles, USA

Oscar Peterson

Oscar Peterson Plays George Gershwin [CD, Verve, 529 698-2]
Oscar Peterson Plays The George Gershwin Songbook [LP, Verve, 823 249-1]
[Musicians: Barney Kessel: Guitar, Ray Brown: Bass, Oscar Peterson: Piano.]

A Foggy Day (Gershwin/Gershwin)
Fascinating Rhythm (Gershwin/Gershwin)
I Got Rhythm (Gershwin/Gershwin)
I Was Doing All Right (Gershwin/Gershwin)
It Ain't Necessarily So (Gershwin/Gershwin)
I've Got A Crush On You (Gershwin/Gershwin)
Love Walked In (Gershwin/Gershwin)
Oh, Lady, Be Good! (Gershwin/Gershwin)
'S Wonderful (Gershwin/Gershwin)
Somebody Loves Me (Gershwin/Gershwin)
Strike Up The Band (Gershwin/Gershwin)
The Man I Love (Gershwin/Gershwin)

20 November 1952 [Estimated]   Los Angeles, USA

Oscar Peterson

Oscar Peterson Plays Cole Porter [LP, Clef, MGC 603]
Oscar Peterson Plays Cole Porter [LP, MFP, MFP 1025]
[Musicians: Barney Kessel: Guitar, Oscar Peterson: Piano, Ray Brown: Bass.]

- Anything Goes (Porter)
- Begin the Beguine (Porter)
- Every Time We Say Goodbye (Porter)
- I Love You (Porter)
- In the Still of the Night (Porter)
- I've Got You Under My Skin (Porter)
- Just One of Those Things (Porter)
- Let's Do It (Porter)
- Love for Sale (Porter)
- Night and Day (Porter)
- So Near Yet So Far (Porter)
- What is This Thing Called Love (Porter)

---

24 November 1952 [Estimated]   Los Angeles, USA

Oscar Peterson

Oscar Peterson Plays Duke Ellington [LP, Columbia, 33CX10012]
Oscar Peterson Plays Duke Ellington [LP, Verve, MGC 606]
Oscar Peterson Plays Duke Ellington [CD, Verve, 559 785-2]
[Musicians: Barney Kessel: Guitar, Oscar Peterson: Piano, Ray Brown: Bass.]

- Cottontail (Ellington)
- Do Nothin' Til You Hear From Me (Ellington/Russell)
- Don't Get Around Much Anymore (Ellington/Russell)
- I Got It Bad (and That Ain't Good) (Ellington/Webster)
- In a Mellow Tone (Ellington)
- John Hardy's Wife (Mercer Ellington)
- Just A-sittin' and A-rockin' (Ellington/Strayhorn/Gaines)
- Prelude to a Kiss (Ellington/Mills/Gordon)
- Rockin' in Rhythm (Ellington)
- Sophisticated Lady (Ellington/Parish/Mills)
- Take the "A" Train (Strayhorn)
- Things Ain't What They Used To Be (Mercer Ellington)

---

26 November 1952 [Estimated]   Los Angeles, USA

Oscar Peterson

Oscar Peterson Plays Irving Berlin [LP, Clef, MGC 604]
Oscar Peterson Plays Irving Berlin [LP, Barclay, GLP 6952]
[Musicians: Barney Kessel: Guitar, Oscar Peterson: Piano, Ray Brown: Bass.]

- Alexander's Ragtime Band (Berlin)
- Always (Berlin)
- Blue Skies (Berlin)
- Cheek to Cheek (Berlin)
- Easter Parade (Berlin)
- How Deep is the Ocean (Berlin)

If I Had You (Berlin)
Isn't It a Lovely Day (Berlin)
I've Got My Love to Keep Me Warm (Berlin)
Remember (Berlin)
Say It Isn't So (Berlin)
The Song is You (Berlin)

28 November 1952   New York, USA

Lester Young

The President Plays with the Oscar Peterson Trio [CD, Verve, 831 670-2]
Lester Young - Pres, Teddy & Oscar [LP, Verve, 2-2502]

[Musicians: Barney Kessel: Guitar, Lester Young: Tenor Saxophone, Oscar Peterson: Piano, Ray Brown: Bass, J.C. Heard: Drums.]

Ad Lib Blues (Young/Peterson)
Almost Like Being In Love (Lerner/Loewe)
I Can't Get Started (Gershwin/Gershwin)
I Can't Give You Anything But Love (Fields/McHugh)
I'm Confessin' (Neilburg/Reynolds/Daugherty)
Indiana (Hanley/MacDonald)
Just You, Just Me (Greer/Klages)
On The Sunny Side Of The Street (McHugh/Fields)
Stardust (Carmichael)
Tea For Two (Youmans/Caesar)
There Will Never Be Another You (Warren/Gordon)
These Foolish Things (Link/Strachey/Marvell)

[Musicians: Barney Kessel: Guitar, Lester Young: Tenor Saxophone/Vocal, Oscar Peterson: Piano, Ray Brown: Bass, J.C. Heard: Drums.]

(It Takes) Two To Tango (Hoffman)

01 December 1952 [Estimated]   Los Angeles, USA

Fred Astaire

The Astaire Story [CD, Verve, 835 649-2]
The Astaire Story [LP, Verve, 2610 056]

[Musicians: Barney Kessel: Guitar, Ray Brown: Bass, Fred Astaire: Vocals, Flip Phillips: Tenor Saxophone, Charlie Shavers: Trumpet, Oscar Peterson: Piano, Alvin Stoller: Drums.]

A Fine Romance (Kern)
Cheek to Cheek (Berlin)
Dancing In The Dark (Dietz/Schwartz)
Fascinating Rhythm (Gershwin/Gershwin)
Fast Dances (Ad Lib)
I Concentrate On You (Porter)
I Love Louisa (Schwartz)
I Used To Be Color Blind (Berlin)
I Won't Dance (Kern)
I'm Putting All My Eggs In One Basket (Berlin)
Isn't This A Lovely Day (Berlin)
I've Got My Eyes On You (Porter)
Let's Call The Whole Thing Off (Gershwin/Gershwin)
Lovely To Look At (Kern)
Medium Dance (Ad Lib)

    New Sun In The Sky (Dietz/Schwartz)
    Nice Work If You Can Get It (Gershwin/Gershwin)
    Night And Day (Porter)
    No Strings (Berlin)
    Puttin' On The Ritz (Berlin)
    'S Wonderful (Gershwin/Gershwin)
    Slow Dances (Ad Lib)
    Steppin' Out With My Baby (Berlin)
    The Carioca (Youmans)
    The Continental (Conrad/Magidson)
    The Way You Look Tonight (Kern)
    They All Laughed (Gershwin/Gershwin)
    Top Hat, White Tie And Tails (Berlin)

Fred Astaire

The Astaire Story* [CD, Verve, 835 649-2]
[Musicians: Barney Kessel: Guitar, Ray Brown: Bass, Fred Astaire: Vocals, Flip Phillips: Tenor Saxophone, Charlie Shavers: Trumpet, Oscar Peterson: Piano, Alvin Stoller: Drums.]

    A Foggy Day (Gershwin/Gershwin)
    A Needle In A Haystack (Conrad)
    Change Partners (Berlin)
    I'm Building Up To An Awful Let Down (Astaire)
    Jam Session (Instrumental) (Ad Lib)
    Not My Girl (Astaire)
    Oh, Lady Be Good (Gershwin/Gershwin)
    So Near Yet So Far (Porter)
    They Can't Take That Away From Me (Gershwin/Gershwin)
    You're Easy To Dance With (Berlin)

---

04 December 1952   New York, USA

Benny Carter

Benny Carter Cosmopolite [CD, Verve, 314-521673-2]
[Musicians: Barney Kessel: Guitar, Ray Brown: Bass, J.C. Heard: Drums, Oscar Peterson: Piano, Benny Carter: Alto Saxophone.]

    I Get A Kick Out Of You (Porter)
    Imagination (Van Heusen)
    Pick Yourself Up (Kern)
    Street Scene (Newman)

---

13 December 1952   New York, USA

Roy Eldridge

Dale's Wail [LP, Verve, VE-2-2531]
[Musicians: Barney Kessel: Guitar, Roy Eldridge: Trumpet, Oscar Peterson: Organ, Ray Brown: Bass, J.C. Heard: Drums.]

    Little Jazz (Eldridge/Harding)
    Rockin' Chair (Carmichael)
    Roy's Riff (Eldridge)
    Wrap Your Trouble in Dreams (Barnes/Koehler/Moll)

13 January 1953   **Los Angeles, USA**

June Christy

This is June Christy [LP, Capitol, T 1006]
[Musicians: Barney Kessel: Guitar, June Christy: Vocals, Uan Rasey: Trumpet, Shorty Rogers: Trumpet, Joe Triscari: Trumpet, Harry Betts: Trombone, Tommy Pederson: Trombone, Si Zentner: Trombone, Gus Bivona: Alto Saxophone, Bud Shank: Alto Saxophone, Bob Cooper: Tenor Saxophone, Ted Nash: Tenor Saxophone, Chuck Gentry: Baritone Saxophone, Milt Raskin: Piano, Phil Stephens: Bass, Alvin Stoller: Drums, Pete Rugolo: Arranger/Conductor.]

    Great Scott

    I Lived When I Met You

---

19 January 1953   **New York, USA**

Oscar Peterson

Oscar Peterson & Art Tatum [LP, Session Disc, SR 120]
[Musicians: Barney Kessel: Guitar, Oscar Peterson: Piano, Ray Brown: Bass, Charlie Shavers: Trumpet.]

    Heat Wave (Berlin)

    You Go To My Head (Coots/Gillespie)

[Musicians: Barney Kessel: Guitar, Oscar Peterson: Piano, Ray Brown: Bass.]

    Sidewalks Of New York (East Side, West Side) (Blake/Lawler)

    Swinging 'Till The Girls Come Home

---

23 January 1953   **New York, USA**

Oscar Peterson

Oscar Peterson & Art Tatum [LP, Session Disc, SR 120]
[Musicians: Barney Kessel: Guitar, Oscar Peterson: Piano, Ray Brown: Bass.]

    Body And Soul (Green/Heyman/Sour/Eyton)

    The Man I Love (Gershwin/Gershwin)

---

26 January 1953   **New York, USA**

Oscar Peterson

Canadian Keys [LP, Alto, AL 718]
[Musicians: Barney Kessel: Guitar, Oscar Peterson: Piano, Ray Brown: Bass.]

    Surrey With The Fringe On Top (Rodgers/Hammerstein)

    Tenderly (Lawrence/Gross)

    The Continental (Magidson/Conrad)

---

03 March 1953   **Paris, France**

Lester Young

Prez's Hat [LP, Philology, 214 W 6]
[Musicians: Barney Kessel: Guitar, Lester Young: Tenor Saxophone, Oscar Peterson: Piano, Ray Brown: Bass, J.C. Heard: Drums.]

    Blues In C (Young)

    I Cover The Waterfront (Heyman/Green)

    Lester Leaps In (Young)

    These Foolish Things (Marvell/Strachey/Link)

14 March 1953　　　　　　　　　　　　**Lausanne, Switzerland**

Oscar Peterson
JATP Lausanne 1953 [CD, TCB, TCB-114450]
[Musicians: Barney Kessel: Guitar, Oscar Peterson: Piano, Ray Brown: Bass, J.C. Heard: Drums, Ella Fitzgerald: Vocals, Lester Young: Tenor Saxophone, Charlie Shavers: Trumpet.]

　　Lester Leaps In (Young)

[Musicians: Barney Kessel: Guitar, Oscar Peterson: Piano, Ray Brown: Bass, J.C. Heard: Drums, Ella Fitzgerald: Vocals.]

　　A Tisket - A Tasket (Fitzgerald/Alexander)
　　It's Only A Paper Moon (Arlen)
　　Lady Be Good (Gershwin/Gershwin)
　　Someone To Watch Over Me (Gershwin/Gershwin)
　　St. Louis Blues (Handy)
　　Why Don't You Do Right (Lee)
　　You Belong To Me (King/Stewart/Price)

[Musicians: Barney Kessel: Guitar, Oscar Peterson: Piano, Ray Brown: Bass.]

　　My Heart Stood Still (Rodgers/Hart)
　　Oscar's Tune (Peterson)
　　The Continental   (Magidson)
　　The Man I Love (Gershwin/Gershwin)
　　The Surrey With The Fringe On Top (Rodgers/Hammerstein)

Oscar Peterson
Oscar Peterson & Friends [CD, TCB, TCB-02162]
[Musicians: Barney Kessel: Guitar, Oscar Peterson: Piano, Ray Brown: Bass, J.C. Heard: Drums, Willie Smith: Alto Saxophone, Lester Young: Tenor Saxophone, Charlie Shavers: Trumpet.]

　　C - Jam Blues (Ellington)
　　Cottontail (Ellington)
　　Dark Eyes (Traditional)
　　Idaho (Stone)
　　Medley - I Cover The Waterfront (Green/Heyman)
　　　　Indian Summer (Herbert)
　　　　Isn't This A Lovely Day (Berlin)
　　Tea For Two (Youmans)

---

20 April 1953　　　　　　　　　　　　**New York, USA**

Roy Eldridge
Dale's Wail [LP, Verve, VE-2-2531]
[Musicians: Barney Kessel: Guitar, Roy Eldridge: Trumpet, Oscar Peterson: Organ, Ray Brown: Bass, Jo Jones: Drums.]

　　Dale's Wail (Eldridge)
　　Love for Sale (Porter)
　　Oscar's Arrangement (Eldridge)
　　The Man I Love (Gershwin/Gershwin)

---

24 April 1953　　　　　　　　　　　　**Chicago, USA**

Oscar Peterson
At The Blue Note Chicago [CD, Jazz Band, EBCD 2111-2]
[Musicians: Barney Kessel: Guitar, Ray Brown: Bass, Oscar Peterson: Piano.]

　　Heat Wave (Berlin)
　　Mood (Peterson)

The Man I Love (Gershwin/Gershwin)

01 May 1953 — Chicago, USA

Oscar Peterson

At The Blue Note Chicago [CD, Jazz Band, EBCD 2111-2]
[Musicians: Barney Kessel: Guitar, Ray Brown: Bass, Oscar Peterson: Piano.]

Anything Goes (Porter)
Heat Wave (Berlin)
The Continental (Magidson/Conrad)

21 May 1953 — New York, USA

Ben Webster

King Of The Tenors [CD, Verve, 519 806-2]
[Musicians: Barney Kessel: Guitar, Ben Webster: Tenor Saxophone, Oscar Peterson: Piano, Ray Brown: Bass, J.C. Heard: Drums.]

Bounce Blues (Alt) (Webster)
Bounce Blues (Webster)
Cottontail (Ellington)
Danny Boy (Weatherly)
Poutin' (Webster)

Oscar Peterson

Romance [LP, Verve, 2304.473]
Oscar Peterson Sings [LP, Verve, MGC 145]
Romance [CD, Verve, POCJ-2573]
[Musicians: Barney Kessel: Guitar, Oscar Peterson: Vocals & Piano, Ray Brown: Bass.]

Autumn In New York (Duke)
I Can't Give You Anything But Love (McHugh/Fields)
I Hear Music (Lane/Loesser)
I'm Glad There Is You (Madeira/Dorsey)
One For My Baby (And One More For The Road) (Mercer/Arlen)
Polka Dots And Moonbeams (Burke/Van Heusen)
Spring Is Here (Rodgers/Hart)
The Things We Did Last Summer (Styne/Cahn)

23 July 1953 — Los Angeles, USA

Barney Kessel

Swing Guitars [LP, Verve, MGV8124]
The Barney Kessel Quartet [EP, Clef, EP-182]
The Barney Kessel Quartet [78, Clef, 89054]
[Musicians: Barney Kessel: Guitar, Jimmy Wyble: Guitar, Marty Corb: Bass, Shelly Manne: Drums.]

All The Things You Are (Kern)
Crazy Rhythm (Caesar/Meyer/Kahn)
East Of The Sun (Bowman)
Heat Wave (Berlin)

14 August 1953   Los Angeles, USA

June Christy

June Christy [CD, Capitol, CP32-5307 (Japan)]

[Musicians: Barney Kessel: Guitar, June Christy: Vocals, Maynard Ferguson: Trumpet, Conrad Gozzo: Trumpet, Shorty Rogers: Trumpet, Jimmy Zito: Trumpet, Milt Bernhart: Trombone, Herbie Harper: Trombone, Tommy Pederson: Trombone, George Roberts: Trombone, Gus Bivona: Alto Saxophone, Bud Shank: Alto Saxophone, Bob Cooper: Tenor Saxophone, Ted Nash: Tenor Saxophone, Chuck Gentry: Baritone Saxophone, Jeff Clarkson: Piano, Joe Mondragon: Bass, Frank Carlson: Drums, Pete Rugolo: Arranger/Conductor.]

    Not I
    Whee Baby
    Why Do You Have To Go Home?
    You're Making Me Crazy

June Christy

Something Cool [CD, Capitol, 7243 5 34069 2 9]
Something Cool [LP, Capitol, T 516]

[Musicians: Barney Kessel: Guitar, June Christy: Vocals, Maynard Ferguson: Trumpet, Conrad Gozzo: Trumpet, Shorty Rogers: Trumpet, Jimmy Zito: Trumpet, Milt Bernhart: Trombone, Herbie Harper: Trombone, Tommy Pederson: Trombone, George Roberts: Trombone, Gus Bivona: Alto Saxophone, Bud Shank: Alto Saxophone, Bob Cooper: Tenor Saxophone, Ted Nash: Tenor Saxophone, Chuck Gentry: Baritone Saxophone, Jeff Clarkson: Piano, Joe Mondragon: Bass, Frank Carlson: Drums, Pete Rugolo: Arranger/Conductor.]

    Something Cool (Barnes)

---

14 September 1953   Los Angeles, USA

Louis Bellson

Louis Bellson - Skin Deep [CD, Verve, 314 559 825-2]
Louis Bellson - Skin Deep [LP, Verve, MGV 8137]

[Musicians: Barney Kessel: Guitar, Harry Edison: Trumpet, Maynard Ferguson: Trumpet, Conrad Gozzo: Trumpet, Ray Linn: Trumpet, Hoyt Bohannon: Trombone, Herbie Harper: Trombone, Tommy Pederson: Trombone, Benny Carter: Alto Saxophone, Willie Smith: Alto Saxophone, Wardell Gray: Tenor Saxophone, Bumps Myers: Tenor Saxophone, Bob Lawson: Baritone Saxophone, Jimmy Rowles: Piano, John Simmons: Bass, Don Redman: Arranger.]

    Caxton Hall Swing (Bellson)
    For Europeans Only (Dameron)
    Phalanges (Terry)
    Skin Deep (Bellson)

---

14 November 1953   Los Angeles, USA

Barney Kessel

Easy Like [LP, Contemporary, C 3511]
Easy Like [CD, Contemporary, OJCCD 153-2]

[Musicians: Barney Kessel: Guitar, Bud Shank: Flute, Arnold Ross: Piano, Harry Babasin: Bass, Shelly Manne: Drums.]

    Bernardo (Kessel)
    Just Squeeze Me (Ellington)
    Tenderly (Lawrence/Gross)
    Vicky's Dream (Kessel)

---

19 December 1953   Los Angeles, USA

Barney Kessel

Easy Like [LP, Contemporary, C 3511]
Easy Like [CD, Contemporary, OJCCD 153-2]

[Musicians: Barney Kessel: Guitar, Bud Shank: Flute, Arnold Ross: Piano, Harry Babasin: Bass, Shelly Manne: Drums.]

    I Let a Song Go Out of My Heart (Ellington)

Lullaby of Birdland (Shearing)

Salute to Charlie Christian (Kessel)

What is There to Say? (Harburg/Duke)

01 February 1954 [Estimated]   Los Angeles, USA

Red Callender

Red Callender Quintet [LP, Cash, 105]

[Musicians: Barney Kessel: Guitar, Red Callender: Bass, Unknown: Organ, Joe Howard: Tenor Saxophone, Unknown: Drums.]

Blue Melody

Dolphin's Theme

01 April 1954   Los Angeles, USA

Anita O'Day

Anita O'Day Swings Cole Porter [CD, Verve, 849 266-2]

[Musicians: Barney Kessel: Guitar, Anita O'Day: Vocals, Arnold Ross: Piano, Monty Budwig: Bass, Jackie Mills: Drums.]

Just One Of Those Things (Porter)

15 April 1954 [Estimated]   Los Angeles, USA

Anita O'Day

An Evening With Anita O'Day [LP, Columbia, 10068]

[Musicians: Barney Kessel: Guitar, Anita O'Day: Vocals, Arnold Ross: Piano, Monty Budwig: Bass, Jackie Mills: Drums.]

Frankie and Johnny (Leighton)

Gypsy In My Soul (Boland)

Just One Of Those Things (Porter)

The Man I Love (Gershwin)

26 May 1954   Los Angeles, USA

Billy May And His Orchestra

Billy May And His Orchestra [LP, Capitol, 2846]

[Musicians: Barney Kessel: Guitar, Conrad Gozzo: Trumpet, Maynard Ferguson: Trumpet, Pete Candoli: Trumpet, Uan Rasey: Trumpet, Manny Klein: Trumpet, Si Zentner: Trombone, Tommy Pederson: Trombone, Murray McEarchen: Trombone, Ed Kusby: Trombone, Willie Schwartz: Alto Saxophone, Skeets Herfurt: Alto Saxophone, Ted Nash: Tenor Saxophone, Chuck Gentry: Baritone Saxophone, Paul Smith: Piano, Joe Mondragon: Bass, Alvin Stoller: Drums.]

Anything Can Happen Mambo

Hernando's Hideaway

Billy May And His Orchestra

Billy May And His Orchestra [LP, Capitol, SAL 9027]

[Musicians: Barney Kessel: Guitar, Conrad Gozzo: Trumpet, Maynard Ferguson: Trumpet, Pete Candoli: Trumpet, Uan Rasey: Trumpet, Manny Klein: Trumpet, Si Zentner: Trombone, Tommy Pederson: Trombone, Murray McEarchen: Trombone, Ed Kusby: Trombone, Willie Schwartz: Alto Saxophone, Skeets Herfurt: Alto Saxophone, Ted Nash: Tenor Saxophone, Chuck Gentry: Baritone Saxophone, Paul Smith: Piano, Joe Mondragon: Bass, Alvin Stoller: Drums.]

La Bomba

Billy May And His Orchestra

The Best Of Billy May [LP, Capitol, MFP 3609]

[Musicians: Barney Kessel: Guitar, Conrad Gozzo: Trumpet, Maynard Ferguson: Trumpet, Pete Candoli: Trumpet, Uan Rasey: Trumpet, Manny Klein: Trumpet, Si Zentner: Trombone, Tommy Pederson: Trombone, Murray McEarchen: Trombone, Ed Kusby: Trombone, Willie Schwartz: Alto Saxophone, Skeets Herfurt: Alto Saxophone, Ted Nash: Tenor Saxophone, Chuck Gentry: Baritone Saxophone, Paul Smith: Piano, Joe Mondragon: Bass, Alvin Stoller: Drums.]

Hi-Fi (May)

189

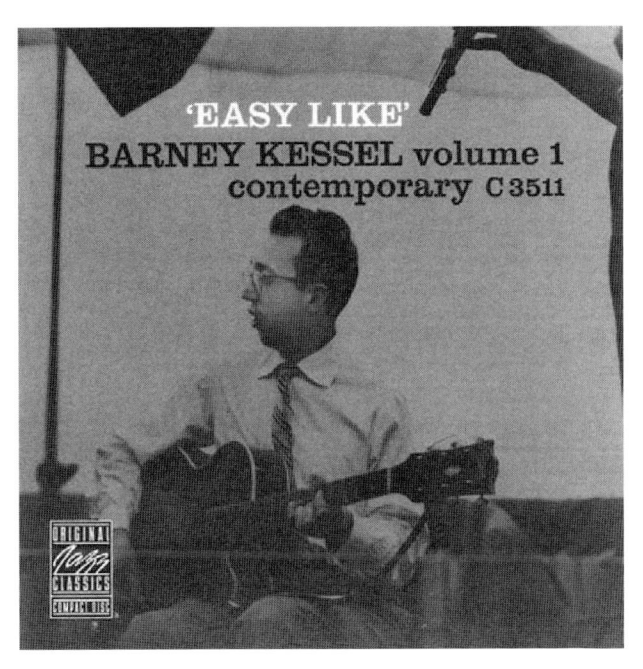

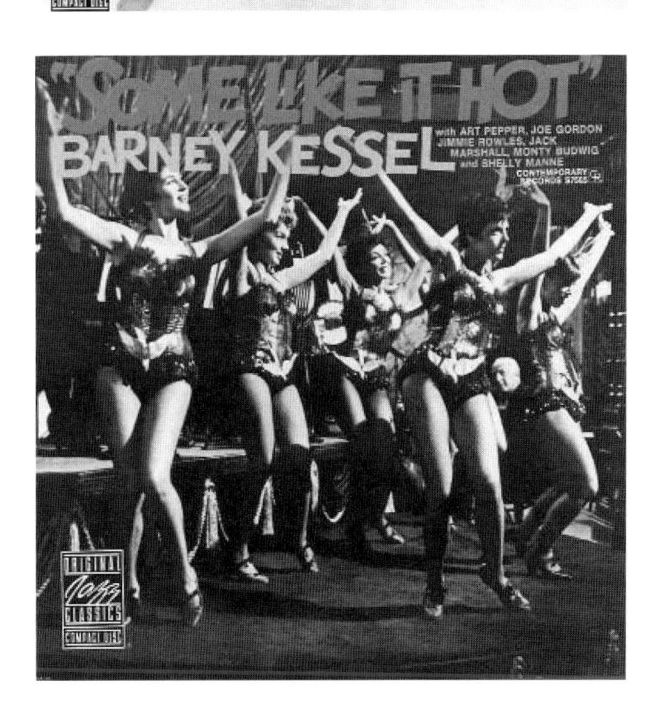

MUSIC TO LISTEN
TO BARNEY KESSEL BY

THE POLL WINNERS: BARNEY KESSEL
WITH SHELLY MANNE AND RAY BROWN
CONTEMPORARY S7535

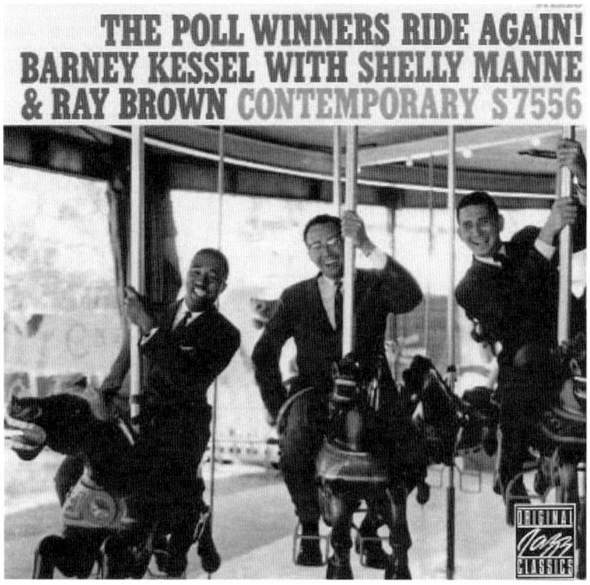
THE POLL WINNERS RIDE AGAIN!
BARNEY KESSEL WITH SHELLY MANNE
& RAY BROWN CONTEMPORARY S7556

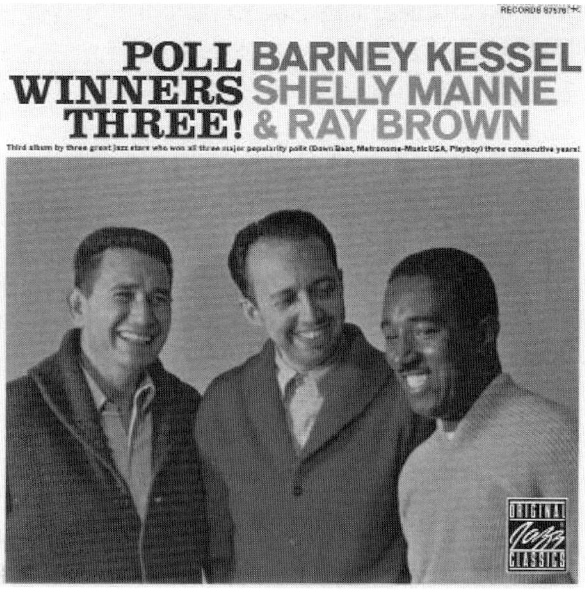
POLL WINNERS THREE!
BARNEY KESSEL
SHELLY MANNE
& RAY BROWN
Third album by three great jazz stars who won all three major popularity polls (Down Beat, Metronome-Music USA, Playboy) three consecutive years!

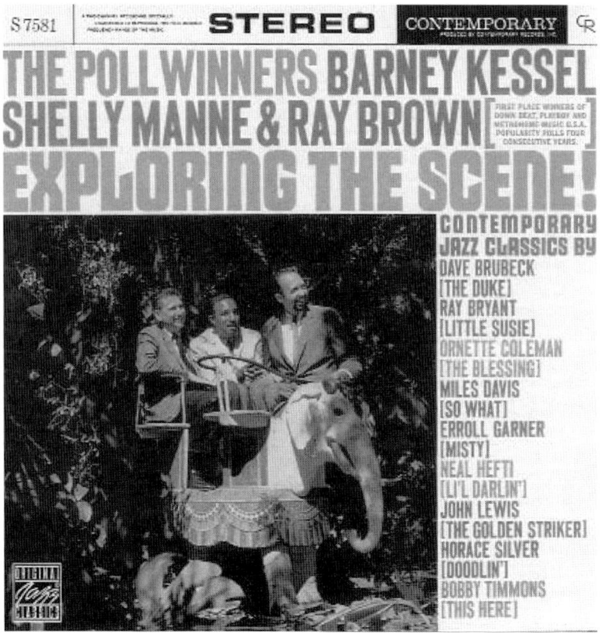
S7581
STEREO
CONTEMPORARY
THE POLL WINNERS BARNEY KESSEL
SHELLY MANNE & RAY BROWN
FIRST PLACE WINNERS OF DOWN BEAT, PLAYBOY AND METRONOME-MUSIC U.S.A. POPULARITY POLLS FOUR CONSECUTIVE YEARS.
EXPLORING THE SCENE!
CONTEMPORARY
JAZZ CLASSICS BY
DAVE BRUBECK
[THE DUKE]
RAY BRYANT
[LITTLE SUSIE]
ORNETTE COLEMAN
[THE BLESSING]
MILES DAVIS
[SO WHAT]
ERROLL GARNER
[MISTY]
NEAL HEFTI
[LI'L DARLIN']
JOHN LEWIS
[THE GOLDEN STRIKER]
HORACE SILVER
[DOODLIN']
BOBBY TIMMONS
[THIS HERE]

CONTEMPORARY
RECORDS S7635
THE POLL WINNERS
STRAIGHT AHEAD
BARNEY KESSEL
RAY BROWN

01 June 1954 [Estimated]   Los Angeles, USA

Johnny Holiday

Johnny Holiday Sings [CD, Contemporary, CCD-14091-2]

[Musicians: Barney Kessel: Guitar, Johnny Holiday: Vocals, Bud Shank: Alto Saxophone, Harry Babasin: Bass, Shelly Manne: Drums, Other Orchestral Musicians: Unidentified, Russ Garcia: Conductor.]

- Baby, Baby All The Time (Troup)
- Come Rain Or Come Shine (Arlen/Mercer)
- I'll Never Be The Same (Malneck/Signorelli/Kahn)
- I'll Never Smile Again (Lowe)
- Julie Is Her Name (Troup)
- Please Remember (Gross/Troup)
- She Does'nt Laugh Like You (Suessdorf/Worth/Carter)
- Speak Low (Weill/Nash)

---

04 June 1954   Los Angeles, USA

Barney Kessel

Barney Kessel Plays Standards [LP, Contemporary, C3512]
Barney Kessel Plays Standards [CD, Contemporary, OJCCD238]

[Musicians: Barney Kessel: Guitar, Bob Cooper: Tenor Saxophone, Claude Williamson: Piano, Monty Budwig: Bass, Shelly Manne: Drums.]

- A Foggy Day (Gershwin/Gershwin)
- On A Slow Boat To China (Loesser)
- Prelude To A Kiss (Ellington)
- Speak Low (Weill/Nash)

---

01 July 1954   Los Angeles, USA

Barney Kessel

Barney Kessel Plays Standards [LP, Contemporary, C3512]
Barney Kessel Plays Standards [CD, Contemporary, OJCCD238]

[Musicians: Barney Kessel: Guitar, Bob Cooper: Tenor Saxophone, Claude Williamson: Piano, Monty Budwig: Bass, Shelly Manne: Drums.]

- 64 Bars on Wilshire Boulevard (Kessel)
- Barney's Blues (Kessel)
- How Long Has This Been Going On (Gershwin/Gershwin)
- Our Love Is Here To Stay (Gershwin/Gershwin)

---

25 August 1954   Los Angeles, USA

Harry Geller

For Cat Dancers Only [LP, RCA, LPM-3228]

[Musicians: Barney Kessel: Guitar, Conrad Gozzo: Trumpet, Maynard Ferguson: Trumpet, Frank Beach: Trumpet, Murray McEachern: Trombone, Milt Bernhardt: Trombone, Pullman Pederson: Trombone, Marshall Cram: Trombone, Jack Dumont: Alto Saxophone, Benny Carter: Alto Saxophone, Freddie Simon: Tenor Saxophone, Bumps Myers: Tenor Saxophone, Marty Berman: Saxophone, Dale Issenhuth: Baritone Saxophone, Paul Smith: Piano, Joe Comfort: Bass, Charles Blackwell: Drums, Harry Geller: Arranger/Conductor, Roselle Gayle: Vocals.]

- Ballin' Boogie
- Stackerlee
- Take All
- The Cats Walk

26 August 1954   Los Angeles, USA

Harry Geller

For Cat Dancers Only [LP, RCA, LPM-3228]

[Musicians: Barney Kessel: Guitar, Conrad Gozzo: Trumpet, Maurice Harris: Trumpet, Frank Beach: Trumpet, Joe Howard: Trombone, Milt Bernhardt: Trombone, Lloyd Ulyate: Trombone, Marshall Cram: Trombone, Jack Dumont: Alto Saxophone, Benny Carter: Alto Saxophone, Freddie Simon: Tenor Saxophone, Bumps Myers: Tenor Saxophone, Ted Nash: Tenor Saxophone, Dale Issenhuth: Baritone Saxophone, Paul Smith: Piano, Joe Comfort: Bass, Charles Blackwell: Drums, Harry Geller: Arranger/Conductor.]

     Pink Champagne
     Please Don't Tease
     Rock-O-Joy
     Zonk

---

03 September 1954   Los Angeles, USA

Billie Holliday

The Complete Billie Holiday 10 CD set [CD, Verve, 517658]

[Musicians: Barney Kessel: Guitar, Billie Holiday: Vocals, Harry Edison: Trumpet, Willie Smith: Alto Saxophone, Bobby Tucker: Piano, Red Callender: Bass, Chico Hamilton: Drums.]

     I Cried For You (Arnheim/Lyman/Freed)
     Love Me or Leave Me (Kahn/Donaldson)
     P.S. I Love You (Jenkins/Mercer)
     Softly
     Stormy Blues
     Too Marvellous for Words (Mercer/Whiting)
     What A Little Moonlight Can Do (Woods)
     Willow Weep For Me (Ronell)

---

11 September 1954   Los Angeles, USA

Shorty Rogers

The Rarest Shorty Rogers [LP, RCA, NL 70110]

[Musicians: Barney Kessel: Guitar, Shorty Rogers: Trumpet, Milt Bernhart: Trombone, Bob Enevoldsen: Trombone, Lennie Niehaus: Alto Saxophone, Bud Shank: Alto Saxophone, Zoot Sims: Tenor Saxophone, Jimmy Giuffre: Tenor Saxophone, Pete Jolly: Piano, Curtis Counce: Bass, Shelly Manne: Drums.]

     Cool Sunshine (Rogers)
     Elaine's Lullaby (Rogers)
     Loki (Rogers)

---

01 October 1954 [Estimated]   Los Angeles, USA

Paul Desmond

Paul Desmond Quartet & Quintet [CD, Fantasy, OJCCD-712-2]
Desmond [LP, Fantasy, LP 321]
Purple Moon [LP, Ember, CJS 814]

[Musicians: Barney Kessel: Guitar, Bob Bates: Bass, Joe Dodge: Drums, Sue Allen: Vocals, Bill Brown: Vocals, Loulie Jean Norman: Vocals, Bernie Parkie: Vocals, Bill Thompson: Vocals, Gloria Wood: Vocals, Paul Desmond: Alto Saxophone.]

     Garden In The Rain (Dyrenforth)
     Soon (Gershwin)
     Winky (Bates)

01 December 1954   Los Angeles, USA

Kid Ory

Kid Ory's Creole Jazz Band [CD, Good Time Jazz, GTCD 12008-2]
Kid Ory's Creole Jazz Band [LP, Good Time Jazz, GTJ L-12008]
[Musicians: Barney Kessel: Guitar, Kid Ory: Trombone, Alvin Alcorn: Trumpet, George Probert: Clarinet, Don Ewell: Piano, Ed Garland: Bass, Minor Hall: Drums.]

- A Closer Walk With Thee (Trad)
- A Good Man Is Hard To Find (Green)
- Copenhagen (Davis)
- Indiana (Hanley)
- Mississippi Mud (Barris)
- Royal Garden Blues (Williams)
- Savoy Blues (Ory)
- Shake That Thing (Jackson)
- Tin Roof Blues (New Orleans Rhythm Kings)

Kid Ory

This Kid's The Greatest! [CD, Good Time Jazz, GTCD 12045-2]
[Musicians: Barney Kessel: Guitar, Alvin Alcorn: Trumpet, George Probert: Clarinet, Don Ewell: Piano, Ed Garland: Bass, Minor Hall: Drums, Kid Ory: Trombone.]

- Ballin' The Jack (Burris)
- Four Or Five Times (Hellmann)
- How Come You Do Me Like You Do (Bergere)

---

01 January 1955 [Estimated]   Los Angeles, USA

Milt Rogers & His Orchestra

The Ultimate In Percussion [LP, Dot, DLP 25319]
[Musicians: Barney Kessel: Guitar, Milt Rogers: Piano, Jack Burger: Bongos & Percussion, Roy Harte: Drums, Ralph Hansell: Vibraphone, Justin Gordon: Reeds, Larry Breen: Bass, Gene Garf: Accordion & Piano, Don Ferris: Organ.]

- Amapola (Lacalle)
- Baia (Barroso)
- Chicago (Fisher)
- Chinatown My Chinatown (Jerome)
- How High The Moon (Hamilton)
- In A Little Spanish Town (Lewis)
- Laura (Raskin)
- On A Slow Boat To China (Loesser)
- Pagan Love Song (Freed)
- Perdido (Tizol)
- Summertime (Gershwin)
- Zing! Went The Strings Of My Heart (Hanley)

---

01 February 1955 [Estimated]   Los Angeles, USA

Karl Keller

The Sonorous Sounds of Karl Keller [LP, Kamak, KAM2003]
[Musicians: Barney Kessel: Guitar, Karl Keller: Hammond Organ, William Caulkins: Flute, Ted Nash: Flute, Emil Richards: Vibraphone/Marimba, Clifford Hills: Bass, Louis Singer: Drums, Carlos Mejia: Latin Percussion.]

- Baubles, Bangles And Beads (Wright/Forrest)
- I Want A Little Girl (Mencher/Moll)
- Indian Love Call (Harbach/Hammerstein)

I've Got A Crush On You (Gershwin/Gershwin)

Lazy Love (Shaffer Smith/Roach)

Misirlou (Roubanis)

Navarak (Shaffer Smith)

Now And Then (Shaffer Smith/Keane)

28 March 1955   Los Angeles, USA

Barney Kessel

To Swing Or Not To Swing [LP, Contemporary, C3513]

To Swing Or Not To Swing [CD, Contemporary, OJCCD317]

[Musicians: Barney Kessel: Guitar, Al Hendrickson: Rhythm Guitar, Red Mitchell: Bass, Jimmy Rowles: Piano, Irv Cottler: Drums.]

Begin The Blues (Kessel)

Don't Blame Me (Fields/McHugh)

Embraceable You (Gershwin)

Midnight Sun (Hampton/Burke)

[Musicians: Barney Kessel: Guitar, Harry Edison: Trumpet, Bill Perkins: Tenor Saxophone, Jimmy Rowles: Piano, Al Hendrickson: Rhythm Guitar, Red Mitchell: Bass, Shelly Manne: Drums.]

Contemporary Blues (Kessel)

Happy Feeling (Kessel)

Wail Street (Kessel)

[Musicians: Barney Kessel: Guitar, Harry Edison: Trumpet, George Auld: Tenor Saxophone, Jimmy Rowles: Piano, Al Hendrickson: Rhythm Guitar, Red Mitchell: Bass, Irv Cottler: Drums.]

12th Street Rag (Bowman)

Indiana (Hanley/Macdonald)

Louisiana (Razaf)

Moten Swing (Moten)

[Musicians: Barney Kessel: Guitar, Red Mitchell: Bass, Al Hendrickson: Rhythm Guitar, Jimmy Rowles: Piano, Irv Cottler: Drums.]

Begin The Blues (Kessel)

13 April 1955   Los Angeles, USA

Claire Austin

When Your Lover Has Gone [CD, Contemporary, OJCCD - 1711-2]

When Your Lover Has Gone [LP, Contemporary, C-5002]

[Musicians: Barney Kessel: Guitar, Claire Austin: Vocals, Bob Scobey: Trumpet, Stan Wrightsman: Piano, Morty Corb: Bass, Shelly Manne: Drums.]

Can't We Talk Over It (Washington/Young)

I'll Never Be The Same (Kahn/Malneck)

My Melancholy Baby (Norton/Wartson/Burnett)

When Your Lover Has Gone (Swan)

21 April 1955   Los Angeles, USA

Kitty White

A New Voice in Jazz [LP, EmArcy, MG36020]

A New Voice in Jazz [CD, Fresh Sound, FSR-CD 465]

[Musicians: Barney Kessel: Guitar, Kitty White: Vocals, George Auld: Tenor Saxophone, Gerald Wiggins: Piano, Red Callender: Bass, Chico Hamilton: Drums.]

Among My Souvenirs (DeSilve/Brown/Henderson)

If You Were Mine (Mercer/Malnek)

Let's Go Around Together (Wright/Ecton)
Out Of This World (Arlen/Mercer)
Porgy (Fields/McHugh)
See Saw (Robinson)
Skylark (Carmichael/Mercer)
So Many Beautiful Men (White/White)
Softly (Beal/Greene)
With Every Breath I Take (Robins/Rayner)
With The Wind And Rain In Your Hair (Lawrence/Edwards)

01 May 1955 [Estimated] Los Angeles, USA

Jackie and Roy

Spring Can Really Hang You Up The Most [CD, Black Lion, BLCD 760904]
Jackie and Roy [LP, Vogue, VA 16011]

[Musicians: Barney Kessel: Guitar, Red Mitchell: Bass, Shelly Manne: Drums, Jackie Cain: Vocals, Roy Kral: Piano.]

Bill's Bit (Holman)
Daahoud (Brown)
I Wish I Were In Love Again (Rodgers)
Lazy Afternoon (Seigmeister)
Let's Take A Walk Around The Block (Arlen)
Listen Little Girl (Landesman)
Lover (Rodgers)
Mine (Gershwin)
Says My Heart (Lane)
Spring Can Really Hang You Up The Most (Landesman)
Tiny Told Me (Kral)
You Smell So Good (Stone)

09 May 1955 Los Angeles, USA

Ray Anthony

Ray Anthony Orchestra [LP, Capitol, 3147]

[Musicians: Barney Kessel: Guitar, Ray Anthony: Trumpet, Zeke Zarchey: Trumpet, Conrad Gozzo: Trumpet, Manny Klein: Trumpet, Uan Rasey: Trumpet, Murray McEarchern: Trombone, Wilbur Schwartz: Trombone, Gus Bivona: Alto Saxophone, Maxwell Davis: Tenor Saxophone, Ted Nash: Tenor Saxophone, Leo Anthony: Baritone Saxophone, Arnold Ross: Piano, Don Simpson: Bass, Alvin Stoller: Drums.]

Learnin' The Blues
Pete Kelly's Blues

Ray Anthony

Ray Anthony Plays Arrangements by George Williams [CD, Lonehill Jazz, LHJ10194]

[Musicians: Barney Kessel: Guitar, Ray Anthony: Trumpet, Zeke Zarchey: Trumpet, Conrad Gozzo: Trumpet, Manny Klein: Trumpet, Uan Rasey: Trumpet, Murray McEarchern: Trombone, Wilbur Schwartz: Trombone, Gus Bivona: Alto Saxophone, Maxwell Davis: Tenor Saxophone, Ted Nash: Tenor Saxophone, Leo Anthony: Baritone Saxophone, Arnold Ross: Piano, Don Simpson: Bass, Alvin Stoller: Drums.]

Swingin' On Campus (Anthony)

17 May 1955 — Los Angeles, USA

Ray Anthony

Ray Anthony Plays Arrangements by George Williams [CD, Lonehill Jazz, LHJ10194]

[Musicians: Barney Kessel: Guitar, Ray Anthony: Trumpet, Zeke Zarchey: Trumpet, Conrad Gozzo: Trumpet, Manny Klein: Trumpet, Uan Rasey: Trumpet, Murray McEarchern: Trombone, Wilbur Schwartz: Trombone, Gus Bivona: Alto Saxophone, Maxwell Davis: Tenor Saxophone, Ted Nash: Tenor Saxophone, Leo Anthony: Baritone Saxophone, Arnold Ross: Piano, Don Simpson: Bass, Alvin Stoller: Drums.]

At Sundown (Donaldson)
If I Had You (Shapiro/Campbell/Connelly)
Pick Yourself Up (Kern/Fields)

18 May 1955 — Los Angeles, USA

Jack Millman

Jazz Studio 4 [LP, Decca, DL 8156]
Jack Millman and his All-Stars [CD, Fresh Sound Records, FSR-CD 502]
Blowing Up A Storm [CD, Progressive, PCD-7085]

[Musicians: Barney Kessel: Guitar, Jack Millman: Trumpet, Jack Montrose: Tenor Saxophone, Maynard Ferguson: Valve Trombone, Buddy Collette: Alto Saxophone, Curtis Counce: Bass, Chico Hamilton: Drums, Frank Flynn: Vibraphone.]

Bambi (Millman)

01 June 1955 — Los Angeles, USA

Ray Anthony

Ray Anthony Plays Arrangements by George Williams [CD, Lonehill Jazz, LHJ10194]

[Musicians: Barney Kessel: Guitar, Ray Anthony: Trumpet, Zeke Zarchey: Trumpet, Conrad Gozzo: Trumpet, Manny Klein: Trumpet, Uan Rasey: Trumpet, Murray McEarchern: Trombone, Wilbur Schwartz: Trombone, Gus Bivona: Alto Saxophone, Maxwell Davis: Tenor Saxophone, Ted Nash: Tenor Saxophone, Leo Anthony: Baritone Saxophone, Arnold Ross: Piano, Don Simpson: Bass, Alvin Stoller: Drums.]

Ain't Misbehavin' (Waller/Brook/Razaf)
Am I Blue? (Akst/Clarke)
I've Found A New Baby (Palmer/Williams)
On The Alamo (Jones/Kahn)

20 June 1955 — California, USA

Howard Rumsey All Stars

Lighthouse At Laguna [LP, Contemporary, C-3509]
Lighthouse At Laguna [CD, Contemporary, OJCCD-406-2]

[Musicians: Barney Kessel: Guitar, Howard Rumsey: Bass, Frank Rosolino: Trombone, Bud Shank: Alto Saxophone, Bob Cooper: Tenor Saxophone, Claude Williamson: Piano, Stan Levey: Drums.]

'Round Midnight (Monk)

01 July 1955 [Estimated] — Los Angeles, USA

Roy Clark

Stringin' Along with the Blues [LP, Capitol, T2535]

[Musicians: Barney Kessel: Guitar, Howard Roberts: Guitar, Earl Palmer: Drums, Red Callender: Bass, Gene Garf: Piano, Roy Clark: Vocals.]

Blues Stay Away From Me (Delmore)
Finger Lickin' (Clark)
Hold It (Butler)
Honky Tonk (Doggett)

I Almost Lost My Mind (Hunter)
Just A Closer Walk With Thee (Traditional)
Overdue Blues, Part VII (Clark)
South (Hayes)
St. Louis Blues (Handy)
The Frankie And Johnnie Blues (Clark)
Turkey In The Straw (Traditional)
Worried Mind (Daffan)

01 August 1955   Los Angeles, USA

Julie London

Julie Is Her Name [CD, EMI, 7-99804-2]
Julie Is Her Name [LP, London, HA-U2005]
Julie Is Her Name [LP, Liberty, LRP 3006]
[Musicians: Barney Kessel: Guitar, Ray Leatherwood: Bass, Julie London: Vocals.]

Can't Help Lovin' That Man (Kern)
Cry Me A River (Hamilton)
Easy Street (Jones)
Gone With The Wind (Magidson/Wrubel)
I Love You (Porter)
I Should Care (Stordahl/Weston/Cahn)
I'm Glad There Is You (Madeira/Dorsey)
I'm In The Mood For Love (Fields/McHugh)
It Never Entered My Mind (Rodgers/Hart)
Laura (Mercer/Raskin)
No Moon At All (Evans/Mann)
'S Wonderful (Gershwin/Gershwin)
Say It Isn't So (Berlin)

02 August 1955   Los Angeles, USA

Art Tatum

Art Tatum [LP, Columbia, 33CX 10115]
[Musicians: Barney Kessel: Guitar, Harry Edison: Trumpet, Lionel Hampton: Vibraphone, Art Tatum: Piano, Red Callender: Bass, Buddy Rich: Drums.]

What Is This Thing Called Love? (Porter)

07 August 1955   Los Angeles, USA

Art Tatum

The Tatum Group Masterpieces * [CD, Pablo, PACD-2405-428-2]
[Musicians: Barney Kessel: Guitar, Red Callender: Bass, Buddy Rich: Drums, Harry Edison: Trumpet, Lionel Hampton: Vibraphone, Art Tatum: Piano.]

September Song (Alt) (Weill/Anderson)
What Is This Thing Called Love (Alt) (Porter)

Art Tatum

The Tatum Group Masterpieces [CD, Pablo, PACD-2405-428-2]
The Tatum Group Masterpieces [LP, Pablo De Luxe, 2310 731]
[Musicians: Barney Kessel: Guitar, Red Callender: Bass, Buddy Rich: Drums, Harry Edison: Trumpet, Lionel Hampton: Vibraphone, Art Tatum: Piano.]

Deep Purple (De Rose/Parish)

Plaid (Edison/Hampton/Tatum)
　　　September Song (Weill/Anderson)
　　　Somebody Loves Me (Gershwin/De Sylva/MacDonald)
　　　Verve Blues (Edison/Hampton/Tatum)
　　　What Is This Thing Called Love (Porter)

---

17 August 1955　　　　　　　　　　**Los Angeles, USA**

The Four Freshmen

The Four Freshmen & Five Trombones [CD, Collectors' Choice Music, 72438-19175-2-7]
The Four Freshmen & Five Trombones [LP, Capitol, SM-11639]

[Musicians: Barney Kessel: Guitar, Frank Rosolino: Trombone, Harry Betts: Trombone, Milt Bernhart: Trombone, Tommy Pederson: Trombone, George Roberts: Trombone, Claude Williamson: Piano, Shelly Manne: Drums, Joe Mondragon: Bass, Bob Flanigan: Vocals, Trombone, Bass, Don Barbour: Vocals, Guitar, Ross Barbour: Vocals, Drums, Ken Errair: Vocals, Trumpet, Bass, Pete Rugolo: Arranger/Conductor.]

　　　Love Is Just Around the Corner (Robin/Gensler)

---

22 August 1955　　　　　　　　　　**Los Angeles, USA**

The Four Freshmen

The Four Freshmen & Five Trombones [CD, Collectors' Choice Music, 72438-19175-2-7]
The Four Freshmen & Five Trombones [LP, Capitol, SM-11639]

[Musicians: Barney Kessel: Guitar, Frank Rosolino: Trombone, Harry Betts: Trombone, Milt Bernhart: Trombone, Tommy Pederson: Trombone, George Roberts: Trombone, Claude Williamson: Piano, Shelly Manne: Drums, Joe Mondragon: Bass, Bob Flanigan: Vocals, Trombone, Bass, Don Barbour: Vocals, Guitar, Ross Barbour: Vocals, Drums, Ken Errair: Vocals, Trumpet, Bass, Pete Rugolo: Arranger/Conductor.]

　　　Angel Eyes (Dennis/Brent)
　　　I Remember You (Schertzinger/Mercer)
　　　Mam'selle (Gordon/Goulding)
　　　Speak Low (Weill/Nash)

---

23 August 1955　　　　　　　　　　**Los Angeles, USA**

Billie Holiday

Music For Torching [CD, Verve, 527 455-2]
Billie Holiday Volume 4 [LP, Verve Super, 2304 114]

[Musicians: Barney Kessel: Guitar, Harry Edison: Trumpet, Benny Carter: Alto Saxophone, Jimmy Rowles: Piano, John Simmons: Bass, Larry Bunker: Drums.]

　　　(I Don't Stand a) Ghost of a Chance (with You) (Young/Crosby/Washington)
　　　I Don't Want to Cry Any More (Schertzinger)
　　　It Had to Be You (Jones/Kahn)
　　　Nice Work if You Can Get It (Gershwin/Gershwin)
　　　Please Don't Talk About Me When I'm Gone (Clare/Stept)
　　　Prelude to a Kiss (Ellington/Mills/Gordon)
　　　When Your Lover Has Gone (Swan)

[Musicians: Barney Kessel: Guitar, John Simmons: Bass, Larry Bunker: Drums, Jimmy Rowles: Piano.]

　　　Gone with the Wind (Magidson/Wrubel)

The Four Freshmen

The Four Freshmen & Five Trombones [CD, Collectors' Choice Music, 72438-19175-2-7]
The Four Freshmen & Five Trombones [LP, Capitol, SM-11639]

[Musicians: Barney Kessel: Guitar, Frank Rosolino: Trombone, Harry Betts: Trombone, Milt Bernhart: Trombone, Tommy Pederson: Trombone, George Roberts: Trombone, Claude Williamson: Piano, Shelly Manne: Drums, Joe Mondragon: Bass, Bob Flanigan: Vocals, Trombone, Bass, Don Barbour: Vocals, Guitar, Ross Barbour: Vocals, Drums, Ken Errair: Vocals, Trumpet, Bass, Pete Rugolo: Arranger/Conductor.]

　　　Guilty (Akst/Kahn/Whiting)

BEST PLUCKING IN TOWN
BARNEY KESSEL
GRANT GREEN
OSCAR MOORE
MUNDELL LOWE

The Tatum Group Masterpieces
ART TATUM
LIONEL HAMPTON
HARRY EDISON
BUDDY RICH
RED CALLENDER
BARNEY KESSEL

Verve
JAZZ AT THE PHILHARMONIC
Oscar Peterson
The Trio Set
BARNEY KESSEL · HERB ELLIS · RAY BROWN

SWING GUITARS
OSCAR MOORE
COLUMBIA
BARNEY KESSEL
TAL FARLOW

SESSIONS, LIVE
BARNEY KESSEL
HARRY BABASIN

reprise
including MOON RIVER and other themes from the film
BREAKFAST AT TIFFANYS
BARNEY KESSEL & HIS MEN

easy
moments

what's new...
BARNEY KESSEL?

BOSSA NOVA
BARNEY
KESSEL
PLUS BIG BAND
reprise

JUNKO
&
BARNEY

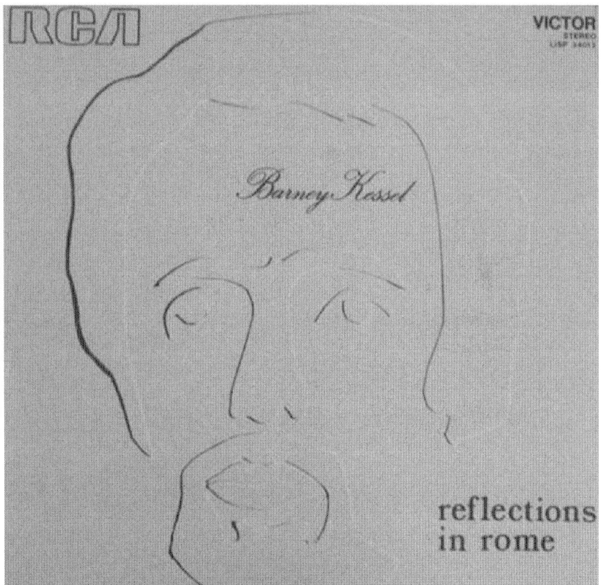
RCA
VICTOR
STEREO
Barney Kessel
reflections
in rome

SHINY STOCKINGS
BARNEY KESSEL
LOB

The Last Time I Saw Paris (Kern/Hammerstein)
You Stepped Out Of A Dream [3] (Brown/Kahn)

25 August 1955   Los Angeles, USA

Billie Holiday

Music For Torching [CD, Verve, 527 455-2]

[Musicians: Barney Kessel: Guitar, Harry Edison: Trumpet, Benny Carter: Alto Saxophone, Jimmy Rowles: Piano, John Simmons: Bass, Larry Bunker: Drums.]

    A Fine Romance (Alt) (Kern)
    A Fine Romance (Master Take) (Kern)
    Come Rain or Come Shine (Mercer/Arlen)
    I Get A Kick out of You (Porter)
    Isn't This a Lovely Day (Berlin)

[Musicians: Barney Kessel: Guitar, Harry Edison: Trumpet, Larry Bunker: Drums, Jimmy Rowles: Piano, John Simmons: Bass.]

    I Got a Right to Sing the Blues (Arlen)

[Musicians: Barney Kessel: Guitar, John Simmons: Bass, Larry Bunker: Drums, Jimmy Rowles: Piano.]

    Everything I Have Is Yours (Burton)
    I Hadn't Anyone till You (Stanley)

[Musicians: Barney Kessel: Guitar, Larry Bunker: Drums, Benny Carter: Alto Saxophone, Jimmy Rowles: Piano, John Simmons: Bass.]

    What's New? (Haggart)

29 August 1955   Los Angeles, USA

The Four Freshmen

The Four Freshmen & Five Trombones [CD, Collectors' Choice Music, 72438-19175-2-7]
The Four Freshmen & Five Trombones [LP, Capitol, SM-11639]

[Musicians: Barney Kessel: Guitar, Frank Rosolino: Trombone, Harry Betts: Trombone, Milt Bernhart: Trombone, Tommy Pederson: Trombone, George Roberts: Trombone, Claude Williamson: Piano, Shelly Manne: Drums, Joe Mondragon: Bass, Bob Flanigan: Vocals, Trombone, Bass, Don Barbour: Vocals, Guitar, Ross Barbour: Vocals, Drums, Ken Errair: Vocals, Trumpet, Bass, Pete Rugolo: Arranger/Conductor.]

    Love (Martin/Blane)
    Our Love Is Here To Stay (Gershwin/Gershwin)
    Somebody Loves Me (Gershwin/Gershwin)
    You Made Me Love You (I Didn't Want To Do It) (McCarthy/Monaco)

01 September 1955   Los Angeles, USA

Buddy Rich & Sweets Edison

Buddy and Sweets [LP, Columbia, 33CX 10080]
Buddy and Sweets [LP, Norgan, MGN 1038]

[Musicians: Barney Kessel: Guitar, Buddy Rich: Drums, Harry Edison: Trumpet, John Simmons: Bass, Jimmy Rowles: Piano.]

    All Sweets (Edison)
    Barney's Bugle (Rich)
    Easy Does It (Oliver)
    Nice Work If You Can Get It (Gershwin/Gershwin)
    Now's The Time (Parker)
    Yellow Rose of Brooklyn (Rich)
    You're Getting To Be A Habit With Me   (Warren)

12 September 1955 — Los Angeles, USA

Barney Kessel

Barney Kessel Plays Standards [LP, Contemporary, C3512]
Barney Kessel Plays Standards [CD, Contemporary, OJCCD238]

[Musicians: Barney Kessel: Guitar, Bob Cooper: Tenor Saxophone, Hampton Hawes: Piano, Red Mitchell: Bass, Chuck Thompson: Drums.]

- I Didn't Know What Time It Was (Rodgers/Hart)
- Jeepers Creepers (Warren/Mercer)
- My Old Flame (Coslow/Johnson)
- You Stepped Out Of A Dream (Brown/Kahn)

---

30 September 1955 — Los Angeles, USA

George Auld

Georgie Auld Orchestra [LP, EmArcy, MG36060]
Georgie Auld and His Hollywood All Stars [CD, Fresh Sounds, FSR2222]

[Musicians: Barney Kessel: Guitar, Maynard Ferguson: Trumpet, Conrad Gozzo: Trumpet, Vito Mangano: Trumpet, Ray Linn: Trumpet, Tommy Pederson: Trombone, Frank Rosolino: Trombone, Si Zentner: Trombone, Skeets Herfurt: Alto Saxophone, Gus Bivona: Alto Saxophone, George Auld: Tenor Saxophone, Babe Russin: Tenor Saxophone, Bob Dawes: Baritone Saxophone, Bob Lawson: Baritone Saxophone, Paul Smith: Piano, Joe Comfort: Bass, Irving Cottler: Drums.]

- If I Loved You (Rodgers/Hammerstein)
- My Blue Heaven (Donaldson/Whiting)
- They Can't Take That Away From Me (Gershwin/Gershwin)

---

06 October 1955 — Los Angeles, USA

Betty Bennett

Nobody Else But Me [LP, Atlantic, 1226]
Betty Bennett/Lurlean Hunter [CD, Collectables, COL-CD-6623]
Shorty Rogers & Andre Previn - In Collaboration [CD, Fresh Sounds, FSR 2227]

[Musicians: Barney Kessel: Guitar, Betty Bennett: Vocals, Shorty Rogers: Trumpet & Flugelhorn, Frank Rosolino: Trombone, Harry Klee: Alto Saxophone, Bob Cooper: Tenor Saxophone, Jimmy Giuffre: Baritone Saxophone, André Previn: Piano, Ralph Pena: Bass, Shelly Manne: Drums.]

- You Took Advantage of Me (Rodgers/Hart)
- My Man's Gone Now (Gershwin/Gershwin)
- Mountain Greenery (Rodgers/Hart)
- You're Driving Me Crazy (Donaldson)

---

07 October 1955 — Los Angeles, USA

Betty Bennett

Nobody Else But Me [LP, Atlantic, 1226]
Betty Bennett/Lurlean Hunter [CD, Collectables, COL-CD-6623]
Shorty Rogers & Andre Previn - In Collaboration [CD, Fresh Sounds, FSR 2227]

[Musicians: Barney Kessel: Guitar, Betty Bennett: Vocals, Shorty Rogers: Trumpet & Flugelhorn, Frank Rosolino: Trombone, Harry Klee: Alto Saxophone, Bob Cooper: Tenor Saxophone, Jimmy Giuffre: Baritone Saxophone, André Previn: Piano, Ralph Pena: Bass, Irv Cottler: Drums.]

- Island in the West Indies (Duke/Gershwin)
- Tomorrow Mountain (Ellington/La Touche)
- Treat Me Rough (Gershwin/Gershwin)
- Sidewalks of Cuba (Oakland/Parish/Mills)

01 November 1955 [Estimated] Los Angeles, USA

Thelma Gracen
Thelma Gracen [LP, EmArcy, MG36096]
[Musicians: Barney Kessel: Guitar, Thelma Gracen: Vocals, Quentin Anderson: Trombone, George Auld: Tenor Saxophone, Lou Levy: Piano, Joe Comfort: Bass, Sid Balkin: Drums.]

- I'll Get By (Turk/Ahlert)
- I'll Never Be The Same (Kahn/Maineck/Signcelli)
- I'll Remember April (Raye/De Paul/Johnston)
- I'm Yours (Mellin)
- Just You, Just Me (Klages/Greer)
- Let There Be Love (Grant/Rand)
- More Than You Know (Youmans/Eilscu/Rose)
- Night And Day (Porter)
- Out Of Nowhere (Heyman/Green)
- People Will Say We're In Love (Rodgers/Hammerstein)
- Solitude (De Lange/Ellington/Mills)
- Tea For Two (Youmans/Caesar/Harbach)

07 November 1955 Los Angeles, USA

George Auld
Georgie Auld Orchestra [LP, EmArcy, MG36060]
Georgie Auld and His Hollywood All Stars [CD, Fresh Sounds, FSR2222]
[Musicians: Barney Kessel: Guitar, Maynard Ferguson: Trumpet, Conrad Gozzo: Trumpet, Mannie Klein: Trumpet, Ray Linn: Trumpet, Tommy Pederson: Trombone, Frank Rosolino: Trombone, Si Zentner: Trombone, Skeets Herfurt: Alto Saxophone, Gus Bivona: Alto Saxophone, George Auld: Tenor Saxophone, Babe Russin: Tenor Saxophone, Bob Dawes: Baritone Saxophone, Chuck Gentry: Baritone Saxophone, Paul Smith: Piano, Joe Comfort: Bass, Irving Cottler: Drums.]

- Dinah (Akst/Young)
- For You (Burke/Dubin)
- In The Land Of Hi-FI (Auld/May)
- Tippin' In (Smith)
- Until The Real Thing Comes Along 1 (Chaplin/Nichols/Cahn/Holiner/Freema

11 November 1955 Los Angeles, USA

George Auld
Georgie Auld Orchestra [LP, EmArcy, MG36060]
Georgie Auld and His Hollywood All Stars [CD, Fresh Sounds, FSR2222]
[Musicians: Barney Kessel: Guitar, Maynard Ferguson: Trumpet, Conrad Gozzo: Trumpet, Vito Mangano: Trumpet, Ray Linn: Trumpet, Tommy Pederson: Trombone, Frank Rosolino: Trombone, Si Zentner: Trombone, Skeets Herfurt: Alto Saxophone, Gus Bivona: Alto Saxophone, George Auld: Tenor Saxophone, Babe Russin: Tenor Saxophone, Bob Dawes: Baritone Saxophone, Chuck Gentry: Baritone Saxophone, Paul Smith: Piano, Joe Comfort: Bass, Irving Cottler: Drums.]

- A Sunday Kind Of Love (Belle/Leonatd/Rhodes/Prima)
- I May Be Wrong (Sullivan/Ruskin)
- Love Is Just Around The Corner (Gensler/Robin)
- Swingin' In The Moore Park (May)

06 December 1955   Los Angeles, USA

Anita O'Day

Anita [LP, Verve, MGV-2000]
Anita O'Day - This is Anita [CD, Verve, 829 261-2]

[Musicians: Barney Kessel: Guitar, Paul Smith: Piano/Celeste, Joe Mondragon: Bass, Alvin Stoller: Drums, Anita O'Day: Vocals.]

- As Long As I Live (Arlen/Koehler)
- Beautiful Love (Young/Van Alstyne/King/Gillespie)
- Fine and Dandy (Swift/James)
- Who Cares? (Gershwin/Gershwin)

---

07 December 1955   Los Angeles, USA

Anita O'Day

Anita [LP, Verve, MGV-2000]
Anita O'Day - This is Anita [CD, Verve, 829 261-2]

[Musicians: Barney Kessel: Guitar, Paul Smith: Piano/Celeste, Joe Mondragon: Bass, Alvin Stoller: Drums, Milt Bernhart: Trombone, Si Zentner: Trombone, Joe Howard: Trombone, Lloyd Elliott: Trombone, Corky Hale: Harp, Unknown: String Section, Anita O'Day: Vocals.]

- A Nightingale Sang in Berkeley Square (Maschwitz/Sherman)
- I Can't Get Started (Duke/Gershwin)
- I Fall In Love Too Easily (Styne/Cahn)
- Time After Time (Styne/Cahn)

---

08 December 1955   Los Angeles, USA

Anita O'Day

Anita [LP, Verve, MGV-2000]
Anita O'Day - This is Anita [CD, Verve, 829 261-2]

[Musicians: Barney Kessel: Guitar, Paul Smith: Piano/Celeste, Joe Mondragon: Bass, Alvin Stoller: Drums, Milt Bernhart: Trombone, Si Zentner: Trombone, Joe Howard: Trombone, Lloyd Elliott: Trombone, Corky Hale: Harp, Unknown: String Section, Anita O'Day: Vocals.]

- Honeysuckle Rose (Waller/Razaf)
- I'll See You In My Dreams (Jones/Kahn)
- No Moon At All (Mann/Evans)
- You're The Top (Porter)

Anita O'Day

Anita O'Day Swings Cole Porter [CD, Verve, 849 266-2]

[Musicians: Barney Kessel: Guitar, Milt Bernhart: Trombone, Lloyd Elliot: Trombone, Si Zentner: Trombone, Joe Howard: Trombone, Paul Smith: Piano, Joe Mondragon: Bass, Alvin Stoller: Drums, Anita O'Day: Vocals.]

- You're The Top (Porter)

---

16 December 1955   Los Angeles, USA

Shorty Rogers

Just A Few [CD, Giants Of Jazz, CD 53208]

[Musicians: Barney Kessel: Guitar, Shorty Rogers: Flugelhorn, Harry Edison: Trumpet, Bud Shank: Alto Saxophone, Pete Jolly: Piano, Leroy Vinnegar: Bass, Shelly Manne: Drums.]

- Blues Way Down There (Rogers)
- Blues Way Up There (Rogers)
- Dickie's Dream (Basie)
- Moten Swing (Moten)

26 January 1956   Los Angeles, USA

Sonny Criss

The Complete Imperial Sessions [CD, Blue Note, 24564]
Sonny Criss Jazz U.S.A. [LP, Liberty, LP 9006]

[Musicians: Barney Kessel: Guitar, Kenny Drew: Piano, Bill Woodson: Bass, Chuck Thompson: Drums, Sonny Criss: Alto Saxophone.]

- Alabamy Bound (Henderson)
- Blue Friday (Criss)
- Criss Cross (Kessel)
- Easy Living (Rainger)
- Ham's Blues (Criss)
- More Than You Know (Youmans)
- Something's Gotta Give (Mercer)
- Sunday (Miller)
- Sweet Georgia Brown (Bernie)
- These Foolish Things (Strachey)
- West Coast Blues (Criss)
- Willow Weep For Me (Ronnell)

07 February 1956   Los Angeles, USA

Ella Fitzgerald

Ella Fitzgerald Sings The Cole Porter Songbook [CD, Verve, 314 537257 2]

[Musicians: Barney Kessel: Guitar, Ella Fitzgerald: Vocals, Milt Bernhart: Trombone, Joe Howard: Trombone, Pete Candoli: Trumpet, Conrad Gozzo: Trumpet, Harry Edison: Trumpet, Maynard Ferguson: Trumpet, Bud Shank: Alto Saxophone, Ted Nash: Tenor Saxophone, Bob Cooper: Tenor Saxophone, Chuck Gentry: Baritone Saxophone, Paul Smith: Piano, Joe Mondragon: Bass, Alvin Stoller: Drums, Buddy Bregman: Arranger/Conductor, Lloyd Ulyate: Trombone, George Roberts: Bass Trombone, Herb Geller: Alto Saxophone.]

- From This Moment On (Porter)
- It's Alright With Me (Porter)
- Just One Of Those Things (Porter)
- Ridin'High (Porter)
- Too Darn Hot (Porter)

[Musicians: Barney Kessel: Guitar, Ella Fitzgerald: Vocals, Paul Smith: Piano, Joe Mondragon: Bass, Alvin Stoller: Drums.]

- Easy To Love (Porter)
- Get Out Of Town (Porter)

[Musicians: Barney Kessel: Guitar, Ella Fitzgerald: Vocals, Ted Nash: Flute, Bob Cooper: Oboe, Paul Smith: Piano/Celeste, Joe Mondragon: Bass, Alvin Stoller: Drums, Corky Hale: Harp, Unknown: String Section, Misha Russell: Concert Master, Buddy Bregman: Arranger/Conductor.]

- Do I Love You? (Porter)
- Ev'ry Time We Say Goodbye (Porter)
- I Am In Love (Porter)
- I Love Paris (Porter)
- Why Can't You Behave? (Porter)

08 February 1956 Los Angeles, USA

Ella Fitzgerald

Ella Fitzgerald Sings The Cole Porter Songbook [CD, Verve, 314 537257 2]

[Musicians: Barney Kessel: Guitar, Ella Fitzgerald: Vocals, Milt Bernhart: Trombone, Joe Howard: Trombone, Lloyd Ulyate: Trombone, George Roberts: Bass Trombone, Harry Edison: Trumpet, Pete Candoli: Trumpet, Maynard Ferguson: Trumpet, Conrad Gozzo: Trumpet, Chuck Gentry: Baritone Saxophone, Bud Shank & Herb Geller: Alto Saxophones, Bob Cooper: Tenor Saxophone/Oboe, Ted Nash: Tenor Saxophone, Paul Smith: Piano, Joe Mondragon: Bass, Alvin Stoller: Drums & Percussion, Corky Hale: Harp, Buddy Bregman: Arranger/Conductor, Misha Russell Concert Master & Unknown: String Section.]

- Ace In The Hole (Porter)
- All Through The Night (Porter)
- Anything Goes (Porter)
- Begin The Beguine (Porter)
- I'm Always True To You In My Fashion (Porter)
- Love For Sale (Porter)
- You Do Something To Me (Porter)

[Musicians: Barney Kessel: Guitar, Ella Fitzgerald: Vocals, Milt Bernhart: Trombone, Joe Howard: Trombone, Pete Candoli: Trumpet, Conrad Gozzo: Trumpet, Harry Edison: Trumpet, Maynard Ferguson: Trumpet, Bud Shank: Alto Saxophone, Ted Nash: Tenor Saxophone, Chuck Gentry: Baritone Saxophone, Paul Smith: Piano, Joe Mondragon: Bass, Alvin Stoller: Drums, Herb Geller: Alto Saxophone, Bob Cooper: Tenor Saxophone, George Roberts: Bass Trombone, Corky Hale: Harp, Misha Russell Concert Master & Unknown: String Section, Buddy Bregman: Arranger/Conductor.]

- Love For Sale (Porter)

---

09 February 1956 Los Angeles, USA

Ella Fitzgerald

Ella Fitzgerald Sings The Cole Porter Songbook [CD, Verve, 314 537257 2]

[Musicians: Barney Kessel: Guitar, Ella Fitzgerald: Vocals, Milt Bernhart: Trombone, Joe Howard: Trombone, Lloyd Ulyate: Trombone, George Roberts: Bass Trombone, Harry Edison: Trumpet, Pete Candoli: Trumpet, Maynard Ferguson: Trumpet, Conrad Gozzo: Trumpet, Chuck Gentry: Baritone Saxophone, Bud Shank & Herb Geller: Alto Saxophones, Bob Cooper: Tenor Saxophone/Oboe, Ted Nash: Tenor Saxophone, Paul Smith: Piano, Joe Mondragon: Bass, Alvin Stoller: Drums & Percussion, Corky Hale: Harp, Buddy Bregman: Arranger/Conductor, Misha Russell Concert Master & Unknown: String Section.]

- In The Still Of The Night (Porter)

[Musicians: Barney Kessel: Guitar, Ella Fitzgerald: Vocals, Milt Bernhart: Trombone, Joe Howard: Trombone, Lloyd Ulyate: Trombone, George Roberts: Bass Trombone, Paul Smith: Piano, Joe Mondragon: Bass, Alvin Stoller: Drums, Buddy Bregman: Arranger/Conductor.]

- All Of You (Porter)
- Don't Fence Me In (Porter)
- I've Got You Under My Skin (Porter)
- What Is This Thing Called Love? (Porter)

[Musicians: Barney Kessel: Guitar, Ella Fitzgerald: Vocals, Milt Bernhart: Trombone, Joe Howard: Trombone, Pete Candoli: Trumpet, Conrad Gozzo: Trumpet, Harry Edison: Trumpet, Maynard Ferguson: Trumpet, Bud Shank: Alto Saxophone, Ted Nash: Tenor Saxophone, Chuck Gentry: Baritone Saxophone, Paul Smith: Piano, Joe Mondragon: Bass, Alvin Stoller: Drums, Herb Geller: Alto Saxophone, Bob Cooper: Tenor Saxophone, George Roberts: Bass Trombone, Corky Hale: Harp, Misha Russell & Unknown: String Section, Buddy Bregman: Arranger/Conductor.]

- I Concentrate On You (Porter)
- It's De-Lovely (Porter)
- So In Love (Porter)

[Musicians: Barney Kessel: Guitar, Ella Fitzgerald: Vocals, Paul Smith: Piano, Joe Mondragon: Bass, Alvin Stoller: Drums.]

- I Get A Kick Out Of You (Porter)
- Let' Do It (Porter)
- You're The Top (Porter)

14 February 1956   **Los Angeles, USA**

Milt Jackson

Ballads & Blues [CD, Collectables, COL-CD 6257]
Ballads & Blues [LP, London, LTZ-K15064]
[Musicians: Barney Kessel: Guitar, Milt Jackson: Vibraphone, Percy Heath: Bass, Lawrence Marable: Drums.]

- Gerry's Blues (Jackson)
- The Song Is Ended (Berlin)
- These Foolish Things (Link)

---

16 February 1956   **Los Angeles, USA**

Claire Austin

When Your Lover Has Gone [CD, Contemporary, OJCCD - 1711-2]
When Your Lover Has Gone [LP, Contemporary, C-5002]
[Musicians: Barney Kessel: Guitar, Claire Austin: Vocals, Bob Scobey: Trumpet, Stan Wrightsman: Piano, Morty Corb: Bass, Shelly Manne: Drums.]

- Come Rain or Come Shine (Arlen/Mercer)
- I'm Thru With Love (Kahn/Malneck)
- Lover, Come Back To Me (Hammerstein/Romberg)
- Someone To Watch Over Me (Gershwin/Gershwin)
- The House Is Haunted (Rose/Adlam)
- What Is This Thing Called Love? (Porter)

---

23 February 1956   **Los Angeles, USA**

Barney Kessel

Easy Like [CD, Contemporary, OJCCD 153-2]
[Musicians: Barney Kessel: Guitar, Buddy Collette: Flute, Claude Williamson: Piano, Red Mitchell: Bass, Shelly Manne: Drums.]

- Easy Like [Alt] (Kessel)
- North of the Border [Alt] (Kessel)

Barney Kessel

Easy Like [LP, Contemporary, C 3511]
Easy Like [CD, Contemporary, OJCCD-153-2]
[Musicians: Barney Kessel: Guitar, Buddy Collette: Flute, Claude Williamson: Piano, Red Mitchell: Bass, Shelly Manne: Drums.]

- April in Paris (Harburg/Duke)
- Easy Like (Kessel)
- North of the Border (Kessel)
- That's All (Haynes/Brandt)

---

21 March 1956   **Los Angeles, USA**

Nellie Lutcher

Our New Nellie [LP, Liberty, LRP 3014]
Nellie Lutcher [CD, Collectables, COL-CD-2788]
[Musicians: Barney Kessel: Guitar, Nellie Lutcher: Vocals/Piano, Cappy Lewis: Trombone, Red Norvo: Vibraphone, Paul Smith: Piano, Ulysees Livingstone: Guitar, Mike Rubin: Bass, Alvin Stoller: Drums.]

- It Had To Be You   (Kahn/Jones)
- On The Sunny Side Of The Street   (McHugh/Fields)
- Someone To Watch Over Me   (Gershwin/Gershwin)

    The Nearness Of You   (Washington/Carmichael)
    This Can't Be Love   (Rodgers/Hart)

---

27 March 1956   Los Angeles, USA

Ella Fitzgerald

Ella Fitzgerald Sings The Cole Porter Songbook [CD, Verve, 314 537257 2]

[Musicians: Barney Kessel: Guitar, Ella Fitzgerald: Vocals, Milt Bernhart: Trombone, Joe Howard: Trombone, Pete Candoli: Trumpet, Conrad Gozzo: Trumpet, Harry Edison: Trumpet, Maynard Ferguson: Trumpet, Bud Shank: Alto Saxophone, Ted Nash: Tenor Saxophone, Chuck Gentry: Baritone Saxophone, Paul Smith: Piano, Joe Mondragon: Bass, Alvin Stoller: Drums, Herb Geller: Alto Saxophone, Bob Cooper: Tenor Saxophone, George Roberts: Bass Trombone, Corky Hale: Harp, Misha Russell Concert Master & Unknown: String Section, Buddy Bregman: Arranger/Conductor.]

    Night And Day (Porter)

[Musicians: Barney Kessel: Guitar, Ella Fitzgerald: Vocals, Paul Smith: Piano, Joe Mondragon: Bass, Alvin Stoller: Drums.]

    I Concentrate On You (Alternate Take) (Porter)
    Let's Do It (Alternate Take) (Porter)
    You're The Top (Alternate Take) (Porter)

---

01 April 1956 [Estimated]   Los Angeles, USA

Murray Arnold

Overheard In A Cocktail Lounge [LP, American, ALP 102]

[Musicians: Barney Kessel: Guitar, Murray Arnold: Piano, Arthur Netzel: Bass, Carl Maus: Drums.]

    Consternation (Shearing)
    Hurry, Hurry (Arnold/Myrow)
    Moonlight (Conrad)
    Overheard In A Cocktail Lounge (Myrow)

---

11 April 1956   Los Angeles, USA

George Auld

Georgie Auld Orchestra [LP, EmArcy, MG36060]
Georgie Auld and His Hollywood All Stars [CD, Fresh Sounds, FSR2222]

[Musicians: Barney Kessel: Guitar, Maynard Ferguson: Trumpet, Conrad Gozzo: Trumpet, Vito Mangano: Trumpet, Ray Linn: Trumpet, Tommy Pederson: Trombone, Frank Rosolino: Trombone, Milt Bernhardt: Trombone, Skeets Herfurt: Alto Saxophone, Willie Smith: Alto Saxophone, George Auld: Tenor Saxophone, Babe Russin: Tenor Saxophone, Irving Roth: Baritone Saxophone, Bob Lawson: Baritone Saxophone, Paul Smith: Piano, Joe Comfort: Bass, Irving Cottler: Drums.]

    Frankie and Johnny (P.D.)
    Too Marvellous For Words (Whiting/Mercer)

---

12 April 1956   Los Angeles, USA

George Auld

Georgie Auld Orchestra [LP, EmArcy, MG36060]
Georgie Auld and His Hollywood All Stars [CD, Fresh Sounds, FSR2222]

[Musicians: Barney Kessel: Guitar, Maynard Ferguson: Trumpet, Conrad Gozzo: Trumpet, Vito Mangano: Trumpet, Ray Linn: Trumpet, Tommy Pederson: Trombone, Frank Rosolino: Trombone, Milt Bernhardt: Trombone, Skeets Herfurt: Alto Saxophone, Willie Smith: Alto Saxophone, George Auld: Tenor Saxophone, Babe Russin: Tenor Saxophone, Irving Roth: Baritone Saxophone, Bob Lawson: Baritone Saxophone, Paul Smith: Piano, Joe Comfort: Bass, Irving Cottler: Drums.]

    Got A Date With An Angel (Waller/Miller/Gray)
    Old Rockin' Chair (Carmichael)

Rod McKuen with the Barney Kessel Orchestra

Songs For A Lazy Afternoon [LP, Liberty, LR 3011]

[Musicians: Barney Kessel: Guitar, Rod McKuen: Vocals, Tommy Tedesco: Guitar, Unknown: Harmonica, Unknown: Bass, Unknown: Percussion, Unknown: Vocal Group.]

- John Hardy (McKuen)
- Lazy Afternoon (Latouche/Moross)
- Puttin' On The Style (Kessel/McKuen)
- The Birds Courting Song (McKuen)
- With A 'No' That Sounds Like A 'Yes' (Gilkyson)

---

17 April 1956 — Los Angeles, USA

Buddy Collette

Man of Many Parts [CD, Contemporary, OJCCD-239-2]
Man of Many Parts [LP, Contemporary, C3522]

[Musicians: Barney Kessel: Guitar, Buddy Collette: Alto & Tenor Saxophone, clarinet, flute, Ernie Freeman: Piano, Joe Comfort: Bass, Larry Bunker: Drums.]

- Cheryl Ann (Collette)
- Jungle Pipe (Collette)
- St. Andrews Place Blues (Collette)
- Zan (Collette)

---

23 April 1956 — Los Angeles, USA

Earl Bostic

Earl Bostic [LP, King, LP 525]

[Musicians: Barney Kessel: Guitar, Earl Bostic: Alto Saxophone, Elmon Wright: Trumpet, Johnny Coles: Trumpet, Benny Golson: Tenor Saxophone, Larry Bunker: Vibraphone, Stash O'Laughlin: Piano, George Tucker: Bass, Chester Jones: Drums.]

- Harlem Nocturne (Hagen/Rogers)
- I Hear A Rhapsody (Frajos/Gasparre/Baker)
- Roses Of Picardy (Weatherly/Wood)
- Where Or When (Rodgers/Hart)

---

26 April 1956 — Los Angeles, USA

Rod McKuen with the Barney Kessel Orchestra

Songs For A Lazy Afternoon [LP, Liberty, LR 3011]

[Musicians: Barney Kessel: Guitar, Rod McKuen: Vocals, Tommy Tedesco: Guitar, Unknown: Harmonica, Unknown: Bass, Unknown: Percussion, Unknown: Vocal Group.]

- All Around Trinidad (Kessel/McKuen/Rohr)
- Bimini (McKuen)
- Colorado Trail (McKuen)
- Jaydee (McKuen)
- Sinner Man (Holt/Baxter)

---

01 May 1956 [Estimated] — Los Angeles, USA

Dorothy Collins

Songs by Dorothy Collins [LP, Coral, CRL57106]

[Musicians: Barney Kessel: Guitar, Dorothy Collins: Vocals, Unknown: Bass, Unknown: Drums/Vibraphone.]

- But Not For Me (Gershwin/Gershwin)
- Come Rain Or Come Shine (Arlen/Mercer)

Guess I'll Hang My Tears Out To Dry (Styne/Cahn)
Here I Am In Love Again (Charlap/Sweeney)
I See Your Face Before Me (Schwartz/Dietz)
It Never Entered My Mind (Rodgers/Hart)
Out Of This World (Arlen/Mercer)
Sometimes I'm Happy (Youmans/Caesar)
The Lady's In Love With You (Lane/Loesser)
The Sky Fell Down (Heyman/Alter)
When Your Lover Has Gone (Swan)
You Took Advantage of Me (Rodgers/Hart)

---

17 May 1956   Los Angeles, USA

Rod McKuen with the Barney Kessel Orchestra

Songs For A Lazy Afternoon [LP, Liberty, LR 3011]

[Musicians: Barney Kessel: Guitar, Rod McKuen: Vocals, Tommy Tedesco: Guitar, Unknown: Harmonica, Unknown: Bass, Unknown: Percussion, Unknown: Vocal Group.]

Aunt Louise (McKuen)
Follow The Drinking Gourd (Kessel/McKuen)
Happy Is A Boy Named Me (McKuen)

---

19 May 1956   Los Angeles, USA

George Auld

Georgie Auld Orchestra [LP, EmArcy, MG36060]
Georgie Auld and His Hollywood All Stars [CD, Fresh Sounds, FSR2222]

[Musicians: Barney Kessel: Guitar, Maynard Ferguson: Trumpet, Conrad Gozzo: Trumpet, Vito Mangano: Trumpet, Ray Linn: Trumpet, Tommy Pederson: Trombone, Frank Rosolino: Trombone, Milt Bernhardt: Trombone, Skeets Herfurt: Alto Saxophone, Gus Bivona: Alto Saxophone, George Auld: Tenor Saxophone, Babe Russin: Tenor Saxophone, Irving Roth: Baritone Saxophone, Bob Lawson: Baritone Saxophone, Andre Previn: Piano, Joe Comfort: Bass, Irving Cottler: Drums.]

Back Home In Indiana (Hanley/MacDonald)
Rosetta (Hines/Woode)

---

21 May 1956   Los Angeles, USA

Buddy DeFranco

Wailers [LP, Norgran, MGN 1085]
Wailers [CD, Definitive, DRCD11253]

[Musicians: Barney Kessel: Guitar, Buddy DeFranco: Clarinet, Harry Edison: Trumpet, Jimmy Rowles: Piano, Bob Stone: Bass, Bobby White: Drums.]

A Fine Romance (Kern/Fields)
Angel Eyes (Dennis/Brent)
Cheek To Cheek (Berlin)
How Long Has This Been Going On? (Gershwin/Gershwin)
I Won't Dance (Kern/Harbach/Fields/McHugh/Hammerstein)
Let's Call The Whole Thing Off (Gershwin/Gershwin)
Moonlight On The Ganges (Wallace/Myers)
Perfidia (Dominguez/Leeds)
Sweet's Blues (Edison)

211

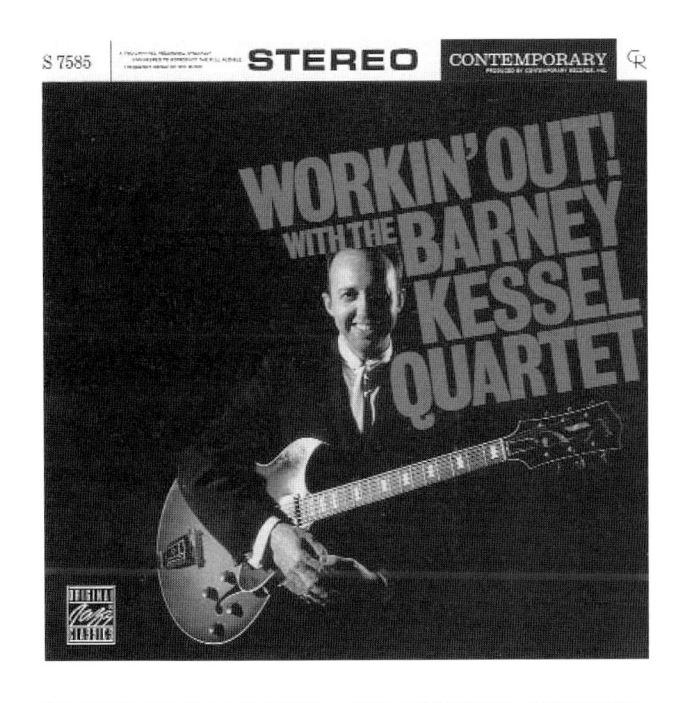

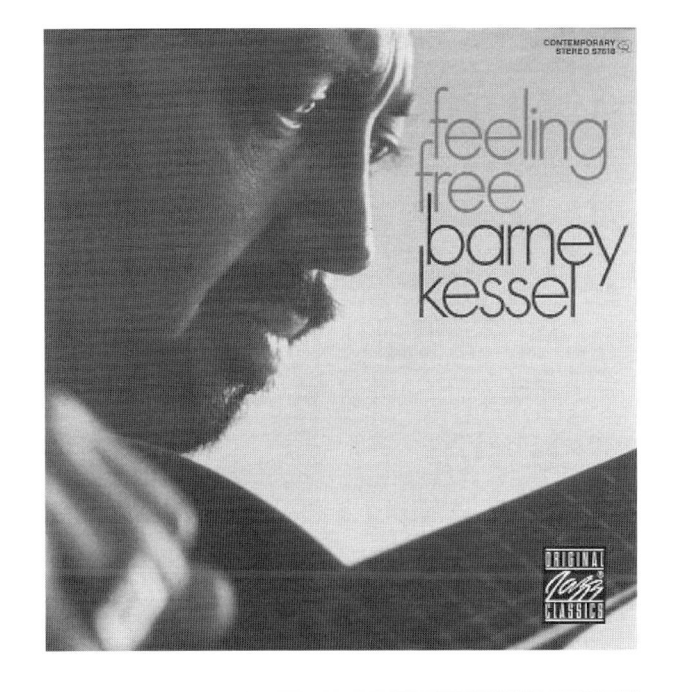

212

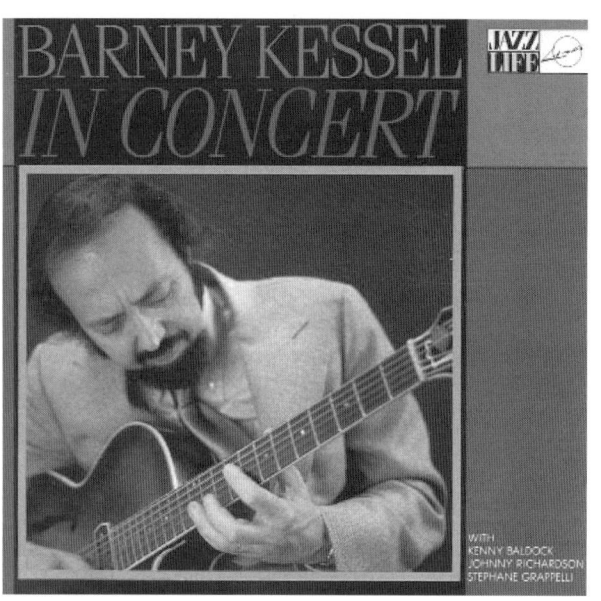

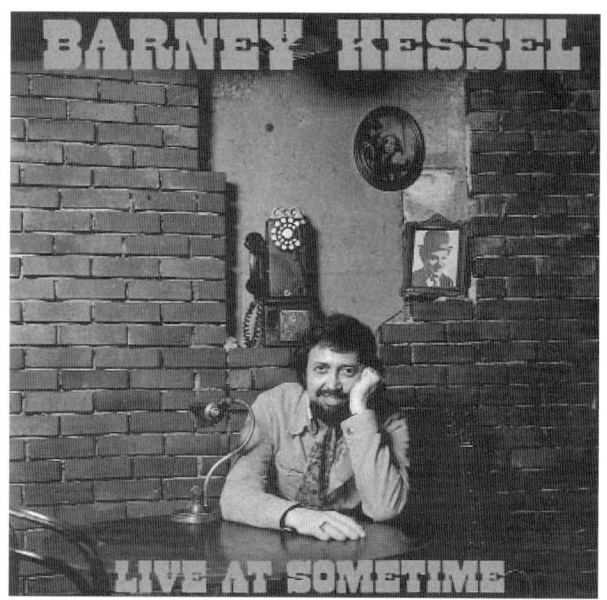

26 May 1956   Los Angeles, USA

George Auld
Georgie Auld Orchestra [LP, EmArcy, MG36060]
Georgie Auld and His Hollywood All Stars [CD, Fresh Sounds, FSR2222]
[Musicians: Barney Kessel: Guitar, Maynard Ferguson: Trumpet, Conrad Gozzo: Trumpet, Vito Mangano: Trumpet, Ray Linn: Trumpet, Tommy Pederson: Trombone, Frank Rosolino: Trombone, Milt Bernhardt: Trombone, Skeets Herfurt: Alto Saxophone, Gus Bivona: Alto Saxophone, George Auld: Tenor Saxophone, Babe Russin: Tenor Saxophone, Irving Roth: Baritone Saxophone, Bob Lawson: Baritone Saxophone, Andre Previn: Piano, Joe Comfort: Bass, Irving Cottler: Drums.]

- Blue Lou (Sampson/Mills)
- I Get A Kick Out Of You (Porter)
- Laura (Raskin/Mercer)
- Prisoners Song (Massey)
- Sweet Lorraine (Burwell/Parish)
- Sweet Sue (Harris/Young)

01 June 1956 [Estimated]   Los Angeles, USA

Earl Grant
Earl Grant [45EP, Prince Records, PR1202X]
[Musicians: Barney Kessel: Guitar, Earl Grant: Vocals, Gerald Wiggins: Piano, Joe Comfort: Bass, Irv Cottler: Drums.]

- Moonlight In Vermont (Blackburn/Suessdorf)

Earl Grant
Earl Grant [45EP, Prince Records, PR1202Y]
[Musicians: Barney Kessel: Guitar, Earl Grant: Vocals, Gerald Wiggins: Piano, Joe Comfort: Bass, Irv Cottler: Drums.]

- Walking In The Summer Rain (Van Winkle/De Lory)

Jeri Simpson
Jeri Simpson [45, Sun-Kist, S-700/701]
[Musicians: Barney Kessel: Guitar, Jeri Simpson: Vocals, Ray Leatherwood: Bass.]

- In My Black Lace (Simpson/Simpon)
- Sugar

11 June 1956   Los Angeles, USA

Bing Crosby
Bing Sings While Bregman Swings [CD, Verve, 31454 93672]
[Musicians: Barney Kessel: Guitar, Bing Crosby: Vocals, Pete Candoli: Trumpet, Harry Edison: Trumpet, Maynard Ferguson: Trumpet, Conrad Gozzo: Trumpet, Milt Bernhart: Trombone, Francis Howard: Trombone, George Roberts: Trombone, Frank Rosolino: Trombone, Lloyd Ulyate: Trombone, Herb Geller: Alto Saxophone, Bud Shank: Alto Saxophone, Bob Cooper: Tenor Saxophone, Chuck Gentry: Baritone Saxophone, Lew Raderman: Violin, Virginia Majewski: Viola, Edgar Lustgarden: Cello, Paul Smith: Piano, Joe Mondragon: Bass.]

- Blue Room (Rodgers/Hart)
- 'Deed I Do (Rose)
- I've Got Five Dollars (Rodgers/Hart)
- Jeepers Creepers (Warren)
- Nice Work If You Can Get It (Gershwin/Gershwin)
- The Song Is You (Kern)

12 June 1956 — Los Angeles, USA

Bing Crosby

Bing Sings While Bregman Swings [CD, Verve, 31454 93672]

[Musicians: Barney Kessel: Guitar, Bing Crosby: Vocals, Pete Candoli: Trumpet, Harry Edison: Trumpet, Maynard Ferguson: Trumpet, Conrad Gozzo: Trumpet, Milt Bernhart: Trombone, Francis Howard: Trombone, George Roberts: Trombone, Frank Rosolino: Trombone, Lloyd Ulyate: Trombone, Herb Geller: Alto Saxophone, Bud Shank: Alto Saxophone, Bob Cooper: Tenor Saxophone, Chuck Gentry: Baritone Saxophone, Lew Raderman: Violin, Virginia Majewski: Viola, Edgar Lustgarden: Cello, Paul Smith: Piano, Joe Mondragon: Bass.]

- Cheek to Cheek (Berlin)
- Have You Met Miss Jones? (Rodgers/Hart)
- Heat Wave (Berlin)
- Mountain Greenery (Rodgers/Hart)
- September In The Rain (Warren)
- They All Laughed (Gershwin/Gershwin)

---

01 July 1956 [Estimated] — Los Angeles, USA

Doris Day

Day By Day [LP, Columbia, CL 942]
Doris Day - Two Classic Albums [CD, Columbia, 475749 2]

[Musicians: Barney Kessel: Guitar, Ted Nash: Alto & Tenor Saxophones, Frank Flynn: Vibraphone, Paul Weston: Arranger/Conductor, Unknown: Band & Strings Personnel.]

- Autumn Leaves (Kosma/Prevert/Mercer)
- But Beautiful (Burke/Van Heusen)
- But Not For Me (Gershwin/Gershwin)
- Day By Day (Schwartz)
- Don't Take Your Love From Me (Nemo)
- Gone With The Wind (Magidson/Wrubel)
- Gypsy In My Soul (Bpland/Jaffe)
- Hello, My Lover, Goodbye (Heyman/Green)
- I Hadn't Anyone Till You (Noble)
- I Remember You (Mercer/Schertzinger)
- The Song Is You (Kern/Hammerstein)
- There Will Never Be Another You (Warren/Gordon)

---

10 July 1956 [Estimated] — Los Angeles

Henri Rene & His Orchestra

Music for Bachelors [CD, RCA BMG, 74321637032]

[Musicians: Barney Kessel: Guitar, Unknown: Orchestra, Henri Rene: Conductor.]

- Comme Ci, Comme Ca (Whitney/Kramer/Coquairla)
- Dinner For One Please, James (Carr)
- Easy To Love (Porter)
- Time On My Hands (Adamson/Gordon/Youmans)

## 01 August 1956 [Estimated]	Los Angeles, USA

Ernie Andrews

Ernie Andrews [CD, GNP Crescendo, GNPD 2274]

[Musicians: Barney Kessel: Guitar, Ernie Andrews: Vocals, Marshal Royal: Alto Saxophone, William Green: Alto Saxophone, Buddy Collette: Tenor Saxophone/Flute, Jewell Grant: Baritone Saxophone, Harry Edison: Trumpet, Pete Candoli: Trumpet, John Anderson: Trumpet, Milt Bernhardt: Trombone, Gerald Wiggins: Piano, Curtis Counce: Bass, Jackie Mills: Drums, Benny Carter: Arranger/Conductor.]

 In The Dark (Broonzy)
 Lover Come Back To Me (Romberg/Hammerstein)
 Round Midnight (Williams/Monk/Hanighen)
 Song of the Wanderer (Robbins/Moret)
 Squeeze Me (Ellington/Gaines)
 Sunset Eyes (Edwards/Wayne)

## 06 August 1956	Los Angeles, USA

Barney Kessel

Music To Listen To Barney Kessel [LP, Contemporary, C3521]
Music To Listen To Barney Kessel [CD, Contemporary, OJCCD746]

[Musicians: Barney Kessel: Guitar, Buddy Collette: Flute, Julie Cobb: Oboe, George Smith: Clarinet, Howard Terry: Clarinet, Justin Gordon: Clarinet, André Previn: Piano, Buddy Clark: Bass, Shelly Manne: Drums.]

 Fascinating Rhythm (Gershwin/Gershwin)
 Gone With The Wind (Magidson/Wrubel)
 I Love You (Porter)
 Makin' Whoopee (Donaldson/Kahn)

## 10 August 1956	Los Angeles, USA

Barney Kessel

Live Sessions [LP, Calliope, CAL3023]

[Musicians: Barney Kessel: Guitar, Jimmy Rowles: Piano, Leroy Vinnegar: Bass, Irv Kluger: Drums.]

 Fascinating Rhythm (Gershwin/Gershwin)
 Laura (Mercer/Raksin)
 The ABC Blues (Kessel)

## 14 August 1956	Los Angeles, USA

Billie Holiday

All Or Nothing At All [CD, Verve, 529-226-2]
Billie Holiday Volume 6 [LP, Verve Super, 2304 116]

[Musicians: Barney Kessel: Guitar, Billie Holiday: Vocals, Harry Edison: Trumpet, Ben Webster: Tenor Saxophone, Jimmy Rowles: Piano, Joe Mondragon: Bass, Alvin Stoller: Drums.]

 Cheek to Cheek (Berlin)
 Do Nothin' till You Hear from Me (Ellington/Russell)
 Ill Wind (You're Blowin Me No Good) (Koehler/Arlen)
 Speak Low (Weill/Wash)

---

15 August 1956　　　　　　　　**Los Angeles, USA**

Ella Fitzgerald

Jazz At The Hollywood Bowl [LP, Verve, MGV 8231-2]
[Musicians: Barney Kessel: Guitar, Ella Fitzgerald: Vocals, Paul Smith: Piano, Joe Mondragon: Bass, Alvin Stoller: Drums.]

- Air Mail Special   (Mundy/Christian)
- I Can't Give You Anything But Love   (Fields/McHugh)
- Just One Of Those Things   (Porter)
- Little Girl Blue   (Rodgers/Hart)
- Love For Sale   (Porter)
- Too Close For Comfort   (Bock/Holofcener/Weiss)

---

18 August 1956　　　　　　　　**Los Angeles, USA**

Billie Holiday

All Or Nothing At All [CD, Verve, 529-226-2]
Billie Holiday Volume 6 [LP, Verve Super, 2304 116]
[Musicians: Barney Kessel: Guitar, Billie Holiday: Vocals, Harry Edison: Trumpet, Ben Webster: Tenor Saxophone, Jimmy Rowles: Piano, Red Mitchell: Bass, Alvin Stoller: Drums.]

- All Or Nothing at All (Lawrence/Altman)
- April in Paris (Duke/Harburg)
- Sophisticated Lady (Ellington/Parish/Mills)
- We'll Be Together Again (Fisher/Laine)

---

01 September 1956 [Estimated]　　**Los Angeles, USA**

Dorothy Carless

The Carless Torch [CD, Hifi Record/Fresh Sound, R 403 CD]
[Musicians: Barney Kessel: Guitar, Dorothy Carless: Vocals, Unknown: Bass, Unknown: Drums/Vibraphone.]

- Baby, Baby, You're The One (Murray)
- Bidin' My Time (Gershwin/Gershwin)
- Ev'ry Time We Say Goodbye (Porter)
- For Every Man There's A Woman (Arlen/Robin)
- Hello, My Lover, Goodbye (Green/Heyman)
- Here Lies Love (Raigner/Robin)
- I Don't Want To Cry Anymore (Schertzinger)
- I'll Never Be The Same (Kahn/Malneck/Signorelli)
- It's Easy To Remember (Rodgers/Hart)
- It's Too Late Now (Lane/Lerner)
- Love Letters In The Sand (Coots/Kenny)
- My Old Flame (Johnston/Coslow)

---

04 September 1956　　　　　　　**Los Angeles, USA**

Ella Fitzgerald

Day Dream - Best of Duke Ellington [CD, Verve, 527-223-2]
Duke Ellington Songbook Volume 2 [LP, Verve, VE 2-2540]
Ella Fitzgerald [CD, Giants of Jazz, CD 53255]
[Musicians: Barney Kessel: Guitar, Ella Fitzgerald: Vocals, Ben Webster: Tenor Saxophone, Stuff Smith: Violin, Paul Smith: Piano, Joe Mondragon: Bass, Alvin Stoller: Drums.]

- Cottontail (Ellington)
- It Don't Mean A Thing (If It Ain't Got That Swing) (Ellington/Mills)

    Just Squeeze Me (Ellington/Gaines)

    Rocks in My Bed (Ellington)

[Musicians: Barney Kessel: Guitar, Ella Fitzgerald: Vocals.]

    Azure (Ellington/Mills)

    Solitude (Ellington/De Lange/Mills)

Ben Webster & Harry Edison

Walkin' With Sweets [LP, Verve, Select 2317 109]

[Musicians: Barney Kessel: Guitar, Harry Edison: Trumpet, Ben Webster: Tenor Saxophone, Jimmy Rowles: Piano, Joe Mondragon: Bass, Alvin Stoller: Drums.]

    Hollering at the Watkins (Edison)

    How Deep is the Ocean (Berlin)

    K.M.Blues (Edison)

    Love is Here to Stay (Gershwin/Gershwin)

    Opus 711 (Edison)

    Studio Call (Edison)

    Used To Be Basie (Edison)

    Walkin' With Sweets (Edison)

    Willow Weep For Me (Ronell)

---

16 September 1956   Los Angeles, USA

Ella Fitzgerald

Duke Ellington Songbook Volume 2 [LP, Verve, VE 2-2540]
Ella Fitzgerald [CD, Giants of Jazz, CD 53255]

[Musicians: Barney Kessel: Guitar, Ella Fitzgerald: Vocals, Ben Webster: Tenor Saxophone, Stuff Smith: Violin, Paul Smith: Piano, Joe Mondragon: Bass, Alvin Stoller: Drums.]

    Do Nothing Till You Hear from Me (Ellington/Russell)

    Don't Get Around Much Anymore (Ellington/Russell)

    I Let a Song Go Out of My Heart (Ellington/Nemo/Mills/Redmond)

    Just A Sittin' and A Rockin' (Ellington/Strayhorn/Gaines)

    Prelude to a Kiss (Ellington/Mills/Gordon)

    Satin Doll (Ellington)

    Sophisticated Lady (Ellington/Parish/Mills)

[Musicians: Barney Kessel: Guitar, Ella Fitzgerald: Vocals.]

    In a Sentimental Mood (Ellington/Mills/Kurz)

---

15 October 1956   Los Angeles, USA

Barney Kessel

Music To Listen To Barney Kessel [LP, Contemporary, C3521]
Music To Listen To Barney Kessel [CD, Contemporary, OJCCD746]

[Musicians: Barney Kessel: Guitar, Ted Nash: Flute, Jules Jacobs: Oboe, George Smith: Clarinet, Howard Terry: Bassoon, Jimmy Rowles: Piano, Red Mitchell: Bass, Shelly Manne: Drums.]

    Blues For A Playboy (Kessel)

    Cheerful Little Earful (Warren/Gershwin/Rose)

    My Reverie (Debussy/Clinton)

29 October 1956 — Los Angeles, USA

Pete Rugolo and his Orchestra

Out On A Limb [LP, EmArcy, MC 36115]
Adventures In Sound - Pete Rugolo [CD, Fresh Sounds, FSR2221]

[Musicians: Barney Kessel: Guitar, Bud Shank: Flute & Oboe, Harry Klee: Alto Saxophone & Oboe, Bob Cooper: Tenor Saxophone & Oboe, Dave Pell: Tenor Saxophone, Milt Bernhart: Trombone, Jimmy Giuffre: Baritone Saxophone, Joe Mondragon: Bass.]

- Smoke Gets In Your Eyes (Kern/Harbach)

[Musicians: Barney Kessel: Guitar, Ed Leddy: Trumpet, Don Fagerquist: Trumpet, Maynard Ferguson: Trumpet, Ray Linn: Trumpet, Milt Bernhart: Trombone, Herbie Harper: Trombone, Frank Rosolino: Trombone, George Roberts: Bass Trombone, John Cave: French Horn, John Grass: French Horn, Jay McAllister: Tuba, Harry Klee: Alto Saxophone, Bud Shank: Alto Saxophone, Bob Cooper: Tenor Saxophone, Dave Pell: Tenor Saxophone, Jimmy Giuffre: Baritone Saxophone, Russ Freeman: Piano, Joe Mondragon: Bass, Shelly Manne: Drums.]

- Ballade For Drums (Rugolo)
- Nancy (Van Heusen/Silvers)
- Repetitious Riff (Rugolo)
- Sunday, Monday Or Always (Van Heusen/Burke)

Sarah Vaughan

Sarah Vaughan Sings Broadway [CD, Verve, 314 526 464-2]

[Musicians: Barney Kessel: Guitar, Sarah Vaughan: Vocals, James Decker: French Horn, Milt Bernhart: Trombone, Joe Howard: Trombone, Ed Kusby: Trombone, George Roberts: Trombone, Ronnie Lang: Alto Saxophone/Woodwind, Ted Nash: Tenor Saxophone/Woodwind, Harry Klee: Woodwind, Champ Webb: Woodwind, George Greeley: Piano, Larry Breen: Bass, Louis Singer: Drums, Katharine Julyie: Harp, Hal Mooney: Arranger/Conductor, 17 Piece: String Section.]

- Autumn In New York (Duke)
- Bewitched (Rodgers/Hart)
- Dancing In The Dark (Scwartz/Dietz)
- Little Girl Blue (Rodgers/Hart)
- My Darling, My Darling (Loesser)
- You're My Everything (Warren/Dixon/Young)

---

30 October 1956 — Los Angeles, USA

Pete Rugolo Orchestra

Reeds In Hi-Fi [LP, Mercury, MG 20260]
Adventures In Sound - Pete Rugolo [CD, Fresh Sounds, FSR2221]

[Musicians: Barney Kessel: Guitar, Bud Shank: Alto Saxophone/Flute, Harry Klee: Alto Saxophone/Flute, Ted Nash: Tenor Saxophone/Oboe, Dave Pell: Tenor Saxophone/Bass Clarinet, Chuck Gentry: Baritone Saxophone, Babe Russin: Woodwinds, Leonard Hartman: Woodwinds, Lloyd Mildebrandt: Woodwinds, Alex Gershunoff: Woodwinds, Morris Bercoy: Woodwinds, Katherine Julyle: Harp, Joe Mondragon: Bass, Shelly Manne: Drums.]

- Collaboration (Rugolo/Kenton)
- If You Could See Me Now (Dameron/Sigman)
- Impressionism (Rugolo)
- Interlude (Rugolo)
- Spring Is Here (Rodgers/Hart)
- Theme For Alto (Rugolo)

Sarah Vaughan

Sarah Vaughan Sings Broadway [CD, Verve, 314 526 464-2]

[Musicians: Barney Kessel: Guitar, Sarah Vaughan: Vocals, James Decker: French Horn, Milt Bernhart: Trombone, Joe Howard: Trombone, Ed Kusby: Trombone, George Roberts: Trombone, Ronnie Lang: Alto Saxophone/Woodwind, Ted Nash: Tenor Saxophone/Woodwind, Harry Klee: Woodwind, Champ Webb: Woodwind, George Greeley: Piano, Larry Breen: Bass, Louis Singer: Drums, Katharine Julyie: Harp, Hal Mooney: Arranger/Conductor, 17 Piece: String Section.]

- All The Things You Are (Kern)
- Can't We Be Friends (Swift/James)
- Homework (Berlin)
- It Never Entered My Mind (Rodgers/Hart)

The Touch Of Your Hand (Kern/Harbach)

They Say It's Wonderful (Berlin)

---

31 October 1956　　　　　　　　Los Angeles, USA

Pete Rugolo Orchestra

Brass In Hi Fi [LP, Mercury, MG-20261]

Adventures In Sound - Pete Rugolo [CD, Fresh Sounds, FSR2221]

[Musicians: Barney Kessel: Guitar, Clarence Karella: Tuba, Don Fagerquist: Trumpet, Pete Candoli: Trumpet, Ray Linn: Trumpet, Maynard Ferguson: Trumpet, Frank Rosolino: Trombone, Herbie Harper: Trombone, Milt Bernhardt: Trombone, John Cave: French Horn, Fred Fox: French Horn, John Graas: French Horn, George Roberts: Bass Trombone, André Previn: Piano, Joe Mondragon: Bass, Larry Bunker: Drums & Percussion, Pete Rugolo: Leader/Arranger.]

All The Things You Are (Kern/Hammerstein)

Brass At Work (Rugolo)

Godchild (Wallington)

My Mother's Eyes (Baer/Gilbert)

Pete Rugolo Orchestra

Reeds In Hi-Fi [LP, Mercury, MG 20260]

Adventures In Sound - Pete Rugolo [CD, Fresh Sounds, FSR2221]

[Musicians: Barney Kessel: Guitar, Bud Shank: Alto Saxophone/Flute, Harry Klee: Alto Saxophone & Piccolo, Bob Cooper: Tenor Saxophone & Oboe, Dave Pell: Tenor Saxophone & Bass Clarinet, Chuck Gentry: Baritone Saxophone, Babe Russin: Woodwinds, Leonard Hartman: Woodwinds, Lloyd Mildebrandt: Woodwinds, Alex Gershunoff: Woodwinds, Morris Bercoy: Woodwinds, Andre Previn: Piano, Joe Mondragon: Bass, Shelly Manne: Drums, Pete Rugolo: Leader/Arranger.]

Igor Beaver (Rugolo)

Our Waltz (Rose)

Polytonal Blues (Rugolo)

Walkin' Shoes (Mulligan)

Yardbird Suite (Parker)

Sarah Vaughan

Sarah Vaughan Sings Broadway [CD, Verve, 314 526 464-2]

[Musicians: Barney Kessel: Guitar, Sarah Vaughan: Vocals, Vince De Rosa: French Horn, Murray McEarchen: Trombone, Dick Noel: Trombone, Tommy Pederson: Trombone, George Roberts: Trombone, Ronnie Lang: Alto Saxophone/Woodwind, Ted Nash: Tenor Saxophone/Woodwind, Gene Cipriani: Woodwind, Justin Gordon: Woodwind, Ray Sherman: Piano, Joe Mondragon: Bass, Larry Bunker: Drums, Ann Mason: Harp, Hal Mooney: Arranger/Conductor, 18 Piece: String Section.]

A Ship Without A Sail (Rodgers/Hart)

A Tree In The Park (Rodgers/Hart)

He's Only Wonderful (Fain/Harburg)

Let's Take An Old Fashioned Walk (Berlin)

My Heart Stood Still (Rodgers/Hart)

My Ship (Weill/Gershwin)

---

01 November 1956　　　　　　　　Los Angeles, USA

Sarah Vaughan

Sarah Vaughan Sings Broadway [CD, Verve, 314 526 464-2]

[Musicians: Barney Kessel: Guitar, Sarah Vaughan: Vocals, Vince De Rosa: French Horn, Murray McEarchen: Trombone, Dick Noel: Trombone, Tommy Pederson: Trombone, George Roberts: Trombone, Ronnie Lang: Alto Saxophone/Woodwind, Ted Nash: Tenor Saxophone/Woodwind, Gene Cipriani: Woodwind, Justin Gordon: Woodwind, Ray Sherman: Piano, Joe Mondragon: Bass, Larry Bunker: Drums, Ann Mason: Harp, Hal Mooney: Arranger/Conductor, 18 Piece: String Section.]

But Not For Me (Gershwin/Gershwin)

If I Loved You (Rodgers/Hammerstein)

Lost In The Stars (Weill/Anderson)

Love Is A Random Thing (Fain/Marion,Jnr)

Poor Butterfly (Hubbell/Golden)

September Song (Weill/Anderson)

02 November 1956   Los Angeles, USA

Pete Rugolo Orchestra

Brass In Hi Fi [LP, Mercury, MG-20261]
Adventures In Sound - Pete Rugolo [CD, Fresh Sounds, FSR2221]

[Musicians: Barney Kessel: Guitar, Pete Rugolo: Arranger/Leader, Don Fagerquist: Trumpet, Pete Candoli: Trumpet, Ray Linn: Trumpet, Maynard Ferguson: Trumpet, Frank Rosolino: Trombone, Herbie Harper: Trombone, Milt Bernhardt: Trombone, John Cave: French Horn, Vince De Rosa: French Horn, John Graas: French Horn, George Roberts: Bass Trombone, Clarence Karella: Tuba, Claude Williamson: Piano, Joe Mondragon: Bass, Larry Bunker: Percussion.]

     A Rose For David (Rugolo)
     Everything Happens to Me (Dennis/Addair)
     Salute (Rugolo)
     Song For Tuba (Rugolo)
     Temptation (Freed/Brown)

Sarah Vaughan

Sarah Vaughan Sings Broadway [CD, Verve, 314 526 464-2]

[Musicians: Barney Kessel: Guitar, Sarah Vaughan: Vocals, Ann Mason: Harp, Murray McEarchen: Trombone, Ed Kusby: Trombone, Randall Miller: Trombone, George Roberts: Trombone, Ronnie Lang: Alto Saxophone/Woodwind, Ted Nash: Tenor Saxophone/Woodwind, Harry Klee: Woodwind, Justin Gordon: Woodwind, George Greeley: Piano, Joe Mondragon: Bass, Larry Bunker: Drums, Frank Beach: Trumpet, John Best: Trumpet, Pete Candoli: Trumpet, Manny Klein: Trumpet, 14 Piece: String Section, Hal Mooney: Arranger/Conductor.]

     Comes Love (Browm/Stept/Tobias)
     If This Isn't Love (Lane/Harburg)
     It's De-lovely (Porter)
     It's Got To Be Love (Rodgers/Hart)
     It's Love (Bernstein/Comden/Green)
     Lucky In Love (Brown/DeSylva/Henderson)

08 November 1956   Los Angeles, USA

Charlie Barnet

Charlie Barnet and his Orchestra [LP, World Record Club, TP 303]
Charlie Barnet Lonely Street [CD, LoneHill Jazz, LHJ10303]

[Musicians: Barney Kessel: Guitar, Maynard Ferguson: Trumpet, Ollie Mitchell: Trumpet, Carlton McBeath: Trumpet, Gene Duerneyer: Trumpet, Diz Mullins: Trumpet, Charlie Barnet: Alto, Soprano & Tenor Saxophones, Willie Smith: Alto Saxophone, Bill Holman: Tenor Saxophone, Bill Trujillo: Tenor Saxophone, Dick Paladino: Alto & Baritone Saxophones, Bob Burgess: Trombone, Dick Nash: Trombone, Ray Anderson: Trombone, Bob Dawes: Baritone Saxophone, Norman Pockrandt: Piano, Red Wooten: Bass, Alvin Stoller: Drums.]

     Blue Rose (Ellington)
     Hear Me Talking To You (Rainey)
     Lemon Twist (Troup)
     Lumby (May)

04 December 1956   Los Angeles, USA

Barney Kessel

Music To Listen To Barney Kessel [LP, Contemporary, C3521]
Music To Listen To Barney Kessel [CD, Contemporary, OJCCD746]

[Musicians: Barney Kessel: Guitar, Red Mitchell: Bass, Shelly Manne: Drums.]

     Laura (Mercer/Raksin)

[Musicians: Barney Kessel: Guitar, Ted Nash: Flute, Jules Jacobs: Oboe, George Smith: Clarinet, Howard Terry: Bassoon, Claude Williamson: Piano, Red Mitchell: Bass, Shelly Manne: Drums.]

     Indian Summer (Herbert/Dubin)
     Love Is For The Very Young (Raksin)

Mountain Greenery (Rodgers/Hart)

11 December 1956 [Estimated]   Los Angeles, USA

Buddy DeFranco

Buddy DeFranco Sextet [LP, Norgran, MGN 1085]
[Musicians: Barney Kessel: Guitar, Buddy DeFranco: Clarinet, Harry Edison: Trumpet, Jimmy Rowles: Piano, Bob Stone: Bass, Bobby White: Drums.]

- A Fine Romance (Kern/Fields)
- Angel Eyes (Dennis)
- Cheek To Cheek (Berlin)
- How Long Has This Been Going On? (Gershwin/Gershwin)
- I Won't Dance (Kern/Harbach/Fields/McHugh/Hammerstein)
- Let's Call The Whole Thing Off (Gershwin/Gershwin)
- Moonlight On The Ganges (Wallace/Myers)
- Perfidia (Dominguez/Leeds)
- Sweets Blues (Edison)

18 December 1956   Los Angeles, USA

Anita O'Day

Pick Yourself Up [CD, Verve, 517 329-2]
Pick Yourself Up [LP, Verve, MGV2043]
[Musicians: Barney Kessel: Guitar, Anita O'Day: Vocals, Harry Edison: Trumpet, Larry Bunker: Vibraphone, Paul Smith: Piano, Joe Mondragon: Bass, Alvin Stoller: Drums.]

- Don't Be That Way (Goodman)
- I Used to Be Color Blind (Berlin)
- Let's Face the Music and Dance (Alt) (Berlin)
- Let's Face the Music and Dance (Berlin)
- Pick Yourself Up (Kern)

20 December 1956   Los Angeles, USA

Anita O'Day

Pick Yourself Up [CD, Verve, 314 517 329-2]
[Musicians: Barney Kessel: Guitar, Anita O'Day: Vocals, Pete Candoli: Trumpet, Conte Candoli: Trumpet, Frank Rosolino: Trombone, Bud Shank: Alto Saxophone, Stan Getz: Tenor Saxophone, Jimmy Giuffre: Baritone Saxophone, Paul Smith: Piano, Joe Mondragon: Bass, Alvin Stoller: Drums.]

- I Never Had A Chance (Berlin)
- I Won't Dance (Kern/McHugh/Hammerstein)
- Let's Begin (Kern/Harbach)
- Stompin' At The Savoy (Goddman/Webb/Razaf/Sampson)
- Sweet Georgia Brown (Pinkard/Bernie/Casey)

03 January 1957   Los Angeles, USA

Billie Holiday

All Or Nothing At All [CD, Verve, 529-226-2]
Embraceable You [LP, Verve, 817 359-1]
[Musicians: Barney Kessel: Guitar, Billie Holiday: Vocals, Harry Edison: Trumpet, Ben Webster: Tenor Saxophone, Jimmy Rowles: Piano, Red Mitchell: Bass, Alvin Stoller: Drums.]

- A Foggy Day (Gershwin/Gershwin)
- I Wished on the Moon (Rainger/Parker)

Moonlight in Vermont (Suessdorf/Blackburn)

04 January 1957   Los Angeles, USA

Billie Holiday

All Or Nothing At All [CD, Verve, 529-226-2]
Embraceable You [LP, Verve, 817 359-1]

[Musicians: Barney Kessel: Guitar, Billie Holiday: Vocals, Harry Edison: Trumpet, Ben Webster: Tenor Saxophone, Jimmy Rowles: Piano, Red Mitchell: Bass, Alvin Stoller: Drums.]

- Comes Love (Alt) (Brown)
- Comes Love (Brown)
- I Didn't Know What Time It Was (Rodgers/Hart)
- Just One of Those Things (Porter)

07 January 1957   Los Angeles, USA

Billie Holiday

All Or Nothing At All [CD, Verve, 529-226-2]
Embraceable You [LP, Verve, 817 359-1]

[Musicians: Barney Kessel: Guitar, Billie Holiday: Vocals, Harry Edison: Trumpet, Ben Webster: Tenor Saxophone, Jimmy Rowles: Piano, Joe Mondragon: Bass, Alvin Stoller: Drums.]

- Body and Soul (Green/Sour/Heyman/Eyton)
- But Not For Me (Gershwin/Gershwin)
- Darn That Dream (De Lange/Van Heusen)
- Day In, Day Out (Mercer/Bloom)

08 January 1957   Los Angeles, USA

Billie Holiday

All Or Nothing At All [CD, Verve, 529-226-2]
Embraceable You [LP, Verve, 817 359-1]

[Musicians: Barney Kessel: Guitar, Alvin Stoller: Drums, Harry Edison: Trumpet, Ben Webster: Tenor Saxophone, Jimmy Rowles: Piano, Joe Mondragon: Bass.]

- Just Friends (instrumental) (Klenner/Lewis)

[Musicians: Barney Kessel: Guitar, Billie Holiday: Vocals, Harry Edison: Trumpet, Ben Webster: Tenor Saxophone, Jimmy Rowles: Piano, Joe Mondragon: Bass, Alvin Stoller: Drums.]

- Just One Of Those Things (Porter)
- Love Is Here to Stay (Gershwin/Gershwin)
- One For My Baby (And One More For The Road) (Mercer/Arlen)
- Say It Isn't So (Berlin)
- Stars Fell on Alabama (Parish/Perkins)

09 January 1957   Los Angeles, USA

Billie Holiday

All Or Nothing At All [CD, Verve, 529-226-2]
Embraceable You [LP, Verve, 817 359-1]

[Musicians: Barney Kessel: Guitar, Billie Holiday: Vocals, Harry Edison: Trumpet, Ben Webster: Tenor Saxophone, Jimmy Rowles: Piano, Joe Mondragon: Bass, Larry Bunker: Drums.]

- Embraceable You (Gershwin/Gershwin)
- Gee, Baby, Ain't I good to You? (Matthew)
- Let's Call The Whole Thing Off (Gershwin/Gershwin)
- They Can't Take That Away From Me (Gershwin/Gershwin)

11 January 1957   Los Angeles, USA

Woody Herman

Songs For Hip Lovers [CD, Verve, 314 559 872-2]

[Musicians: Barney Kessel: Guitar, Harry Edison: Trumpet, Ben Webster: Tenor Saxophone, Jimmy Rowles: Piano, Joe Mondragon: Bass, Larry Bunker: Drums, Woody Herman: Vocals.]

- Alone Together (Schwartz)
- Bidin' My Time (Gershwin)
- Moon Song (Johnston)
- Willow Weep For Me (Ronell)

12 January 1957   Los Angeles, USA

Woody Herman

Songs For Hip Lovers [CD, Verve, 314 559 872-2]

[Musicians: Barney Kessel: Guitar, Harry Edison: Trumpet, Ben Webster: Tenor Saxophone, Jimmy Rowles: Piano, Joe Mondragon: Bass, Larry Bunker: Drums, Woody Herman: Vocals.]

- Louise (Whiting)
- Makin' Whoopee (Donaldson)

14 January 1957   Los Angeles, USA

Paul Smith

Softly, Baby [CD, Jasmine Records, CD JAS 311]
Softly, Baby [LP, Capitol, T829]

[Musicians: Barney Kessel: Guitar, Stan Levey: Drums, Joe Mondragon: Bass, Paul Smith: Piano.]

- Blues a la P.T (Smith)
- Easy To Love (Porter)
- I Didn't Know What Time It Was (Rodgers/Hart)
- I Got Rhythm (Gershwin/Gershwin)
- I'll Remember April (Raye/DePaul/Johnston)
- Invitation (Bronislau/Kaper)
- Long Live Phineas (Smith)
- Taking A Chance On Love (Duke/Latouche/Fetter)
- The Man I Love (Gershwin/Gershwin)

15 January 1957   Los Angeles, USA

Rose Murphy

Not Cha-Cha But Chi-Chi [LP, Verve, MGV 2070]
Not Cha-Cha But Chi-Chi [CD, Polydor KK, POCJ 2663]

[Musicians: Barney Kessel: Guitar, Rose Murphy: Vocals/Piano, Willie Smith: Alto Saxophone, Bruce Lawrence: Bass, Alvin Stoller: Drums.]

- Honeysuckle Rose (Razaf/Waller)
- If You Were Only Mine (Brown/Freed)
- In A Shanty In Old Shanty Town (Young/Siras/Little)
- Mr Wonderful (Holfcener/Weiss/Bock)
- You Were Meant for Me (Freed/Brown)

22 January 1957 Los Angeles, USA

Rose Murphy

Not Cha-Cha But Chi-Chi [LP, Verve, MGV 2070]
Not Cha-Cha But Chi-Chi [CD, Polydor KK, POCJ 2663]
[Musicians: Barney Kessel: Guitar, Rose Murphy: Vocals/Piano, Willie Smith: Alto Saxophone, Bruce Lawrence: Bass, Alvin Stoller: Drums.]

- By The Waters Of Minnetonka (Lieurance/Cavanass)
- Coquette (Kahn/Lombardo/Green)
- I Ain' Got Nobody (Williams/Graham)
- Pennies From Heaven (Johnston/Burke)
- Please Don't Talk About Me When I'm Gone (Stept/Clare)
- Sweet Georgia Brown (Pinkard/Bernie/Casey)
- Sympathetic Little Star (Razal/Murphy/Fink)
- Watcha Gonna Lose (Murphy/Peter)

---

26 January 1957 Los Angeles, USA

Red Norvo

Music to Listen to Red Norvo By [CD, Contemporary, OJCCD 1015-2]
Music to Listen to Red Norvo By [LP, Contemporary, C 7534]
[Musicians: Barney Kessel: Guitar, Red Norvo: Vibraphone, Buddy Collette: Flute, Bill Smith: Clarinet, Red Mitchell: Bass, Shelly Manne: Drums.]

- Poeme (Montrose)
- Red Sails (Kessel)
- The Red Broom (Norvo)

---

09 February 1957 Los Angeles, USA

Red Norvo

Music to Listen to Red Norvo By [CD, Contemporary, OJCCD 1015-2]
Music to Listen to Red Norvo By [LP, Contemporary, C 7534]
[Musicians: Barney Kessel: Guitar, Red Norvo: Vibraphone, Buddy Collette: Flute, Bill Smith: Clarinet, Red Mitchell: Bass, Shelly Manne: Drums.]

- Paying The Dues Blues (Niehaus)
- Rubricity (Tatro)

---

01 March 1957 [Estimated] Los Angeles, USA

Mel Tormé

California Suite [CD, Avenue Jazz, R2 75824]
[Musicians: Barney Kessel: Guitar, Pete Candoli: Trumpet, Don Fagerquist: Trumpet, Bob Enevoldsen: Trombone, Dave Pell: Tenor Saxophone, Max Bennett: Bass, Mel Lewis: Drums, Alvin Stoller: Drums, Loulie Jean Norman: Vocals, T & R Van Horne: Vocals, R Carmichael: Vocals, Mel Torme: Vocals.]

- Atlantic City Boardwalk (Tormé)
- Coney Island (Tormé)
- Got The Date On The Golden Gate (Tormé)
- L.A (Tormé)
- La Jolla (Tormé)
- Nothing To Do (But Shed A Tear) (Tormé)
- Poor Little Extra Girl (Tormé)
- San Fernando Valley (Tormé)
- Six O'Clock (It's Time To Leave The Set) (Tormé)

The Territory (The Soil Was Good) (Tormé)
They Go To San Diego (Tormé)
West Coast Is The Best Coast (reprise) (Tormé)
West Coast Is The Best Coast (Tormé)

---

02 March 1957   **Los Angeles, USA**

Red Norvo

Music to Listen to Red Norvo By [CD, Contemporary, OJCCD 1015-2]
Music to Listen to Red Norvo By [LP, Contemporary, C 7534]
[Musicians: Barney Kessel: Guitar, Red Norvo: Vibraphone, Buddy Collette: Flute, Bill Smith: Clarinet, Red Mitchell: Bass, Shelly Manne: Drums.]

Divertimento - 1st Movement (Smith)
Divertimento - 2nd Movement (Smith)
Divertimento - 3rd Movement (Smith)
Divertimento - 4th Movement (Smith)

---

05 March 1957   **Los Angeles, USA**

Ben Webster

The Soul Of Ben Webster [CD, Verve, 527 475-2]
Gee, Baby Ain't I Good to You [LP, Verve, MGV 8211]
[Musicians: Barney Kessel: Guitar, Harry Edison: Trumpet, Oscar Peterson: Piano, Ray Brown: Bass, Alvin Stoller: Drums.]

Blues for Piney Brown (Edison)
Blues for the Blues (Alt) (Edison)
Blues for the Blues (Edison)
Gee, Baby, Ain't I Good to You? (Redman)
You're Getting to Be a Habit with Me (Warren)

---

07 March 1957   **Los Angeles, USA**

Stuff Smith

Stuff Smith [CD, Verve, 314 521 676-2]
[Musicians: Barney Kessel: Guitar, Stuff Smith: Violin, Oscar Peterson: Piano, Ray Brown: Bass, Alvin Stoller: Drums.]

In A Mellotone (Ellington)

Stuff Smith

Stuff Smith [LP, Verve, 2304 536]
Stuff Smith [CD, Verve, 314 521 676-2]
[Musicians: Barney Kessel: Guitar, Stuff Smith: Violin, Oscar Peterson: Piano, Ray Brown: Bass, Alvin Stoller: Drums.]

Desert Sands (Smith)
It Don't Mean A Thing (If It Ain't Got That Swing) (Ellington)
Soft Winds (Goodman)
Time And Again (Smith)

---

12 March 1957   **Los Angeles, USA**

Stuff Smith

Stuff Smith [CD, Verve, 314 521 676-2]
[Musicians: Barney Kessel: Guitar, Stuff Smith: Violin, Oscar Peterson: Piano, Ray Brown: Bass, Alvin Stoller: Drums.]

Body and Soul (Green/Heyman/Sour/Eyton)
Heat Wave (Berlin)

Stuff Smith

Stuff Smith [LP, Verve, 2304 536]
Stuff Smith [CD, Verve, 314 521 676-2]
[Musicians: Barney Kessel: Guitar, Stuff Smith: Violin, Oscar Peterson: Piano, Ray Brown: Bass, Alvin Stoller: Drums.]

    I Know That You Know (Harbach)
    Things Ain't What They Used To Be (Ellington)

---

18 March 1957   Los Angeles, USA

Barney Kessel

The Poll Winners [LP, Contemporary, S7535]
The Poll Winners [CD, Contemporary, OJCCD156-2]
The Poll Winners [XRCD, Contemporary, JVCXR 0019-2]
[Musicians: Barney Kessel: Guitar, Ray Brown: Bass, Shelly Manne: Drums.]

    Don't Worry 'Bout Me (Koehler/Bloom)
    Green Dolphin Street (Kaper)
    It Could Happen To You (Burke/Van Heusen)
    Jordu (Jordan)
    Mean To Me (Turk/Ahlert)
    Minor Mood (Kessel)
    Nagasaki (Dixon/Warren)
    Satin Doll (Ellington)
    You Go To My Head (Coots/Gillespie)

---

21 March 1957   Los Angeles, USA

Josephine Premice With The Barney Kessel Orchestra

Caribe - Josephine Premice Sings Calypso [LP, Verve, MGV 2067]
[Musicians: Barney Kessel: Guitar, Josephine Premice: Vocals, Ben Tucker: Bass, Uknown: Other Musicians.]

    Chicken Gumbo (Merrick/Willoughby/Evans)
    Island Wind (Hunter/Emig)
    It Never Happens To Me (Elly)
    No, No Joe (Kessel/Marshall)
    Rookombey (Premice)
    Song Of The Jumbies (Premice)
    Taking A Chance On Love (Duke/Fetter/Latouche)
    Talk T' Me (Skylar/Fields)
    The Man I Love (Gershwin/Gershwin)
    The Thief (Norvas)
    T'is Only A Matter Of Mind Over Matter (Brana/Sanford/Mysels)
    Two Ladies In De Shade Of The Banana Tree (Arlen/Capote)

---

18 April 1957   Los Angeles, USA

Woody Herman

Woody Herman Sings [EP, Verve, 10053]
[Musicians: Barney Kessel: Guitar, Woody Herman: Vocals, Ted Nash: Tenor Saxophone, Herb Geller: Alto Saxophone, Harry Edison: Trumpet, Jimmy Rowles: Piano, Joe Mondragon: Bass, Alvin Stoller: Drums.]

    House Built On A Strong Foundation
    I Wonder

01 May 1957 [Estimated]   Los Angeles, USA

Dory Previn & Andre Previn

The Leprechauns Are Upon Me [LP, Verve, MGV 2101]
[Musicians: Barney Kessel: Guitar, André Previn: Keyboard, Unknown: Bass, Dory Previn: Vocals.]

- Lonely Girl In London (DePaul/Dory Previn)

[Musicians: Barney Kessel: Guitar, André Previn: Piano, Unknown: Bass, Dory Previn: Vocals.]

- Care Free Love (Dory Previn)
- Forget Me (Henderson/Dory Previn)
- Gooney Bird (Dory Previn)
- Just For Now (Previn/Dory Previn)
- Leprechauns Are Upon Me (Dory Previn)
- Let Me Show You Off (Saunders/Dory Previn)
- Mandy Sides (Raksin/Dory Previn)
- My Heart Is A Hunter (Previn/Dory Previn)
- No (Murray/Dory Previn)
- Sea Shells (Saunders/Dory Previn)
- Warm Winter Day (Saunders/Dory Previn)

[Musicians: Barney Kessel: Guitar, Unknown: Bass, Dory Previn: Vocals.]

- Can't We Be Enemies (DePaul/Dory Previn)

---

01 June 1957 [Estimated]   Los Angeles, USA

Helen Grayco

After Midnight [LP, VIK, LX 1066]
After Midnight [CD, RCA Records, 74321638202]
[Musicians: Barney Kessel: Guitar, Helen Grayco: Vocals, Lee Robinson: Alto Saxophone, Gerald Wiggins: Piano, Larry Bunker: Vibraphone, Joe Mondragon: Bass, Alvin Stoller: Drums, Russ Garcia: Arranger, Judd Conlon: Conductor.]

- Black Coffee (Webster/Burke)
- Ev'ry Time We Say Goodbye (Porter)
- Glad To Be Unhappy (Rodgers/Hart)
- Good Morning Heartache (Higginbotham/Drake/Fisher)
- Last Night When We Were Young (Arlen/Yarburg)
- Midnight Sun (Mercer/Burke/Hampton)
- Mood Indigo (Ellington/Mills/Bigard)
- Take Me In Your Arms (Parrish/Makush)
- We'll Be Together Again (Fischer/Laine)
- While We're Young (Engvick/Wilder/Palitz)
- You Don't Know What Love Is (Raye/DePaul)
- You're My Thrill (Clare/Gorney)

Buddy Mel

Buddy Mel Vocalist [EP, Shad, S-101]
[Musicians: Barney Kessel: Guitar, Buddy Mel: Vocalist, Skeets Herfurt: Saxophone, Buddy Cole: Piano/Organ, Don Whitaker: Bass, Alvin Stoller: Drums.]

- Carolina Walkin' Down The Street (Shad Fry)
- Rain In The Night (Yaw/Galbraith)

Buddy Mel

Buddy Mel Vocalist [EP, Shad, S-102]
[Musicians: Barney Kessel: Guitar, Buddy Mel: Vocalist, Skeets Herfurt: Saxophone, Buddy Cole: Piano/Organ, Don Whitaker: Bass, Alvin Stoller: Drums.]

- In My Frame Of Mind (Shad Fry)

The Blues Won't Bother Me

08 June 1957 [Estimated]   Los Angeles, USA

Universal-International Orchestra

Touch Of Evil - Soundtrack [LP, Challenge, CHL-602]

Touch Of Evil - Soundtrack [CD, Movie Sound, MSCD-401]

[Musicians: Barney Kessel: Guitar, Pete Candoli: Trumpet, Plas Johnson: Tenor Saxophone, Dave Pell: Baritone Saxophone, Red Norvo: Vibraphone, Ray Sherman: Piano, Jack Costanzo: Bongoes, Joseph Gershenson: Conductor, Unknown: Other Musicians.]

- Background For Murder (Mancini)
- Bar Room Rock (Mancini)
- Blue Pianola (Mancini)
- Borderline Montuna (Mancini)
- Flashing Nuisance (Mancini)
- Ku Ku (Mancini)
- Lease Breaker (Mancini)
- Orson Around (Mancini)
- Reflection (Mancini)
- Something For Susan (Mancini)
- Son Of Raunchy (Mancini)
- Strollin' Blues (Mancini)
- The Big Drag (Mancini)
- The Boss (Mancini)
- The Chase (Mancini)

[Musicians: Barney Kessel: Guitar, Pete Candoli: Trumpet, Plas Johnson: Tenor Saxophone, Dave Pell: Baritone Saxophone, Red Norvo: Vibraphone, Ray Sherman: Piano, Jack Costanzo: Bongoes, Rollie Bundock: Bass, Mike Pacheo: Conga Drums, Unknown: Other Musicians, Joseph Gershenson: Conductor.]

- Main Title (Mancini)

11 June 1957   Los Angeles, USA

Benny Carter

Jazz Giant [CD, Original Classics, OJCCD 167-2]

[Musicians: Barney Kessel: Guitar, Benny Carter: Alto Saxophone, Ben Webster: Tenor Saxophone, Frank Rosolino: Trombone, André Previn: Piano, Jimmy Rowles: Piano, Leroy Vinnegar: Bass, Shelly Manne: Drums.]

- Blue Lou (Sampson)
- Old Fashioned Love (Mack)

22 July 1957   Los Angeles, USA

Benny Carter

Jazz Giant [CD, Original Classics, OJCCD 167-2]

[Musicians: Barney Kessel: Guitar, Benny Carter: Alto Saxophone, Ben Webster: Tenor Saxophone, Frank Rosolino: Trombone, André Previn: Piano, Shelly Manne: Drums, Leroy Vinnegar: Bass.]

- A Walkin' Thing (Carter)

[Musicians: Barney Kessel: Guitar, Benny Carter: Trumpet, Ben Webster: Tenor Saxophone, Frank Rosolino: Trombone, Jimmy Rowles: Piano, Shelly Manne: Drums, Leroy Vinnegar: Bass.]

- I'm Coming Virginia (Heywood)

24 July 1957 — Los Angeles, USA

Ella Fitzgerald

First Lady of Song [CD, Verve, 314 517 898 2]

[Musicians: Barney Kessel: Guitar, Ella Fitzgerald: Vocals.]

- Angel Eyes

Ella Fitzgerald

Get Happy [CD, Verve, 523 321-2]

[Musicians: Barney Kessel: Guitar, Pete Candoli: Trumpet, Harry Edison: Trumpet, Ray Linn: Trumpet, George Werth: Trumpet, Milt Bernhart: Trombone, George Roberts: Trombone, Lloyd Ulyate: Trombone, Ben Webster: Tenor Saxophone, Clint Neagley: Alto Saxophone, Arnold Ross: Piano, Joe Mondragon: Bass, Alvin Stoller: Drums, Dorothy Lemsen: Harp, Nine Piece: Woodwind section, Milt Howard: Percussion, Ella Fitzgerald: Vocals, Frank DeVol: Conductor/Arranger, Twenty-Six Piece: String Section.]

- A-Tisket, A-Tasket (Feldman)
- Goody Goody (Malneck/Mercer)
- St. Louis Blues (Handy)
- The Gypsy In My Soul (Boland/Jaffe)
- You Turned The Tables On Me (Alter/Mitchell)

Ella Fitzgerald

Hello Love [LP, Verve, MG VS 6100]
Hello Love [CD, MCA Polygram, POCT-2760]

[Musicians: Barney Kessel: Guitar, Pete Candoli: Trumpet, Harry Edison: Trumpet, Ray Linn: Trumpet, George Werth: Trumpet, Milt Bernhart: Trombone, George Roberts: Trombone, Lloyd Ulyate: Trombone, Ben Webster: Tenor Saxophone, Clint Neagley: Alto Saxophone, Arnold Ross: Piano, Joe Mondragon: Bass, Alvin Stoller: Drums, Dorothy Lemsen: Harp, Nine Piece: Woodwind section, Milt Howard: Percussion, Ella Fitzgerald: Vocals, Frank DeVol: Conductor/Arranger, Twenty-Six Piece: String Section.]

- Moonlight In Vermont (Suessdorf/Blackburn)
- Stairway To The Stars (Malneck/Parish/Signorelli)
- Tenderly (Lawrence/Gross)

---

31 July 1957 — Los Angeles, USA

Barney Kessel

Barney Kessel Quartet [LP, Playboy, PB1957-3]

[Musicians: Barney Kessel: Guitar, Arnold Ross: Bass, Red Mitchell: Bass, Shelly Manne: Drums.]

- A Playboy In Love (Kessel)

---

01 August 1957 [Estimated] — Los Angeles, USA

Page Cavanagh

Swingin' Down The Road From Paris To Rome [LP, Capitol, T1001]

[Musicians: Barney Kessel or Al Hendrickson: Guitar, Page Cavanagh: Piano, Jack Smalley: Bass, Milt Holland: Drums.]

- Anema E Core (Curtis/Akst/Manilo/D'esposito)
- Comme Ci Comme Ca (Coquatrix)
- Domino (Ferrari/Plante)
- Echoes In The Night (Raye/Panzuti/Deani)
- I Only Know I Love You (Stillman/Calise/Rossi)
- If You Love Me, Really Love Me (Monnot)
- Love Theme From 'La Strada' (Galdieri/Rota)
- Mandolino Di Napoli (Raye/DePaul/Mario/Giordano)
- Munasterio E Santa Chiara (Raye/Barberis)
- Petite Waltz (Heyne)
- Pigalle (Ulmer/Kager)

Scalinatella (Wilson/Cioffi)

Souvenir D'Italie (Luttazzi/Scarnicci/Tarabusi)

Tu Voio Ben (Bidoli)

Under Paris Skies (Giraud/Drejac)

[Musicians: Barney Kessel: Guitar, Page Cavanagh: Piano, Jack Smalley: Bass, Milt Holland: Drums.]

C'Est Si Bon (Betti/Hornez)

I Wish You Love (Trenet/Beach)

Kickin' The Can (Raye)

---

06 August 1957   Los Angeles, USA

Barney Kessel

Let's Cook! [LP, Contemporary, S7603]
Let's Cook! [CD, Contemporary, OJCCD 1010-2]

[Musicians: Barney Kessel: Guitar, Frank Rosolino: Trombone, Ben Webster: Tenor Saxophone, Jimmy Rowles: Piano, Leroy Vinnegar: Bass, Shelly Manne: Drums.]

Jersey Bounce (Plater/Johnson/Bradshaw/Wright)

Tiger Rag (Original Dixieland Jazz Band)

---

31 August 1957   Los Angeles, USA

Ella Fitzgerald

Ella Fitzgerald Sings The Rodgers & Hart Songbook [CD, Verve, 314 537258 2]

[Musicians: Barney Kessel: Guitar, Ella Fitzgerald: Vocals, Milt Bernhart: Trombone, Joe Howard: Trombone, Pete Candoli: Trumpet, Conrad Gozzo: Trumpet, Maynard Ferguson: Trumpet, George Roberts: Bass Trombone, Bud Shank: Alto Saxophone, Ted Nash: Tenor Saxophone, Chuck Gentry: Baritone Saxophone, Paul Smith: Piano, Joe Mondragon: Bass, Alvin Stoller: Drums, Buddy Bregman: Conductor.]

A Ship Without A Sail (Rodgers/Hart)

Bewitched (Rodgers/Hart)

Blue Moon (Rodgers/Hart)

Dancing On The Ceiling (Rodgers/Hart)

Ev'rything I've Got (Rodgers/Hart)

Give It Back To The Indians (Rodgers/Hart)

Have You Met Miss Jones? (Rodgers/Hart)

Here In My Arms (Rodgers/Hart)

I Could Write A Book (Rodgers/Hart)

I Didn't Know What Time It Was (Rodgers/Hart)

I Wish I Were In Love Again (Rodgers/Hart)

Isn't It Romantic (Rodgers/Hart)

It Never Entered My Mind (Rodgers/Hart)

I've Got Five Dollars (Rodgers/Hart)

Johnny One Note (Rodgers/Hart)

Little Girl Blue (Rodgers/Hart)

Lover (Monaural Take) (Rodgers/Hart)

Lover (Stereo Take) (Rodgers/Hart)

Manhattan (Rodgers/Hart)

Mountain Greenery (Rodgers/Hart)

My Funny Valentine (Rodgers/Hart)

My Heart Stood Still (Rodgers/Hart)

My Romance (Rodgers/Hart)

Spring Is Here (Rodgers/Hart)

Ten Cents A Dance (Rodgers/Hart)

  The Blue Room (Rodgers/Hart)
  The Lady Is A Tramp (Rodgers/Hart)
  There's A Small Hotel (Rodgers/Hart)
  This Can't Be Love (Rodgers/Hart)
  Thou Swell (Rodgers/Hart)
  To Keep My Love Alive (Rodgers/Hart)
  Wait Till You See Her (Rodgers/Hart)
  Where Or When (Rodgers/Hart)
  With A Song In My Heart (Rodgers/Hart)
  You Took Advantage Of Me (Rodgers/Hart)

10 September 1957   Los Angeles, USA

Jack Montrose All - Stars

The Horn's Full [CD, BMG, 74321 18521 2]

[Musicians: Barney Kessel: Guitar, Jack Montrose: Tenor Saxophone, Red Norvo: Vibraphone, Larry Wooten: Bass, Mel Lewis: Drums.]

  Polka Dots And Moonbeams (Van Heusen)
  Rosanne (Osser)
  Solid Citizen (Montrose)
  The Little House (Montrose)

11 September 1957   Los Angeles, USA

Jack Montrose All - Stars

The Horn's Full [CD, BMG, 74321 18521 2]

[Musicians: Barney Kessel: Guitar, Jack Montrose: Tenor Saxophone, Red Norvo: Vibraphone, Larry Wooten: Bass, Mel Lewis: Drums.]

  Do Nothing Till You Hear From Me (Ellington)
  Goody Goody (Mercer)
  The Horn's Full (Montrose)
  True Blue (Montrose)

26 September 1957   Los Angeles, USA

Woody Herman with Barney Kessel Orchestra

Woody Herman Sings [EP, Verve, 10102]

[Musicians: Barney Kessel: Guitar, Woody Herman: Vocals, George Auld: Tenor Saxophone, Jimmy Rowles: Piano, Joe Mondragon: Bass, Alvin Stoller: Drums, Unknown: Male Vocal Chorus.]

  My Heart Reminds Me (Bargoni/Stillman/Siegel)
  The One I Love Belongs To Somebody Else (Jones/Kahn)

Woody Herman with Barney Kessel Orchestra

Woody Herman Sings [EP, Verve, 10121]

[Musicians: Barney Kessel: Guitar, Woody Herman: Vocals, George Auld: Tenor Saxophone, Jimmy Rowles: Piano, Joe Mondragon: Bass, Alvin Stoller: Drums, Unknown: Male Vocal Chorus.]

  Blue Flame
  Caldonia (Moore/Moine)

07 October 1957　　　　　　　　**Los Angeles, USA**

Benny Carter

Jazz Giant [CD, Original Classics, OJCCD 167-2]
[Musicians: Barney Kessel: Guitar, Benny Carter: Trumpet, Ben Webster: Tenor Saxophone, Frank Rosolino: Trombone, André Previn: Piano, Leroy Vinnegar: Bass, Shelly Manne: Drums.]

　　　How Can You Lose (Carter)

---

29 October 1957　　　　　　　　**Los Angeles, USA**

Buddy DeFranco

Buddy DeFranco Plays Benny Goodman [LP, Verve, MG V-2089]
Buddy DeFranco Plays Benny Goodman [CD, Polydor KK Japan, J25J 25154]
[Musicians: Barney Kessel: Guitar, Buddy DeFranco: Clarinet, George Auld: Tenor Saxophone, Don Fagerquist: Trumpet, Victor Feldman: Vibraphone, Carl Perkins: Piano, Leroy Vinnegar: Bass, Stan Levey: Drums.]

　　　A Smooth One (Goodman)
　　　Airmail Special (Christian?Goodman/Mundy)
　　　Benny's Bugle (Goodman/Basie)
　　　Good-Bye (Jenkins)
　　　Medley: Body and Soul (Green/Heyman/Sour/Eyton)
　　　　　　Memories of You (Razaf/Blake)
　　　　　　Sweet Lorraine (Burnell/Parish)
　　　More Than You Know (Youmans/Eliscu/Rose)
　　　Seven Come Eleven (Christian/Goodman)
　　　Wholly Cats (Goodman)

Buddy DeFranco

Buddy DeFranco Plays Benny Goodman [LP, Verve, MGV2108]
Buddy DeFranco Plays Benny Goodman [CD, Polydor KK Japan, J25J 25154]
[Musicians: Barney Kessel: Guitar, Buddy DeFranco: Clarinet, Don Fagerquist: Trumpet, George Auld: Tenor Saxophone, Carl Perkins: Piano, Leroy Vinnegar: Bass, Stan Levey: Drums, Victor Feldman: Vibraphone.]

　　　The Sheik Of Araby (Smith/Snyder/Wheeler)

---

30 October 1957　　　　　　　　**Los Angeles, USA**

Buddy DeFranco

Buddy DeFranco Plays Benny Goodman [LP, Verve, MG V-2089]
Buddy DeFranco Plays Benny Goodman [CD, Polydor KK Japan, J25J 25154]
[Musicians: Barney Kessel: Guitar, Buddy DeFranco: Clarinet, George Auld: Tenor Saxophone, Don Fagerquist: Trumpet, Larry Bunker: Vibraphone, Carl Perkins: Piano, Leroy Vinnegar: Bass, Bob Neal: Drums.]

　　　Rose Room (Hickman/Williams)

Buddy DeFranco

Buddy DeFranco Plays Benny Goodman [LP, Verve, MGV2108]
Buddy DeFranco Plays Benny Goodman [CD, Polydor KK Japan, J25J 25154]
[Musicians: Barney Kessel: Guitar, Buddy DeFranco: Clarinet, Don Fagerquist: Trumpet, George Auld: Tenor Saxophone, Carl Perkins: Piano, Leroy Vinnegar: Bass, Bob Neal: Drums, Larry Bunker: Vibraphone.]

　　　Oh Lady Be Good (Gershwin/Gershwin)
　　　Soft Winds (Goodman)

Buddy DeFranco

Closed Session Buddy DeFranco [LP, Verve, MG V-8382]
[Musicians: Barney Kessel: Guitar, Buddy DeFranco: Clarinet, George Auld: Tenor Saxophone, Don Fagerquist: Trumpet, Larry Bunker: Vibraphone, Carl Perkins: Piano, Leroy Vinnegar: Bass, Bob Neal: Drums.]

　　　After You've Gone (Layton/Creamer)

Don't Be That Way (Goodman/Sampson/Parrish)
Limehouse Blues (Braham/Furber)
Medley: Poor Butterfly (Hubbell/Golden)
    These Foolish Things (Link/Strachey/Marvell)
    Where Or When (Rodgers/Hart)
My Blue Heaven (Donaldson/Whiting)
Softly As In A Morning Sunrise (Romberg/Hammerstein)
S'Wonderful (Gershwin/Gershwin)
Temptation (Fredd/Brown)

---

31 October 1957   Los Angeles, USA

Buddy DeFranco

Buddy DeFranco Plays Artie Shaw [LP, Verve, MG V-2090]
Buddy DeFranco Plays Artie Shaw [CD, Polydor KK Japan, J25J 25155]
[Musicians: Barney Kessel: Guitar, Buddy DeFranco: Clarinet, Ray Linn: Trumpet, Jimmy Rowles: Piano/Harpsichord, Joe Mondragon: Bass, Alvin Stoller: Drums.]

Concerto For Clarinet (DeFranco)
Keeping Myself For You (Youmans/Clare)
Medley: I Cover The Waterfront (Green/Heyman)
    It Could Happen To You (Burke)
    Someone To Watch Over Me (Gershwin/Gershwin)
My Heart Stood Still (Rodgers/Hart)

Buddy DeFranco

Buddy DeFranco Plays Artie Shaw [LP, Verve, MGV2108]
Buddy DeFranco Plays Artie Shaw [CD, Polydor KK Japan, J25J 25155]
[Musicians: Barney Kessel: Guitar, Buddy DeFranco: Clarinet, Ray Linn: Trumpet, Jimmy Rowles: Piano/Harpsichord, Joe Mondragon: Bass, Alvin Stoller: Drums.]

Dancing In The Dark (Dietz/Schwartz)
Medley: Moonglow (Hudson/Mills/DeLange)
    Time On My Hands (Youmans/Adamson/Gordon)

Buddy DeFranco

Wholly Cats [LP, Verve, MG V-8375]
[Musicians: Barney Kessel: Guitar, Buddy DeFranco: Clarinet, Ray Linn: Trumpet, Jimmy Rowles: Piano, Joe Mondragon: Bass, Alvin Stoller: Drums.]

All The Things You Are (Kern/Hammerstein)
I Surrender Dear (Barris/Clifford)
Night And Day (Porter)
Smoke Gets In Your Eyes (Kern/Harbach)

---

01 November 1957   Los Angeles, USA

Buddy DeFranco

Buddy DeFranco Plays Artie Shaw [LP, Verve, MG V-2090]
Buddy DeFranco Plays Artie Shaw [CD, Polydor KK Japan, J25J 25155]
[Musicians: Barney Kessel: Guitar, Buddy DeFranco: Clarinet, Ray Linn: Trumpet, Paul Smith (Irving Garner): Piano/Harpsichord, Joe Mondragon: Bass, Milt Holland: Drums.]

Frenesi (Dominquez/Charles/Russell)
Stardust (Carmichael/Parish)

Buddy DeFranco

Buddy DeFranco Plays Artie Shaw [LP, Verve, MGV2108]
Buddy DeFranco Plays Artie Shaw [CD, Polydor KK Japan, J25J 25155]
[Musicians: Barney Kessel: Guitar, Buddy DeFranco: Clarinet, Ray Linn: Trumpet, Paul Smith (Irving Garner): Piano/Harpsichord, Joe Mondragon: Bass, Milt Holland: Drums.]

- Cross Your Heart (DeSylva/Gensier)
- Indian Love Call (Frimi/Harbach/Hammerstein)

---

11 November 1957   Los Angeles, USA

Barney Kessel

Let's Cook! [LP, Contemporary, S7603]
Let's Cook! [CD, Contemporary, OJCCD 1010-2]
[Musicians: Barney Kessel: Guitar, Victor Feldman: Vibraphone, Hampton Hawes: Piano, Leroy Vinnegar: Bass, Shelly Manne: Drums.]

- Just In Time (Styne/Comden/Green)
- Let's Cook (Kessel)
- Time Remembered (Duke)

---

27 December 1957   Los Angeles, USA

T-Bone Walker

T-Bone Blues [CD, Atlantic Jazz, 8020-2]
T-Bone Blues [LP, Atlantic, SD 8256]
[Musicians: Barney Kessel: Guitar, R. S. Rankin: Guitar, T-Bone Walker: Guitar, Plas Johnson: Tenor Saxophone, Ray Johnson: Piano, Joe Comfort: Bass, Earl Palmer: Drums.]

- Blues Rock (Walker)
- Evenin' (Parish)
- How Long Blues (Carr)
- Two Bones And A Pick (Walker)
- You Don't Know What You're Doing (Adams)

---

01 January 1958 [Estimated]   Los Angeles, USA

Benny Goodman

Happy Session [CD, Columbia, 14-476523-10]
Happy Session [LP, Columbia, CL 1324]
[Musicians: Barney Kessel: Guitar, Benny Goodman: Clarinet, André Previn: Piano, Leroy Vinnegar: Bass, Frank Capp: Drums.]

- Having A Ball (Goodman)
- You'd Be So Nice To Come Home To (Porter)

---

27 January 1958   Los Angeles, USA

Hampton Hawes

FOUR! [CD, Contemporary, OJCCD-165-2]
FOUR! [LP, Contemporary, S7553]
[Musicians: Barney Kessel: Guitar, Hampton Hawes: Piano, Red Mitchell: Bass, Shelly Manne: Drums.]

- Bow Jest (Mitchell)
- Like Someone in Love (Burke/Van Heusen)
- Love is Just Around The Corner (Robin/Gensier)
- Sweet Sue (Young/Harris)

    The Awful Truth (Hawes)
    Ther Will Never Be Another You (Warren/Gordon)
    Thou Swell (Rodgers/Hart)
    Up Blues (Hawes)
    Yardbird Suite (Parker)

13 March 1958   Los Angeles, USA

Ella Fitzgerald

Ella Fitzgerald Sings The Irving Berlin Song Book [CD, Verve, 314 543830 2]

[Musicians: Barney Kessel: Guitar, Ella Fitzgerald: Vocals, Don Fagerquist: Trumpet, Fred Stuice: Clarinet, Ted Nash: Tenor Saxophone, Babe Russin: Tenor Saxophone, Chuck Gentry: Baritone Saxophone, Gene Cipriani: Woodwind, Paul Smith: Piano, Jack Ryan: Bass, Alvin Stoller: Drums, Paul Weston: Arranger/Conductor.]

    Always (Berlin)
    I'm Putting All My Eggs In One Basket (Berlin)
    Isn't This A Lovely Day (Berlin)
    Let's Go Slumming On Park Avenue (Berlin)
    Russian Lullaby (Berlin)

14 March 1958   Los Angeles, USA

Ella Fitzgerald

Ella Fitzgerald Sings The Irving Berlin Song Book [CD, Verve, 314 543830 2]

[Musicians: Barney Kessel: Guitar, Ella Fitzgerald: Vocals, Don Fagerquist: Trumpet, Matty Matlock: Clarinet, Ted Nash: Tenor Saxophone, Babe Russin: Tenor Saxophone, Chuck Gentry: Baritone Saxophone, Gene Cipriani: Woodwind, Paul Smith: Piano, Jack Ryan: Bass, Alvin Stoller: Drums, Paul Weston: Arranger/Conductor.]

    How's Chances (Berlin)
    I Used To Be Colour Blind (Berlin)
    No Strings (Berlin)
    You Can Have Him (Berlin)

17 March 1958   Los Angeles, USA

Ella Fitzgerald

Ella Fitzgerald Sings The Irving Berlin Song Book [CD, Verve, 314 543830 2]

[Musicians: Barney Kessel: Guitar, Ella Fitzgerald: Vocals, Don Fagerquist: Trumpet, Harry Edison: Trumpet, John Best: Trumpet, Manny Klein: Trumpet, Pete Candoli: Trumpet, Ed Kusby: Trombone, Dick Noel: Trombone, William Schaefer: Trombone, Juan Tizol: Trombone, Chuck Gentry: Baritone Saxophone, Matty Matlock: Clarinet, Ted Nash: Tenor Saxophone, Fred Stulce: Flute, Babe Russin: Tenor Saxophone, Paul Smith: Piano, Jack Ryan: Bass, Alvin Stoller: Drums, Paul Weston: Arranger/Conductor.]

    Change Partners (Berlin)
    Get Thee Behind Me Satan (Berlin)
    How About Me? (Berlin)
    How Deep Is The Ocean? (Berlin)
    Now It Can Be Told (Berlin)
    Reaching For The Moon (Berlin)
    Supper Time (Berlin)
    You Keep Coming Back Like A Song (Berlin)
    You're Laughing At Me (Berlin)

18 March 1958   **Los Angeles, USA**

Ella Fitzgerald

Ella Fitzgerald Sings The Irving Berlin Song Book [CD, Verve, 314 543830 2]

[Musicians: Barney Kessel: Guitar, Ella Fitzgerald: Vocals, Don Fagerquist: Trumpet, Harry Edison: Trumpet, John Best: Trumpet, Manny Klein: Trumpet, Pete Candoli: Trumpet, Ed Kusby: Trombone, Dick Noel: Trombone, William Schaefer: Trombone, Juan Tizol: Trombone, Chuck Gentry: Baritone Saxophone, Matty Matlock: Clarinet, Ted Nash: Tenor Saxophone, Fred Stulce: Flute, Babe Russin: Tenor Saxophone, Paul Smith: Piano, Jack Ryan: Bass, Alvin Stoller: Drums, Paul Weston: Arranger/Conductor.]

    All By Myself (Berlin)
    Blue Skies (Berlin)
    Cheek To Cheek (Berlin)
    Heat Wave (Berlin)
    It' A Lovely Day Today (Berlin)
    I've Got My Love To Keep Me Warm (Berlin)
    Lazy (Berlin)
    Let's Face The Music And Dance (Berlin)
    Puttin' On The Ritz (Berlin)
    The Song Is Ended (Berlin)
    You Forgot To Remember (Berlin)

Ella Fitzgerald

Get Happy [CD, Verve, 523 321-2]

[Musicians: Barney Kessel: Guitar, John Best: Trumpet, Pete Candoli: Trumpet, Harry Edison: Trumpet, Don Fagerquist: Trumpet, Manny Klein: Trumpet, Ed Kusby: Trombone, Dick Noel: Trombone, William Schaefer: Trombone, Juan Tizol: Valve Trombone, Chuck Gentry: Reeds, Matty Matlock: Reeds, Ted Nash: Reeds, Babe Russin: Reeds, Fred Stulce: Reeds, Paul Smith: Piano, Joe Mondragon: Bass, Alvin Stoller: Drums, Ella Fitzgerald: Vocals.]

    Blue Skies (Berlin)

---

19 March 1958   **Los Angeles, USA**

Ella Fitzgerald

Ella Fitzgerald Sings The Irving Berlin Song Book [CD, Verve, 314 543830 2]

[Musicians: Barney Kessel: Guitar, Ella Fitzgerald: Vocals, Fred Stulce: Flute, Harry Edison: Trumpet, Leonard Hartman: Woodwind, Matty Matlock: Clarinet, Ted Nash: Tenor Saxophone, Paul Smith: Piano, Joe Mondragon: Bass, Alvin Stoller: Drums, Paul Weston: Arranger/Conductor.]

    Alexander's Ragtime Band (Berlin)
    Let Yourself Go (Berlin)
    Top Hat, White Tie, And Tails (Berlin)

Ella Fitzgerald

Get Happy [CD, Verve, 523 321-2]

[Musicians: Barney Kessel: Guitar, Harry Edison: Trumpet, Leonard Hartman: Flute, Matty Matlock: Flute, Ted Nash: Flute, Fred Stulce: Flute, Paul Smith: Piano, Joe Mondragon: Bass, Alvin Stoller: Drums, Paul Weston: Arranger/Conductor.]

    Swingin' Shepherd Blues (Roberts/Jacobs/Koffman)

---

02 April 1958   **Los Angeles, USA**

Buddy DeFranco

Generalissimo [LP, Verve, MGV 8363]

[Musicians: Barney Kessel: Guitar, Buddy DeFranco: Clarinet, Harry Edison: Trumpet, Bob Hardaway: Tenor Saxophone, Jimmy Rowles: Piano, Curtis Counce: Bass, Alvin Stoller: Drums.]

    Between The Devil And The Deep Blue Sea (Arlen/Koehler)
    Blue Lou (Sampson/Mills)
    Funky's Uncle (Kessel/DeFranco)
    Medley: How Can We Be Wrong? (Schwartz/Stillman/Dietz)

Lullaby Of The Leaves (Petkere/Young)
Round Midnight (Monk/Hanighen/Williams)
Yesterdays (Kern/Harbach)
You Don't Know What Love Is (Raye/DePaul)
Sunday (Conn/Miller/Stein/Krueger)
Tea For Two (Youmans/Caesar/Harbach)

---

04 April 1958   **Los Angeles, USA**

Buddy DeFranco

Live Date [LP, Verve, MGV8383]

[Musicians: Barney Kessel: Guitar, Buddy DeFranco: Clarinet, Herbie Mann: Tenor Saxophone/Flute, Victor Feldman: Vibraphone/Piano, Pete Jolly: Piano/Accordion, Scott LeFaro: Bass, Stan Levey: Drums.]

Blues For Space Travellers (Kessel)
Crazy Rhythm (Caesar/Meyer/Kahn)
Lullaby Of Birdland (Shearing/Forster)
Medley: I'm Glad There Is You (Madeira/Dorsey)
    There's No You (Adair/Hopper/Dergen)
    These Foolish Things (Marvell/Strachey/Link)
My Funny Valentine (Rodgers/Hart)
Oh Lady Be Good (Gershwin/Gershwin)
Satin Doll (Ellington)
Tin Reed Blues (DeFranco)

---

05 April 1958   **Los Angeles, USA**

Buddy DeFranco

Bravura [LP, Verve, MGV 8315]

[Musicians: Barney Kessel: Guitar, Buddy DeFranco: Clarinet, Harry Edison: Trumpet, Herbie Mann: Flute/Bass Clarinet, Jimmy Rowles: Piano, Joe Mondragon: Bass, Mel Lewis: Drums.]

Ja-Da 1 (Carelton)
Just Squeeze Me (Ellington/Gains)
Lulu's Back In Town (Warren/Dubin)
Medley: Darn That Dream (DeLange/Van Heusen)
    Honey (Whiting/Simons/Gillespie)
    How Long Has This Been Going On? (Gershwin/Gershwin)
    Now I Lay Me Down To Dream (Howard/Fiorito)
    Old Folks (Hill/Robison)
    Please (Robin/Rainger)
    This Love Of Mine (Sinatra/Sanacola)
    Witty (DeFranco)
Undecided (Shavers/Robin)

---

21 April 1958   **Los Angeles, USA**

Benny Carter

Jazz Giant [CD, Original Classics, OJCCD 167-2]

[Musicians: Barney Kessel: Guitar, Benny Carter: Alto Saxophone, Leroy Vinnegar: Bass, Shelly Manne: Drums, André Previn: Piano.]

Blues My Naughty Sweetie Gives To Me (Swanstone/McCarron/Morgan)

[Musicians: Barney Kessel: Guitar, Benny Carter: Trumpet, Shelly Manne: Drums, Leroy Vinnegar: Bass, André Previn: Piano.]

Ain't She Sweet (Ager/Yellen)

01 May 1958 [Estimated]   Los Angeles, USA

Barney Kessel

Barney Kessel - Military Swing [CD, JazzBank Archives, MTCJ-1094]

[Musicians: Barney Kessel: Guitar, Frank Patchen: Piano, Albert Stinson: Bass, Shelly Manne: Drums, Victor Feldman: Vibraphone & Percussion.]

- Hungarian Dance No. 5 (Brahms)
- Ritual Fire Dance (De Falla)
- Serenade To Servicemen (Stinson)

05 May 1958 [Estimated]   Los Angeles, USA

Candoli Brothers

Candoli Brothers [LP, Colpix, CLP 502]

[Musicians: Barney Kessel: Guitar, Conte Candoli: Trumpet, Pete Candoli: Trumpet, Jimmy Rowles or John Williams: Piano, Red Mitchell or Joe Mondragon: Bass, Alvin Stoller: Drums.]

- Bell, Book And Candle
- Herb Shop
- I Wish I Could Shimmy Like My Sister Kate
- Only Human
- Pywackert-Queenie-Girl
- Send Me Nikki
- Shep Hook
- Shep Hooked
- Stormy Weather Polka
- The Spell
- Way Out Calypso
- Where Pywackert
- Zodiac Blues
- Zodiac Serenade

30 May 1958   Los Angeles, USA

Peggy Lee

Things Are Swingin' [CD, Capitol, 7243 5 97071 2 9]

[Musicians: Barney Kessel: Guitar, Peggy Lee: Vocals, Uan Rasey: Trumpet, Pete Candoli: Trumpet, Mannie Klein: Trumpet, Bob Enevoldsen: Valve Trombone, Milt Bernhardt: Trombone, Justin Gordon: Reeds, George Smith: Reeds, Joe Harnell: Piano, Joe Mondragon: Bass, Shelly Manne: Drums.]

- Alone Together (Dietz/Schwartz)
- I'm Beginning To See The Light (Ellington/Hodges/George/James)
- It's A Wonderful World (Adamson/Savitt/Watson)

01 June 1958 [Estimated]   Los Angeles, USA

Benny Carter

Aspects Benny Carter [CD, Capitol, 7243 8 52677 2 7]

[Musicians: Barney Kessel: Guitar, Benny Carter: Alto Saxophone/Trumpet, Al Porcini: Trumpet, Stu Williamson: Trumpet, Ray Triscari: Trumpet, Joe Gordon: Trumpet, Frank Rosolino: Trombone, Tommy Pederson: Trombone, Russ Bown: Trombone, Buddy Collette: Reeds, Bill Green: Reeds, Jewel Grant: Reeds, Plas Johnson: Reeds, Gerald Wiggins: Piano, Joe Comfort: Bass, Shelly Manne: Drums.]

- June Is Busting Out All Over (Mono Take) (Rodgers/Hammerstein)
- June Is Busting Out All Over (Rodgers/Hammerstein)
- March Wind (Carter)

Roses In December (Magidson/Oakland/Jessel)
Sleigh Ride In July (Burke/Van Heusen)
Something For October (Carter)
Swingin' In November (Mono Take) (Carter)
Swingin' In November (Carter)

---

20 June 1958   Los Angeles, USA

Jimmy Rowles

Let's Get Acquainted With Jazz [CD, V.S.O.P., #VSOP 11 CD]
Let's Get Acquainted With Jazz [LP, Tampa, TP-8]
El Tigre [LP, Parker, PLP 832]
Barney Kessel with Jimmy Rowles Sextet [EP, Sonet, SXP2841]

[Musicians: Barney Kessel: Guitar, Jimmy Rowles: Piano, Red Mitchell: Bass, Mel Lewis: Drums, Harold Land: Tenor Saxophone, Larry Bunker: Vibraphone.]

East Of The Sun (Bowman)
Lullaby Of Birdland (Shearing)
Perdido (Tizol)
The Blues (Take One) (Rowles)
The Blues (Take Two) (Rowles)
The Cobra (Rowles)

[Musicians: Barney Kessel: Guitar, Jimmy Rowles: Piano, Red Mitchell: Bass, Mel Lewis: Drums, Pete Candoli: Trumpet.]

All For You (Scherman)
Body And Soul (Green/Heyman/Sour/Eyton)
Cheeta's For Two (Rowles)
El Tigre (Rowles)
Tea For Two (Youmans/Caesar)

---

28 July 1958   Los Angeles, USA

Bing Crosby & Rosemary Clooney

Fancy Meeting You Here - Crosby-Clooney [CD, BMG Bluebird, 09026-63859-2]

[Musicians: Barney Kessel: Guitar, Buddy Cole: Piano, Frank Beach: Trumpet, Pete Candoli: Trumpet, Uan Rasey: Trumpet, Shorty Sherock: Trumpet, Simon Zentner: Trombone, Murray McEarchen: Trombone, Ed Kusby: Trumpet, George Roberts: Trombone, Ted Nash: Tenor Saxophone, Willie Schwartz: Tenor Saxophone, Buddy Collette: Alto Saxophone, Jules Jacobs: Alto Saxophone, Fred Falensby: Baritone Saxophone, Phil Stephens: Tuba, Joe Mondragon: Bass, Alvin Stoller: Drums, Ralph Hansell: Percussion, Milt Holland: Percussion.]

Brazil (Russell/Barroso)
How About You (Freed/Lane)
Love Won't Let You Get Away (Cahn/Van Heusen)
On a Slow Boat to China (Loesser)

---

07 August 1958   Los Angeles, USA

Bing Crosby & Rosemary Clooney

Fancy Meeting You Here - Crosby-Clooney [CD, BMG Bluebird, 09026-63859-2]

[Musicians: Barney Kessel: Guitar, Buddy Cole: Piano, Frank Beach: Trumpet, Pete Candoli: Trumpet, Uan Rasey: Trumpet, Manny Klein: Trumpet, Simon Zentner: Trombone, Murray McEarchen: Trombone, Ed Kusby: Trumpet, George Roberts: Trombone, Ted Nash: Tenor Saxophone, Willie Schwartz: Tenor Saxophone, Buddy Collette: Alto Saxophone, Jules Jacobs: Alto Saxophone, Fred Falensby: Baritone Saxophone, Red Callender: Tuba, Joe Mondragon: Bass, Alvin Stoller: Drums, Ralph Hansell: Percussion, Milt Holland: Percussion.]

Calcutta (Livingston/Evans)
Fancy Meeting You Here (Cahn/Van Heusen)
Hindustan (Wallace/Weeks)

It Happened in Monterey (Wayne/Rose)

11 August 1958 Los Angeles, USA

Bing Crosby & Rosemary Clooney

Fancy Meeting You Here - Crosby-Clooney [CD, BMG Bluebird, 09026-63859-2]

[Musicians: Barney Kessel: Guitar, Buddy Cole: Piano, Frank Beach: Trumpet, Pete Candoli: Trumpet, Uan Rasey: Trumpet, Shorty Sherock: Trumpet, Simon Zentner: Trombone, Murray McEarchen: Trombone, Ed Kusby: Trumpet, George Roberts: Trombone, Jules Kinsler: Tenor Saxophone, Willie Schwartz: Tenor Saxophone, Buddy Collette: Alto Saxophone, Jules Jacobs: Alto Saxophone, Fred Falensby: Baritone Saxophone, Phil Stephens: Tuba, Ralph Pena: Bass, Larry Bunker: Drums, Ralph Hansell: Percussion, Milt Holland: Percussion.]

    I Can't Get Started (Gershwin/Duke)
    Isle of Capri (Kennedy/Grosz)
    Love Won't Let You Get Away (Alt) (Cahn/Van Heusen)
    Say "Si Si" (Lecuona/Stillman/Luban)
    You Came A Long Way From St. Louis (Brooks/Russell)

19 August 1958 Los Angeles, USA

Barney Kessel

The Poll Winners Ride Again [LP, Contemporary, S3114]
The Poll Winners Ride Again [CD, Contemporary, OJCCD607-2]

[Musicians: Barney Kessel: Guitar, Shelly Manne: Drums, Ray Brown: Bass.]

    Angel Eyes (Dennis)
    Be Deedle Dee Do (Kessel)
    Custard Puff (Brown)
    Foreign Intrigue (Kessel)
    Spring Is Here (Rodgers/Hart)
    The Merry Go Round Broke Down (Franklin)
    The Surrey With The Fringe On Top (Rodgers/Hart)
    Volare (Migliacci/Modugno/Parrish)
    When The Red Red Robin (Woods)

31 August 1958 Los Angeles, USA

Henry Mancini

The Music From Peter Gunn [CD, Buddha/BMG, 7446599610 2]
The Music From Peter Gunn [LP, RCA Victor, LSP-1956]

[Musicians: Barney Kessel: Guitar, Henry Mancini: Conductor, Conrad Gozzo: Trumpet, Pete Candoli: Trumpet, Frank Beach: Trumpet, Uan Rasey: Trumpet, Milt Bernhardt: Trombone, Dick Nash: Trombone, Karl De Karske: Trombone, Jimmy Priddy: Trombone, Plas Johnson: Saxophones, Ted Nash: Saxophones, John Williams: Piano, Al Hendrickson: Rhythm Guitar, Rolly Bundock: Bass, Jack Sperling: Drums, Larry Bunker: Vibraphone.]

    Dreamsville (Mancini)
    Session At Pete's Pad (Mancini)

04 September 1958 Los Angeles, USA

Benny Goodman

Benny Rides Again! [CD, MCA, CHD-31264]

[Musicians: Barney Kessel: Guitar, Benny Goodman: Clarinet, Andre Previn: Piano, Leroy Vinneger: Bass, Frank Capp: Drums.]

    Everything I'Ve Got

Benny Goodman

Swing International [LP, Jazztone, SJS 743]
Benny Rides Again! [CD, MCA, CHD-31264]
[Musicians: Barney Kessel: Guitar, Benny Goodman: Clarinet, Andre Previn: Piano, Leroy Vinneger: Bass, Frank Capp: Drums.]

    Stereo Stomp (Goodman)

---

08 September 1958   Los Angeles, USA

Benny Goodman

Benny Goodman 1958-1967 Era [LP, Festival, Double 246]
[Musicians: Barney Kessel: Guitar, Benny Goodman: Clarinet, Russ Freeman: Piano, Leroy Vinnegar: Bass, Frank Capp: Drums.]

    Avalon (Jolson/Rose/De Sylva)
    It's All Right With Me (Porter)
    Poor Butterfly (Hebbell/Golden)

---

16 October 1958   Los Angeles, USA

Shorty Rogers

Boots Brown And His Blockbusters [LP, RCA Victor, 20-7399]
[Musicians: Barney Kessel: Guitar, Shorty Rogers: Trumpet, Gil Bernal: Saxophones, Jimmy Rowles: Piano, Bill Pitman: Guitar, Milt Norman: Guitar, Red Callender: Bass, Shelly Manne: Drums, Larry Bunker: Percussion.]

    Corn Shuckin'
    Jim Twangy
    Trollin'

---

17 October 1958   Los Angeles, USA

Peggy Lee

I Like Men [LP, Capitol, T1131]
I Like Men/ Sugar 'N' Spice [CD, EMI, 7243 4 96729 2 5]
[Musicians: Barney Kessel: Guitar, Peggy Lee: Vocals, Jack Marshall: Conductor/Arranger, Benny Carter: Alto Saxophone, Pete Candoli: Trumpet, Jack Sheldon: Trumpet, Milt Bernhardt: Trombone, Frank Rosolino: Trombone, Jimmy Rowles: Piano, Unknown: Bass, Shelly Manne: Drums.]

    Charley, My Boy (Fiorito/Kahn)
    I'm Just Wild About Harry (Blake/Sissle)
    My Man (Charles/Pollock/Willemet)
    Oh Johnny, Oh Johnny Oh! (Olman/Rose)

---

19 October 1958   Los Angeles, USA

Peggy Lee

I Like Men [LP, Capitol, T1131]
I Like Men/ Sugar 'N' Spice [CD, EMI, 7243 4 96729 2 5]
[Musicians: Barney Kessel: Guitar, Peggy Lee: Vocals, Jack Marshall: Conductor/Arranger, Benny Carter: Alto Saxophone, Pete Candoli: Trumpet, Jack Sheldon: Trumpet, Milt Bernhardt: Trombone, Frank Rosolino: Trombone, Jimmy Rowles: Piano, Unknown: Bass, Shelly Manne: Drums.]

    I Like Men (Lee/Marshall)
    I Love To Love (Baker)
    It's so Nice To Have A Man Around The House (Elliot)
    So In Love (Porter)

20 October 1958   Los Angeles, USA

Sonny Rollins

Sonny Rollins and the Contemporary Leaders [CD, Contemporary, OJCCD-340-2]
Sonny Rollins and the Contemporary Leaders [LP, Contemporary, S-7564]
Sonny Rollins and the Contemporary Leaders [XRCD, JVC XRCD2, VICJ-60244]

[Musicians: Barney Kessel: Guitar, Sonny Rollins: Tenor Saxophone, Hampton Hawes: Piano, Leroy Vinnegar: Bass, Shelly Manne: Drums, Victor Feldman: Vibraphone.]

- You (Adamson/Donaldson)

[Musicians: Barney Kessel: Guitar, Sonny Rollins: Tenor Saxophone, Hampton Hawes: Piano, Leroy Vinnegar: Bass, Shelly Manne: Drums.]

- Alone Together (Schwartz/Dietz)
- How High The Moon (Lewis/Hamilton)
- In The Chapel In The Moonlight (Hill)
- I've Found A New Baby (Alt) (Palmer/Williams)
- I've Found A New Baby (Palmer/Williams)
- I've Told Ev'ry Little Star (Kern/Hammerstein)
- Rock-A-Bye Your Baby With A Dixie Melody (Lewis/Schwartz/Young)
- The Song Is You (Alt) (Kern/Hammerstein)
- The Song Is You (Kern/Hammerstein)

---

22 October 1958   Los Angeles, USA

Peggy Lee

I Like Men [LP, Capitol, T1131]
I Like Men/ Sugar 'N' Spice [CD, EMI, 7243 4 96729 2 5]

[Musicians: Barney Kessel: Guitar, Peggy Lee: Vocals, Jack Marshall: Conductor/Arranger, Benny Carter: Alto Saxophone, Pete Candoli: Trumpet, Jack Sheldon: Trumpet, Milt Bernhardt: Trombone, Frank Rosolino: Trombone, Jimmy Rowles: Piano, Unknown: Bass, Shelly Manne: Drums.]

- Bill (Hammerstein/Kern/Wodehouse)
- Good-For-Nothin' Joe (Bloom/Koehler)
- Jim (Petrillo/Samuels/Shawn)
- When A Woman Loves A Man (Hanighen/Jenkins)

---

24 October 1958   Los Angeles, USA

Bobby Troup

Bobby Troup and his Stars of Jazz [LP, RCA Victor, NL45669]

[Musicians: Barney Kessel: Guitar, Benny Carter: Alto Saxophone, Bob Cooper: Tenor Saxophone, Chuck Gentry: Baritone Saxophone, Bill Holman: Tenor Saxophone, Paul Horn: Alto Saxophone, Plas Johnson: Tenor Saxophone, Richie Kamuca: Tenor Saxophone, Bud Shank: Alto Saxophone, Buddy Childers: Trumpet, Conte Candoli: Trumpet, Pete Candoli: Trumpet, Ollie Mitchell: Trumpet, Al Porcino: Trumpet, Shorty Rogers: Trumpet, Ray Triscari: Trumpet, Stu Williamson: Trumpet, Milt Bernhart: Trombone, Harry Betts: Trombone, Bob Enevoldsen: Trombone.]

- As Long As I Live (Koehler/Arlen)
- Is You Is Or Is You Ain't My Baby (Jordan/Austin)
- Please Be Kind (Cahn/Chaplin)

01 November 1958 [Estimated]　　Los Angeles, USA

Jack Marshall

Soundsville! [LP, Capitol, T1194]

[Musicians: Barney Kessel: Guitar, Don Fagerquist: Trumpet, Manny Klein: Trumpet, Uan Rasey: Trumpet, Milt Bernhart: Trombone, Bob Enevoldsen: Valve Trombone, George Roberts: Bass Trombone, Justin Gordon: Saxophones, George Smith: Saxophones, Milt Raskin: Piano, Jack Marshall: Guitar/Zither/Arranger, Joe Mondragon: Bass, Mike Rubin: Bass, Shelly Manne: Drums, Larry Bunker: Percussion, Lou Singer: Percussion, Milt Holland: Percussion.]

- Baby It's Cold Outside (Loesser)
- Clouds (Kahn/Donaldson)
- Hot Sombrero (Marshall)
- Mimi (Rodgers/Hart)
- Should I? (Brown/Freed)
- Sonante (Marshall)
- The River Kwai March (Alford)
- The Third Man Theme (Karas/Lord)
- Tiptoe Through The Tulips (Burke/Dubin)
- Walking Around (Marshall)
- Whistle While You Work (Churchill/Morey)
- Whistlin' Blues (Marshall)

---

10 November 1958　　Los Angeles, USA

Bobby Troup

Bobby Troup and his Stars of Jazz [LP, RCA Victor, NL45669]

[Musicians: Barney Kessel: Guitar, Benny Carter: Alto Saxophone, Bob Cooper: Tenor Saxophone, Chuck Gentry: Baritone Saxophone, Bill Holman: Tenor Saxophone, Paul Horn: Alto Saxophone, Plas Johnson: Tenor Saxophone, Richie Kamuca: Tenor Saxophone, Bud Shank: Alto Saxophone, Buddy Childers: Trumpet, Conte Candoli: Trumpet, Pete Candoli: Trumpet, Ollie Mitchell: Trumpet, Al Porcino: Trumpet, Shorty Rogers: Trumpet, Ray Triscari: Trumpet, Stu Williamson: Trumpet, Milt Bernhart: Trombone, Harry Betts: Trombone, Bob Enevoldsen: Trombone.]

- Oh! You Crazy Moon (Burke/Van Heusen)
- Tip-Toe Thru The Tulips With Me (Burke/Dubin)
- Tulip Or Turnip (George/Ellington)

---

24 November 1958　　Los Angeles, USA

Candoli Brothers

Sessions Live [LP, Calliope, CAL 3025]

[Musicians: Barney Kessel: Guitar, Conte Candoli: Trumpet, Pete Candoli: Trumpet, Jimmy Rowles: Piano, Joe Mondragon: Bass, Alvin Stoller: Drums.]

- Chef Shook (Candoli)
- My Funny Valentine (Rodgers/Hart)
- Rockin' Boogie (Candoli)

---

03 December 1958　　Los Angeles, USA

Bobby Troup

Bobby Troup and his Stars of Jazz [LP, RCA Victor, NL45669]

[Musicians: Barney Kessel: Guitar, Benny Carter: Alto Saxophone, Bob Cooper: Tenor Saxophone, Chuck Gentry: Baritone Saxophone, Bill Holman: Tenor Saxophone, Paul Horn: Alto Saxophone, Plas Johnson: Tenor Saxophone, Richie Kamuca: Tenor Saxophone, Bud Shank: Alto Saxophone, Buddy Childers: Trumpet, Conte Candoli: Trumpet, Pete Candoli: Trumpet, Ollie Mitchell: Trumpet, Al Porcino: Trumpet, Shorty Rogers: Trumpet, Ray Triscari: Trumpet, Stu Williamson: Trumpet, Milt Bernhart: Trombone, Harry Betts: Trombone, Bob Enevoldsen: Trombone.]

- Back In Your Own Back Yard (Rose/Jolson/Dreyer)
- Free and Easy (Mancini/Troup)

I'm Thru With Love (Livingston/Malneck/Kahn)

Perdido (Tizol/Lengsfelder/Drake)

Sent For You Yesterday (Rushing/Basie/Durham)

Take Me Out To The Ball Game (Von Tilzer/Norworth)

05 December 1958   Los Angeles, USA

Candoli Brothers

Bell, Book And Candoli [LP, DOT, DLP 3168]
Bell, Book And Candoli [LP, MCA Impulse, MCA-29064]
Jazz Horizons [CD, Lone Hill Jazz, LHJ10167]

[Musicians: Barney Kessel: Guitar, Conte Candoli: Trumpet, Pete Candoli: Trumpet, Jimmy Rowles: Piano, Joe Mondragon: Bass, Alvin Stoller: Drums.]

- Bell, Book And Candoli (Candoli)
- Boulevard Of Broken Dreams (Warren/Dubin)
- Hey Bellboy (Candoli)
- I May Be Wrong (Ruskin/Sullivan)
- Night Walk (Candoli)
- Old Devil Moon (Harburg/Lane)
- Pagoda (Candoli)
- Pavanne (Gould)
- Spanish Carnival (Candoli)
- What Is This Thing Called Love? (Porter)

The Trombones, Inc.

The Trombones, Inc. [LP, Warner Bros., WS 1272]

[Musicians: Barney Kessel: Guitar, George Roberts: Trombone, Joe Howard: Trombone, Herbie Harper: Trombone, Frank Rosolino: Trombone, Dick Nash: Trombone, Ken Shroyer: Trombone, Ed Kusby: Trombone, Tommy Pederson: Trombone, Murray McEachern: Trombone, Marshall Cram: Trombone, Marty Paich: Piano, Red Mitchell: Bass, Mel Lewis: Drums, Mike Pacheco: Bongos, Warren Barker: Leader, Alvino Rey: Producer.]

- Impossible (Allen)
- Lassus Trombone (Fillmore)
- Old Devil Moon (Harburg/Lane)

09 December 1958   Los Angeles, USA

Shorty Rogers

Chances Are It Swings [CD, RCA, 74321433902]

[Musicians: Barney Kessel: Guitar, Shorty Rogers: Trumpet, Don Fagerquist: Trumpet, Conte Candoli: Trumpet, Al Porcino: Trumpet, Ollie Mitchell: Trumpet, Ray Triscari: Trumpet, Bob Enevoldsen: Valve Trombone, Harry Betts: Trombone, Dick Nash: Trombone, Ken Shroyer: Bass Trombone, Paul Horn: Clarinet, Bud Shank: Clarinet, Bill Holman: Tenor Saxophone, Richie Kamuca: Tenor Saxophone, Chuck Gentry: Baritone Saxophone, Gene Estes: Vibraphone, Pete Jolly: Piano, Howard Roberts: Guitar, Joe Mondragon: Bass.]

- Chances Are (Allen)
- It's Not For Me To Say (Allen)
- Lilac Chiffon (Allen)
- No Such Luck (Allen)

12 December 1958   Los Angeles, USA

Shorty Rogers

Chances Are It Swings [CD, RCA, 74321433902]

[Musicians: Barney Kessel: Guitar, Shorty Rogers: Trumpet, Don Fagerquist: Trumpet, Conte Candoli: Trumpet, Al Porcino: Trumpet, Ollie Mitchell: Trumpet, Ray Triscari: Trumpet, Bob Enevoldsen: Valve Trombone, Harry Betts: Trombone, Dick Nash: Trombone, Ken Shroyer: Bass Trombone, Paul Horn: Clarinet, Bud Shank: Clarinet, Bill Holman: Tenor Saxophone, Richie Kamuca: Tenor Saxophone, Chuck Gentry: Baritone Saxophone, Gene Estes: Vibraphone, Pete Jolly: Piano, Howard Roberts: Guitar, Joe Mondragon: Bass.]

     Everybody Loves A Lover (Allen)
     My Very Good Friend In The Looking Glass (Allen)
     Who Needs You (Allen)
     You Know How It Is (Allen)

---

19 December 1958   Los Angeles, USA

Barney Kessel

Carmen [CD, Contemporary, OJCCD-269-2]
Carmen [LP, Contemporary, SCA5011]

[Musicians: Barney Kessel: Guitar, André Previn: Piano, Joe Mondragon: Bass, Shelly Manne: Drums, Buddy Collette: Flute, Bill Smith: Clarinet, Jules Jacobs: Oboe, Pete Terry: Bassoon, Justin Gordon: Flute.]

     A Pad on the Edge of Town (Bizet (arr. Kessel))
     Flowersville (Bizet (arr. Kessel))
     Free as a Bird (Bizet (arr. Kessel))
     There's No Place Like (Bizet (arr. Kessel))
     Viva el Toro! (Bizet (arr. Kessel))

[Musicians: Barney Kessel: Guitar, André Previn: Piano, Joe Mondragon: Bass, Shelly Manne: Drums, Ray Linn: Trumpet, Harry Betts: Trombone, Herb Geller: Alto Saxophone, Chuck Gentry: Baritone Saxophone, Justin Gordon: Tenor Saxophone.]

     Swingin' the Toreador (Bizet (arr. Kessel))
     The Gypsy's Hip (Bizet (arr. Kessel))

---

20 December 1958   Los Angeles, USA

Shorty Rogers

Chances Are It Swings [CD, RCA, 74321433902]

[Musicians: Barney Kessel: Guitar, Shorty Rogers: Trumpet, Don Fagerquist: Trumpet, Conte Candoli: Trumpet, Al Porcino: Trumpet, Ollie Mitchell: Trumpet, Ray Triscari: Trumpet, Bob Enevoldsen: Valve Trombone, Harry Betts: Trombone, Dick Nash: Trombone, Ken Shroyer: Bass Trombone, Paul Horn: Clarinet, Bud Shank: Clarinet, Bill Holman: Tenor Saxophone, Richie Kamuca: Tenor Saxophone, Chuck Gentry: Baritone Saxophone, Red Norvo: Vibraphone, Pete Jolly: Piano, Howard Roberts: Guitar, Monty Budwig: Bass.]

     A Very Special Love (Allen)
     Comes To Me (Allen)
     I Just Don't Know (Allen)
     Teacher, Teacher (Allen)

---

22 December 1958   Los Angeles, USA

Barney Kessel

Carmen [CD, Contemporary, OJCCD-269-2]
Carmen [LP, Contemporary, SCA5011]

[Musicians: Barney Kessel: Guitar, André Previn: Piano, Joe Mondragon: Bass, Shelly Manne: Drums, Victor Feldman: Vibraphone.]

     Carmen's Cool (Bizet (arr. Kessel))
     If You Dig Me (Bizet (arr. Kessel))

01 January 1959 [Estimated]   Los Angeles, USA

Claudia Thompson

Goodbye To Love [CD, Fresh Sounds/Edison, E500 CD]

[Musicians: Barney Kessel: Guitar, Benny Carter: Alto Saxophone, Joe Howard: Trombone, Harry Betts: Trombone, Ed Kusby: Trombone, George Roberts: Trombone, Paul Smith: Piano, Joe Mondragon: Bass, Alvin Stoller: Drums, Claudia Thompson: Vocals.]

- Blue Prelude (Jenkins)
- Fan Me (Russell)
- Gloomy Sunday (Javor)
- Some Of These Days (Brooks)
- The Morning After (Coslow)

[Musicians: Barney Kessel: Guitar, Ted Nash: Alto Saxophone, Mike Rubin: Bass, Claudia Thompson: Vocals.]

- Stormy Weather (Koehler)

[Musicians: Barney Kessel: Guitar, Ted Nash: Flute, Nino Rossi: Cello, Arnold Ross: Piano, Mike Rubin: Bass, Dick Shanahan: Drums, Claudia Thompson: Vocals.]

- Goodbye (Jenkins)
- If I Should Lose You (Kahn)

---

10 January 1959 [Estimated]   Los Angeles, USA

Cathy Hayes

The Angels Sing [CD, Fresh Sound, FSR-CD 55]
It`s All Right With Me [LP, HiFi Record, R 416]

[Musicians: Barney Kessel: Guitar, Cathy Hayes: Vocals, Larry Bunker: Vibraphone, Howard Roberts: Rhythm Guitar, Monty Budwig: Bass, Shelly Manne: Drums, Conte Candoli: Trumpet, Bill Perkins: Tenor Saxophone, Ted Nash: Tenor Saxophone, Bud Shank: Alto Saxophone, Justin Gordon: Baritone Saxophone, Jimmy Rowles: Piano.]

- Down in the Depths
- Happiness is Just a Thing Called Joe (Arlen/Harburg)
- Tangerine (Mercer/Schertzinger)
- Wonder Why
- You Smell So Good

[Musicians: Barney Kessel: Guitar, Cathy Hayes: Vocals, Larry Bunker: Vibraphone, Howard Roberts: Rhythm Guitar, Monty Budwig: Bass, Shelly Manne: Drums.]

- Blue Moods
- Last Night When We Were Young (Warren/Bacall)
- My Old Flame (Coslow/Johnston)
- You Don't Know What Love Is

[Musicians: Barney Kessel: Guitar, Cathy Hayes: Vocals, Monty Budwig: Bass, Mel Lewis: Drums.]

- If I Were A Bell (Loesser)
- The Angels Sing (Elman/Mercer)
- You And The Night And The Music (Deitz/Schwartz)

---

20 January 1959 [Estimated]   Los Angeles, USA

Van Alexander

The Home Of Happy Feet [LP, Capitol, ST 1243]
Van Alexander [CD, Capitol/EMI, 7243 35211 2]

[Musicians: Barney Kessel: Guitar, Conrad Gozzo: Trumpet, Klein Sherock: Trumpet, Milt Bernhart: Trombone, Joe Howard: Trombone, Chuck Gentry: Saxophones, Plas Johnson: Saxophones, Ronnie Lang: Saxophones, Abe Most: Saxophones, Ray Sherman: Piano, Joe Mondragon: Bass, Shelly Manne: Drums.]

- A-Tisket, A-Tasket (Fitzgerald)
- I Would Do Anything For You (Hopkins)
- Until The Real Thing Comes Along (Holinger)

Uptown Rhapsody (Hill)

[Musicians: Barney Kessel: Guitar, Conrad Gozzo: Trumpet, Manny Klein: Trumpet, Uan Rasey: Trumpet, Shorty Sherock: Trumpet, Joe Howard: Trombone, Ed Kusby: Trombone, Tommy Pederson: Trombone, Ken Shroyer: Trombone, Paul Horn: Saxophones, Julie Jacob: Saxophones, Plas Johnson: Saxophones, Abe Most: Saxophones, Butch Stone: Saxophones, Paul Smith: Piano, Joe Comfort: Bass, Irv Cottler: Drums.]

Chant Of The Weed (Redman)

East St. Louis Toodle-do (Ellington)

Let's Get Together (Webb)

Ride, Red, Ride (Millinder)

[Musicians: Barney Kessel: Guitar, Manny Klein: Trumpet, Shorty Sherock: Trumpet, Milt Bernhart: Trombone, Chuck Gentry: Saxophones, Plas Johnson: Saxophones, Ronnie Lang: Saxophones, Abe Most: Saxophones, Geoff Clarkson: Piano, Joe Mondragon: Bass, Shelly Manne: Drums.]

Christopher Columbus (Razaf)

Organ Grinder's Swing (Hudson)

Stompin' At The Savoy (Goodman)

Undecided (Shanery)

---

03 February 1959　　　　　　Los Angeles, USA

Shorty Rogers

The Wizard Of Oz [CD, RCA Records, 74321453792]

[Musicians: Barney Kessel: Guitar, Shorty Rogers: Trumpet, Al Porcino: Trumpet, Conte Candoli: Trumpet, Don Fagerquist: Trumpet, Bob Enevoldsen: Valve Trombone, Frank Rosolino: Trombone, Harry Betts: Trombone, Ken Shroyer: Bass Trombone, Bud Shank: Alto Flute, Herb Geller: Alto Flute, Bill Holman: Tenor Saxophone, Jimmy Giuffre: Clarinet, Larry Bunker: Vibraphone, Pete Jolly: Piano, Joe Mondragon: Bass, Mel Lewis: Drums.]

Blues In The Night (Arlen/Mercer)

Get Happy (Arlen/Koehler)

Let's Fall In Love (Arlen/Koehler)

That Old Black Magic (Arlen/Mercer)

[Musicians: Barney Kessel: Guitar, Shorty Rogers: Trumpet, Don Fagerquist: Trumpet, Bob Enevoldsen: Valve Trombone, Frank Rosolino: Trombone, Herb Geller: Tenor Saxophone, Jimmy Giuffre: Clarinet, Larry Bunker: Vibraphone, Pete Jolly: Piano, Joe Mondragon: Bass, Mel Lewis: Drums.]

Ding Dong! The Witch Is Dead (Arlen/Harburg)

If I Only Had A Brain (Arlen/Harburg)

My Shining Hour (Arlen/Mercer)

Over The Rainbow (Arlen/Harburg)

The Jitterbug (Arlen/Harburg)

The Merry Old Land Of Oz (Arlen/Harburg)

We're Off To See The Wizard (Arlen/Harburg)

---

01 March 1959 [Estimated]　　　　　　Los Angeles, USA

Vicky Lane

I Swing For You [LP, RCA Victor, LPM-2056]
I Swing For You [CD, RCA Victor, 74321938542]

[Musicians: Barney Kessel: Guitar, Vicky Lane: Vocals, Pete Candoli: Trumpet, Jimmy Rowles or Johnny Williams: Piano, Joe Mondragon: Bass, Alvin Stoller: Drums, Larry Bunker: Percussion, Milt Holland: Percussion, Lou Singer: Percussion, Ralph Hansell: Percussion, Johnny Cyr: Percussion, Gene Estes: Percussion.]

I Love You (Porter)

Long Ago and Far Away (Kern/Gershwin)

Love Isn't Born (It's Made) (Loesser/Schwartz)

My Heart Stood Still (Rodgers/Hart)

My Romance (Hart/Rodgers)

Our Very Own (Young/Elliott)

Right As The Rain (Arlen/Harburg)

The Song Is You (Kern/Hammerstein)

> The Trolley Song (Martin/Blane)
> They Say It's Wonderful (Berlin)
> This Heart of Mine (Kalmar/Ruby)
> You Hit The Spot (Gordon/Revel)

---

26 March 1959   Los Angeles, USA

Ella Fitzgerald

Ella Fitzgerald Sings The Gershwin Songbook [CD, Verve, 825-024-2]

[Musicians: Barney Kessel: Guitar, Ella Fitzgerald: Vocals, Don Fagerquist: Trumpet, Dick Nash: Trombone, Tommy Pederson: Trombone, James Priddy: Trombone, George Roberts: Bass Trombone, Ronnie Lang: Alto Saxophone, Paul Smith: Piano, Joe Comfort: Bass, Larry Bunker: Drums, Mel Lewis: Drums, Alvin Stoller: Drums, Katherine Julyie: Harp, Nelson Riddle: Conductor/Arranger, 17 Piece: String Section, 5 Piece: Woodwind Section, James Decker: French Horn, Vincent DeRosa: French Horn.]

> But Not For Me (Gershwin/Gershwin)
> Let's Call The Whole Thing Off (Gershwin/Gershwin)
> Let's Kiss And Make Up (Gershwin/Gershwin)
> Looking For A Boy (Gershwin/Gershwin)
> Lorelei (Gershwin/Gershwin)
> Love Walked In (Gershwin/Gershwin)
> My One And Only (Gershwin/Gershwin)
> Nice Work If You Can Get It (Gershwin/Gershwin)
> Someone To Watch Over Me (Gershwin/Gershwin)
> They All Laughed (Gershwin/Gershwin)

---

30 March 1959   Los Angeles, USA

Barney Kessel

Some Like It Hot [CD, Victor Japan 20 Bit, VICJ-60769]
Some Like It Hot [CD, Contemporary, OJCCD168]

[Musicians: Barney Kessel: Guitar, Joe Gordon: Trumpet, Art Pepper: Clarinet, Jimmy Rowles: Piano, Jack Marshall: Guitar, Monty Budwig: Bass, Shelly Manne: Drums.]

> Running Wild (Alternate Take) (Grey/Wood/Gibbs)
> Sweet Sue (Alternate Take) (Young/Harris)

Barney Kessel

Some Like It Hot [LP, Contemporary, S3565]
Some Like It Hot [CD, Contemporary, OJCCD168]
Some Like It Hot [CD, Victor Japan 20 Bit, VICJ-60769]

[Musicians: Barney Kessel: Guitar, Joe Gordon: Trumpet, Art Pepper: Clarinet, Jimmy Rowles: Piano, Jack Marshall: Guitar, Monty Budwig: Bass, Shelly Manne: Drums.]

> By The Beautiful Sea (Carroll/Atteridge)
> Down Among The Sheltering Palms (Brockman/Olman)
> I Wanna Be Loved By You (Stothart)
> Runnin' Wild (Grey/Harrington-Grey/Woods)
> Some Like It Hot (Malneck)
> Sugar Blues (Sampson)
> Sweet Georgia Brown (Bernie/Pinkard/Casey)
> Sweet Sue (Young)

01 April 1959 [Estimated]　　　Los Angeles, USA

Barney Kessel

Barney Kessel - Military Swing [CD, JazzBank Archives, MTCJ-1094]

[Musicians: Barney Kessel: Guitar, Frank Patchen: Piano, Albert Stinson: Bass, Shelly Manne: Drums, Victor Feldman: Vibraphone & Percussion.]

- Army Rocks And Navy Rolls (Kessel)
- High In The Sky (Stinson)
- Waltz In Spingtime (Kessel)

---

03 April 1959　　　Los Angeles, USA

Barney Kessel

Some Like It Hot [LP, Contemporary, M3565]
Some Like It Hot [CD, Contemporary, OJCCD168]
Some Like It Hot [CD, Victor Japan 20 Bit, VICJ-60769]

[Musicians: Barney Kessel: Guitar, Monty Budwig: Bass.]

- I'm Through With Love (Kahn)
- Stairway To The Stars (Parish)

---

23 April 1959　　　Los Angeles, USA

Mel Torme and the Meltones

Back In Town [LP, Verve, MGV-2120]
Back In Town [LP, Verve (France), 2304-384]

[Musicians: Barney Kessel: Guitar, Mel Torme: Vocals, Jack Sheldon: Trumpet, Art Pepper: Alto/Tenor Saxophone, Joe Gibbons: Guitar, Al Hendrickson: Guitar, Bill Pitman: Guitar, Tony Rizzi: Guitar, Vic Feldman: Vibraphone, Marty Paich: Keyboards, Red Mitchell: Bass, Alvin Stoller: Drums, The Meltones: Vocal Group.]

- A Bunch of The Blues (Mandel/Kahn)
- A Smooth One (Goodman/Royal)
- Baubles, Bangles And Beads (Wright/Forrest)
- Don't Dream Of Anybody But Me (Hefti/Howard)
- Hit The Road To Dreamland (Arlen/Mercer)
- It Happened In Monterey (Wayne/Rose)
- I've Never Been In Love Before (Loesser)
- Makin' Whoopee (Donaldson/Kahn)
- Some Like It Hot (Biondi/Krupa/Loesser)
- Truckin' (Bloom/Koehler)
- What Is This Thing Called Love (Porter)

---

01 May 1959 [Estimated]　　　Los Angeles, USA

Claudia Thompson

Goodbye To Love [CD, Fresh Sounds/Edison, E500 CD]

[Musicians: Barney Kessel: Guitar, Red Mitchell: Bass, Claudia Thompson: Vocals.]

- Body And Soul (Green)
- Gloomy Sunday (Javor)
- I Was Yours (Idriss)
- I'm Through With Love (Livingston)
- You Call It Madness (Dubois)

19 May 1959 — Los Angeles, USA

Bobby Darin

This is Darin [CD, Atlantic, 82628-2]

[Musicians: Barney Kessel: Guitar, Bobby Darin: Vocals, Al Porcino: Trumpet, Stu Williamson: Trumpet, Ray Triscari: Trumpet, Conte Candoli: Trumpet, Milt Bernhart: Trombone, Bob Enevoldsen: Trombone, Joe Cadeno: Trombone, Ken Shroyer: Trombone, Ted Nash: Tenor Saxophone, Bud Shank: Alto Saxophone, Buddy Collette: Tenor Saxophone, Richard Berhke: Piano, Joe Mondragon: Bass, Alvin Stoller: Drums, Twelve Piece: String Section.]

- Down With Love (Harburg/Lane)
- My Gal Sal (Dresser)
- The Gal That Got Away (Arlen/Gershwin)

20 May 1959 — Los Angeles, USA

Bobby Darin

This is Darin [CD, Atlantic, 82628-2]
This is Darin [LP, Atco, 33-115]

[Musicians: Barney Kessel: Guitar, Bobby Darin: Vocals, Milt Bernhart: Trombone, Buddy Collette: Alto Saxophone, Gene Cipriani: Tenor Saxophone, Richard Berhke: Piano, Joe Mondragon: Bass, Alvin Stoller: Drums, Twenty-One Piece: String Section.]

- Black Coffee (Webster/Burke)
- Pete Kelly's Blues (Cahn/Heindorf)

21 May 1959 — Los Angeles, USA

Bobby Darin

This is Darin [CD, Atlantic, 82628-2]
This is Darin [LP, Atco, 33-115]

[Musicians: Barney Kessel: Guitar, Bobby Darin: Vocals, Milt Bernhart: Trombone, Bob Enevoldsen: Trombone, Joe Cadeno: Trombone, Ken Shroyer: Trombone, Al Porcino: Trumpet, Stu Williamson: Trumpet, Ray Triscari: Trumpet, Conte Candoli: Trumpet, Mel Flory: Alto Saxophone, Charles Kennedy: Alto Saxophone, Jack Schwarz: Tenor Saxophone, Bill Perkins: Tenor Saxophone, Joe Maini: Baritone Saxophone, Richard Berhke: Piano, Max Bennett: Bass, Mel Lewis: Drums.]

- Caravan (Tizol/Ellington/Mills)
- Don't Dream of Anybody But Me (Howard/Hefti)
- Have You Got Any Castles Baby (Mercer/Whiting)

22 May 1959 [Estimated] — Los Angeles, USA

Bobby Darin

This is Darin [CD, Atlantic, 82628-2]
This is Darin [LP, Atco, 33-115]

[Musicians: Barney Kessel: Guitar, Bobby Darin: Vocals, Milt Bernhart: Trombone, Bob Enevoldsen: Trombone, Joe Cadeno: Trombone, Ken Shroyer: Trombone, Al Porcino: Trumpet, Stu Williamson: Trumpet, Ray Triscari: Trumpet, Conte Candoli: Trumpet, Mel Flory: Alto Saxophone, Charles Kennedy: Alto Saxophone, Jack Schwarz: Tenor Saxophone, Bill Perkins: Tenor Saxophone, Joe Maini: Baritone Saxophone, Richard Berhke: Piano, Max Bennett: Bass, Mel Lewis: Drums.]

- All Nite Long (Harris)
- Clementine (Harris)
- Guys and Dolls (Loesser)
- I Can't Give You Anything But Love (Fields/McHugh)

01 June 1959   **Los Angeles, USA**

Jack Marshall Band

Jazz From Two Sides [LP, Concept, VL5]

[Musicians: Barney Kessel: Guitar, Pete Candoli: Trumpet, Milt Bernhart: Trombone, Bud Shank: Alto Saxophone, Justin Gordon: Basson, Milt Raskin: Piano, Red Mitchell: Bass, Shelly Manne: Drums.]

     A Song (Marshall)

     Angry Young Men (Marshall)

     Heebie Jeebies (Armstrong)

     I've Found A New Baby (Williams)

     Looking at the World Through Rose Colored Glasses (Malie)

     Stuttin' With Some Barbecue (Armstrong)

---

04 July 1959   **Los Angeles, USA**

Elmer Bernstein

Staccato [LP, Capitol, T1287]

Staccato/Paris Swings [CD, DRG, 19110.2]

[Musicians: Barney Kessel: Guitar, Pete Candoli: Trumpet, Don Fagerquist: Trumpet, Si Zentner: Trombone, Dick Nash: Trombone, Ted Nash: Reeds, Dave Pell: Reeds, Gene Cipriano: Reeds, John Williams: Piano, Red Mitchell: Bass, Shelly Manne: Drums, Larry Bunker: Vibraphone.]

     Like Having Fun (Bernstein)

     Night Mood (Bernstein)

     Pursuit (Bernstein)

     Walk A Lonely Street (Bernstein)

---

05 July 1959   **Los Angeles, USA**

Elmer Bernstein

Staccato [LP, Capitol, T1287]

Staccato/Paris Swings [CD, DRG, 19110.2]

[Musicians: Barney Kessel: Guitar, Pete Candoli: Trumpet, Don Fagerquist: Trumpet, Uan Rasey: Trumpet, Milt Bernhardt: Trombone, Dick Nash: Trombone, Joe Howard: Trombone, George Roberts: Trombone, Vince DeRosa: French Horn, Dick Perissi: French Horn, Gene Cipriano: Reeds, Marty Berman: Reeds, Chuck Gentry: Reeds, Dave Pell: Reeds, Ted Nash: Reeds, Lou Singer: Percussion, John Williams: Piano, Bob Bain: Guitar, Red Mitchell: Bass, Shelly Manne: Drums.]

     Deadly Game (Bernstein)

     Greenwich Village Rumble (Bernstein)

     Staccato's Theme (Bernstein)

     Thinking of Baby (Bernstein)

---

08 July 1959   **Los Angeles, USA**

Elmer Bernstein

Staccato [LP, Capitol, T1287]

Staccato/Paris Swings [CD, DRG, 19110.2]

[Musicians: Barney Kessel: Guitar, Pete Candoli: Trumpet, Larry Bunker: Vibraphone, John Williams: Piano, Red Mitchell: Bass, Shelly Manne: Drums.]

     MacDougal Street Special (Bernstein)

     One Before Closing (Bernstein)

     Poi and Juice (Bernstein)

     The Jazz at Waldo's (Bernstein)

01 October 1959 [Estimated]   Los Angeles, USA

Bobby Christian

Bobby Christian - In Action [LP, Golden Era Records, GER LP-15057]
[Musicians: Barney Kessel: Guitar, Bobby Christian: Percussion/Vibraphone, Pete Candoli: Trumpet, Manny Klein: Trumpet, Conrad Gozzo: Trumpet, Shorty Sherock: Trumpet, Ed Kusby: Trombone, Unknown: Other Musicians.]

- Sandu (Brown)

---

05 October 1959   Los Angeles, USA

Elmer Bernstein

Paris Swings [LP, Capitol, ST 1288]
Staccato/Paris Swings [CD, DRG, 19110.2]
[Musicians: Barney Kessel: Guitar, Ted Nash: Reeds, Andre Previn: Piano, Red Mitchell: Bass, Shelly Manne: Drums, Larry Bunker: Vibraphone.]

- Darling, Je Vous Aime Beaucoup. (Baker)
- La Vie en Rose (Piaf)
- Symphony (Rogers)
- Valentina (Chevalier)

---

06 October 1959   Los Angeles, USA

Elmer Bernstein

Paris Swings [LP, Capitol, ST 1288]
Staccato/Paris Swings [CD, DRG, 19110.2]
[Musicians: Barney Kessel: Guitar, Ted Nash: Reeds, Andre Previn: Piano, Red Mitchell: Bass, Shelly Manne: Drums, Larry Bunker: Vibraphone.]

- Adieu d'amour (Bernstein)
- I Love Paris (Porter)
- Paris in the Spring (Gordon/Revel)

---

12 October 1959   Los Angeles, USA

Elmer Bernstein

Paris Swings [LP, Capitol, ST 1288]
Staccato/Paris Swings [CD, DRG, 19110.2]
[Musicians: Barney Kessel: Guitar, Ted Nash: Reeds, Andre Previn: Piano, Red Mitchell: Bass, Shelly Manne: Drums, Larry Bunker: Vibraphone.]

- April in Paris (Duke)
- Autumn Leaves (Mercer)
- Pauvre Moi, Pauvre Moi
- Souvenir du printemps (Bernstein)
- Under Paris Skies

---

02 November 1959   Los Angeles, USA

Barney Kessel

Poll Winners Three! [LP, Contemporary, S7576]
Poll Winners Three! [CD, Contemporary, OJCCD692-2]
[Musicians: Barney Kessel: Guitar, Shelly Manne: Drums, Ray Brown: Bass.]

- Crisis (Kessel)
- Easy Living (Robin)

I Hear Music (Lane/Loesser)
I'm Afraid The Masquerade Is Over (Wrubel)
It's All Right With Me (Porter)
Mack The Knife (Weill)
Minor Mystery (Brown)
Raincheck (Strayhorn)
Soft Winds (Goodman)
The Little Rhumba (Manne)

23 December 1959 Los Angeles, USA

Anita O'Day

Anita O'Day - Compact Jazz [CD, Verve, 314 517 954-2]

[Musicians: Barney Kessel: Guitar, Anita O'Day: Vocals, Red Nichols: Cornet, Moe Schneider: Trombone, Heinie Beau: Clarinet, Benny Carter: Alto Saxophone, Eddie Miller: Tenor Saxophone, Jess Stacy: Piano, Morty Corb: Bass, Gene Krupa: Drums.]

Memories of You (Blake/Razaf)

01 January 1960 [Estimated] Los Angeles, USA

Peanuts Hucko

Stealin' Apples [LP, Zodiac, ZR1020]

[Musicians: Barney Kessel: Guitar, Pete Jolly: Piano, Arnold Fishkind: Bass, Earl Palmer: Drums, Max Bennett: Fender Bass.]

A 'Bien Tot (Hucko)
A Summer's Love (Ashton)
First Friday (Hucko)
Just A Closer Walk With Thee (Traditional)
Sweet Home Suite (Hucko)

08 January 1960 Los Angeles, USA

Paul Smith

The Sound Of Music [LP, Verve, MGV(S6)2128]
The Sound Of Music [CD, Verve Japan, POCJ-2585]

[Musicians: Barney Kessel: Guitar, Paul Smith: Piano, Morty Corb: Bass, Irv Cottler: Drums.]

An Ordinary Couple (Rodgers/Hammerstein)
Climb Every Mountain (Rodgers/Hammerstein)
Do-Re-Mi (Rodgers/Hammerstein)
Edelweiss (Rodgers/Hammerstein)
How Can Love Survive? (Rodgers/Hammerstein)
Maria (Rodgers/Hammerstein)
My Favourite Things (Rodgers/Hammerstein)
No Way To Stop It (Rodgers/Hammerstein)
So Long, Farewell (Rodgers/Hammerstein)
The Lonely Goat Herd (Rodgers/Hammerstein)
The Sound Of Music (Rodgers/Hammerstein)

01 February 1960 [Estimated] Los Angeles, USA

Paul Weston Orchestra

Mood for 12 [LP, Columbia, CL 693]
Easy Jazz [LP, Corinthian, COR-109]
Two Classic Albums from Paul Weston [CD, Collectors' Choice, CCM073-2]
[Musicians: Barney Kessel: Guitar, Paul Weston: Arranger/Conductor, Unknown: Musicians.]

My Funny Valentine (Rodgers/Hart)

---

01 May 1960 [Estimated] Los Angeles, USA

Barney Kessel

Barney Kessel - Military Swing [CD, JazzBank Archives, MTCJ-1094]
[Musicians: Barney Kessel: Guitar, Arnold Ross: Piano, Monty Budwig: Bass, Frankie Capp: Drums.]

Constellation (Shearing)
Hurry Arnold (Ross)
Morning Dew (Wallington)

---

01 June 1960 [Estimated] Los Angeles, USA

Jackie Cain and Roy Kral

Sweet and Low Down [LP, Columbia, CL 1469]
[Musicians: Barney Kessel: Guitar, Jackie Cain: Vocals, Roy Kral: Piano, Al McKibbon: Bass, Frank Butler: Drums, Larry Bunker: Vibraphone, Anthony Ortega: Alto Saxophone/Flute.]

Cheek to Cheek (Berlin)
Chicago (Fisher)
Experiment (Porter)
Fun Life (Wolf)
Hallelujah! (Robin)
Mountain Greenery (Rodgers/Hart)
'S Wonderful (Gershwin/Gershwin)
Sweet and Low Down (Gershwin/Gershwin)
They Can't Take That Away From Me (Gershwin/Gershwin)
Wingin' with the Wind (Kral)

---

19 July 1960 Los Angeles, USA

Barney Kessel

Swingin' Party At Contemporary [LP, Contemporary, S7613]
Swingin' Party At Contemporary [CD, Contemporary, OJCCD-1066-2]
[Musicians: Barney Kessel: Guitar, Marvin Jenkins: Piano, Gary Peacock: Bass, Ron Lunberg: Drums.]

Bluesology (Jackson)
Joy Spring (Brown)
Lover Man (Davis/Ramirez/Sherman)
Miss Memphis (Jenkins)
New Rhumba (Jamal)
Now's The Time (Parker)

01 September 1960　　　　　　　Los Angeles, USA

Barney Kessel

Exploring The Scene [LP, Contemporary, S7581]
Exploring The Scene [CD, Contemporary, OJCCD-969-2]
[Musicians: Barney Kessel: Guitar, Ray Brown: Bass, Shelly Manne: Drums.]

- Doodlin' (Silver)
- Li'l Darlin (Hefti)
- Little Susie (Bryant)
- Misty (Garner)
- So What (Davis)
- The Blessing (Coleman)
- The Duke (Brubeck)
- The Golden Striker (Lewis)
- This Here (Timmons)

---

06 September 1960　　　　　　　Los Angeles, USA

Helen Humes

Songs I Like To Sing [CD, Contemporary, OJCCD-171-2]
Songs I Like To Sing [LP, Contemporary, S 7582]
[Musicians: Barney Kessel: Guitar, Helen Humes: Vocals, Ben Webster: Tenor Saxophone, André Previn: Piano, Leroy Vinnegar: Bass, Shelly Manne: Drums, Harry Betts: Trombone, Bob Fitzpatrick: Trombone, Art Pepper: Alto Saxophone/Clarinet, Bill Hood: Baritone Saxophone, Al Porcino: Trumpet, Ray Triscari: Trumpet, Stu Williamson: Trumpet, Jack Sheldon: Trumpet.]

- Don't Worry About Me (Alt) (Bloom/Koehler)
- Don't Worry About Me (Bloom/Koehler)
- I Want a Roof Over My Head (Brooks)
- Love Me or Leave Me (Kahn/Donaldson)
- Mean to Me (Turk/Ahlert)
- Million Dollar Secret (Humes)
- Please Don't Talk About Me When I'm Gone (Stept/Clare)
- St. Louis Blues (Handy)
- You're Driving Me Crazy (Donaldson)

---

08 September 1960　　　　　　　Los Angeles, USA

Helen Humes

Songs I Like To Sing [CD, Contemporary, OJCCD-171-2]
[Musicians: Barney Kessel: Guitar, Helen Humes: Vocals, Ben Webster: Tenor Saxophone, André Previn: Piano, Leroy Vinnegar: Bass, Shelly Manne: Drums, James Getoff: Violin, Joseph Stepansky: Violin, Alvin Dinkin: Viola, Eleanor Slatkin: Cello.]

- Every Now And Then (Sherman)
- If I Could Be With You (Creamer)
- Imagination (Burke)
- My Old Flame (Johnston)

01 October 1960 [Estimated]   Los Angeles, USA

Ann Richards

Ann Richards: Ann, Man! [CD, Atco, AMCY-1071]
Ann Richards: Ann, Man! [CD, Collectables, COL-CD-6321]
Ann Richards: Ann, Man! [LP, Atco, 33-136]
[Musicians: Barney Kessel: Guitar, Ann Richards: Vocals, Jack Sheldon: Trumpet, Red Callender: Bass, Larry Bunker: Drums.]

- An Occasional Man (Martin/Blane)
- And That's All (Thorpe)
- Evil Gal Blues (Feather)
- I Couldn't Sleep a Wink Last Night (Adamson/McHugh)
- Is You Is or Is You Ain't My Baby (Austin/Jordan)
- Love is a Word for the Blues (Feather/Hyman/Raskin)
- The Masquerade is Over (Magidson/Wrubel)
- Yes Sir, That's My Baby (Kahn/Donaldson)

[Musicians: Barney Kessel: Guitar, Ann Richards: Vocals.]

- Bewitched (Rodgers/Hart)
- How Do I Look in Blue (Roland/Richards)
- There's a Lull in My Life (Gordon/Revel)
- You Go To My Head (Coots/Gillespie)

---

01 January 1961 [Estimated]   Los Angeles, USA

Dinah Washington

Unforgettable [CD, Mercury, 314 510 602-2]
[Musicians: Barney Kessel: Guitar, Ernie Freeman: Piano, Rene Hall: Rhythm Guitar, Red Callender: Bass, Earl Palmer: Drums, Dinah Washington: Vocals, Unknown: String Section, Belford C. Hendricks: Arranger/Conductor.]

- Congratulations To Someone (Alfred)
- Our Love Is Here To Stay (Gershwin/Gershwin)
- Surprise Party (Hillard)

---

02 January 1961 [Estimated]   Los Angeles, USA

Dinah Washington

Dinah Washington [LP, Mercury, MG21119]
[Musicians: Barney Kessel: Guitar, Ernie Freeman: Piano, Rene Hall: Rhythm Guitar, Red Callender: Bass, Earl Palmer: Drums, Dinah Washington: Vocals, Unknown: String Section, Belford C. Hendricks: Arranger/Conductor.]

- An Affair To Remember (Warren/Adamson/McCarey)
- Blue Skies (Berlin)
- Cabin In The Sky (Duke/Latouche)
- Love Is A Many Splendoured Thing (Webster/Fain)
- Love Letters (Young/Heyman)
- On Green Dolphin Street (Caper/Washington/Randi/Quest)
- Pagan Love Song (Brown/Freed)
- Six Bridges To Cross
- Stormy Weather (Arlen/Kohler)
- Three Coins In The Fountain (Styne/Cahn)

04 January 1961 [Estimated]   Los Angeles, USA

Dinah Washington

Dinah Washington [CD, Mercury, MG 838960-2]
[Musicians: Barney Kessel: Guitar, Ernie Freeman or Joe Zawinul: Piano, Rene Hall: Rhythm Guitar, Red Callender or Jimmy Rowser: Bass, Earl Palmer: Drums, Dinah Washington: Vocals, Unknown: String Section, Belford C. Hendricks: Arranger/Conductor.]

- Am I The Fool?
- As Long As You're In My Arms
- Aw, Come On, Kiss Me
- I Can't Believe You're In Love With Me (Gaskill/McHugh)
- I Was Telling Him About You
- I've Got Your Love To keep Me Warm (Berlin)
- Softly Baby
- This Heart Of Mine (Warren/Freed)

09 January 1961   Los Angeles, USA

Barney Kessel

Workin' Out! [LP, Contemporary, S7585]
Workin' Out! [CD, Contemporary, OJCCD-970-2]
[Musicians: Barney Kessel: Guitar, Marvin Jenkins: Piano, Jerry Good: Bass, Stan Pepper: Drums.]

- My Funny Valentine (Rodgers/Hart)
- My Man's Gone Now (Gershwin/Gershwin)
- New Rhumba (Jamal)
- Pedal Point (Kessel)
- Spanish Scenery (Kessel)
- Summertime (Gershwin/Gershwin)
- The Good Li'l Man (Jenkins)
- When Johnny Comes Marching Home (Gilmore)

19 January 1961   Los Angeles, USA

Anita O'Day

Travlin' Light' - Anita O'Day [LP, Verve, V-2157]
Anita O'Day - Compact Jazz [CD, Verve, 314 517 954-2]
[Musicians: Barney Kessel: Guitar, Don Fagerquist: Trumpet, Ben Webster: Tenor Saxophone, Jimmy Rowles: Piano, Buddy Clark: Bass, Mel Lewis: Drums, Anita O'Day: Vocals.]

- God Bless The Child (Holiday/Herzog)
- Miss Brown To You (Whiting/Rainger/Robin)
- Remember (Berlin)
- Some Other Spring (Herzog/Kitchings)
- The Moon Looks Down And Laughs (Ruby/Calman/Silvers)
- What A Little Moonlight Can Do (Woods)

01 February 1961 [Estimated]   Los Angeles, USA

Paul Weston Orchestra

Solo Mood [LP, Columbia, CL 879]
Easy Jazz [LP, Corinthian, COR-109]
Two Classic Albums from Paul Weston [CD, Collectors' Choice, CCM073-2]
[Musicians: Barney Kessel: Guitar, Paul Weston: Arranger/Conductor, Unknown: Musicians.]

    Autumn In New York (Duke)

---

01 March 1961 [Estimated]   Los Angeles, USA

Sylvia Telles

Sylvia Telles USA [LP, Fontana, 6485 102]
Sylvia Telles USA [CD, Philips Japan, PHCA-4202]
[Musicians: Barney Kessel: Guitar, Sylvia Telles: Vocals, Joe Mondragon: Bass.]

    Manha de Carnaval (Bonfa/Maria)
    Meu Amanha (Menescal/de Oliveira)
    Sabado em Copacabana (Caymmi/Guinle)

---

01 April 1961 [Estimated]   Los Angeles, USA

Mahalia Jackson

Everytime I Feel The Spirit [LP, Columbia, CS8443]
[Musicians: Barney Kessel: Guitar, Mahalia Jackson: Vocals, Dorothy Simmons or Louis Weaver: Organ, Mildred Falls: Piano, John Williams: Conductor, Unknown: Other Musicians.]

    Everytime I Feel The Spirit I Pray (Jackson)
    Have You Any Time For Jesus? (Hill/Range)
    I Know Prayer Changes Things (Hill/Range)
    I Want To Be A Christian (Jackson)
    Little David Play Your Harp (Jackson)
    Rockin' In Jerusalem (Jackson)
    The Love of Song (Jackson)
    The Only Hope We Have (Aikans/Fafayette)
    Trail To Heaven (Spectra)
    What A Difference Since My Heart's Been Changed (Rubert/Anderson)

---

01 May 1961 [Estimated]   Los Angeles, USA

Luis Rivera

Las Vegas - Luis Rivera [LP, Cash, LP-1002]
[Musicians: Barney Kessel: Guitar, Luis Rivera: Hammond Organ, Larry Bunker: Vibraphone, Willie Smith: Alto Saxophone, Carey Visor: Tenor Saxophone, Gene Gammage: Drums.]

    I'm Gone (Pleasure/Jones)
    Our Love Is Here To Stay (Gershwin/Gershwin)
    Rough Riding (Fitzgerald/Jones)
    The Riviera (Rivera)

01 June 1961 [Estimated] Los Angeles, USA

Barney Kessel

Barney Kessel - Military Swing [CD, JazzBank Archives, MTCJ-1094]
[Musicians: Barney Kessel: Guitar, Frank Patchen: Piano, Victor Feldman: Vibraphone, Herb Mickman: Bass, Victor Feldman: Vibraphone & Percussion, Stan Levey: Drums, Pete Candoli: Trumpet, Plas Johnson: Alto Saxophone.]

- C Jam Blues (Ellington)

Mahalia Jackson

Mahalia Jackson - Live in Concert [DVD, ZYX Music, DVD 3030]
[Musicians: Barney Kessel: Guitar, Mahalia Jackson: Vocals, Louise Weaver: Piano, Edward Robinson: Organ, Red Mitchell: Bass, Shelly Manne: Drums.]

- Come On Children Let's Sing (Smith)
- Didn't It Rain (Martin)
- God will Take Care Of Thee (Traditional)
- Highway To Heaven (Traditional)
- I Asked The Lord (Traditional)
- I Believe (Drake/Graham/Shirl/Stillman)
- Joshua fit The Battle Of Jericho (Traditional)
- Just As I Am (Bradbury/Elliot)
- Lord, Don't Move The Mountain (Traditional)
- My Faith Look Up To Thee (Traditional)
- My Lord And I (Traditional)
- Somebody Bigger Than You And I (Burke/Heath/Lange)
- Tell It, Sing It, Shout It (Traditional)
- The Lord's Prayer (Malotte)
- The Rosary (Traditional)
- You'll Never Walk Alone (Rodgers/Hammerstein)

23 January 1962 Los Angeles, USA

Barney Kessel

Breakfast At Tiffany's [LP, Reprise, R 6019]
[Musicians: Barney Kessel: Guitar, Paul Horn: Alto Saxophone/Flute, Victor Feldman: Marimba, Chuck Berghofer: Bass, Earl Palmer: Drums.]

- Bossa Nova (Mancini)
- Breakfast At Tiffany's (Mancini)
- Holly (Mancini)
- Hub Caps And Tail Lights (Mancini)
- Latin Go Lightly (Mancini)
- Loose Caboose (Mancini)
- Moon River (Mancini)
- Moon River Cha Cha (Mancini)
- Sally's Tomato (Mancini)
- Something For Cat (Mancini)
- The Big Blowout (Mancini)
- The Big Heist (Mancini)

[Musicians: Barney Kessel: Guitar/Banjo, Paul Horn: Alto Saxophone/Flute, Victor Feldman: Marimba, Chuck Berghofer: Bass, Earl Palmer: Drums.]

- Mr. Yunioshi (Mancini)

26 March 1962   **Los Angeles, USA**

Billie Holiday

Solitude [CD, Verve, 519 810-2]
Solitude [LP, Clef, MGC 690]
[Musicians: Barney Kessel: Guitar, Billie Holiday: Vocals, Charlie Shavers: Trumpet, Flip Phillips: Tenor Saxophone, Oscar Peterson: Piano, Alvin Stoller: Drums.]

- Blue Moon (Rodgers/Hart)
- East of the Sun (and West of the Moon) (Brooks)
- Easy to Love (Porter)
- Everything I Have Is Yours (Lane/Adamson)
- I Only Have Eyes for You (Warren/Dubin)
- Love for Sale (Porter)
- Moonglow (De Lange/Hudson/Mills)
- Solitude (Ellington/De Lange/Mills)
- Tenderly (Gross/Lawrence)
- These Foolish Things (Remind Me of You) (Link/Strachey/Maschwitz)
- You Go To My Head (Coots/Gillespie)
- You Turned the Tables on Me (Alter/Mitchell)

---

16 July 1962   **Los Angeles, USA**

Barney Kessel

Bossa Nova! [LP, Reprise, R-6049]
[Musicians: Barney Kessel: Guitar, Ray Johnson: Organ, Unknown: Big Band Musicians.]

- A String Of Pearls (Gray)
- Bye Bye Blues (Lown)
- Heartaches (Klenner/Hoffman)
- It Ain't Necessarily So (Gershwin/Gershwin)
- Ja-da (Carleton)
- Love For Sale (Porter)
- Muskrat Ramble (Ory)
- Summertime (Gershwin/Gershwin)
- Sweet Georgia Brown (Casey)
- They Can't Take That Away From Me (Gershwin/Gershwin)
- Tumbling Tumbleweeds (Nolan)
- You Came A Long Way From St. Louis (Brooks)

---

07 August 1962   **Los Angeles, USA**

Sarah Vaughan

The Intimate Sarah Vaughan [LP, Roulette, 2682 032]
The Intimate Sarah Vaughan [LP, Vogue, VJD 543]
[Musicians: Barney Kessel: Guitar, Joe Comfort: Bass, Sarah Vaughan: Vocals.]

- All I Do Is Dream Of You (Brown)
- All Or Nothing At All (Lawrence)
- Baby Won't You Please Come Home (Williams)
- Goodnight Sweetheart (Noble)
- I Understand (Gannon)
- Just In Time (Comden)
- Just Squeeze Me (Ellington)

Key Largo (Carter)
The Very Thought Of You (Noble)
When Lights Are Low (Carter)
When Sunny Gets Blue (Fisher)

---

01 January 1963 [Estimated] Los Angeles, USA

Barney Kessel

Contemporary Latin Rhythms [LP, Reprise, R-6073]

[Musicians: Barney Kessel: Guitar, Conte Candoli: Trumpet, Paul Horn: Alto Saxophone, Victor Feldman: Vibraphone, Emil Richards: Marimba, Al Hendrickson: Guitar, Bill Pitman: Guitar, Red Mitchell: Bass, Stan Levey: Drums, Frank Capp: Percussion, Edward Talamantes: Percussion, Francisco Aguabella: Percussion.]

Blues In The Night (Arlen/Mercer)
Days Of Wine And Roses (Mancini/Mercer)
Every Time I Hear This Song (Kessel)
Lady Bird (Dameron)
Latin Dance Band No. 1 (Kessel)
Love (Martin/Blane)
One Note Samba (Jobim/Hendricks)
Quizas, Quizas, Quizas (Davis/Farres)
The Peanut Vendor (Sunshine/Gilbert/Simon)
Twilight In Acapulco (Kessel)

---

15 January 1963 Los Angeles, USA

Jackie Davis

Easy Does It [LP, Warner Brothers, W1492]

[Musicians: Barney Kessel: Guitar, Jackie Davis: Organ, Joe Comfort: Bass, Earl Palmer: Drums.]

Blues In The Night (Arlen/Mercer)
Easy Does It (Oliver/Young)
Five Minutes More (Styne/Cahn)
If I Could Be With You One Hour Tonight (Creamer/Johnson)
In The Wee Small Hours Of The Morning (Mann/Hilliard)
Lonely Wine (Wells)
Midnight Sun (Burke/Hampton/Mercer)
Night Train (Forrest/Washington/Simpkins)
One For My Baby (Arlen/Mercer)
'Round Midnight (Hanighen/Williams/Monk)
Sleepy Time Gal (Lorenzo/Whiting/Alden/Egan)
St. Louis Blues (Handy)

---

30 January 1963 Los Angeles, USA

Vi Redd

Vi Redd: Lady Soul [LP, ATCO, 33-157]

[Musicians: Barney Kessel: Guitar, Vi Redd: Alto Saxophone, Bill Perkins: Tenor Saxophone, Jennell Hawkins: Organ, Leroy Vinnegar: Bass, Leroy Harrison: Drums.]

Lady Soul (Redd)
Salty Papa Blues (Feather)
Your Love Is Like The Wind (Smith)

01 February 1963 [Estimated]   Los Angeles, USA

Erroll Garner

A New Kind Of Love [CD, Telarc, CD-83383]

[Musicians: Barney Kessel: Guitar, Carroll Lewis: Trumpet, Dick Nash: Trombone, Dick Noel: Trombone, George Roberts: Trombone, Bob Enevoldsen: Trombone, Ted Nash: Woodwind, Gene Cipriani: Woodwind, Harry Klee: Woodwind, Ronnie Lang: Woodwind, Chuck Gentry: Woodwind, Buddy Collette: Woodwind, Red Mitchell: Bass, Larry Bunker: Drums & Percussion, Irving Cottler: Drums & Percussion, Alvin Stoller: Drums & Percussion.]

- Fashion Interlude (Garner)
- In The Park in Paree (Rainger)
- Louise (Whiting)
- Mimi (Rodgers/Hart)
- Paris Mist (Bossa Nova) (Garner)
- Paris Mist (Waltz-Swing) (Garner)
- Steve's Song (Garner)
- The Tease (Garner)
- Theme from A New Kind Of Love (All Yours) (Garner)
- You Brought a New Kind of Love to Me (Fain)

---

01 March 1963 [Estimated]   Los Angeles, USA

Buddy Greco

Buddy Greco Sings For Intimate Moments [LP, Epic, BN 26057]

[Musicians: Barney Kessel: Guitar, Buddy Greco: Vocals, Dave Grusin: Piano, Bud Shank: Tenor Saxophone, Joe Mondragon: Bass, Shelly Manne: Drums, Unknown: Vocal Chorus.]

- As Long As She Needs Me (Bart)
- Call Me Irresponsible (Cahn/Van Heusen)
- Days Of Wine And Roses (Mancini/Mercer)
- Desafinado (Hendricks/Cavanaugh/Mendoco/Jobim)
- I Wanna Be Around (Vimmerstedt/Mercer)
- If Ever I Would Leave You (Lerner/Loewe)
- Lollipops And Roses (Velona)
- Moon River (Mancini/Mercer)
- The Good Life (Distel/Reardon)
- This Is All I Ask (Jenkins)
- Wishing Star (Carroll/Ray)

---

12 June 1963   Los Angeles, USA

Sarah Vaughan

The Lonely Hours [LP, Roulette, SR 52104]

[Musicians: Barney Kessel: Guitar, Sarah Vaughan: Vocals, Benny Carter: Arranger/Conductor, Vince De Rosa: French Horn, Dick Perissi: French Horn, John Cave: French Horn, Bill Hinshaw: French Horn, Red Callender: Tuba, Jimmy Rowles: Piano, Joe Comfort: Bass, Alvin Stoller: Drums.]

- Always On My Mind (Green/Newell)
- If I Had You (Berlin)
- What'll I Do (Berlin)
- You're Driving Me Crazy (Donaldson)

13 June 1963   Los Angeles, USA

Sarah Vaughan

The Lonely Hours [LP, Roulette, SR 52104]

[Musicians: Barney Kessel: Guitar, Sarah Vaughan: Vocals, Benny Carter: Arranger/Conductor, Shorty Sherock: Trumpet, Carmell Jones: Trumpet, Conrad Gozzo: Trumpet, Bobby Bryant: Trumpet, Ed Kusby: Trombone, Dick Nash: Trombone, Buddy Collette: Reeds, Bill Green: Reeds, Plas Johnson: Reeds, Willie Schwartz: Reeds, Bill Hood: Reeds, Jimmy Rowles: Piano, Tommy Tedesco: Guitar, Red Callender: Bass, Alvin Stoller: Drums.]

     I'll Never Be The Same (Kahn/Malneck/Signorelli)
     Lonely Hours (Glaser/Solomon)
     So Long, My Love (Cahn/Spence)
     Solitude (Ellington/DeLange/Mills)

---

01 October 1963 [Estimated]   Los Angeles, USA

Harry Fields - Caloric All - Stars

Bach to Rock [LP, Capitol Custom, SUB-2236/2237]

[Musicians: Barney Kessel: Guitar, Shelly Manne: Drums, Bobby Haynes: Bass, Gene Estes: Percussion, Harry Fields: Piano, Pete Candoli: Trumpet, Plas Johnson: Alto Saxophone, Victor Feldman: Vibraphone, Stan Levey: Drums, Sue Evans: Harp.]

     C Jam Blues (Ellington)

[Musicians: Barney Kessel: Guitar, Shelly Manne: Drums, Bobby Haynes: Bass, Gene Estes: Percussion, Harry Fields: Piano.]

     Harry Plays Bach #4 (Fields)
     Harry's Rock (Fields)
     Hungarian Dance #5 (Brahms)
     Jazz Sonata (Fields)
     Ritual Fire Dance (De Falla)
     Springtime of Love (Fields)
     Wondrous (Fields)

---

01 May 1964 [Estimated]   Los Angeles, USA

Charles Cochran

'Round Midnight [LP, Ava, A/AS44]

[Musicians: Barney Kessel: Guitar, Charlie Cochran: Vocals, Harry Edison: Trumpet, Gerald Wiggins: Piano, Bob West: Bass, Jackie Mills: Drums.]

     All The Things You Are (Kern/Hammerstein)
     I Think I Fell In Love Today (Harrell/Whyte)
     I'm Afraid The Masquerade Is Over (Magidson/Wrubel)
     I've Got Your Number (Leigh/Coleman)
     Just Friends (Lewis/Klenner)
     On Green Dolphin Street (Washington/Kaper)
     'Round Midnight (Hanighan/Monk/Williams)
     Spring Can Really Hang You Up The Most (Wolf/Landesman)
     Sunday (Conn/Miller/Krueger/Styne)
     The Late Late Show (Alfred/Berlin)

---

01 June 1964 [Estimated]   Los Angeles, USA

Dean Martin

Dream With Dean [LP, Reprise, R 6123]
Dream With Dean [CD, Collector's Choice, CCM-254-2]

[Musicians: Barney Kessel: Guitar, Ken Lane: Piano, Red Mitchell: Bass, Irv Cottler: Drums, Dean Martin: Vocals.]

     Baby Won't You Please Come Home (Williams)

Blue Moon (Rodgers/Hart)
Everybody Loves Somebody (Lane)
Fools Rush In (Bloom)
'Gimmie' a Little Kiss (Turk)
Hands Across the Table (Delettre)
I Don't Know Why (Ahlert)
If You Were the Only Girl (Ayer)
I'll Buy That Dream (Wrubel)
I'm Confessin' (Daughety/Reynolds/Neiburg)
My Melancholy Baby (Burnett)
Smile (Chaplin)

01 August 1964 [Estimated]   Los Angeles, USA

Pete Jolly

Hello Jolly! [LP, Ava Records, AS 51]

[Musicians: Barney Kessel: Rhythm Guitar, Pete Jolly: Piano, Bud Shank: Alto Saxophone, Bob Hardaway: Alto Saxophone, Bill Robinson: Saxophone, John Lowe: Saxophone, Bill Perkins: Tenor Saxophone, Bob Edmondson: Trombone, Mike Barone: Trombone, Ernie Tack: Bass Trombone, Jim Zito: Trumpet, Lee Katzman: Trumpet, Jules Chaiken: Trumpet, Oliver Mitchell: Trumpet, Chuck Berghofer: Bass, Norm Jeffries: Drums, 12 Piece: String Section.]

A Sleepin' Bee (Arlen/Capote)
Blues Two Ways (Grove)
Here' That Rainy Day (Burke/Van Heusen)
People (Styne/Merrill)
Sweet September (McGuffie/Phillips/Stanley)
The First of May (Grove)
The Grass is Greener (Smith/Maxwell)
The Moment of Truth (Satterwhite/Scott)

19 October 1964   Los Angeles, USA

Ella Fitzgerald

Ella Fitzgerald Sings The Johnny Mercer Song Book [CD, Verve, 539 057-2]

[Musicians: Barney Kessel: Guitar, Ella Fitzgerald: Vocals, Carroll Lewis: Trumpet, Vito Mangano: Trumpet, George Seaburg: Trumpet, Shorty Sherock: Trumpet, Dick Nash: Trombone, Tommy Pederson: Trombone, Tommy Shepard: Trombone, George Roberts: Bass Trombone, John Cave: French Horn, Buddy Collette: Flute, Harry Klee: Flute, Buddy DeFranco: Clarinet, Abe Most: Clarinet, Plas Johnson: Tenor Saxophone, Babe Russin: Tenor Saxophone, Norman Benno: Oboe, Seymour Schoneberg: Oboe, Lloyd Hildebrand: Bassoon.]

Dream (Mercer)
Early Autumn (Burns/Mercer)
Trav'lin Light (Mundy/Mercer)

21 October 1964   Los Angeles, USA

Ella Fitzgerald

Ella Fitzgerald Sings The Johnny Mercer Song Book [CD, Verve, 539 057-2]

[Musicians: Barney Kessel: Guitar, Ella Fitzgerald: Vocals, Carroll Lewis: Trumpet, Vito Mangano: Trumpet, George Seaburg: Trumpet, Shorty Sherock: Trumpet, Milt Bernhart: Trombone, Tommy Pederson: Trombone, Tommy Shepard: Trombone, George Roberts: Bass Trombone, John Cave: French Horn, Buddy Collette: Flute, Harry Klee: Flute, Buddy DeFranco: Clarinet, George Smith: Clarinet, Plas Johnson: Tenor Saxophone, Babe Russin: Tenor Saxophone, Norman Benno: Oboe, Seymour Schoneberg: Oboe, Lloyd Hildebrand: Bassoon.]

I Remember You (Schertzinger/Mercer)
Laura (Raksin/Mercer)
Something's Gotta Give (Mercer)
Too Marvelous for Words (Whiting/Mercer)

When A Woman Loves A Man (Hanighen/Mercer)

23 October 1964   Los Angeles, USA

Ella Fitzgerald

Ella Fitzgerald [EP, Verve, VK 10340]
[Musicians: Barney Kessel: Guitar, Ella Fitzgerald: Vocals, Unknown: Other Instrumentalists, Arranger and Conductor: Barney Kessel.]

    I'm Fallin' In Love (Kessel)

    Ringo Beat (Fitzgerald)

16 December 1964   Los Angeles, USA

Mel Torme

That's All: A Lush Romantic Album [LP, Columbia, CL 2318]
That's All: A Lush Romantic Album [CD, Columbia, CK 65165]
That's All: A Lush Romantic Album [CD, Columbia, CK 53779]
[Musicians: Barney Kessel: Guitar, Mel Torme: Vocals, James Decker: French Horn, Richard Perissi: French Horn, Gene Cipriani: Woodwind, Plas Johnson: Woodwind, John Gray: Guitar, Rollie Bundock: Bass, Jack Sperling: Drums, Elizabeth Ershoff: Harp, Louis Adrian: Percussion, Dale Anderson: Percussion, Sol Babitz: Percussion, Robert Mersey: Leader/Arranger, 15 Piece: String Section.]

    Do I Love You?   (Rodgers/Hammerstein)

    Isn't A Pity? (Gershwin/Gershwin)

    My Romance (Rodgers/Hart)

    The Folks That Live On The Hill   (Kern/Hammerstein)

    The Nearness Of You   (Carmichael/Washington)

19 December 1964   Los Angeles, USA

Mel Torme

That's All: A Lush Romantic Album [LP, Columbia, CL 2318]
That's All: A Lush Romantic Album [CD, Columbia, CK 65165]
That's All: A Lush Romantic Album [CD, Columbia, CK 53779]
[Musicians: Barney Kessel: Guitar, Mel Torme: Vocals, James Decker: French Horn, Richard Perissi: French Horn, Gene Cipriani: Woodwind, Plas Johnson: Woodwind, John Gray: Guitar, Rollie Bundock: Bass, Jack Sperling: Drums, Elizabeth Ershoff: Harp, Louis Adrian: Percussion, Dale Anderson: Percussion, Sol Babitz: Percussion, Robert Mersey: Leader/Arranger, 15 Piece: String Section.]

    I've Got You Under My Skin (Porter)

    That's All (Bland/Haymes)

    What Is There To Say? (Duke/Harburg)

01 May 1965 [Estimated]   Los Angeles, USA

Joseph Mullendore Studio Orchestra

Honey West - Original TV Soundtrack [LP, ABC, S 532]
Honey West - Original TV Soundtrack [CD, Harkit, HRKCD 8150]
[Musicians: Barney Kessel: Guitar, Buddy Collette: Alto Saxophone, Wilbur Schwartz: Alto Saxophone, Plas Johnson: Tenor Saxophone, William Green: Tenor Saxophone, Larry Sullivan: Trumpet, George Werth: Trumpet, Don Fagerquist: Trumpet, Carroll Lewis: Trumpet, Tom Shepard: Trombone, Tom Pederson: Trombone, Barrett O'Hara: Trombone, Albert Anderson: Trombone, Richard Nash: Trombone, Paul Smith: Piano, Red Callender: Bass, Alvin Stoller: Drums, Tommy Gumina: Accordion, John Grey: Guitar, William Ulyate: Baritone Saxophone.]

    Bolero (Mullendore)

    Jazzito (Mullendore)

    Lots of Pluck (Mullendore)

    Preludium to Mayhem (Mullendore)

Sam Goes (Honey) West (Mullendore)
Serape (Mullendore)
Silk 'N' Honey (Mullendore)
Sweet Honey (Mullendore)
The Ocelot (Mullendore)
Wait And See (Mullendore)
Wild Honey (Mullendore)

22 June 1965   Los Angeles, USA

Bill Henderson

When My Dreamboat Comes Home [LP, Verve, V/V6-8619]

[Musicians: Barney Kessel: Guitar, Bill Henderson: Vocals, Milt Bernhardt: Trombone, Dick Nash: Trombone, Dick Noel: Trombone, Barrett O`Hara: Trombone, John Pisano: Guitar, Lou Morrell: Guitar, Michael Lang: Piano, William Plummer: Bass, Larry Bunker: Drums, Nine-Piece: String Section, Rene Hall: Conductor/Arranger.]

Lay Down Your Weary Tune (Dylan)
When You`re Smiling (Styne/Merrill)
Who`s Sorry Now (Snyder/Ruby/Kalmar)

01 July 1965 [Estimated]   Los Angeles, USA

Barney Kessel

On Fire [LP, Emerald, EST 2401]
On Fire [CD, Venus, TKCZ-79531]

[Musicians: Barney Kessel: Guitar, Jerry Scheff: Bass, Frank Capp: Drums.]

Just In Time (Styne/Comden/Green)
One Mint Julep (Toombs)
Recado Bossa Nova (Gift Of Love) (Antonio/Ferreira)
Slow Burn (Kessel)
Sweet Baby (Kessel)
The Shadow Of Your Smile (Webster/Mandel)
Who Can I Turn To? (Newley/Bricusse)

02 March 1966   Los Angeles, USA

Benny Carter

Additions to Further Definitions [LP, MCA/Jasmine Records, JAS 57]
Additions to Further Definitions [CD, Impulse, 12292]

[Musicians: Barney Kessel: Guitar, Benny Carter: Alto Saxophone, Bud Shank: Alto Saxophone, Buddy Collette: Tenor Saxophone, Teddy Edwards: Tenor Saxophone, Bill Hood: Baritone Saxophone, Don Abney: Piano, Alvin Stoller: Drums, Ray Brown: Bass.]

Come On Back (Carter)
Fantastic That's You (Gates)
If Dreams Come True (Goodman)
Prohibido (Carter)

01 April 1966 [Estimated] Los Angeles, USA

John Anderson

Time Will Tell [LP, Tangerine, TRC 1506]

[Musicians: Barney Kessel: Guitar, Bobby Bryant: Trumpet, John Audino: Trumpet, Anthony Terran: Trumpet, Melvin Moore: Trumpet, Harry 'Sweets' Edison: Trumpet, Lou Blackburn: Trombone, Pete Myers: Trombone, Ernest Tack: Trombone, Harold Land: Saxophone, Teddy Edwards: Saxophone, Carrington Visor: Saxophone, Walter Benton: Saxophone, Jewell Grant: Saxophone, William Green: Piccolo, Buddy Collette: Flute, Jack Wilson: Piano, Robert West: Bass, Mel Lee: Drums, John Anderson: Leader.]

- Brasilia (Anderson)
- Frantic Fiesta (Simon)

---

01 April 1967 [Estimated] Los Angeles, USA

Lou Rawls

Too Much! Lou Rawls [LP, Capitol, CAP (S) T2713]

[Musicians: Barney Kessel: Guitar, Lou Rawls: Vocals, Freddie Hill: Trumpet, Tony Terran: Trumpet, Teddy Edwards: Saxophone, Jim Horn: Saxophone, Gerald Wiggins: Piano, James Bond: Bass, Earl Palmer: Drums, H.B. Barnum: Conductor, Unknown: Other Musicians.]

- Dead End Street (Axelrod/Raleigh)
- I Just Want To Make Love To You (Dixon)
- I Wanna Little Girl (Moll/Mencher)
- I'll Take Time (Anderson)
- The Twelfth Of Never (Webster/Livingston)
- Then You Can Tell Me Goodbye (Loudermilk)
- Uphill Climb To The Bottom (Enzel)
- Why Do I Love You So? (Alexander)
- Yes It Hurts (Doesn't It) (Raleigh/Barnum)
- You're Always On My Mind (Alexander)
- You're Takin' My Bag (Loudermilk)

---

01 May 1967 [Estimated] Tokyo, Japan

Herbie Mann

Herbie Mann's Song Book Complete Bossa Nova [LP, Union (Japan), UPS-26]

[Musicians: Barney Kessel: Guitar, Herbie Mann: Flute, Roy Ayers: Vibraphone, Earl May: Bass, Ed Carr: Drums.]

- Girl From Ipanema (Jobim/DeMoraes/Gimbel)
- How Insensitive (Jobim/DeMoraes)
- So Danco Samba (Jobim)

---

25 May 1967 Los Angeles, USA

Doris Day

Doris Day - The Love Album [CD, Vision Music, VIS CD2]

[Musicians: Barney Kessel: Guitar, Doris Day: Vocals, Ronnell Bright: Piano, Mike Rubin: Bass, Irving Cottler: Drums, Unknown: String Section, Sidney F. Feller: Conductor.]

- All Alone (Berlin)
- Are You Lonesome Tonight (Handman/Turk)
- Faded Summer Love (Baxter)
- For All We Know (Coots/Lewis)
- If I Had My Life To Live Over (Tobias/Jaffe/Vincent)
- Let Me Call You Sweetheart (Friedman/Whitson)
- Life Is Just A Bowl Of Cherries (Henderson/Brown)

Oh, How I Miss You Tonight (Burke/Fisher/Davis)
Sleepy Lagoon (Lawrence/Coates)
Snuggled On Your Shoulder (Lombardo/Young)
Street Of Dreams (Young/Lewis)
Wonderful One (Whiteman)

05 November 1967 — Berlin, Germany

Barney Kessel

Guitar Workshop - Berlin Jazz Festival [LP, Polydor, (G)15034/MPS68159]
Guitar Workshop - Berlin Jazz Festival [CD, MPS/Polydor, POCJ-2555]
[Musicians: Barney Kessel: Guitar, Jack Lesberg: Bass, Don Lamond: Drums.]

Medley: Manha De Carnival/Samba de Orfeu (Jobim)
On A Clear Day (Burton/Lane)

[Musicians: Barney Kessel: Guitar, Jim Hall: Guitar.]

You Stepped Out Of A Dream (Brown/Khan)

07 November 1967 — Paris, France

Barney Kessel

Guitar Workshop - Paris Jazz Festival [CD, Blu Jazz, BJ008CD]
[Musicians: Barney Kessel: Guitar, Jack Lesberg: Bass, Don Lamond: Drums.]

Medley - Manha de Carnaval/Samba de Orfeu (Jobim)
On A Clear Day (Lane)

01 February 1968 — Los Angeles, USA

Mel Torme

A Day In The Life Of Bonnie And Clyde [LP, Liberty, LST 7560]
[Musicians: Barney Kessel: Guitar, Mel Torme: Vocals, Buddy Childers: Trumpet, Frank Rosolino: Trombone, George Auld: Saxophones, Dave Pell: Saxophones, John Audino: Unknown Instrument, Bill Green: Unknown Instrument, Gene DiNovi: Piano/Organ, Mike Deasy: Guitar, Herb Ellis: Guitar, Ray Pohlman: Bass, John Cyr: Drums, Frank Capp: Percussion, Lincoln Mayorga: Arranger/Conductor.]

A Day In The Life Of Bonnie And Clyde (Torme)
Annie Doesn't Live Here Anymore (Burke/Spina/Young)
Brother, Can You Spare A Dime? (Harburg/Gorney)
Button Up Your Overcoat (DeSylva/Brown/Henderson)
Cab Driver (Parks)
I Concentrate On You (Porter)
I Found A Million Dollar Baby (Dixon/Rose/Warren)
Little White Lies (Donaldson)
The Music Goes 'Round and Around (Riley/Farley/Hodgson)
We're In The Money (Warren/Dubin)
With Plenty Of Money And You (Warren/Dubin)
You're The Cream In My Coffee (DeSylva/Brown/Henderson)

01 June 1968 [Estimated]   Los Angeles, USA

Buddy Anderson Sings

Buddy Anderson Sings [EP, Bijou Records, BR001]
[Musicians: Barney Kessel: Guitar, Buddy Anderson: Vocals, Mike Rubini: Piano/Organ, Al McKibbon: Bass, Chuck Piscatello: Drums, Harry Fields: Arranger.]

     Bittersweet Champagne (Anderson)
     How Could I Love You So? (Anderson)
     Stop For Just A Second (Anderson)
     Take Care My Love (Anderson)

---

29 October 1968   London, England

Barney Kessel

Swinging Easy [LP, Black Lion, BLP30107]
Autumn Leaves [CD, Black Lion, BLCD760112]
Autumn Leaves [LP, Black Lion, BLP60112]
[Musicians: Barney Kessel: Guitar, Kenny Napper: Bass, John Marshall: Drums.]

     I Will Wait For You (Legrand)
     Watch The Birds Go By (Kessel)
     Watch What Happens (Legrand)
     You're The One For Me (Kessel)

---

30 October 1968   London, England

Barney Kessel

Swinging Easy [LP, Black Lion, BLP30107]
Autumn Leaves [CD, Black Lion, BLCD760112]
Autumn Leaves [LP, Black Lion, BLP60112]
[Musicians: Barney Kessel: Guitar, Kenny Napper: Bass, John Marshall: Drums.]

     Aquarius (Radi/Ragno/McDermot)
     Autumn Leaves (Kosma)
     On A Clear Day (Lerner/Lane)
     On A Clear Day (Lerner/Lane)

---

31 October 1968   London, England

Barney Kessel

Blue Soul [LP, Black Lion, BLP30161]
Autumn Leaves [CD, Black Lion, BLCD760112]
Autumn Leaves [LP, Black Lion, BLP60112]
[Musicians: Barney Kessel: Guitar, Kenny Napper: Bass, John Marshall: Drums.]

     Quail Beat (Kessel)

Barney Kessel

Swinging Easy [LP, Black Lion, BLP30107]
Autumn Leaves [CD, Black Lion, BLCD760112]
Autumn Leaves [LP, Black Lion, BLP60112]
[Musicians: Barney Kessel: Guitar, Kenny Napper: Bass, John Marshall: Drums.]

     Corcovado (Jobim)
     The Look Of Love (Bacharach)

02 November 1968   London, England

Barney Kessel

Hair Is Beautiful [LP, Polydor, 583725]

[Musicians: Barney Kessel: Guitar, Kenny Salmon: Organ, Ike Isaacs: Guitar, Tony Campo: Bass, Barry Morgan: Drums.]

     Ain't Got Me (Radi/Ragno/McDermot)
     Donna (Radi/Ragno/McDermot)
     Good Morning Starshine (Radi/Ragno/McDermot)
     Hare Krishna (Radi/Ragno/McDermot)
     I Got Life (Radi/Ragno/McDermot)
     Walkin In Space (Radi/Ragno/McDermot)

[Musicians: Barney Kessel: Guitar, Steve Gray: Organ, Ike Isaacs: Guitar, Tony Campo: Bass, Barry Morgan: Drums.]

     Aquarius (Radi/Ragno/McDermot)
     Easy To Be Hard (Radi/Ragno/McDermot)
     Frank Mills (Radi/Ragno/McDermot)
     Where Do I Go (Radi/Ragno/McDermot)

---

26 February 1969   New York, USA

Newport Jazz Festival All Stars

George Wein's Newport All-Stars [LP, Atlantic Records, SD 1533]
George Wein's Newport All-Stars [CD, Collectable's, COL-CD-6194]

[Musicians: Barney Kessel: Guitar, George Wein: Piano, Ruby Braff: Cornet, Red Norvo: Vibraphone, Tal Farlow: Guitar & Bass Guitar, Larry Ridley: Bass, Don Lamond: Drums.]

     Blue Boy (Kessel)
     Ja-Da (Carleton)
     Sunny (Hebb)

---

27 February 1969 [Estimated]   New York, USA

Newport Jazz Festival All Stars

George Wein's Newport All-Stars [LP, Atlantic Records, SD 1533]
George Wein's Newport All-Stars [CD, Collectable's, COL-CD-6194]

[Musicians: Barney Kessel: Guitar, George Wein: Piano, Ruby Braff: Cornet, Red Norvo: Vibraphone, Tal Farlow: Guitar & Bass Guitar, Larry Ridley: Bass, Don Lamond: Drums.]

     Am I Blue (Clarke)
     Exactly Like You (McHugh)
     In A Little Spanish Town (Lewis)
     My Melancholy Baby (Burnett)
     These Foolish Things (Link)
     Topsy (Battle)

[Musicians: Barney Kessel: Guitar, George Wein: Piano/Vocals, Ruby Braff: Cornet, Red Norvo: Vibraphone, Tal Farlow: Guitar & Bass Guitar, Larry Ridley: Bass, Don Lamond: Drums.]

     Nobody Knows You When You Are Down And Out (Cox)

---

12 March 1969   Los Angeles, USA

Barney Kessel

Feeling Free [LP, Contemporary, S7618]
Feeling Free [CD, Contemporary, OJCCD-1043-2]

[Musicians: Barney Kessel: Guitar, Bobby Hutcherson: Vibraphone, Chuck Domanico: Bass, Elvin Jones: Drums.]

     Blue Grass (Kessel)

Great Guitars
Charlie Byrd • Barney Kessel • Herb Ellis
Recorded Live at the Concord Summer Festival

BARNEY
KESSEL
BLACK LION
AQUARIUS
The music from Hair

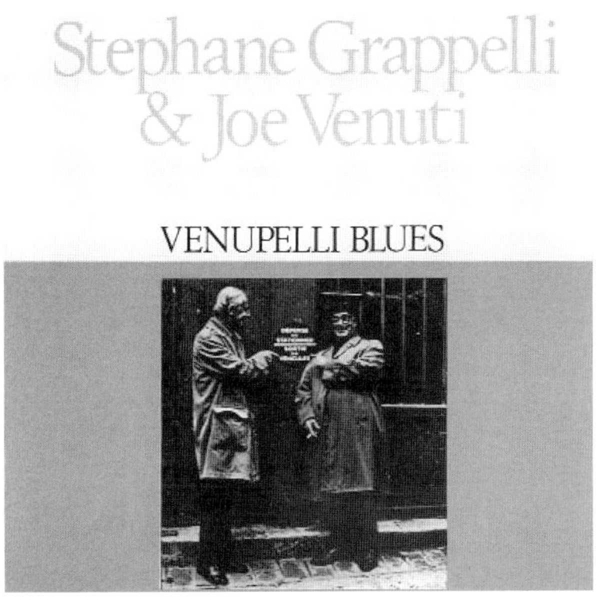
Stephane Grappelli
& Joe Venuti
VENUPELLI BLUES

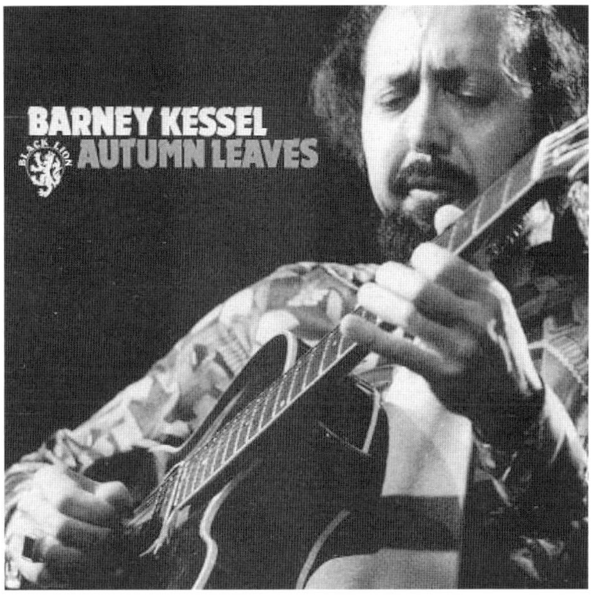
BARNEY KESSEL
BLACK LION
AUTUMN LEAVES

STEPHANE
GRAPPELLI
MEETS
BARNEY
KESSEL
BLACK LION

STEPHANE GRAPPELLI-
BARNEY KESSEL
LIMEHOUSE
BLUES
BLACK LION

BARNEY KESSEL
Just Friends

berlin festival
guitar workshop
baden powell
barney kessel
jim hall
buddy guy
elmer snowden

PARIS GUITAR
JAZZ FESTIVAL
Elmer SNOWDEN, Buddy GUY,
Barney KESSELL, Jim HALL,
George BENSON
LIVE

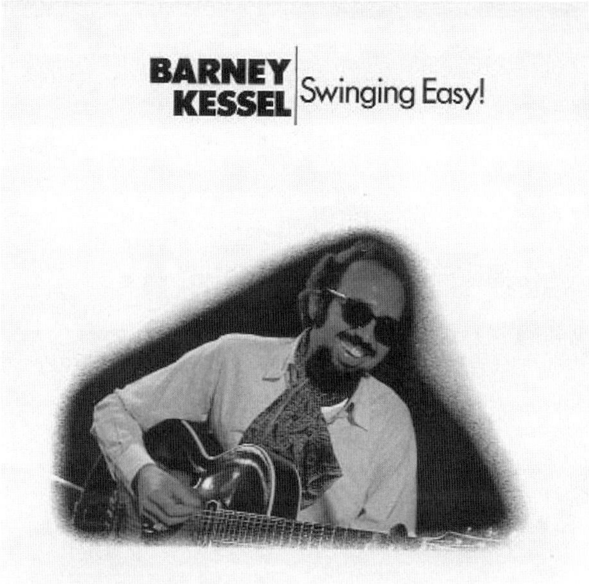
BARNEY
KESSEL
Swinging Easy!

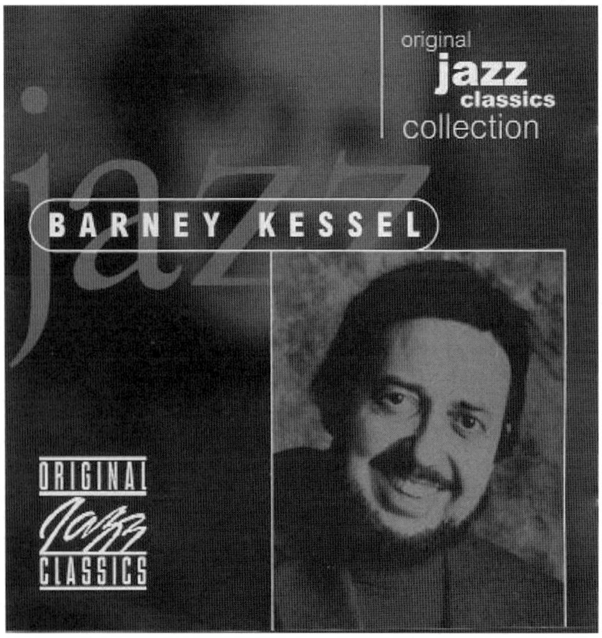
original
jazz
classics
collection
jazz
BARNEY KESSEL
ORIGINAL
Jazz
CLASSICS

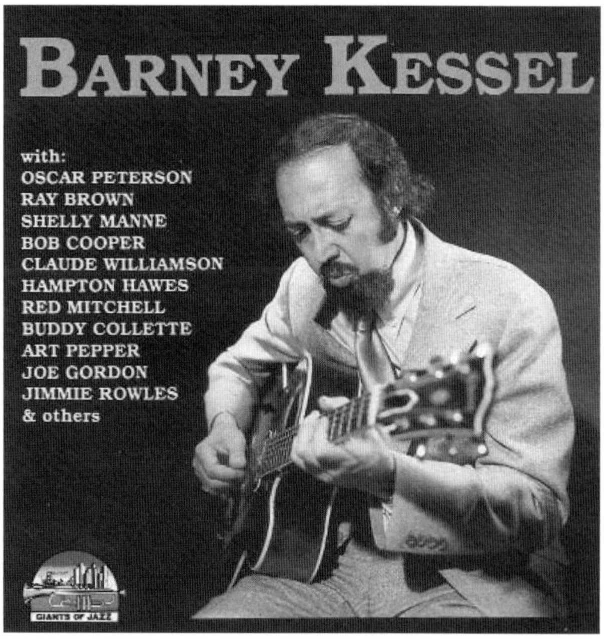
BARNEY KESSEL
with:
OSCAR PETERSON
RAY BROWN
SHELLY MANNE
BOB COOPER
CLAUDE WILLIAMSON
HAMPTON HAWES
RED MITCHELL
BUDDY COLLETTE
ART PEPPER
JOE GORDON
JIMMIE ROWLES
& others
GIANTS OF JAZZ

Blues Up, Down And All Around (Kessel)
　　　Moving Up (Kessel)
　　　The Sound Of Silence (Simon)
　　　This Guy's In Love With You (Bacharach)
　　　Two Note Samba (Kessel)

---

01 May 1969 [Estimated]　　　　　　　Rome, Italy

Barney Kessel - Carlo Pes Duo

Easy Moments [LP, Gemeli, GG ST.10.025LP]

[Musicians: Barney Kessel: Guitar, Carlo Pes: Guitar.]

　　　Both Ways (Kessel/Pes)
　　　Clouds (Kessel/Pes)
　　　Easy Moments (Kessel/Pes)
　　　Good Brothers (Kessel/Pes)
　　　Hummin' Dobro (Kessel/Pes)
　　　Just Simple (Kessel/Pes)
　　　Lonely Walks (Kessel/Pes)
　　　Memories (Kessel/Pes)
　　　My Winter (Kessel/Pes)
　　　Runnin' Notes (Kessel/Pes)
　　　South Border (Kessel/Pes)
　　　Swingin' Partners (Kessel/Pes)

---

07 May 1969　　　　　　　Rome, Italy

Barney Kessel

Kessel's Kit [LP, RCA, SF8098]
Barney Kessel [LP, RCA Victor, 730-710]
Guitarra [CD, BMG Japan, 37262]

[Musicians: Barney Kessel: Guitar, Antonello Vannucchi: Organ, Carlo Pes: Guitar, Giovanni Tommaso: Electric Bass, Ciro Cicco: Drums, Vincenzo Restuccia: Percussion.]

　　　Amelia (Kessel)
　　　B J's Samba (Kessel)
　　　Freeway (Kessel)
　　　From My Heart (Kessel)
　　　Lison (Kessel)
　　　Malibu (Kessel)
　　　Meu Irmao (Kessel)
　　　On The Riviera (Kessel)
　　　Swing Samba (Kessel)

Barney Kessel

Reflections In Rome [LP, RCA, LISP 34012 (Italy)]
Barney Kessel [LP, Amiga, 8 55 447 (Germany)]

[Musicians: Barney Kessel: Guitar, Giovanni Tommaso: Bass, Daniel Humair: Drums, Vincenzo Restuccia: Drums.]

　　　Caliente Blues (Kessel)
　　　Carlo's Dream (Kessel)
　　　Free Wheeling (Kessel)
　　　Minor Major Mode (Kessel)
　　　Minor Mode (Kessel)
　　　Mysterioso Impromptu (Kessel)

Reflections In Rome (Kessel)
Shufflin' The Blues (Kessel)
The Opener (Kessel)

01 June 1969 [Estimated]　　　　Los Angeles, USA

Chet Baker

At Albert's House [LP, Bainbridge, BT 1040]
At Albert's House [LP, Beverly Hills, BH 1134 LP]
[Musicians: Barney Kessel: Guitar, Paul Smith: Piano, Jim Hughart: Bass, Frank Capp: Drums, Chet Baker: Trumpet.]

A Man Who Used To Be (Allen)
Albert's House (Allen)
End Of The Line (Allen)
Farewell, San Francisco (Fitch)
How Dare You, Sir (Allen)
I Should Have Told You So (Allen)
Life (Allen)
Never Had This Feeling Before (Allen)
Nice Little Girls (Allen)
Pretty People (Allen)
Sunday In Town (Allen)
Time (Allen)

16 June 1969　　　　Paris, France

Barney Kessel

What's New [LP, Mercury, 135720]
[Musicians: Barney Kessel: Guitar, Eddy Louiss: Organ, Carlo Pes: Guitar, Guy Pettersen: Bass, Bernard Lubat: Percussion, Emile Boza: Percussion, Pierre-Alain Dahan: Drums.]

Blues All Night Long (Kessel)
Holiday In Rio (Kessel)

18 June 1969　　　　Paris, France

Barney Kessel

What's New [LP, Mercury, 135720]
[Musicians: Barney Kessel: Guitar, George Arvanitas: Organ, Carlo Pes: Guitar, Guy Pettersen: Bass, Pierre-Alain Dahan: Drums, Bernard Lubat: Percussion, Michel Delaporte: Percussion.]

Blues For Bird (Kessel)
I See You (Baker)

[Musicians: Barney Kessel: Guitar, Stephane Grappelli: Violin, Maurice Vander: Piano, Michel Gaudry: Bass, Marcel Blanche: Drums, Carlo Pes: Guitar, Unknown: String Section.]

Nuages (Reinhardt)
What's New (Haggart/Burke)

23 June 1969　　　　Paris, France

Barney Kessel & Stephane Grappelli

I Remember Django [LP, Black Lion, BLP3010]
I Remember Django [CD, Black Lion, BLC760150CD]
[Musicians: Barney Kessel: Guitar, Stephane Grappelli: Violin, Nini Rosso: Rhythm Guitar, Michel Gaudry: Bass, Jean-Louis Viale: Drums.]

Et Maintenant (Becaud)

Honeysuckle Rose (Waller)
I Can't Get Started (Gershwin)
I Found A New Baby (Palmer)
I Remember Django (Kessel)
It's Only A Paper Moon (Arlen)
More Than You Know (Youmans)
What A Difference A Day Made (Grever)

Barney Kessel & Stephane Grappelli

Limehouse Blues [CD, BLC, 760158CD]

[Musicians: Barney Kessel: Guitar, Stephane Grappelli: Violin, Nini Rosso: Rhythm Guitar, Michel Gaudry: Bass, Jean-Louis Viale: Drums.]

Blues For George (Kessel)
Copa Cola (Kessel)
Honeysuckle Rose (Take 2) (Razaf/Waller)
I Got Rhythm (Gershwin/Gershwin)
Perdido (Tizol/Lenk/Drake)

Barney Kessel & Stephane Grappelli

Limehouse Blues [LP, Black Lion, BLP 30129]
Limehouse Blues [CD, BLC, 760158CD]

[Musicians: Barney Kessel: Guitar, Stephane Grappelli: Violin, Nini Rosso: Rhythm Guitar, Michel Gaudry: Bass, Jean-Louis Viale: Drums.]

How High The Moon? (Hamilton/Lewis)
It Don't Mean A Thing (Ellington)
Limehouse Blues (Furber)
Little Star (Kessel)
Out Of Nowhere (Heyman/Green)
Tea For Two (Youmans/Caesar/Harbach)
Undecided (Shavers)
Willow Weep For Me (Ronell)

---

26 June 1969   Paris, France

Barney Kessel

What's New [LP, Mercury, 135720]

[Musicians: Barney Kessel: Guitar, Michel Gaudry: Bass, Jean-Louis Viale: Drums.]

Blue Fountain (Kessel)
Blues A La Carte (Kessel)
Chez Roger (Kessel)
Cool Groove (Kessel)

---

18 September 1969   Los Angeles, USA

Barney Kessel

Blue Soul [LP, Black Lion, BLP30161]
Autumn Leaves [CD, Black Lion, BLCD760112]

[Musicians: Barney Kessel: Guitar, Teddy Edwards: Tenor Saxophone, Jimmy Rowles: Piano.]

Blue Soul (Kessel)
Comin' Home (Kessel)
Shufflin (Kessel)
Stumblin' Around (Kessel)

08 October 1969 **Tokyo, Japan**

Newport Festival Jazz All Stars

Newport Jazz All Stars in Japan [LP, Union (Japan), UPS-49]
[Musicians: Barney Kessel: Guitar, Ruby Braff: Cornet, Red Norvo: Vibraphone, George Wein: Piano, Joe Venuti: Violin, Larry Ridley: Bass, Cliff Leeman: Drums.]

- Autumn Leaves (Kosma/Prevert/Mercer)
- Body And Soul (Green/Heyman/Sour/Eyton)
- Fly Me To The Moon (Howard)
- Honeysuckle Rose (Razaf/Waller)
- I Surrender Dear (Clifford/Barris)
- Perdido (Tizol/Lenk/Drake)
- Russian Lullaby (Berlin)
- Stardust (Carmichael/Parish)
- Summertime (Gershwin/Gershwin)

---

20 October 1969 **Paris, France**

Ruby Braff and Red Norvo

Swing That Music [LP, Affinity, AFF (D) 45]
Swing That Music [CD, Affinity, CD AFF 776]
[Musicians: Barney Kessel: Guitar, Red Norvo: Vibraphone, George Wein: Piano, Larry Ridley: Bass, Don Lamond: Drums.]

- Confessin' (Reynolds/Neiburg)
- Lullaby Of The Leaves (Petkere/Young)
- Rose Room (Williams/Hickman)
- Spider's Webb (Webb)
- Sunday (Miller/Cohn/Stein/Kreuger)
- The Girl From Ipanema (Jobim/Gimbel/Morales)
- Wrap Your Troubles In Dreams (Barris/Moll/Koehler)

[Musicians: Barney Kessel: Guitar, Ruby Braff: Cornet, George Wein: Piano, Larry Ridley: Bass, Don Lamond: Drums.]

- (Was I To Blame For) Falling In Love With You (Newman/Kahn/Young)
- Cornet Chop Suey (Armstrong)
- It's Wonderful (Smith/Parish)
- I've Got A Feelin' I'm Fallin' (Waller/Rose/Link)
- Someday You'll Be Sorry (Armstrong)
- Swing That Music (Armstrong)
- Thankful (Cahn/Chaplin)
- When It's Sleepytime Down South (Rene/Rene/Muse)

---

22 October 1969 **Paris, France**

Stephane Grappelli and Joe Venuti

Venupelli Blues [LP, Affinity, Aff 29]
Venupelli Blues [CD, Charly/Affinity, 73]
[Musicians: Barney Kessel: Guitar, Stephane Grappelli: Violin, Joe Venuti: Violin, George Wein: Piano, Larry Ridley: Bass, Don Lamond: Drums.]

- After You've Gone (Creamer/Layton)
- I Can't Give You Anything But Love (Fields/McHugh)
- I'll Never Be The Same (Khan/Malneck/Signorelli)
- My One And Only Love (Wood/Mellin)
- Tea For Two (Youmans/Caesar)
- Undecided (Robin/Shavers)

Venupelli Blues (Venuti/Grappelli)

29 October 1969   Basle, Switzerland

Newport Festival Jazz All Stars

Newport Jazz All Stars: Tribute To The Duke [LP, MPS (Germany), 15255]
[Musicians: Barney Kessel: Guitar, Ruby Braff: Cornet, Red Norvo: Vibraphone, George Wein: Piano, Joe Venuti: Violin, Kenny Burrell: Guitar, Larry Ridley: Bass, Don Lamond: Drums.]

    Day Dream (Ellington)
    Deed I Do (Hirsch Rose)
    I Got It Bad And That Ain't Good (Ellington)
    If I Could Be With You One Hour Tonight (Creamer/Johnson)
    Just A-Sittin' And A Rockin' (Ellington)
    Rose Room (Williams/Hickman)
    Sophisticated Lady (Ellinfton)
    Sweet Georgia Brown (Pinkard/Bernie/Casey)
    Things Ain't What They Used To Be (Ellington)
    Undecided (Robin/Shavers)

01 November 1969   London, UK

Barney Kessel

Barney Kessel Trio at Ronnie Scott's [LP, PRIVATE RECORDING, BBC 1]
[Musicians: Barney Kessel: Guitar, Larry Ridley: Bass, Don Lamond: Drums.]

    Autumn Leaves (Kosma/Prevert/Mercer)
    Baubles, Bangles And Beads (Wright/Forest)
    You Stepped Out Of A Dream (Brown/Khan)

05 November 1969   Berlin, Germany

Newport Festival Jazz All Stars

Newport Jazz All Stars: European Concert [LP, Unique Jazz (Italy), 28]
[Musicians: Barney Kessel: Guitar, Ruby Braff: Cornet, Red Norvo: Vibraphone, George Wein: Piano, Joe Venuti: Violin, Kenny Burrell: Guitar, Larry Ridley: Bass, Don Lamond: Drums.]

    C Jam Blues (Ellington)
    Don't Get Around Much Anymore (Ellington)
    Medley: I Want To Be Happy (Youmans/Caesar/Harbach)
        In A Sentimental Mood (Ellington)
        Sophisticated Lady (Ellington)
        Take The A Train (Strayhorn)
    Perdido (Tizol/Lenk/Drake)
    Rockin' In Rhythm (Ellington)
    Satin Doll (Ellington)

01 April 1971 [Estimated]   Italy

SoundTrack - Permette? Rocco Papaleo

SoundTrack - Permette? Rocco Papaleo [LP, Cam, SAG 9037]
SoundTrack - Permette? Rocco Papaleo [CD, Cam, CSE 103]
[Musicians: Barney Kessel: Guitar, Carlo Pes: Guitar, Gino Marinacci: Flute, Unknown: Other Musicians.]

    Little Shakie Girl (Trovaioli/Pes)
    The Loop (Trovaioli/Pes)

15 May 1972   **Los Angeles, USA**

Barney Kessel & Joe Pass

Live at Donte's [LP, Not Issued, Pisano 001C]

[Musicians: Barney Kessel: Guitar, Joe Pass: Guitar, John Heard: Bass, Frank Severino: Drums.]

    Blues 1 (Kessel/Pass)
    Blues 2 (Kessel/Pass)
    Georgia on My Mind (Carmichael)
    Here's That Rainy Day (Burke/Van Heusen)
    Lover Man (Davis/Ramirez/Sherman)
    Soon (Gershwin)
    Stella by Starlight (Young/Washington)
    The More I See You (Gordon/Warren)

01 November 1972 [Estimated]   **Los Angeles, USA**

Les Strand

The Winners: Les Strand & The Yamaha [LP, Yamaha, YR5001]

[Musicians: Barney Kessel: Guitar, Les Strand: Organ, Shelly Manne: Drums.]

    A Foggy Day   (Gershwin/Gershwin)
    Close To You (Bacharach/David)
    Eleanor Rigby (Lennon/McCartney)
    For Cathy (Strand)
    I Don't Know How To Love Him (Webber/Rice)
    I'll Remember April   (Raye/De Paul/Johnston)
    My Funny Valentine   (Rodgers/Hart)
    Yamaha Blues (Feather)
    Yesterday   (Lennon/McCartney)

27 December 1972   **Los Angeles, USA**

Oscar Peterson

History Of An Artist Volume 1 [LP, Pablo, SD2625-702]
History Of An Artist [CD, Pablo, 2625-702]

[Musicians: Barney Kessel: Guitar, Oscar Peterson: Piano, Ray Brown: Bass.]

    Okie Blues (Peterson)

Oscar Peterson

History Of An Artist Volume 2 [LP, Pablo, 2310-895]
History Of An Artist Volume [CD, Pablo, 2625-702]

[Musicians: Barney Kessel: Guitar, Oscar Peterson: Piano, Ray Brown: Bass.]

    Ma He's Making Eyes at Me (Clare/Conrad)
    Wes' Tune (Montgomery)

05 June 1973   **Stockholm, Sweden**

Barney Kessel

Two Way Conversation [LP, Sonet, SNTF681]
Two Way Conversation [CD, EmArcy, 602498148853]

[Musicians: Barney Kessel: Guitar, Red Mitchell: Bass.]

    Summertime (Gershwin/Gershwin)

Two Way Conversation (Kessel)

Walkin' And Talkin' (Kessel)

04 July 1973   Montreux, Switzerland

Barney Kessel

Black Lion at Montreux [LP, Black Lion, BLP30148]
Barney Kessel in Concert [CD, Laser CD, 15011]
[Musicians: Barney Kessel: Guitar, Kenny Baldock: Bass, Johnny Richardson: Drums.]

Old Devil Moon (Lane/Harburg)

[Musicians: Barney Kessel: Guitar, Stephane Grappelli: Violin.]

Tea for Two (Youmans/Caesar)

Barney Kessel

Summertime In Montreux [LP, Black Lion, BLP30151]
Barney Kessel in Concert [CD, Laser CD, 15011]
[Musicians: Barney Kessel: Guitar, Kenny Baldock: Bass, Johnny Richardson: Drums, Brian Lemon: Piano, Danny Moss: Tenor Saxophone.]

Bridging The Blues (Kessel)

[Musicians: Barney Kessel: Guitar, Kenny Baldock: Bass, Johnny Richardson: Drums, Brian Lemon: Piano.]

It's A Blue World (Wright)

Summertime (Gershwin/Gershwin)

[Musicians: Barney Kessel: Guitar, Kenny Baldock: Bass, Johnny Richardson: Drums.]

Laura (Raksin/Mercer)

[Musicians: Barney Kessel: Guitar.]

In The Garden Of Love (Kessel)

Yesterday (Lennon)

01 August 1973 [Estimated]   Germany

Barney Kessel

Alan Broadbent & Friends [LP, BBC Radioplay Music, TAIR 78002]
[Musicians: Barney Kessel: Guitar, Lucas Lindholm: Bass, Tony Inzalaco: Drums.]

Star Eyes (Raye/De Paul)

27 September 1973   Stockholm, Sweden

Barney Kessel

Just Friends [LP, Sonet, SNTF685]
Just Friends [CD, Sonet, SNT 685CD]
[Musicians: Barney Kessel: Guitar, Sture Nordin: Bass, Pelle Hulten: Drums.]

Bewitched (Rodgers/Hart)

Days Of Wine And Roses (Mancini/Mercer)

Going Thru Some Changes (Kessel)

Just Friends (Klenner)

Old Devil Moon (Lane)

'Samba' From Black Orpheus (Bonfa)

True Blues (Kessel)

02 October 1973 — Stockholm, Sweden

Barney Kessel

Two Way Conversation [LP, Sonet, SNTF681]
Two Way Conversation [CD, EmArcy, 602498148853]
[Musicians: Barney Kessel: Guitar, Red Mitchell: Bass.]

- Alone Again (Naturally) (O'Sullivan)
- I'm On My Way (Kessel)
- Killing Me Softly With His Song (Gimbel/Fox)
- Wave (Mimosa)

---

28 July 1974 — New York, USA

Great Guitars

Great Guitars [LP, Concord Jazz, CJ4]
Great Guitars [CD, Concord Jazz, CD6004]
[Musicians: Barney Kessel: Guitar, Charlie Byrd: Guitar, Herb Ellis: Guitar, Joe Byrd: Bass, Johnny Rae: Drums.]

- Benny's Bugle (Goodman/Basie)
- Charlie's Blues (Byrd)
- Down Home Blues (Ellis)
- H And B Guitar Boogie (Ellis)
- Latin Groove (Kessel)
- O Barquinho (Menescal)
- Slow Burn (Kessel)
- Topsy (Christian)
- Undecided (Shavers)

---

01 January 1975 [Estimated] — Los Angeles, USA

Barney Kessel

Barney Kessel & Friends [CD, Concord, CCD-6009]
Barney Plays Kessel [LP, Concord, CJ9]
[Musicians: Barney Kessel: Guitar, Chuck Domanico: Bass, Victor Feldman: Vibraphone, Jake Hanna: Drums, Milt Holland: Percussion, Jimmy Rowles: Keyboards, Herbie Steward: Alto Saxophone.]

- For My Love (Kessel)

[Musicians: Barney Kessel: Guitar, Chuck Domanico: Bass, Victor Feldman: Vibraphone, Jake Hanna: Drums, Milt Holland: Percussion, Jimmy Rowles: Piano, Herbie Steward: Flute.]

- Goin' Through Some Changes (Kessel)
- Here's That Sunny Day (Kessel)
- Holiday in Rio (Kessel)
- I'm On My Way (Kessel)
- Love of My Life (Kessel)
- Sea Miner (Kessel)

[Musicians: Barney Kessel: Guitar, Chuck Domanico: Bass, Victor Feldman: Vibraphone, Jake Hanna: Drums, Milt Holland: Percussion, Jimmy Rowles: Piano, Herbie Steward: Soprano Saxophone.]

- Brazilian Beat (Kessel)
- Down in the Swamp (Kessel)

12 December 1975   Los Angeles, USA

The Poll Winners

The Poll Winners - Straight Ahead [LP, Contemporary, S7635]
The Poll Winners - Straight Ahead [CD, Contemporary, OJCCD-409-02]
[Musicians: Barney Kessel: Guitar, Ray Brown: Bass, Shelly Manne: Drums.]

- Blue Boy (Kessel)
- Caravan (Ellington/Tizol/Mills)
- Laura (Mercer/Raskin)
- One Foot Off The Curb (Kessel)
- Someday My Prince Will Come (Churchill/Morey)
- Two Cents (Brown)

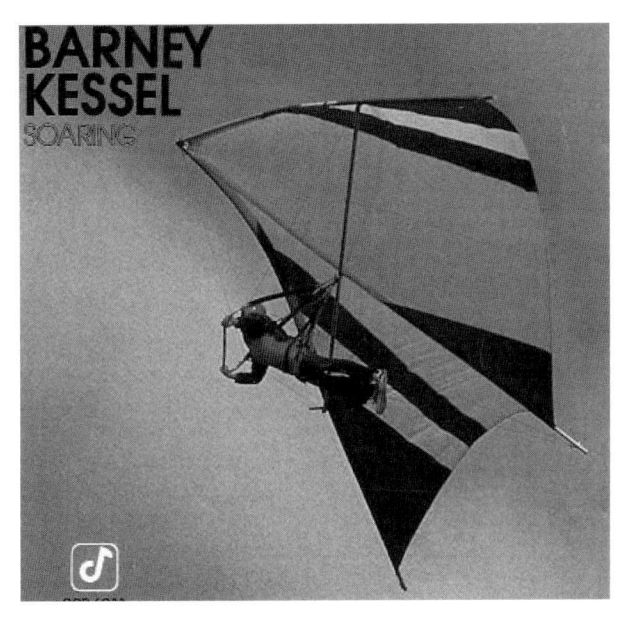

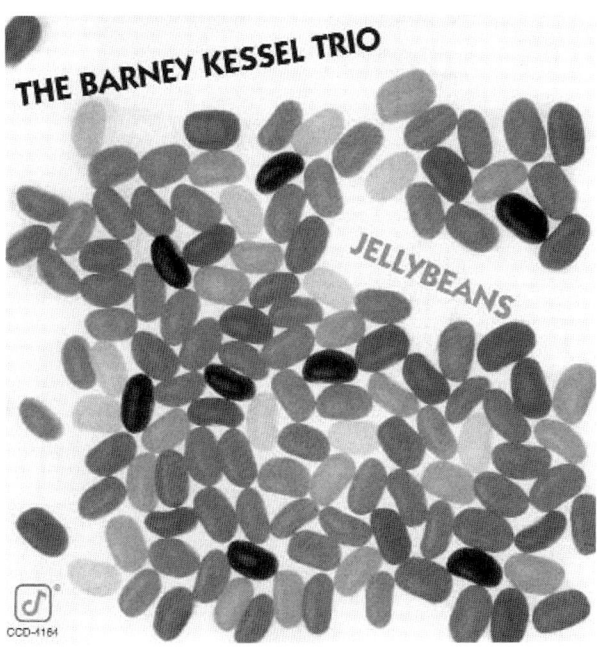

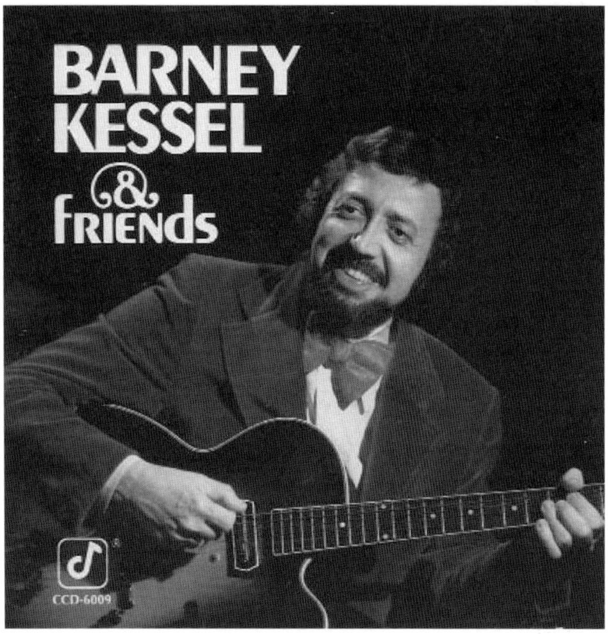
BARNEY
KESSEL
&
FRIENDS
CCD-6009

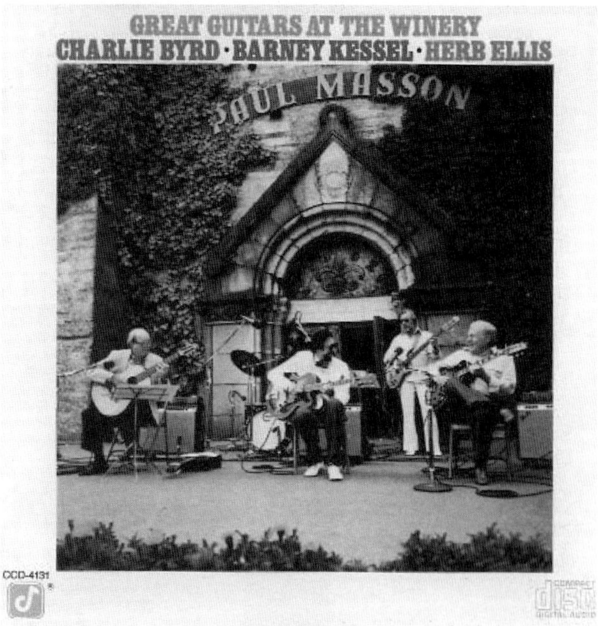
GREAT GUITARS AT THE WINERY
CHARLIE BYRD · BARNEY KESSEL · HERB ELLIS
CCD-4131

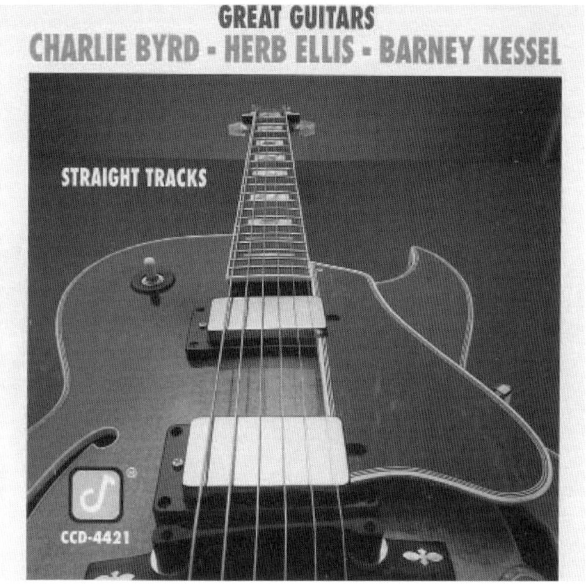
GREAT GUITARS
CHARLIE BYRD - HERB ELLIS - BARNEY KESSEL
STRAIGHT TRACKS
CCD-4421

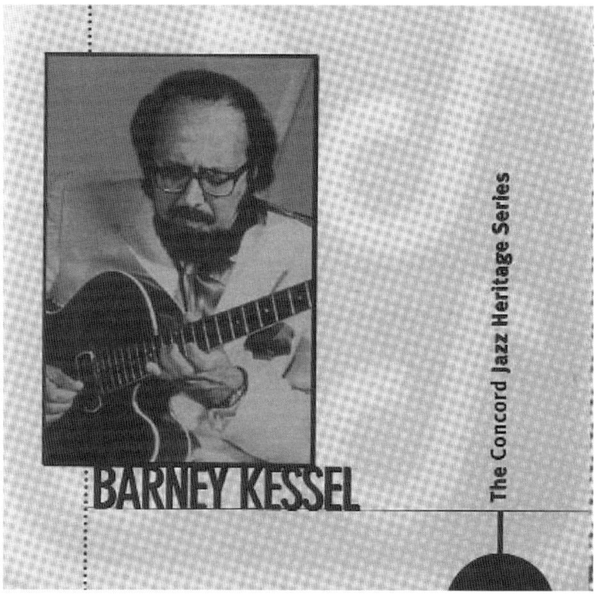
BARNEY KESSEL
The Concord Jazz Heritage Series

GREAT GUITARS
AT
Charlie's
GEORGETOWN
CCD-4209
CHARLIE BYRD • BARNEY KESSEL • HERB ELLIS
*Includes 2 previously unreleased selections.

CHARLIE
BYRD
BARNEY
KESSEL
HERB
ELLIS
GREAT GUITARS II
CCD-4023

01 July 1976 [Estimated]　　　San Francisco, USA

Barney Kessel

Poor Butterfly [LP, Concord Jazz, CJ34]
Poor Butterfly [CD, Concord Jazz, CCD4034]
[Musicians: Barney Kessel: Guitar, Herb Ellis: Guitar, Monty Budwig: Bass, Jake Hanna: Drums.]

- Blueberry Hill (Lewis/Stock/Rose)
- Brigitte (Baker)
- Dearly Beloved (Kern)
- Early Autumn (Mercer)
- Hello (Ellis)
- I'm A Lover (Ellis)
- Make Someone Happy (Comden/Green/Styne)
- Monsieur Armand (Kessel)
- Poor Butterfly (Golden/Hubbell)

10 August 1976 [Estimated]　　　San Francisco, USA

Great Guitars

Great Guitars II [LP, Concord Jazz, CJ-23]
Great Guitars II [CD, Concord Jazz, CD4023]
[Musicians: Barney Kessel: Guitar, Charlie Byrd: Guitar, Herb Ellis: Guitar, Joe Byrd: Bass, Wayne Phillips: Drums.]

- Amparo (Carlos)
- Body And Soul (Heyman)
- Cow Cow Boogie (Raye)
- Lover (Rodgers/Hart)
- Makin' Whoopee (Kahn)
- Medley: Flying Home (Robin)
  - Goin' Out Of My Head (Randazzo)
  - Nuages (Reinhardt)
- On Green Dolphin Street (Washington)
- Outer Drive (Ellis)

25 August 1976　　　San Francisco, USA

Barney Kessel

Soaring [LP, Concord Jazz, CJ33]
Soaring [CD, Concord Jazz, CCD6033]
[Musicians: Barney Kessel: Guitar, Monty Budwig: Bass, Jake Hanna: Drums.]

- Beautiful Love (Young)
- Get Out Of Town (Porter)
- I Love You (Porter)
- Like Someone In Love (Burke)
- Seagull (Kessel)
- Star Eyes (Raye)
- You Go To My Head (Coots)
- You're The One For Me (Kessel)

04 October 1976 — Los Angeles, USA

Barney Kessel & Herb Ellis

Guitar Player [LP, MCA Records, MCA2-6002]
[Musicians: Barney Kessel: Guitar, Herb Ellis: Guitar, Pete Jolly: Piano, Monty Budwig: Bass, Jake Hanna: Drums.]

- Contrary-Ness (Kessel)
- Tea For Two (Youmans/Caesar)
- Two More For The Blues (Ellis)

---

02 February 1977 — Tokyo, Japan

Barney Kessel

By Myself [LP, Victor Japan, SPX-1042]
[Musicians: Barney Kessel: Guitar.]

- Blue Moon (Rodgers/Hart)
- Georgia On My Mind (Carmichael/Carroll)
- Have You Met Miss Jones? (Rodgers/Hart)
- I Can't Get Started (Gershwin/Duke)
- Once I Loved (Jobim/Moraes/Gilbert)
- Samba De Orfeu (Bonfa/Maria)
- Sometimes I'm Happy (Youmans/Caesar/Grey)
- Stompin' At The Savoy (Goodman/Sampson/Webb/Razal)
- That Old Feeling (Fain/Brown)
- What A Difference A Day Made (Grever/Adams)
- Yesterdays (Kern/Harbach)

---

22 February 1977 — Tokyo, Japan

Barney Kessel

Shiny Stockings [LP, LOB, LDC-1004]
[Musicians: Barney Kessel: Guitar, Kunimitsu Inaba: Bass, Tetsujiroh Obara: Drums.]

- Autumn In New York (Duke)
- Manha Do Carnaval (Black Orpheus) (Bonfa)
- Secret Love (Fain/Webster)
- Shiny Stockings (Foster)
- There Is No Greater Love (Jones)
- Triste (Jobim)

---

23 February 1977 — Tokyo, Japan

Barney Kessel

Live At Sometime [LP, Trio Records, PAP9062]
Live At Sometime [CD, Trio, STCD4157]
[Musicians: Barney Kessel: Guitar, Kunimitsu Inaba: Bass, Tetsujiroh Obara: Drums.]

- Barniana (Almeida)
- Body & Soul (Green)
- Bye Bye Blackbird (Henderson)
- Feelings (Albert)
- Georgia On My Mind (Carmichael)
- Girl From Ipanema (Jobim)
- Softly As In A Morning Sunrise (Romberg)

Stella By Starlight (Young)
What Is This Thing Called Love (Porter)
Willow Weep For Me (Ronell)

06 March 1977   Tokyo, Japan

Barney Kessel

Junko & Barney [LP, Trio Records, PAP-9060]
[Musicians: Barney Kessel: Guitar, Junko Mine: Vocals, Kunimitsu Inaba: Bass, Tetsujiroh Obara: Drums.]

As Time Goes By (Hupfeld)
Johnny Guitar (Young)
Love Letters (Young)
Our Love Is Here To Stay (Gershwin/Gershwin)
'S Wonderful (Gershwin/Gershwin)
Speak Low (Weill)
The Shadow Of Your Smile (Mandel)
The Very Thought Of You (Noble)
The Way We Were (Hamlish)
Time After Time (Styne)

01 July 1978 [Estimated]   Los Angeles, USA

Great Guitars

Great Guitars - Straight Tracks [LP, Concord Jazz, CJD1002]
Great Guitars - Straight Tracks [CD, Concord Jazz, CCD4421]
[Musicians: Barney Kessel: Guitar, Charlie Byrd: Guitar, Herb Ellis: Guitar, Joe Byrd: Bass, Wayne Phillips: Drums.]

Clouds (Donaldson)
Favela (Jobim)
Gravy Waltz (Brown)
I'm Putting All My Eggs In One Basket (Berlin)
It Might As Well Be Spring (Rodgers/Hart)
Kingston Cutie (Kessel)
Little Rock Getaway (Sullivan)
Um Abraco No Bonfa (Gilberto)

27 March 1979   Ames, Iowa, USA

Great Guitars

Great Guitars At The Maintenance Shop [VID, K Jazz Video, KJ126]
[Musicians: Barney Kessel: Guitar, Charlie Byrd: Guitar, Herb Ellis: Guitar, Joe Byrd: Bass, Wayne Philips: Drums.]

Alfie (Bacharach)
Aqua De Berber (Jobim)
Caranosa
Days Of Wine And Roses (Mancini/Mercer)
Favela (Jobim)
Flying Home (Goodman/Hampton/DeLange)
Goin' Out Of My Head (Randazzo/Weinstein)
Meditation (Jobim)
Nuages (Reinhardt)
Outer Drive (Ellis)
Tangerine (Mercer/Schertzinger)

Great Guitars

Great Guitars At The Maintenance Shop [VID, K Jazz Video, KJ131]
[Musicians: Barney Kessel: Guitar, Charlie Byrd: Guitar, Herb Ellis: Guitar, Joe Byrd: Bass, Wayne Philips: Drums.]

- Clouds (Kahn/Donaldson)
- Etude For Guitar (Byrd)
- Is'nt This A Lovely Day (Berlin)
- Jitterbug Waltz (Waller/Maltby Jnr)
- Kingston Kutie (Kessel)
- Little Rock Getaway (Sullivan)
- Oh Lady Be Good (Gershwin/Gershwin)
- Sesame Street (Raposo/Stone/Bruce)
- Seven Come Eleven (Christian/Goodman)
- Undecided (Shavers)

Great Guitars

Great Guitars At The Maintenance Shop [VID, K Jazz Video, KJ132]
[Musicians: Barney Kessel: Guitar, Charlie Byrd: Guitar, Herb Ellis: Guitar, Joe Byrd: Bass, Wayne Philips: Drums.]

- Benny's Bugle (Goodman/Basie)
- Concerto in D - First Movement (Vivaldi)
- Django (Lewis)
- I'm Putting All My Eggs In One Basket (Berlin)
- It Might As Well Be Spring (Rodgers/Hart)
- Lover (Porter)
- Make Someone Happy (Conden/Green/Styne)
- Slow Burn (Kessel)
- St. Thomas (Rollins)
- Vou Vivendo

---

09 April 1979   Los Angeles, USA

Paul Smith

The Good Life [LP, Voss, D1 72937]
The Good Life [LP, Discwasher, DR004-D]
The Good Life [CD, Voss, D2 72937]
[Musicians: Barney Kessel: Guitar, Paul Smith: Piano, Frank Capp: Drums, Monty Budwig: Bass.]

- Boppo For J.J. (Smith)
- Here's That Rainy Day (Burke/Van Heusen)
- I Hadn't Anyone 'Til You (Noble)
- Madame Butterfly (Harling)
- Perdido (Tizol/Lenk/Drake)
- Send In The Clowns (Sondheim)
- Someday My Prince Will Come (Churchill)
- The Fourth Way (Kessel)
- The Good Life (Distel)
- What I Did For Love (Hamlish)

01 October 1979 [Estimated] Suddeutscher Rundfunk, G

Barney Kessel and the Erwin Lehn Big Band

A Tribute To Barney Kessel Vol.1 [CD, Edition Musikat, 4 022228 850003]
[Musicians: Barney Kessel: Guitar, Musicians Unknown: Erwin Lehn Radio Big Band.]
- Have You Met Miss Jones? (Rodgers/Hart)
- Misty (Garner)

01 July 1980 Saratoga, Califonia, USA

Great Guitars

At The Winery: Great Guitars [LP, Concord Jazz, CJ131]
At The Winery: Great Guitars [CD, Concord Jazz, CCD4131]
[Musicians: Barney Kessel: Guitar, Charlie Byrd: Guitar, Herb Ellis: Guitar, Joe Byrd: Bass, Jimmie Smith: Drums.]
- Air Mail Special (Mundy)
- Body And Soul (Green)
- Broadway (DeSylva)
- Just In Time (Comden)
- Sheik Of Araby (Smith)
- So Danco Samba (Jobim)
- Straighten Up And Fly Right (Cole)
- The Talk Of The Town (Kahn)
- You Took Advantage Of Me (Rodgers)

01 April 1981 [Estimated] San Francisco, USA

Barney Kessel

Jelly Beans [LP, Concord Jazz, CJ164]
Jelly Beans [CD, Concord Jazz, CCD4146]
[Musicians: Barney Kessel: Guitar, Bob Maize: Bass, Jimmie Smith: Drums.]
- I've Never Been In Love Before (Loesser)
- Jelly Beans (Kessel)
- Juarez After Dark (Kessel)
- Mermaid (Kessel)
- My Foolish Heart (Young)
- Shiny Stockings (Foster)
- St.Thomas (Rollins)
- Stella By Starlight (Washington)

02 April 1981 [Estimated] San Francisco, USA

Barney Kessel

Solo - Barney Kessel [LP, Concord Jazz, CJ221]
Solo - Barney Kessel [CD, Concord Jazz, CCD0221]
[Musicians: Barney Kessel: Guitar.]
- Alfie (Bacharach)
- Brazil (Barroso)
- Everything Happens To Me (Adair)
- Happy Little Song (Kessel)
- Jellybeans (Kessel)
- Manha De Carnaval (Bonfa)

    People (Merrill)
    What Are You Doing The Rest Of Your Life (Legrand)
    You Are The Sunshine Of My Life (Wonder)

01 May 1981 [Estimated]   Los Angeles, USA

Julie London

Sharky's Machine: Film Soundtrack [LP, Warner Bros., BSK 3653]
[Musicians: Barney Kessel: Guitar, Ray Brown: Bass, Shelly Manne: Drums, Julie London: Vocals.]

    My Funny Valentine (Rodgers/Hart)

27 September 1981   Los Angeles, USA

Zoot Sims

Art 'N' Zoot [CD, Pablo, PACD-2310-957-2]
[Musicians: Barney Kessel: Guitar, Zoot Sims: Tenor Saxophone, Victor Feldman: Piano, Ray Brown: Bass, Billy Higgins: Drums.]

    Broadway (Woode/McCrae/Bird)
    The Girl From Ipanema (Jobim/DeMoraes)

01 August 1982 [Estimated]   Washington D.C, USA

Great Guitars

Great Guitars At Charlie's Georgetown [LP, Concord Jazz, CJ209]
Great Guitars At Charlie's Georgetown [CD, Concord Jazz, CCD-4209]
[Musicians: Barney Kessel: Guitar, Charlie Byrd: Guitar, Herb Ellis: Guitar, Joe Byrd: Bass, Chuck Redd: Drums.]

    Change Partners (Berlin)
    Get Happy (Arlen/Koehler)
    New Orleans (Carmichael)
    Old Folks (Hill)
    Opus One (Oliver)
    Trouble In Mind (Jones)
    When The Saints Go Marching In (Byrd)
    Where Or When (Rodgers/Hart)

20 February 1987   Berkeley, CA, USA

Barney Kessel

Spontaneous Combustion [CD, Contemporary, CDD-14033]
[Musicians: Barney Kessel: Guitar, Monty Alexander: Piano, John Clayton: Bass, Jeff Hamilton: Drums.]

    Shaw 'Nuff (Gillespie/Parker)

Barney Kessel

Spontaneous Combustion [LP, Contemporary, C14033]
Spontaneous Combustion [CD, Contemporary, CDD-14033]
[Musicians: Barney Kessel: Guitar, Monty Alexander: Piano, John Clayton: Bass, Jeff Hamilton: Drums.]

    Ah, Sweet Mystery Of Live (Young/Herbert)
    Almost The Blues (Kessel)
    Bluesy (Kessel)
    Everything I Have Is Yours (Lane/Adamson)
    Get Me To The Church On Time (Lerner/Loewe)
    Moonlight Walk (Kessel)

'Round Midnight (Monk)
Star Fire (Kessel)

15 March 1988 — Berkeley, CA, USA

Barney Kessel

Red Hot And Blues [LP, Contemporary, C14044]
Red Hot And Blues [CD, Contemporary, CCD14044-2]
[Musicians: Barney Kessel: Guitar, Bobby Hutcherson: Vibraphone, Kenny Barron: Piano, Rufus Reid: Bass, Ben Riley: Drums.]

Barniana (Almeida)
Blues For Bird (Kessel)
By Myself (Dietz/Schwartz)
I'm Glad There Is You (Mertz/Dorsey)
It's You Or No One (Cahn/Styne)
Messin' With The Blues (Kessel)
Rio (Kessel)
You've Changed (Carey/Fischer)

01 July 1988 [Estimated] — La Jolla, California, USA

Barney Kessel

Club Date - Guitarists Collection [LD, Media Rings Corp., MGLP-1023]
[Musicians: Barney Kessel: Guitar, Bob Magnusson: Bass, Sherman Ferguson: Drums.]

Brazil/A Day In The Life Of A Fool Medley (Barroso/Bonfa)
I've Grown Accustomed To Her Face (Lerner/Loewe)
Wave (Jobim)

[Musicians: Barney Kessel: Guitar, Herb Ellis: Guitar, Bob Magnusson: Bass, Sherman Ferguson: Drums.]

Body And Soul (Green/Hayman)
Lover Man (Davis/Ramirez/Sherman)
Sheik Of Araby (Snyder)
The Flintstones (Barbera/Goodwin/Hanna)

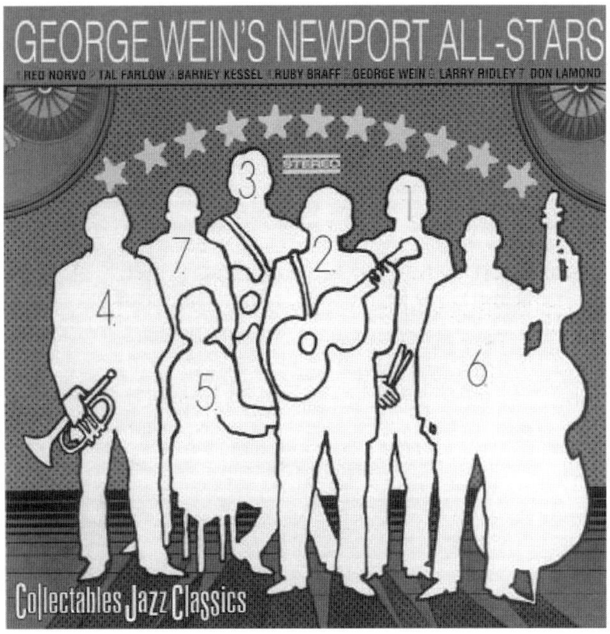
GEORGE WEIN'S NEWPORT ALL-STARS
RED NORVO TAL FARLOW BARNEY KESSEL RUBY BRAFF GEORGE WEIN LARRY RIDLEY DON LAMOND
Collectables Jazz Classics

Barney Kessel
Autumn Leaves
24 BIT REMASTERED

barney kessel
PLAYS FOR LOVERS

A JAZZ HOUR WITH
BARNEY KESSEL
It's A Blue World
ON A CLEAR DAY, YOU CAN SEE FOREVER
THE LOOK OF LOVE | HONEYSUCKLE ROSE
HOW HIGH THE MOON
BLUE WORLD | AND MANY OTHERS

Barney Kessel
I Got Rhythm
ORIGINAL
Jazz
STANDARDS

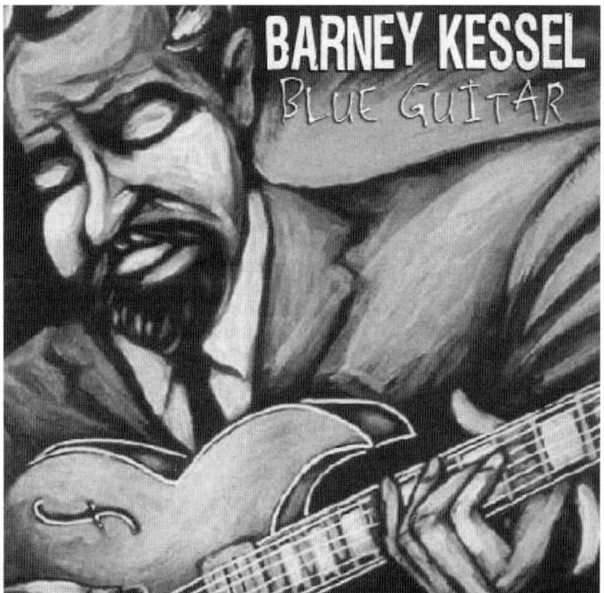
BARNEY KESSEL
BLUE GUITAR

BARNEY KESSEL - A JAZZ LEGEND

Compilation CDs

In recent years several compilation CDs of Barney Kessel have been issued by various companies. These include tracks selected from different Barney Kessel's many recordings over very many years. They can be an ideal introduction to the artistry of this great jazz guitarist. Here is a selected list:

The Artistry of Barney Kessel	Contemporary	FCD-60-021
Barney Kessel	Giants of Jazz	CD 53116
A Jazz Hour with Barney Kessel	Jazz Hour	JHR 73526
Barney Kessel	Original Jazz Classics	OJCX 010
Salute to Charlie Christian	Past Perfect	220304-203
Barney Kessel – Master of Guitar	Modern Jazz Archive	221957-306
Barney Kessel – I Got Rhythm	Zyx Music	OJSCD 030-2
Barney Kessel	Supreme Jazz	223263-207
Barney Kessel Plays For Lovers	Contemporary	CCD-6022-2
Barney Kessel – Blue Guitar	Fuel 2000	302 061 422 2
Barney Kessel Blues For A Playboy	Cherry Red	FiveFour 25

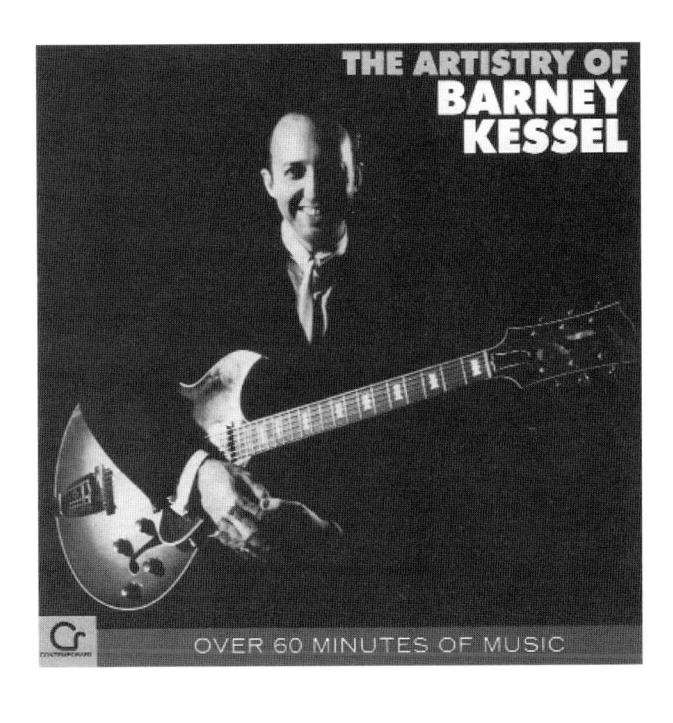

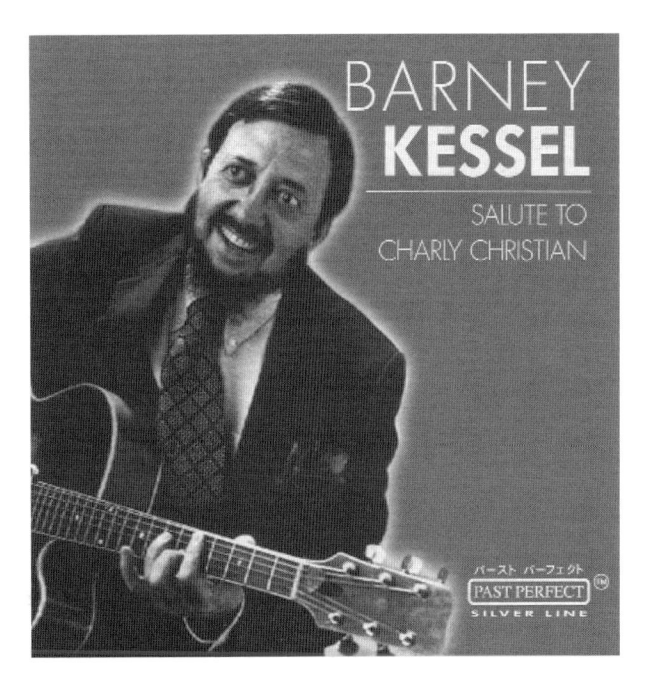

Concert Büro Rolf Schubert presents:

BARNEY KESSEL Trio

The Genius of Guitar

VIDEO RECORDINGS OF BARNEY KESSEL'S TELEVISION PERFORMANCES WHICH HAVE NEVER BEEN RELEASED COMMERCIALLY. HOWEVER PRIVATE COPIES ARE IN CIRCULATION AND SCENES FROM SOME OF THESE ARE FREQUENTLY AVAILABLE ON 'YOU TUBE'.

Barney Kessel Trio on Jazz Scene USA 1962 (26 min)
Host: Oscar Brown Jnr, Barney Kessel (guitar), Buddy Woodson (bass), Stan Levey (drums).
Gypsy In My Soul
Fly Me To The Moon
April In Paris
Danny Boy
One Mint Julep

Barney Kessel Quartet on CBC Vancouver Television Show
Hosted by Howard Bateman. c.1964 (60 min)
Barney Kessel (guitar), Chris Gage (piano), Don Thompson (bass), Terry Clarke (drums), Kenny Colman (vocals).
Recado Bossa Nova
Make Someone Happy
Like Someone in Love
Our Day Will Come
Danny Boy
Nobody Else But Me
*The programme includes a discussion about music, hosted by Howard Bateman, by the musicians and disc jockey Maurice Foisy.

Barney Kessel Trio in Sweden 1967 (8:20 min)
Barney Kessel (guitar), Sture Nordin (bass), Pete Hulten (drums)
On A Clear Day
Manha De Carnaval
Samba De Orfeu

Barney Kessel – 1975 Swedish Television Show (10 min)
Barney Kessel (guitar)
Yes My Darling Daughter

Barney Kessel Trio Stockholm, Sweden 1973 (27 min)
Barney Kessel (guitar), Sture Nordin (bass), Pete Hulten (drums)
Barney's Tune
I Love You
Brazilian Beat (Solo guitar)
The Shadow Of Your Smile
Basie's Blues

Barney Kessel Trio in Switzerland 1979 (66 min)
Barney Kessel (guitar), Jim Richardson (bass), Tony Mann (drums)
Autumn Leaves
Misty
Moose The Mooch
The Shadow Of Your Smile
I Can't Get Started
You Are The Sunshine Of My Life
Stella By Starlight
St. Thomas
Basie's Blues

Wave
Barney's Blues

The Great Guitars in the England 1979 (27 min)
Barney Kessel, Herb Ellis, Charlie Byrd (guitars), Joe Byrd (bass), Wayne Phillips (drums)
Lover
Pato
Nuages
Going Out Of My Head
Flying Home
Clouds
Undecided
Flintstones Theme

Barney Kessel Trio in England 1979 (50 min)
Barney Kessel (guitar), Jim Richardson (bass), Tony Mann(drums)
Autumn Leaves
Misty
Moose The Mooch
The Shadow Of Your Smile
I Can't Get Started
Stella By Starlight
St. Thomas
Basie's Blues

Barney Kessel on 'Pete Appleyard Presents Jazz' Toronto 1979 (46 min)
Barney Kessel (guitar), Pete Appleyard (vibraphone), Gary Cross (piano), Dave Young (bass), Terry Clarke (drums), Joe Williams(vocals) and O.C. Smith (vocals)
I'll Remember April
Come Back Baby Come Back
Shiny Stockings
Where Is The Love
Everyday I Have The Blues
Cherokee
I'm Getting Sentimental Over You
When You're In My Arms
Basie's Blues
The More I See You
When You're Smiling
Fascinating Rhythm

The Great Guitars in Berlin 1981 (50 min)
Barney Kessel, Herb Ellis, Charlie Byrd (guitars), Joe Byrd (bass), Chuck Redd (drums)
It's The Talk Of The Town
Nuages
Going Out Of My Head
Flying Home
Jitterbug Waltz
I'm Getting Sentimental Over You
Favela
Samba De Orfeu
The More I See You
Jumpin' At The Woodside

The Great Guitars at the North Sea Jazz Festival 1982 (29 min)
Barney Kessel, Herb Ellis, Charlie Byrd (guitars), Joe Byrd (bass), Chuck Redd (drums)
It's The Talk Of The Town
Undecided
A Felicidade
Manha De Carnaval
Nuages
Going Out Of My Head
Flying Home

Barney Kessel in Italy #1 c 1990
Barney Kessel (guitar), Jim Richardson (bass), Tony Mann (drums)
I've Grown Accustomed To Her Face

Barney Kessel & Carlo Pes in Italy c.1990
I Love You
Body And Soul
Now's The Time
The Nearness Of You

Barney Kessel, Carlo Pes, unknown 3rd guitarist & unknown bass in Italy c.1990
Theme
Misty
Satin Doll
Just Friends

Barney Kessel in Italy #2 c.1990 (89min)
Barney Kessel with bass and drums
Star Eyes
Wave
The Shadow Of Your Smile
Bye Bye Blackbird
Falling In Love With Love
Satin Doll
Estate
Flintstones Theme

Barney Kessel, Carlo Pes, Third guitarist (unknown)
Theme (Miles Davis)
Nuages
Barney's Blues
Just Friends
Seven Come Eleven

Barney Kessel –
Rare Performances 1962-1991
Vestapol DVD 13013

This is an excellent compilation DVD, commercially available, which includes some licensed scenes from the videos already listed. The contents are as follows:

England 1987
Interview

Jazz Scene USA 1962
Gypsy In My Soul
One Mint Julep

Sweden 1967
On A Clear Day

Sweden 1973
I Love You
Brazilian Beat

England 1974
Here's That Rainy Day

Switzerland 1979
Moose The Mooche
I Can't Get Started
You Are The Sunshine Of My Life

Iowa 1979 - Great Guitars at the Maintenance Shop
Undecided
Kingston Kuties
Seven Come Eleven

Oklahoma Jazz Hall Of Fame, Tulsa 1991
Speech

Vestapol's three DVD *Legends of Jazz Guitar* series include the following footage of Barney Kessel:

Volume 1 #13009
Basie's Blues   Sweden 1973
A Slow Burn (with Herb Ellis)   Iowa, USA 1979
Shadow of your Smile   Sweden 1973

Volume 2 #13033
Blue Mist (with Kenny Burrell and Grant Green)   London, UK 1969
BBC Blues   London, UK 1974

Volume 3 #13043
Medley: Manha De Carnaval & Samba De Orfeu   Denmark 1969
Oh! Lady Be Good (with Herb Ellis)   Iowa, USA 1979
Flintstones Theme (with Herb Ellis)   Cork, Ireland 1980

Norman Granz's historic short film Jammin' The Blues, directed by Gjon Mili, is also available on DVD:
Jammin' The Blues   IDEM IDVD 1057
The Greatest Jazz Films Ever   IDEM IDVD 2869058
Jammin' The Blues   EFOR B0002 T1 EEK
Norman Granz - Improvisation   Eagle Rock EE 39060-9

Tribute to Barney Kessel

University of Oklahoma May 1996

The University of Oklahoma bestowed an honorary doctorate upon Barney Kessel in May, 1996. The following is the transcription of that tribute given by Betty Price, Director of the State Arts Council of Oklahoma, the President of the University David L. Boren and Phyllis Kessel. The following was spoken by Betty Price:

I am very honoured this evening to be here with you to present a man of great talent. You know, without music and art, the world would really be a dull place, kind of like champagne that's lost its effervescence. Barney Kessel, who is known as one of the world's all-time greatest jazz guitarists, has spent his life helping make the world a 'swingingest', happening place.

Barney worked for forty years in Hollywood as an arranger and freelance musician for radio, films and television, per-forming with such diverse talent as Lawrence Welk, the Beach Boys, Barbra Streisand, Liberace, Elvis Presley and Frank Sinatra. That's diversity! He made more than four hundred recordings, both solo and with such jazz artists as Charlie Parker, Billie Holiday, Oscar Peterson, Sarah Vaughn, Ella Fitzgerald, Ben Webster and Sonny Rollins. In the 1940s, he performed with the renowned Artie Shaw, Charlie Barnet and Benny Goodman bands. Known for his brilliant harmonic improvisation, his fluid beat and hard-driving earthy style, critics called Barney one of the 'swingingest' players in jazz.

A winner of all of the major jazz polls, including Downbeat, Metronome and Playboy for several years, he was the most popular jazz guitarist in the 1950s and the 1960s. Jazz aficionados know that he was the first musician to take the jazz guitar and make it the main instrument in a jazz trio. He was also the first to use the guitar to sound like a full jazz orchestra. His landmark 1955 recording with Julie London, 'Julie is her Name', and its memorable 'Cry Me A River', is an early example of his ability to make arrangements which bring out full orchestral tone colours with only a string bass and an electric guitar.

During a 1991 engagement at New York's Village Vanguard Jazz Club, the New York Post wrote that he's one of the finest guitarists in jazz, and the New York Times referred to him as the master of guitar. In that same year, 1991, he was installed in the Oklahoma Jazz Hall of Fame at the historic Greenwood Cultural Center in Tulsa, and I was there. It was a great evening.

A man of many talents, he also is an accomplished composer and arranger, perhaps best known for his jazz classic, Swedish Pastry. As a teacher, he has given seminars and workshops all over the world. Barney served as cultural ambassador for the U.S. State Department in Europe, Asia, the Balkans, South America and Egypt. He toured the world as a solo artist and in groups, performing for two presidents - at the inaugural reception for Ronald Reagan, and at the invitation of President Jimmy Carter in 1981. He's a native of my hometown, Muskogee, and he is truly an Oklahoma treasure. He richly deserves the honorary degree from the University of Oklahoma for his great contribution to the world of jazz. It is my pleasure to present Mr. Barney Kessel.

Barney wrote a short speech in response which he asked his wife Phyllis to read out for him;

I'm very thankful to President Boren and the University of Oklahoma for this honorary degree. I am almost entirely self-educated. I never went beyond the ninth grade, so this honour is particularly meaningful to me. In my life, I have sought to be an inspiration to others, first as a human being, and secondly as a musician. I recognize my importance in the history of jazz, but my priorities are and always have been my spiritual relationship with God, my relation-ship with my wife, my family and friends, and then music, in that order. I am very proud and pleased to be called back home to receive this honour. Thank you.

The following closing comments, during the morning of commencement, were made by the President of the University, David L. Boren.

Jazz is truly America's contribution to music, and Barney Kessel, during your long and distinguished career as one of the world's greatest jazz artists, free-lance musician for radio during the golden age of radio, and arranger for hundreds of films and television productions, you have touched and enriched the lives of countless people around the world and have performed before huge audiences in Europe and Asia. Having performed for two presidents, you are well known both nationally and inter-nationally as an innovative educator, that you have officially been designated by the State Department of the United States as Cultural Ambassador of the United States, because of your artistic creativity, and most of all because of your personal moral values. You have brought great pride to your fellow Oklahomans, and it is a pleasure to award you the degree, Doctor of Humane Letters.

Ladies and Gentlemen - Dr. Barney Kessel.

Barney Kessel c. 1991.

Barney Kessel c.1976.

Guitar PLAYER
The Magazine For Professional And Amateur Guitarists
OCTOBER 1974
75¢
Frets
THEIR HISTORY
INATRA: A DEFENSE BY LEE CASTLE
June 25, 1959 35¢
down beat
Special Guitar Issue
John S. Wilson
ooks At History
Of Jazz Guitar
Musicians Win
Courtroom Gains
In New York, L. A.
Just Jazz Guitar
COLLECTORS EDITION 2
U.S. $10.00 • SEPTEMBER 1997
Barney Kessel
FOR THE ARCHTOP AND
$2.50
Cadence
The American Review of Jazz & Blues
VOL. 13 NO. 8 AUGUST 1987
Inside Interviews With:
Barney Kessel, Pete Peterson and Wade Walton
Book Reviews
Record Reviews
News
crescendo
international
1972
november
30 pence
the musicians' viewpoint

Great Jazz Guitar Books

Django Reinhardt
by **Charles Delaunay**
AM0254S (HL00183208) USA **$35.00**   UK **£19.95**
AM0254H Hard Cover Edition UK £29.95

A deluxe and extended version of the original and best biography of Django Reinhardt. Updated by Charles Delaunay with a correct and complete LP discography, an appendix with new information, and literally dozens of new, and previously unpublished photographs and documents. Essential reading for all guitarists.

Wes Montgomery
by **Adrian Ingram**
AM4553 (HL00332748) USA **$36.99**   UK **£18.50**

Wes Montgomery was unquestionably the most significant jazz guitarist to emerge during the 1960's. During the 70's and 80's he had like Charlie Christian and Django Reinhardt before him, become a major influence on other guitar players. Elements of his style are discernable in many of today's finest players. Although many musicians acknowledge Wes as one of the finest guitar players of the 20th Century there has been until now a lack of detailed biographical and analytical material. The author hopes that this book will be widely read and enjoyed by guitarists and jazz guitar enthusiasts everywhere and that Wes' achievements, so often narrowly categorised as the development of octave playing, will be more fully understood and appreciated. This definitive work is a must for all guitarists and jazz lovers alike.

Solo Flight - The Seminal Electric Guitarist
by **Peter Broadbent**
AM2159S (HL00330937) USA **$29.95**   UK **£15.95**
AM2159H Hard Cover Edition UK £25.00

Charlie Christian is regarded by many jazz historians as one of the major voices that shaped modern jazz in the early 1940s. Even though he tragically died before reaching his 26th birthday, his brilliant improvisations, phenominal rhythmic drive, and blues influenced guitar playing had already changed the course of jazz, and the guitar's place in jazz, for all-time. This second, updated and greatly expanded edition, details the full importance of Charlie Christian's brief life. Peter Broadbent, a talented jazz guitarist himself, has studied all Christian's known recordings for over thirty years. His well-researched biography of the Texan jazz genius reveals many new facts about Charlie Christian's short life and career in music. The discography in this book is certainly the most complete and accurate to be published to date. It corrects for the first time many errors in previous discographies and books. Also included is an impressive and unique collection of photographs and documents to illustrate this important work.

www.fretsonly.com

Essential Jazz Guitar Music

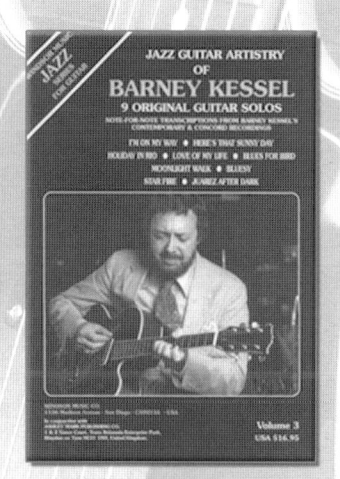

The Jazz Guitar Artistry of Barney Kessel

Volume 1 - AM1305 (HL00699350) **USA $16.95   UK £10.99**

Fourteen original solos by master jazz guitarist, Barney Kessel. Titles are: 'You're the One for Me', 'Study in Parallel, Contrary and Oblique Motion', 'Mermaid', 'Minor Mood', 'Blue Boy', 'Be Deedle De Do', 'Cool Groove', 'Jelly Beans', 'Minor Mode', 'New Blues', 'Blazin'', 'The Fourth Way', 'Lonely Moments' and 'Brazilian Beat'. In standard notation with chord numbers. Also includes a brief biography and a number of photographs.

Volume 2 - AM2183 (HL00330336) **USA $16.95   UK £10.99**

Eight original solos by master jazz guitarist, Barney Kessel. Titles are: 'Contemporary Blues', 'Begin the Blues', 'Barney's Blues', 'Salute to Charlie Christian', 'Vicky's Dream', '64 Bars on Wilshire', 'Foreign Intrigue' and 'Easy Like'. In standard notation with chord numbers. Also includes a brief biography and a number of photographs.

Volume 3 - AM2851 (HL00330588) **USA $16.95   UK £10.99**

Nine original guitar solos by master jazz guitarist, Barney Kessel. Titles are: 'I'm On My Way', 'here's That Sunny Day', 'Holiday in Rio', 'Love of My Life', 'Blues for Bird', 'Moonlight Walk', 'Bluesy', 'Star Fire' and 'Juarez After Dark'.

The Jazz Guitar Artistry of Martin Taylor
AM1116 (HL00490507) **USA $16.95 UK £10.99**

A wonderful book of note for note transcriptions of Martin Taylor's recorded solo guitar performances on his CD release 'A Tribute to Art Tatum'. Titles are: 'Old Man River', 'Time After Time', 'It's Only A Paper Moon', 'All The Things You Are', 'I've Got The World On A String', 'Taking A Chance On Love' and 'Don't Get Around Much Anymore'. All the solos are played fingerstyle by Martin, with many moving bass lines, and as such will be a great source of pleasure to guitarists of many styles, including classical guitarists.

Perfect Pick Technique
AM2324 (HL00695293) **USA 16.95 UK £10.99**

First published 30 years ago, this book remains the finest method available for playing steel-strung guitar, resulting in a flawless basic right-hand technique without limitations. Includes; right-hand analysis of some great jazz guitarists; Pictoral examples of holding & applying the pick; Fifteen groups of exercises covering different aspects of picking technique including; chords, scales, octaves, arpeggios & phrasing; Six solos composed and/or arranged by Ivor Mairants.

Distribution to Good Book and Music Shops throughout North America by Hal Leonard Publishing Corporation,
7777 West Bluemound Road, P.O. Box 13819 Milwaukee, WI 532 13

Distribution to the Rest of the World by Ashley Mark Publishing Company,
1 Vance Court, Trans Britannia Enterprise Park, Blaydon on Tyne, NE21 5NH, United Kingdom
Tel: +44 (0) 191 414 9000   Fax: +44 (0) 191 414 9001   email: mail@ashleymark.co.uk   www.fretsonly.com